APA, July 14, 1980 $5.00

Career Opportunities for Psychologists

Career Opportunities for Psychologists

Expanding and Emerging Areas

Edited by

Paul J. Woods

ψ American Psychological Association

Library of Congress Publication Data

Career opportunities for psychologists.

  Includes bibliographies.
  1. Psychology—Vocational guidance. I. Woods,
Paul J., 1930- II. American Psychological Association.
III. Title.
BF76.C37   150'.23   76-15351

ISBN 0-912704-03-9

Published by the American Psychological Association, Inc.
1200 Seventeenth Street, N.W., Washington, D.C. 20036.

Office of Educational Affairs
J. Russell Nazzaro, *Administrative Officer*

Special Publications Office
Patricia Walsh, *Editor*
Jeanne McManus, *Technical Editor*

Printed in the United States of America.

Contents

Part 4   Engineering/Human Factors/ Industrial/Management

Part 5   Ecology/Environment/Population

Part 6   Miscellaneous

Foreword

If present trends continue, the number of psychologists in the United States will double in the next 10 years. American graduate schools are currently producing about 3,000 doctorates and 5,000 master's in psychology each year. Will the job market be able to absorb this many psychologists?

One of the traditional employment opportunities for psychologists has been college and university teaching. However, faculties are increasingly becoming tenured, and psychology staff are by and large young; therefore, there is little likelihood of substantial turnover. Although psychologists may be underrepresented in terms of student/faculty ratios (as compared with other disciplines), the probability of job expansion is low because of financial exigencies. In sum, the employment outlook in academia is not rosy. Employment opportunities in the human services may provide the best prospects for young psychologists.

The last job survey conducted by APA in June 1974 reported that one out of every five recent PhDs was unemployed at the time of graduation. However, in the traditional academic areas such as experimental, physiological, and social psychology, closer to one out of every three recent PhDs was unemployed at the time of graduation.

It is therefore imperative that graduate students be made aware of new and expanding job possibilities. This book attempts to broaden the horizons for prospective psychologists and to contribute to changes in professional preparation. The book also provides options not ordinarily considered by psychologists wishing to change careers or those who currently may be unemployed or underutilized. In a small way at least, it should help ameliorate what could be called "the new depression" for the highly educated.

J. Russell Nazzaro
Educational Affairs Officer
American Psychological Association

1

Paul J. Woods

Introduction

This book has its origins in the Education and Training Board of the American Psychological Association. In recent years many individuals, boards, and committees expressed concern with the employment prospects of those being turned out by our graduate programs in psychology, but no general attack on the problem was launched. Then we on the Education and Training Board became aware of a startling fact: There are now more people in graduate school studying to become psychologists than there are psychologists in the APA!

To "view with alarm," as we are fond of saying in APA committees, would not help much. It was time for action. And with a little investigation we found that action had already been initiated. Many people, dealing mostly in specialty areas, had been surveying job prospects and speculating on innovative careers. Their efforts could be found in some publications, but many of them chose the outlet of presentation at regional or national meetings. It was necessary to pull their efforts together and to seek out others who might be willing to prepare contributions in areas that had not been covered previously. These efforts, which only began in earnest during June 1975, involved, first of all, contacting everyone who in recent years had made a convention presentation that seemed related to careers for psychologists. We also contacted APA division presidents and graduate department heads and then followed up on a number of other leads.

As a result we collected a number of manuscripts from which those in this book were selected. While wide coverage is available here, no pretense exists on our part that we have exhausted all possible career areas or even included all of the major areas. Thoroughness has been compromised by urgency. We felt a strong need to produce this publication as soon as possible. Some areas are not covered merely because we could not find anyone to prepare a relevant paper or because the papers submitted were judged inappropriate for various reasons. Some other areas have been excluded by a policy decision, namely, not to reproduce any brochures that have already been published by a division of APA.[1]

Paul J. Woods is a Professor in the Department of Psychology, Hollins College.

1. We have some overlap with the divisional brochures, but some areas are not covered at all in this book. However, the following divisions of the APA have brochures available upon request through the Central Office: industrial and organizational psychology, school psychology, counseling psychology, military psychology, and consumer psychology. Those in-

Another policy decision that we made was to limit our attention to careers for people with graduate training. We felt that this level provided sufficient material for discussion without expanding our coverage to the much larger populations of bachelor's-level and Associate-of-Arts-level people. They deserve guidance through a separate publication.

To move on: We have organized the chapters in this book under some general headings. At this point a brief overview might be helpful in guiding the reader to select those of interest or in enticing the reader to taste and explore.

General

I have chosen an optimistic chapter to begin this book. John Stern feels optimistic about the academic marketplace if young PhDs are willing to settle for less prestigious colleges and universities as well as two-year institutions. More generally, his position supports the theme of this book: Many areas exist in which psychologists can be usefully and gainfully employed, and these can be found if we raise our sights beyond "conventional" careers. This chapter touches briefly on areas that are subsequently elaborated upon by others.

Janet Cuca, who headed the APA's Clearinghouse for Information on Human Resources, presents the employment picture from the "hard data" perspective. After making certain assumptions and analyzing trends, she predicts that in order to have full employment of psychologists in 1980, 11,708 *new* jobs will have to be found or created between now and then. That sum works out to approximately 2,000 jobs each year. It is my hope that the other chapters in this book contain valid predictions as to where these jobs will originate.

An unfortunate fact that students and job seekers may all be well aware of is revealed in a questionnaire survey of members of the Western Psychological Association by Michele Wittig and Sharon Nolfi. Differential treatment of males and females continues. Their female respondents reported, for example, that despite having received degrees from equally prestigious institutions they are "much less likely [than men] to be employed in one of the prestigious PhD-granting public universities of the West and less than one third as likely to be a full professor if employed anywhere in academia." Other examples of discrimination are described in graduate school, recruitment and hiring practices, employment conditions, and opportunities for professional performance. The authors' findings and their recommendations deserve serious attention.

The chapter by Kevin Hynes, which deals with job placement mechanisms, has several audiences; it is included here in the hope that it may reach all of them. Of particular interest to the job seeker is advice on the effective use of existing job placement mechanisms.

---

terested in further information on careers in these areas can obtain copies of the brochures by writing to the Educational Affairs Office, American Psychological Association, 1200 Seventeenth Street, N.W., Washington, D.C. 20036.

The final chapter in this section, by Edward Crossman and J. Russell Nazzaro, is "required reading." At the risk of destroying the vita as a "projective technique," they present stylistic suggestions and some actual models derived from a survey of persons who deal with vitae and make important decisions based upon them. Their advice merits serious attention by all job seekers.

Academia

Robert Grinder's chapter, "Unsolicited Letters . . .," has been placed in this section because it deals directly with making employment contacts in higher education, but its general message is relevant for anyone seeking employment. It, therefore, is in the same category of "required reading" as the chapter by Crossman and Nazzaro. His remarks on "blunders" are well worth the attention of the young job seeker and will, I predict, produce smiles and chuckles in many of our more seasoned colleagues—if only APA had an award for humorous writing.

An overall picture of academic employment and growth trends based on data collected by the National Academy of Sciences is presented in the chapter by Helen Astin. She concludes that in spite of a high growth rate in new doctorates in psychology, "psychologists have been about as successful at locating employment as doctorates in other fields." But unless the factors that create the demand for college and university teachers change markedly (and she recognizes the possibility that they might), traditional academic careers will not be available for as large a proportion of our doctorates as in the past. Fortunately, psychologists have more options outside of academia than do our colleagues in many other fields. And Astin is yet another author who supports the general theme of this book by stating "it is important to recognize that our diversity and versatility are part of our strength as a field and that our students should be encouraged to think in terms of alternative careers."

Human Services

I had hopes of obtaining a chapter for this section dealing with the relatively new area known as "community psychology," but our deadline was too close for our possible contributors. Large employment prospects could exist in this area. Interested persons might be able to obtain some information from the APA Division of Community Psychology.

George Albee's chapter developed from his presentation in a symposium entitled "Innovative Roles for Psychologists in Improving the Quality of Life" at the 1975 meeting of the American Association for the Advancement of Science. He presents a general argument predicting both an increasing need for psychological services of all sorts and a large public composed of individuals and organizations willing to pay for them. Human problems will become more "diffuse and ambiguous," and playing the futurology game involves anticipation by prediction and planning.

Some claim that a committee cannot write a paper, but that is just what was done by the Task Force on Health Research of APA's Board of Scientific Affairs. They have produced, in my opinion, one of the most interesting and exciting chapters in this book. Their discussion on the contributions of psychology to health research should be studied carefully by all psychologists, not just those with career decision problems.

Alcoholism and drug abuse are dealt with in the next two chapters. Faye J. Goldberg first asks and then proceeds to tell us why psychologists should occupy roles in the field of substance abuse. Consider the following: (a) Industry is becoming increasingly concerned with alcohol and drug abuse; (b) general, private, military, and veterans' hospitals are developing detoxification programs and treatment facilities; (c) the federal government has consolidated mental health programs and training under the Alcohol, Drug Abuse and Mental Health Administration. Couple the above with the increased abuse of illicit as well as licit drugs and you can see an expanding need for knowledgeable professionals in such areas as administration, training, prevention, treatment, and research.

John Wolfe's chapter deals only with alcoholism and, initially, takes psychologists to task for failing to deal effectively with problems of alcohol abuse because of their own feelings and values about the use of alcohol. If psychologists can approach alcoholic people from a different perspective than they have formerly, a potential exists for real service and valuable opportunities for career involvement.

A number of people wrote the chapter dealing with forensic psychology, which is defined as "the application of psychological principles to the problems and administration of the legal-judicial system—both its criminal justice and civil justice components." This relatively long chapter deals with a complex system. Specially trained psychologists can be intimately involved in its operation and reform. The authors discuss at length the roles of a police department psychologist, a correctional psychologist, and a staff trainer and consultant. They also cover new roles in drug abuse treatment programs and discuss extensively the functions of psychologists in the courts. Forensic psychology's multifaceted challenge should attract large numbers of psychologists in the coming years.

A related chapter by Stanley Brodsky summarizes a conference that dealt with the role and contributions of psychology to the problems of crime, delinquency, and corrections. The book *Psychologists in the Criminal Justice System* was generated by that conference, and in the present chapter the author draws on both the conference and the book to identify "the major issues and directions in psychology and justice."

Engineering, Human Factors, Industrial, Management

Erwin Stanton addresses his chapter to the industrial-organizational psychologist who has traditionally been employed by colleges and universities, consulting firms, government agencies, and business and industry. While some positions will continue to be available in these areas, he suggests that graduate students prepare themselves for alternative career directions. He also believes that the best possible alternative for the industrial-organizational psychologist lies in the area of personnel administration and human resources development. He sees at the present time "a considerable amount of accelerating interest within business and industry in designing and implementing more effective human resources utilization systems, for it is believed that the proper utilization of personnel is the very heart and essence of good business management."

New directions in engineering psychology/human factors are discussed and illustrated in the chapter by Richard Kulp. He defines new directions as emerging areas where increasing members of engineering psychology/ human factors technologists are working in research and development activities. He then provides an overview of career activities in the following general categories: environments, computer systems, systems design, transportation, training, and consumer products. His analysis makes it clear that "new directions in engineering psychology/human factors have emerged over the last decade, and it is these areas that will offer exciting and challenging opportunities for future engineering psychology/human factors technologists."

Computer-based business information systems are the topic of the chapter by William Fox: "An information system is a combination of software, hardware, people, and procedures assigned to receive, store, manipulate, summarize, and present data to a given organization." The author feels that this field has the greatest need for engineering psychology of any field since the beginning of systems related to defense over 35 years ago. But the demands of the new information systems differ in that more emphasis is placed on the person–machine interface, and the future direction for engineering psychology should deal with the "dimensions of human involvement in computer-based information systems." Since we are experiencing a marked growth rate in the use of such systems, we clearly have an expanding area for psychologists with relevant skills.

The final chapter in this section, by H. McIlvaine Parsons, is a definitive description of the field of engineering psychology dealing with its past, present, and future. Technology has produced this hybrid field, which the author identifies by specifying "(a) who the people in it are, (b) what they do, (c) where they are, (d) how they are trained, (e) their substantive interest areas, (f) their techniques, (g) how the field can be distinguished from other disciplinary areas inside and outside psychology, and (h) some of the field's significant characteristics." As I said, it's definitive! Readers interested in this section should also note the first chapter in the next section.

Ecology, Environment, Population

The first chapter, by Bernard Bass and Ruth Bass, bridges Parts 4 and 5 and begins with a brief history of human effects on the environment. Much of the chapter deals with the kinds of research contributions that the authors foresee for the industrial psychologist. Personnel specialists are also needed to deal with job definitions and then recruitment, selection, training, and placement of persons in a wide variety of ecologically related careers. A bright sign appears in the data they report that indicate a willingness among management groups and the public at large to spend money on environmental cleanup and to pay further for conservation efforts.

The next chapter was developed from efforts of the American Psychological Association's Task Force on Environment and Behavior and was prepared by Central Office staff person Willo White. The major part of the chapter consists of a listing of federal agencies whose mandates involve them in concerns for the environment. These mandates are then, in effect, operationalized by input from psychologists whose career activities illustrate the actual tasks in which they are currently engaged. The end result is a rather thorough "directory" that should receive close scrutiny from those interested in this area.

Vaida Thompson and Sidney Newman collaborated on the final chapter in this section, which deals with training and research opportunities in population psychology. The growing interest by psychologists in this area is evidenced by the newly formed APA Division of Population and Environmental Psychology, which now contains over 300 members. The authors argue that while this is clearly an interdisciplinary field, psychologists are uniquely trained to make important contributions. Contraception and migration involve behavior, and it is psychologists who are concerned with "motives, attitudes, values, personal orientations, decision processes, and dyadic interactions" that underlie or are associated with these behaviors. Psychologists also have acquired special methodological and analytical skills that are valuable to this area. This chapter deals with three major topics: What are the areas and issues of research in population psychology? How can psychology trainees—even ones in a "pure" research setting—prepare themselves for work in this area? What postdoctoral training and research support opportunities may assist them toward their goals?

Miscellaneous

The point has been made several times that psychologists by virtue of special skills and perspectives can make unique contributions to particular problem areas or fields of endeavor. The point is again made by Lee Sechrest—this time in relation to program evaluation. At all levels in our society, programs are proposed and then often implemented to deal with particular problems. Unfortunately, "in the usual course of events, programs are implemented in ways that make it impossible to tell whether they conform to the plan, and they remain in force until either funds have expired or the recurrence or persistence of the original problem makes it obvious that the programs are not working. In some cases programs, however effective or ineffective they may be, persist indefinitely because of a lack of any firm information concerning their success or failure." In this chapter the author argues that psychologists have special qualifications to deal with such situations.

Arthur Brayfield and Mark Lipsey describe and discuss a new professional specialty that has been emerging—public affairs psychology. "The core functions of public affairs psychology are to conceptualize, understand, and investigate a public policy issue in its psychological dimensions and to translate that analysis and research into terms and information that a 'consumer' of such knowledge can readily understand and act upon." They see at least three major activities involved in these functions: (a) the creation of knowledge relevant to various public issues, (b) the application of existing psychological knowledge to public issues, and (c) the application of methodology to evaluation and monitoring activities. Opportunities for persons involved with such functions and activities are seen at all levels of government, in specialized nonprofit organizations, and in business and industry. The authors conclude with a discussion of strategies for career entry and the outlook for the future.

A survey of social psychologists led to the chapter by Sheldon Levy. "The primary goal of the survey was to inform academics and nonacademics about each other's employment environments. Another functionally important goal was to provide information to new PhDs about the conditions of employment that exist in a variety of settings." Information was collected on eight major areas ranging from intellectual freedom to job satisfaction and income, and much of the chapter deals with a presentation of the results of the survey.

In another chapter in this section, Kristina Hooper explores the lack of contact that has traditionally been the state of affairs between psychologists and architects and proposes methods by which that situation might be changed. She views the combination of psychology and architecture as a natural one. Contributing to the development of more humane environments should certainly attract the interest of many of our younger colleagues.

The concluding chapter, "Potpourri," presents a number of brief job descriptions from psychologists in nontraditional or innovative roles. Headings can be skimmed by the reader and selections studied as interest dictates.

Overall, I see a fantastic variety of career possibilities throughout the book, and I am optimistic that members of our field will continue to find satisfying and rewarding careers that will demand the full range of their talents.

Part 1 ———————————————

General

2

John A. Stern

An "Optimist" Looks at Employment Opportunities for Psychologists

At the 1975 APA Convention in Chicago, I participated in one symposium devoted to "Jobs for the Recent PhD" and attended two other symposia devoted to the same issue; one was entitled "The Hunter or the Hunted: Job Seeking in Social Psychology," and the other, "Graduate Student Views of Future Directions for Educational Psychology." There was evidence of considerable and justifiable concern about the job market, along with a lot of wailing, rigidity in perception of "the job market," and unwillingness to adapt to changing realities and "social needs." I accepted the challenging task to look at the job market through a particular type of rose-colored glasses, ones which accepted the realities that have been so well demonstrated by wo/manpower surveys of the recent past and that have sought to identify career opportunities in more promising directions than academic psychology. Let me begin with the academic marketplace and work my way up to more promising fields.

The Academic Marketplace

Though projections three years ago were for a severe reduction in academic positions, the crunch does not *appear* to be as severe as was predicted. If our young PhDs are willing to go to less prestigious universities, colleges, and junior colleges, then the opportunities still exist to teach and bootleg a bit of research. They may have to teach more than their role models, their students may not be of the "academic caliber" to which they would like to devote their effort, and support for research may not be as plentiful as that to which they have grown accustomed, but jobs are there. I would like to remind students and their mentors that comparable situations prevailed when I and many of those "mentors" entered the ranks of college students in the mid-1940–1950 era. Professors suddenly were faced with larger classes, with students of questionable "academic caliber," and with students less docile, more demanding, and more "relevance" oriented than they had the pleasure of dealing with during calmer academic years. They weathered the storm, some gracefully, others kicking all the way. They educated herds of "unwashed" characters who would not have been able to

John A. Stern is Director of the Behavior Research Laboratory, Washington University, St. Louis, Missouri.

enter college had it not been for the G.I. Bill of Rights and later social legislation that opened the doors of higher education to a larger segment of American youth.

Let me take a brief side trip into the "ethics" of educating more psychologists than we believe can be absorbed by the marketplace. A number of years ago I asked one of my fellow psychologists (who received his PhD during the Depression of the 1930s) how he had the audacity to work for a PhD in psychology when the job market for such people was non-existent—and who had advised him to go into psychology in the first place. I also asked him what advice he was giving to his new graduate students. This man is a Talmudic scholar and a well-known psychologist, and I was certain of a well-reasoned, highly qualified, and logical answer: His decision to do graduate work in psychology was a function of his interest in the subject matter. His concern was not with the job market. He knew the job market was lousy but he also knew that his burning ambition was to educate himself in an area that happened to be psychology. With respect to making a living, he felt secure in being able to support himself by teaching Hebrew or by working in an office if nothing materialized in psychology. Thus his choice of educational goals had little to do with the job market.

His motivation to become a psychologist was, to say the least, unusual in his lack of concern with job prospects in his field of training. However, most students at that time (at least a 10-year period) must have been, in view of the poor job market, strongly motivated in their desire to become psychologists. Of course, some of them went into graduate work because jobs were not available, but this apparently was a small minority.

To undergraduate students expressing the desire to do graduate work in psychology, I always recount this tale after telling them about current job opportunities. Many of them still decide to do graduate work in psychology—even in physiological psychology—so I suspect that the motives of students today are not so terribly different from students of the 1930s. I present these thoughts to you, some of whom may feel guilty about training students for nonexistent jobs. As long as you are honest and point out the difficulties in the current employment market, the decision about seeking graduate work in psychology is the student's. Thus, I for one am against reducing the number of students entering into graduate work in psychology *if the basis for that decision is predicated on their having to be absorbed into the job market as "conventional" psychologists.* There are other cogent, more rational reasons for retrenchment.

With a bit of organized effort the market for teachers of psychology at the junior college and, yes, the high school level can be successfully exploited as a job market for PhD and hopefully MA psychologists.

Other Job Markets

What other job markets close to home base (academic) are available to enterprising young psychologists, or could be opened up to the psychological community for the benefit of their students and hopefully the marketplace as well? Three types of psychologists that seem to be suffering less from "retrenchment" are developmental psychologists, psychologists concerned with the educational enterprise in general, and psychologists in the world of business. Developmental psychologists are found in schools of home economics or of human development, those concerned with the educational enterprise are found in schools of education, and those in the business schools are located in departments of organizational psychology. If I may be permitted a somewhat personal observation, it appears that my fellow academic associates have for too long looked with myopic and hypercritical eyes at psychologists involved in such enterprises: They are not "pure" researchers; their work smacks of applicability in the real world; they deal with messy constructs and cannot exercise the kind of control that self-respecting psychologists would insist on before they deigned to sully their fingers in such enterprises, etc. We can no longer afford to entertain such narrow perceptions of psychological enterprises and of psychological research.

I suspect that need will be the mother of invention and changing attitudes. Role models, as exemplified in professors of psychology, may not change (hopefully they will) but young PhDs will begin to explore career opportunities in less favored academic climates, such as professional schools, junior colleges, and high schools, and in schools of social work, schools of business, and schools of education and home economics. We in academia will have to mend, build, or rebuild bridges to such educational enterprises, but I am confident that this is possible. I see the current interest of experimental psychology in problems of cognition and information processing as positive signs; these research areas should coordinate well with education, child development, and industrial psychology.

Beyond Academia

What about opportunities outside the academic marketplace? Again, they do exist. They are not necessarily knocking at our door—we may have to go and search them out—but they are there. We have probably done a reasonable job of development in a few areas of "professionalism" such as clinical psychology, community psychology, and school psychology.

Psychology has a lot to contribute to other industries. The fact that psychologists have not made this contribution is probably a function of (a) psychologists not being asked to assume responsibilities in these areas and (b) the lack of "respectability" of such work, be it practice or research.

Let me again briefly digress. One of the puzzles in my career as a psychologist dates back to my entry into the job market when I had opportunities to look at research laboratories in the "real world," both government-affiliated laboratories and those in hospitals and industrial organizations. What always struck me was the defensiveness of psychologists in such positions. They were "ashamed" of being in nonuniversity laboratories, ones with real-world responsibilities. They would invariably tell me that their "mission" was to perform "basic" research, and that is generally all they did. What surprised me was that so many of them were supported as long as they were both in industry and in government.

In the past few years the picture has changed somewhat, and those laboratories still in operation are devoting a good portion of their research effort to practical problems and are solving at least some of them. I predict that the job market in such laboratories will increase over the next decade. We will also see more "private" laboratories develop, ones devoted to doing "contract" research for both the government and the private sector of industry. These then are areas in which I see the job market for experimental psychologists expanding. It is true that life in such organizations is "riskier" than a tenured appointment in a university or government position, but the rewards (including financial) may be as great as, if not greater than, those we in "safe" occupations enjoy.

Promoting Psychology

What can we do about the problem of "not being asked" to work in such areas? We have to do something at both the individual and the group level. At the individual level, I suspect that enterprising, hungry young PhDs will begin knocking at the doors of industry trying to sell their skills; they will have to demonstrate that their skills are directly applicable to that industry. It will take aggressive, persistent effort on the part of young PhDs to gain a receptive ear in an industry that is imaginative enough to see the potential contributions a psychologist can make. Perhaps we need to do some brainstorming in special seminars to sensitize students about possible opportunities in industry and about the search for a position in this "new world." Professors of psychology might seek consulting roles in industry, without pay if necessary, to establish liaison with such organizations in the hope of placing their students in such establishments.

What can the group do? By group I mean organized psychology, specifically organizations such as the American Psychological Association, the Organization of Chairmen of Departments of Psychology, the Divisions of the American Psychological Association, and the state psychological associations. What the groups are doing is complaining. One need only to read divisional newsletters to appreciate this. See, for example, "The Job Market in Psychology: A Survey of Despair" (Kessler, McKenra, Russell, Stang, & Sweet, 1975).

What can be done? Let me give a few examples of what is feasible. APA could generate some "advertising," that is, pamphlets, aimed at specific markets, that would extoll the virtues of psychologists in solving problems relevant to those markets. APA could also see that such material was directed toward relevant individuals. We could organize seminars, or a booth or two at meetings of trade or professional organizations, where we could persuasively demonstrate what psychologists have done and can do in solving relevant problems. We could be more active about placing people in settings where they can demonstrate what psychologists can do. A good example of this is the American Association for the Advancement of Science program of placing young scientists in the offices of federal legislators to work on unspecified problems.

We should survey recent PhDs to find out more about innovative approaches to obtaining jobs and about "unusual" careers on which they have embarked. The clinical psychological enterprise appears to be a viable one (though even here we have our pessimistic prophets) in that it is expanding in a number of new directions (neuropsychology, rehabilitation psychology, biofeedback, medical psychology, to name a few) and is developing new models for training such professionals, ranging from the departments of psychology or universities that offer professional degrees to the new, independent professional schools. The clinical enterprise appears to be thriving.

Let me give a few examples of the kinds of problems being tackled by psychologists, not all of them trained as clinicians. A large number of the solutions to these problems are being generated by experimental psychologists. Some of these psychologists have gone through the "rejuvenation" process of receiving postdoctoral training in clinical psychology; others have through good or bad fortune obtained employment in settings where they were encouraged to develop new treatment and evaluative programs. The application of biofeedback procedures to patients is certainly a burgeoning area, one in which claims are often ahead of reality. Let me give a few reality-oriented examples. Relaxation training to help heroin addicts during the stages of major withdrawal is certainly an innovative use of such a biofeedback procedure. Other examples include retraining persons with fecal or urinary incontinence, teaching patients to control premature ventricular contractions (PVCs), and helping patients with problems of muscular spasticity to relax.

Shifting out of the biofeedback and into the "behavior control" arena we find psychologists training people with chronic pain syndromes to lead more productive and useful lives. We have also seen some imaginative but poorly developed programs in the rehabilitation of youthful and older offenders in training schools and prisons. Some innovative programs in early child and parent education appear to have real payoffs in terms of protecting the child's performance on tests of intelligence from the usual decrements that characterize children born and raised in ghetto areas. These are but a few examples of areas of research and intervention into which psychology can expand.

Social psychology appears to be making some moves toward getting a piece of the community psychology action as well as getting involved in problems of communication. I see these as examples of healthy actions and reactions to a changing job market.

Quality of Life

Along with other "industries," psychology will expand in the area of providing services to consumers. "Quality of life" is becoming a paramount concern ranging from medical ethics to euthanasia and from birth control to conceptions of a philosophy of life that enables more people to have a feeling of satisfaction with the way they spend their productive and retirement years. What kind of services could psychologists perform? Let me give but a few possible examples. More psychologists will be employed in serving retired people, ranging from what Bill Schofield (1964) referred to as "the sale/purchase of friendships"—psychotherapy—to assistance in the planning and running of retirement communities.

Let me take two areas in which the question of quality of life is becoming increasingly important and in which psychology might play a prominent or supporting role, one leading to an expanding job market for psychologists.

Health

Concern in the area of health is manifested, for example, by the mandating and development of peer review organizations (PRO). The peer review process is currently an in-house operation, a self-policing action. Psychologists can be employed in the development of assessment procedures and the development of evaluative tools to see if the health provider is meeting minimal performance criteria. With the increase in government intervention in the health industry we will probably see a shift from self-policing to "other" policing, a policy that we may not like but one that may benefit psychology in a variety of ways.

In the medical arena, quality-of-life considerations include the concern with the cost of providing health services and the development of ancillary health professionals, not only in the areas of mental health but in medicine in general. Again psychology can play a role in evaluating as well as training such personnel. Associated with the development of other health professionals, such as the nurse-practitioner and other paramedical personnel, is the need for changing the attitudes of both consumers and providers of conventional health delivery systems toward the utilization of such personnel. Attitudes must also be changed to get people to accept the concept of health maintenance or preventive health care as contrasted to the current model of the practice of medicine, one principally concerned with the treatment of illness. Here again, psychology can play a major role. It is true that we will be competing with other professionals equally desirous of providing these functions, such as medical sociologists and health educators, but if we are convinced that we can do a better job than those professionals we had better start waving our banners and attracting attention to psychology as the discipline best endowed with the necessary skills to meet such needs.

Rehabilitation

The area of rehabilitation, or habilitation, ranges from helping people with specific types of pain syndromes to aiding people to live happy and socially productive lives where their chances for such a life are otherwise dim.

Rehabilitation also focuses on socially deviant individuals, for example, those in prison. Though for the immediate future the support of rehabilitative programs in prisons appears to be scheduled for belt tightening and retrenchment (Holden, 1975), we suspect that the pendulum will begin swinging in the other direction and that thoughtful programs involving behavior modification approaches (another dirty phrase today) and environmental manipulations will again be supported.

Summary

Let me stop at this point and sum up my convictions:

1. Recipients of PhDs in psychology will find that the academic jobs that were so attractive in the past (e.g., teaching with adequate time and funds to conduct research) will indeed be in short supply.

2. Teaching jobs will continue to be available; however, the options that previously went along with such positions have shrunk considerably.

3. Job markets in areas other than teaching will have to be developed. Such development will occur as a function of individual need and aggressive action on the part of the profession. (a) Enterprising young PhDs with imagination, perseverance, and useful skills will find positions in "industry" or will develop new industries (such as private research laboratories). (b) The profession will react to the threat of low employability of its graduates by developing information and campaigns to let industry know what psychologists can do for them; changing attitudes within the profession about the respectability of teaching in departments without PhD programs and accepting "unconventional" careers such as "applied" research; and responding to "threats" by other professions that encourage deplorable restrictive legislation for the practice of psychological skills.

4. The job market for psychologists in less conventional settings requires considerable development but has the potential to provide jobs for psychologists currently going through psychological education programs.

REFERENCES

Holden, C. Prisons: Faith in "rehabilitation is suffering a collapse." *Science*, 1975, *188*, 815–817.

Kessler, S., McKenra, W., Russell, V., Stang, D., & Sweet, S. A survey of despair. *State Psychological Association Affairs Newsletter*, 1975, 7(1).

Schofield, W. *Psychotherapy: The purchase of friendship.* Englewood Cliffs, N.J.: Prentice-Hall, 1964.

3

Janet Melei Cuca

PhDs in Psychology: Supply and Demand

In considering the future of psychology and the future of employment in psychology, it is well to first look at some events of the past both to note their influences on the wide-ranging course of psychology and to have a framework for looking at the future. Until World War II, psychology was very much an experimental science pursued in the halls of academia. To be sure, psychologists were employed in other settings, but not many.

During the years of the war, however, new doctorates coming out of graduate school, as well as experienced psychologists, were recruited by the federal government to devise screening procedures that could be used on a mass basis to select personnel for various military functions. Once selected, those personnel had to be trained in their assigned tasks as efficiently as possible, and psychologists were recruited to devise the training procedures. If this was not the spawning of what we now call organizational/personnel psychology, it was at least its burgeoning.

After World War II and the Korean War, the federal government, through such programs as Veterans Administration traineeships, again affected the course of psychology by pouring money into the training of psychologists to provide clinical/counseling/rehabilitation services for the returning veterans. As was intended, the number of professional psychologists increased phenomenally. Today it is no longer unusual for a psychologist to be devoted to the full-time provision of services. In fact, the full-time equivalent of 40% is devoted to providing services, an activity that was hardly more than a sideline for the pre-1940 academic psychologist. Circumstances at that time also restricted the provision of services to the more affluent members of society.

Psychology is once again in the throes of adjusting to actions and events with wo/manpower implications that will ultimately change its future course. These events are many: recession of the national economy, reduction of federal support for training in psychology, reduction of federal funds for research and development in the field, and increased interest in the graduate study of psychology. The events are interacting in such a way as to produce imbalances in the supply and demand for psychologists' ser-

Janet Melei Cuca, formerly a Research Associate and Manager of the American Psychological Association's Clearinghouse for Information on Human Resources, is now a Research Associate at the Association of American Medical Colleges, Washington, D.C.

vices, both scientific and professional. Unless there are major turnarounds in these events in the next years, the supply–demand imbalances will continue at least until 1980 and quite likely for some years thereafter.

Many of the factors determining the situation in 1980 have already been set into motion by events that are taking place now or that have taken place in the very recent past. The 1980 doctorates are already in graduate school. Short-run predictions are more accurate than are long-run predictions simply because they are closer to the reality of present and actual events.

Estimating Supply

The supply side of the picture is the easier to pin down since psychologists are made in graduate school, not in heaven. The supply of psychologists is directly related to the noncelestial production of graduate degrees in psychology; therefore, let us consider the number of PhDs that have been awarded in psychology since 1940. The year 1940 was chosen because psychologists who were 64 years old in 1974 and who would, on the average, be retiring in 1975, would have received their PhDs in 1940. That assumption is made on the basis of data from the National Research Council's (NRC) Doctorate Records File (NAS-NRC, 1963; NRC, 1967–1974), which indicate that 30 is the median age at which persons have received doctorates in psychology over the years.

Table 3-1 presents data from two sources on doctorates granted by departments of psychology from 1940 to 1974. The Office of Education data (DHEW, 1975; DHEW, annually) tend to underestimate the actual number of degrees conferred, since that survey gathers data from university registrars. The National Research Council survey (NAS, 1967; NAS–NRC, 1963; NRC, 1967–1974) contacts each degree recipient directly. Completion of its questionnaire has even reached the point of being

TABLE 3-1   *Doctorates Awarded in Psychology: 1940–1974*

Years	National Research Council[a]	Office of Education[b]
1940–44	530	—
1945–49	719	—
1950–54	2,753	2,450
1955–59	3,672	3,079
1960–64	4,408	3,908
1965–69	6,561	5,806
1970–74	11,292	9,113
Total	29,935	24,356

[a]Sources: (a) National Academy of Sciences. *Doctorate recipients from United States universities 1958–1966* (No. 1489). Washington, D.C.: Author, 1967.
(b) National Academy of Sciences-National Research Council. *Doctorate production in U.S. universities, 1920–1962* (No. 1142). Washington, D.C.: Author, 1963.
(c) National Research Council. *Summary report: Doctorate recipients from United States universities.* Washington, D.C.: Author, various years.
[b]Sources: Data are taken from three publications of the Department of Health, Education, and Welfare, Office of Education (OE), National Center for Educational Statistics: (a) *Projections of educational statistics to 1983–84, 1974 edition* (DHEW Publ. NCES 72-209). Washington, D.C.: U.S. Government Printing Office, 1975. (b) *Earned degrees conferred,* published annually. (c) *Biennial survey of education.*

a graduation requirement in a few universities, so its response rate tends to be 100% for all intents and purposes. Another qualification that should be borne in mind is that these data do not include doctorates that are essentially in the field of psychology but that have been awarded by departments other than psychology departments. For example, 482 doctorates in educational psychology and 653 in guidance/counseling/student personnel were awarded by departments of education in 1974. Besides schools and departments of education, schools of business and medicine and departments of human and family relations, among others, also award doctorates in psychology. According to the NRC data, then, the total number of doctorates awarded by departments of psychology from 1940 to 1974 was 29,935.

The number of doctorates awarded, however, whether by departments of psychology or other departments, does not tell the whole story about supply. This discussion has already controlled for retirement by excluding those doctorates 65 years of age or older on the assumption that the average retirement will occur at age 65, even though some psychologists work well past that age and some retire early. We must also take into account the number of psychologists who dropped out of the labor pool due to mortality. Applying the mortality rates for white males (since psychology has over the years been a predominantly white male enterprise) to the NRC figures in Table 3-1 gives an estimated loss of 2,385, which brings the supply to 27,550.

Another phenomenon that affects the size of the labor pool is migration into and out of the field, or more colloquially, "field switching." The National Academy of Sciences' (NAS) 1973 profile of doctoral scientists (NAS, 1974) examined wo/manpower flow from field of degree to field of employment for persons receiving the doctorate from 1930 through 1972. Of those receiving degrees in psychology, only 89% were employed in psychology; the other 11% left the field. The percentage of those leaving the field decreases the more recently the degree was received: Of the 1972 doctorates only 7.5% had left the field by the following year.

The 89% of psychology doctorates who stayed in the field accounted for only 81% of all those employed in the field—which means that there is considerable migration into the field. Most of the in-migration is due to doctorates in the nonsciences (e.g., arts and humanities, education, and other professional fields). Adjusting our estimate of the labor supply by −11% for those who leave the field and 19% for those who enter gives 29,754.

Doctorate holders from foreign universities, whether or not they are United States citizens, should also be taken into account as another element of in-migration. The profile of doctoral scientists (NAS, 1974) indicates that 1.5% of those employed in psychology have foreign doctorates, a percentage that brings the supply to 30,200.

At any particular time, some persons are unavailable for employment and are therefore not considered part of the labor force. Most of these are women taking time out of their careers to bear and raise children. These voluntarily unemployed persons comprise less than one-half of one per-

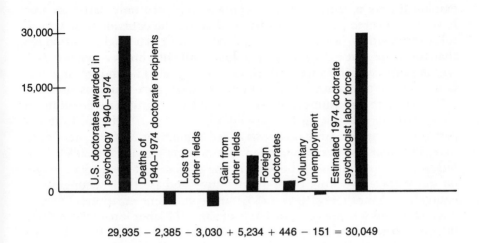

$$29{,}935 - 2{,}385 - 3{,}030 + 5{,}234 + 446 - 151 = 30{,}049$$

Figure 3-1. Estimating the 1974 doctorate psychologist labor force.

cent of doctorates, or 151 persons. Taking these people into account brings the final estimate of the 1974 doctorate psychologists labor force to 30,049. Figure 3-1 is a graphic representation of the various calculations that have just been made.

In the same manner we can estimate the size of the 1980 labor force. Figure 3-2 graphically depicts that operation. Attrition due to deaths and retirement during the 1975–1980 period will diminish the 1974 labor force by 3,501. It is worth noting here that the median age of PhD psychologists is only about 42 years, making psychology a young discipline; that is, replacement openings due to death and retirement will not really be a sizable factor for many years yet.

The United States Office of Education (DHEW, 1975), in its 1974 edition of educational statistics, projected that 16,460 doctorates will be awarded in psychology from 1975 to 1980. Obviously none of these new doctorates will retire, but 96 will be lost due to death and another 1,234 will be employed in other fields. However, 988 nonpsychology doctorates will be employed as psychologists, making a net loss of 246 due to field switching. Foreign doctorates will add 246 to the labor pool and those who voluntarily exclude themselves from the labor force will amount to 247. As a result, the supply will total 42,658 in 1980.

Predicting Demand

The unemployment rate among psychologists, that is, the percentage of all psychologists who want to work but cannot find a position, is about 1% for all doctorate psychologists, although it increases to 3% for new doctorates. Thus 99% of the 1974 pool are employed. Figure 3-3 shows that this 99%

breaks down into 91% who are employed full-time and 8% who are employed only part-time. Those who are employed only part-time may have two or three part-time positions that are the equivalent of a single full-time position, or they may simply be working at a single position less than full-time. The 91% who are employed full-time break down into 60% who are employed in a single full-time position and 31% who are employed in a full-time position as well as in one or more part-time positions.

To estimate the number of single, full-time-equivalent positions in 1974, assume that for the 31% who are employed both full-time and part-time, their part-time positions added 8 hours (or 20%) to their work-load. This increase is the equivalent of 6% more jobs (31% × 20%). Similarly, assume that the 8% who work in one or more part-time positions are, on the average, working three-quarter time and are thus occupying the equivalent of another 6% (8% × 75%) single, full-time positions. Thus, we have 91% plus 6% plus 6%, or 103% of the 1974 labor force with a single full-time position. That works out to 30,950 positions in 1974. If, then, there are going to be 42,658 doctorate psychologists in 1980, as calculated earlier, the discrepancy between 1974 demand and 1980 supply is 11,708. In other words, in order for there to be full employment of the 1980 labor force, 11,708 *new* jobs will have to found or created between now and 1980. Therefore, approximately 2,000 *new* jobs are needed each year.

The Bureau of Labor Statistics (BLS) of the U.S. Department of Labor in 1974 estimated that the average number of openings for psychologists that will occur each year from 1972 to 1985 is 4,300, that is, 1,900 replacements and 2,400 new positions (Department of Labor, 1974). That sounds quite encouraging, doesn't it—4,300 openings each year? But these 4,300 annual openings are for bachelor, master, and doctorate psychologists, who to-

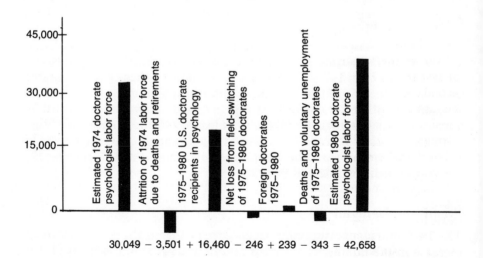

$$30,049 - 3,501 + 16,460 - 246 + 239 - 343 = 42,658$$

Figure 3-2. Estimating the 1980 doctorate psychologist labor force.

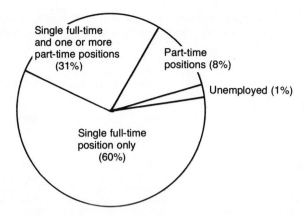

Figure 3-3. Employment status of doctorate psychologist labor force. (Sources: C. A. Boneau & J. M. Cuca. An overview of psychology's human resources: Characteristics and salaries from the 1972 APA survey. *American Psychologist*, 1974, *29*, 821–840; and National Academy of Sciences. *Doctoral scientists and engineers in the United States: 1973 profile*. Washington, D.C.: Author, 1974.)

gether are being produced at a rate of about 70,000 annually. Furthermore, the BLS projections are based on various assumptions about the United States' economy, among which are a 4% unemployment rate and a 3% annual increase in the implicit price deflator for the gross national product. Since the unemployment rate has been up to almost 10% and the quarterly inflation rate up to 12%, it is unlikely that the average rates for the period will work out to the low levels upon which BLS based its projections. So, 4,300 openings for 70,000 applicants is even quite optimistic.

Areas of Demand

Where has the demand for psychologists come from over the years? Table 3-2 shows the settings in which psychologists have been employed over the last 18 or 19 years. Employment in educational settings whether at the secondary level or in higher education is the major component of demand, accounting for over half of all positions throughout the years. The nonacademic positions are distributed more or less equally over all other settings.

The distribution across the various settings has changed somewhat over the years. The percentage of those in education increased approximately 5%, while the percentage of those in government decreased approximately 9%–10%. The percentages of those employed in nonprofit organizations, those in industry and business, and those self-employed all declined about 2%–3%. The most striking feature of Table 3-2 is the more-than-tripled increase in the number of psychologists from 1956–1958 to 1972.

Table 3-3 documents a phenomenon quite central to the issue of supply–demand imbalances. Not only has the percentage of academic

TABLE 3-2   *Doctorate Psychologists by Employment Settings: 1956–1972*

Employment setting	1972[a]	1970[b]	1968[b]	1966[b]	1964[b]	1962[b]	1960[b]	1958–56[b]
Education	12,456	10,465	8,658	7,054	5,818	5,226	4,625	3,534
Federal government	1,583	1,142	1,069	1,048	1,044	1,082	980 }	
Other government	1,614	1,337	916	1,065	882	1,020	838 }	1,556
Nonprofit organizations	1,172	1,334	1,410	1,084	966	961	833	486
Industry and business	1,138	1,194	1,001	735	735	824 }		
Self-employed	1,422	1,293	1,084	856	831	813 }	1,402	779
Military	95	145	142	106	104	127	103	—[c]
Other	141	114	90	165	140	123	280	178
No report of employer	1,015	99	105	132	61	125	—[c]	—[c]
Not employed	608	470	319	300	262	208	0	0
Total	21,210	17,593	14,794	12,545	10,843	10,301	9,061	6,533

[a]Source: American Psychological Association. *1972 manpower survey.* Unpublished data, Washington, D.C., 1972.
[b]Sources: National Science Foundation's biennial series *American science manpower,* 1956–58 (NSF 61-45); 1960 (NSF 62-43); 1962 (NSF 64-16); 1964 (NSF 66-29); 1966 (NSF 68-7); 1968 (NSF 69-38); 1970 (NSF 71-45).
[c]These data were included in the "other" employment settings.

employees with the doctorate increased over the years but so has the percentage of all doctorates employed by academia. This does not mean that the proportion of jobs in academia is increasing, relative to other settings. It does mean that the doctorate is increasingly required for academic positions. Depending upon a positive or negative outlook, this requirement is referred to as "enrichment" or "underemployment." Since 90% of the psychologists employed by colleges and universities have the doctorate, little room for enrichment exists in those settings. The possibilities for increased doctorate employment are greater in the other educational settings, such as two-year colleges, high schools, and school systems, because the percentage of psychologists with the doctorate presently employed in those settings is considerably less than that in colleges and universities.

In all employment settings, positions formerly held by persons without a doctorate are now being filled by PhDs. In a buyer's market, employers can

TABLE 3-3   *Percentage of Doctorates Employed in Educational Settings: 1960–1972*

	Colleges and universities		All educational settings[c]		All psychologists
Year	% in setting with PhD	% of all PhDs employed in setting	% in setting with PhD	% of all PhDs employed in setting	% with PhD
1972[a]	90	54	83	59	78
1970[b]	86	44	70	59	67
1968[b]	83	42	68	59	64
1966[b]	87	40	72	56	66
1964[b]	86	39	71	54	65
1962[b]	84	38	68	51	61
1960[b]	82	36	66	51	59

[a]Source: C. A. Boneau & J. M. Cuca. An overview of psychology's human resources: Characteristics and salaries from the 1972 APA survey. *American Psychologist,* 1974, *29,* 821–840.
[b]Sources: National Science Foundation's biennial series *American science manpower,* 1956–58 (NSF 61-45); 1960 (NSF 62-43); 1962 (NSF 64-16); 1964 (NSF 66-29); 1966 (NSF 68-7); 1968 (NSF 69-38); 1970 (NSF 71-45).
[c]These data include the "colleges and universities" setting.

TABLE 3-4   *Salaries of Positions Offered at Regional Conventions and in the APA Employment Bulletin 1972–1974*

Degree and amount of experience	1972		1973		1974	
	Range	Median	Range	Median	Range	Median
College, university, medical school: academic year						
PhD, with experience	9.5–19.2	14.3	8.5–18.0	11.7	10.0–15.0	11.6
PhD, no experience	9.5–12.5	—[a]	9.0–15.0	11.0	8.0–14.7	11.3
Less than PhD, with experience	9.5–15.5	12.5	7.9–15.0	11.0	8.6–12.0	—[a]
Less than PhD, no experience	7.5–12.5	—[a]	8.0–12.0	10.8	8.0–15.0	10.5
College, university, medical school: calendar year						
PhD, with experience	7.1–26.5	16.8	10.5–20.0	—[a]	11.0–25.0	—[a]
PhD, no experience	9.5–14.0	11.8	10.5–17.5	—[a]	10.5–16.5	—[a]
Less than PhD, with experience	8.0–15.5	12.7	8.5–20.5	—[a]	8.5–13.0	—[a]
Less than PhD, no experience	7.0–13.5	10.2	10.0–18.0	—[a]	10.0–15.0	—[a]
Government						
PhD, with experience	12.0–24.1	18.1	13.7–23.4	16.0	12.0–21.0	16.4
PhD, no experience	8.5–16.0	14.6	8.0–18.7	14.4	10.0–18.0	15.0
Less than PhD, with experience	8.4–23.0	15.7	7.7–21.3	10.5	9.0–27.9	12.7
Less than PhD, no experience	9.4–13.0	—[a]	6.0–18.0	12.0	7.0–16.2	11.6
Hospitals and clinics						
PhD, with experience	7.5–24.5	16.5	12.0–25.0	15.0	13.9–17.5	—[a]
PhD, no experience	12.0–16.6	—[a]	12.0–18.0	—[a]	14.0–15.0	—[a]
Less than PhD, with experience	9.2–15.5	—[a]	9.0–18.5	—[a]	8.9–19.0	12.6
Less than PhD, no experience	10.5–20.5	14.6	10.0–16.5	—[a]	9.3–17.0	—[a]

Source: J. M. Cuca. Placement report: 1973 and 1974. *American Psychologist,* 1975, *30,* 1176–1179.
Note. Salaries are expressed in thousands of dollars.
[a]Data for *N*s less than 25 were not computed.

purchase a higher quality product at the same price. Table 3-4 shows that, in absolute dollar amounts, the median salaries offered in the three years from 1972 to 1974 either remained the same or declined. Actually, when adjusted for inflation, it means that salaries have declined—proof that the market is adjusting to an increased supply.

What is the job market situation by specialty or subfield? Table 3-5 gives the number of doctorates awarded in various subfields for the 10 years from 1965 to 1974. Note that in terms of absolute numbers the experimental, physiological, and psychometrics subfields have declined in doctorate production since 1971, an adjustment to the especially difficult employment situation recently affecting these subfields.

In terms of percentages of all doctorates awarded, however, the 1974 level of doctorate production in physiological psychology is no different than its 1965 level; the level for psychometrics is down only 1%. The most pronounced shifts in the percentage distribution of subfields are as follows: a 9% decline in experimental psychology, a 4% decline in clinical psychol-

TABLE 3-5   *Doctorates Awarded in Psychology by Subfield and Year: 1965–1974*

Subfield	1974	1973	1972	1971	1970	1969	1968	1967	1966	1965
Clinical	751	737	671	616	549	525	483	417	368	335
Counseling and guidance	208	199	151	144	113	108	103	79	57	47
Developmental/ gerontological	171	149	134	113	83	71	60	48	40	28
Educational	124	113	127	99	87	76	69	60	47	36
School	92	108	87	70	45	32	26	30	10	16
Experimental	360	333	352	392	366	321	282	282	268	219
Comparative	29	24	21	15	22	17	17	16	9	11
Physiological	120	122	121	130	116	108	92	86	75	43
Industrial/personnel	83	76	55	68	75	59	46	59	50	37
Personality	59	51	51	46	50	35	27	34	35	28
Psychometrics	27	24	25	36	18	20	18	15	25	17
Social	207	214	183	171	157	177	121	108	107	100
General	215	154	129	127	120	123	87	42	33	31
Other	141	140	155	89	82	56	21	17	9	7
Total	2,587	2,444	2,262	2,116	1,883	1,728	1,452	1,293	1,133	955

Sources: (a) National Academy of Sciences. *Doctorate recipients from United States universities 1958–1966* (No. 1489). Washington, D.C.: Author, 1967.
(b) National Academy of Sciences-National Research Council. *Doctorate production in U.S. universities, 1920–1962* (No. 1142). Washington, D.C.: Author, 1963.
(c) National Research Council. *Summary report: Doctorate recipients from United States universities.* Washington, D.C.: Author, various years.

ogy, 5% increases in the general and "other" categories, and 3% increases in counseling/guidance and developmental/gerontological psychology. In no subfield, however, is the absolute number of doctorates awarded in 1974 less than that for 1965.

The major market for the so-called "scientific" cluster of subfields has been academia, as can be seen in Table 3-6. More than 80% of those in the combined fields of experimental, comparative, and physiological psychology are employed in colleges and universities, as are 79% of those in developmental, 77% of those in personality, and 76% of those in social. While 65% of those in counseling are also employed in colleges and universities, unpublished APA data show that most are employed in student counseling centers as professionals rather than in academic departments as scientists. Only 35% of the clinicians are employed in academia, but 31% and 16%, respectively, are employed in hospitals or clinics and private practice, the traditional settings of clinicians. Industrial/ organizational psychologists are employed equally (42%) in colleges and universities and in consulting firms and business. School psychologists, not unsurprisingly, are employed primarily in schools (56%) and only secondarily in colleges and universities (29%).

Because the demand of the academic market, heretofore the major employer of scientific psychologists, has stabilized while PhD production continues to increase, the supply–demand relationship in "scientific" psychology has suffered severe imbalances. Table 3-7 is from an article headlined "Job Crunch Hits Scientists Harder Than Professionals" (Cuca, 1975) and that title sums up the situation. New doctorates in "scientific" psychology experienced the worst difficulties in finding employment,

TABLE 3-6   *Doctorate Psychologists by Subfield and Employment Setting: 1972*

Subfield	Schools	Junior colleges	Colleges	Universities	Hospitals and clinics	Independent or group practice	Research or consulting organizations	Business and industry	Government agencies	Other	No report	Total
Clinical	177	81	392	1,978	2,103	1,089	98	9	279	139	434	6,779
Counseling	70	102	290	1,056	200	84	39	9	94	40	96	2,080
Community	5	0	14	115	104	4	12	2	67	5	21	349
Developmental	13	22	130	567	23	6	24	1	31	5	61	883
Educational	95	33	211	797	24	12	86	18	45	18	82	1,421
Experimental/comparative/ physiological	5	18	406	1,423	76	3	113	28	86	21	71	2,250
General	3	23	75	109	5	5	7	1	7	3	14	252
Industrial/organizational	7	6	85	577	9	39	368	285	103	35	71	1,585
Personality	2	6	56	208	10	7	8	3	8	8	26	342
Psychometrics	2	2	12	103	7	3	27	20	15	4	8	203
School	444	10	45	184	20	11	6	4	7	2	64	797
Social	7	17	147	752	28	11	65	14	61	21	54	1,177
Other	9	5	34	215	29	14	39	13	26	14	42	440
No report	265	45	179	811	253	134	98	64	111	136	556	2,652
Total	1,104	370	2,076	8,895	2,891	1,422	990	471	940	451	1,600	21,210

Source: American Psychological Association. *1972 manpower survey.* Unpublished data, Washington, D.C., 1972.

TABLE 3-7   *1975 Employment Status of 1974 Doctorates in Psychology*

Subfield	Academic position	Nonacademic position		Postdoctoral study	Employed but not as a psychologist	Unemployed		Unknown	Total
		Traditional	Nontraditional			Seeking employment	Not seeking employment		
Clinical	162	406	13	23	2	18	1	6	631
Counseling	53	76	3	8	—	5	1	—	145
Developmental	62	42	3	10	1	3	1	1	121
Educational	80	25	2	1	1	—	1	—	110
School	16	56	—	—	—	—	—	—	73
Experimental	170	54	6	34	6	15	—	4	289
Comparative	14	—	—	2	1	1	1	—	18
Physiological	46	13	6	29	1	5	1	—	101
Industrial	22	33	4	2	—	—	—	—	61
Personality	24	7	1	9	—	2	—	—	43
Social	102	28	2	8	—	5	—	3	147
Psychometrics	15	6	1	2	—	1	—	—	26
Other	28	14	5	16	1	3	—	2	69
Total	794	760	46	144	12	58	4	16	1,834

Source: J. M. Cuca. Job crunch hits scientists harder than professionals. *APA Monitor*, July 1975, p. 10.

TABLE 3-8   *Number of Degrees Awarded in 1973[a] and Percentage not Placed in Appropriate Employment by Specialty and Degree*

Specialty	Doctorates		Continuing master's	Master's	
	Awarded	% not placed	Awarded	Awarded	% not placed
Clinical	749	19	500	626	7
Comparative/physiological	103	21	74	23	0
Counseling	325	10	279	1,365	4
Developmental	119	4	106	37	16
Educational	134	3	164	342	3
Experimental	402	9	303	209	12
General	14	0	172	404	17
Industrial	76	0	35	103	5
Personality	42	0	10	11	0
Professional	84	0	35	22	5
Psychometrics	13	8	24	8	0
School	142	0	152	333	9
Social	215	2	148	99	12
Other	194	2	182	510	12
Total	2,612	4	2,124	4,102	7

Source: J. M. Cuca. Graduate enrollments leveling off. *APA Monitor*, November 1974, pp. 16; 19.
[a]Estimated from 77% response.

even though "professional" psychologists were not immune. In spite of the difficulties, the majority of new doctorates eventually do find jobs, perhaps jobs not as desirable as those of a few years ago, but jobs.

Out of 1,834 of the 1974 doctorates appearing in Table 3-7 only 58 were unemployed and seeking employment. A disproportionate number of the unemployed, though, were in experimental psychology. Furthermore, a disproportionate number of those in postdoctoral study, sometimes a haven or a delaying tactic for the unemployed, were in experimental and physiological psychology. The number of those in self-designated non-traditional or innovative positions was small in contrast to the number of those in academic and other traditional positions (46 vs. 1,554), perhaps by definition.

Table 3-8 shows the even greater employment difficulties of those who hold the master's degree. These difficulties are due in part to the encroachment of the doctorates on what had been master's-level jobs and in part to the greater number of master's being produced.

Summary

The phenomenon of supply–demand imbalances is not unique to psychology nor does it seem that the situation will improve in the near future. Experts in future research foresee increases, not decreases, in rates of undergraduate and graduate enrollments and in rates of degree completion. Their reasoning is thus: Because the job market is so competitive, the psychologist with a doctorate degree will have an edge over the psychologist with a master's when competing for what used to be a master's-level position. Therefore, students have a greater incentive to complete the doctorate. The other side of the argument, derived from classical economic theory, is that students will consider the years of graduate study not worth the declining job opportunities and salaries, so enrollments and degrees will decline. The rest of this scenario is that, since supply will decline, demand and salaries will respond by increasing again.

This argument assumes a highly elastic supply, that is, that those considering entering the field will make their decisions primarily in terms of monetary considerations. This has been shown to be untrue.

In any case, as was pointed out earlier, we can be fairly confident about short-run predictions and, barring the tremendous increase in academic hiring or the creation of government programs in which psychologists can take part, the signs for employment are not auspicious.

This may be the point in psychology's history when psychologists themselves will determine the future course of the discipline. In the past that course has been, in good part, a response to the stimulus of federal monies—monies to increase the supply of psychologists trained and working in certain areas immediately applicable to urgent national needs. Because of reductions in those monies, increases in the number of psychologists, and other factors, psychologists must now seek new settings and new types of work activities in which their training and expertise can be utilized. While psychologists will always be found in academia and in mental health service settings, these innovative types of work will now give psychology new directions to its course.

Where will psychology be 25 years from now?

REFERENCES

Cuca, J. M. Job crunch hits scientists harder than professionals. *APA Monitor*, July 1975, p. 10.

Department of Health, Education, and Welfare, Office of Education, National Center for Educational Statistics. *Projections of educational statistics to 1983-84, 1974 edition* (NCES 75-209). Washington, D.C.: United States Government Printing Office, 1975.

Department of Health, Education, and Welfare, Office of Education, National Center for Educational Statistics. *Earned degrees conferred.* Washington, D.C.: United States Government Printing Office, published annually.

Department of Labor, Bureau of Labor Statistics. *Occupational manpower and training needs: Revised 1974* (Bulletin 1824). Washington, D.C.: United States Government Printing Office, 1974.

National Academy of Sciences. *Doctorate recipients from United States universities 1958–1966* (No. 1489). Washington, D.C.: Author, 1967.

National Academy of Sciences. *Doctoral scientists and engineers in the United States: 1973 Profile.* Washington, D.C.: Author, March 1974.

National Academy of Sciences-National Research Council. *Doctorate production in U.S. universities, 1920–1962* (No. 1142). Washington, D.C.: Author, 1963.

National Research Council. *Summary report. Doctorate recipients from United States universities.* Washington, D.C.: Author, annually 1967–1974.

4

Michele Andrisin Wittig and Sharon L. Nolfi

Sex Differences in the Training, Recruitment, and Employment of Psychologists

A number of research reports that have appeared in the last five years have empirically documented aspects of the differential treatment accorded to preprofessional and professional women as compared to men. These differences have been noted in terms of admission to graduate school (Colson & Scott, 1970; Epstein, 1971), hiring (Fidell, 1970), and salaries and promotions (Astin, 1972; Astin & Bayer, 1972; Boneau & Cuca, 1974; Ferber & Loeb, 1973; Keiffer & Cullen, 1970; Levitin, Quinn, & Staines, 1971).

The study reported here relates to the already published work documenting broad areas of differential treatment by sex and also concerns itself with assessing psychologists' perceptions of the motives and reasons for differential treatment within the profession of psychology. Four areas of concern, which Mitchell and Starr (1971) identified as requiring further investigation, are examined: graduate school training, recruitment processes, employment conditions, and opportunities for professional performance.

With regard to graduate school training, evidence suggests that a psychology graduate student's progress toward the PhD is facilitated by institutional experiences such as research involvement, assistance from one's thesis adviser, and discussion of career plans with an adviser (Astin, El-Khawas, & Bisconti, 1973). Often, women are not offered equal opportunity to participate in these experiences.

After graduate training is completed, recruitment processes loom as potential areas of differential treatment by sex. When the professional seeks his or her first employment, differential treatment may be evident in rules against nepotism, in unstructured or nonexistent hiring policies, in

Michele Andrisin Wittig is at the Department of Psychology, California State University, Northridge, and Sharon L. Nolfi is at the Department of Higher Education, University of California, Los Angeles.

A more detailed version of this paper was originally submitted as a report to the Status of Women Committee of the Western Psychological Association, Nora Weckler, Chairperson. The authors express their thanks to the Western Psychological Association and the California State University, Northridge, Foundation for financial support and to James S. Fleming for computer programming. Parts of this paper were presented at the 1974 Western Psychological Association Convention in San Francisco. Requests for copies of the original report should be addressed to Michele A. Wittig, Department of Psychology, California State University, Northridge, California 91324.

distorted concepts of "affirmative action," in unavailability of part-time work for parents, or in employers' desires for candidates with geographic mobility (Scott, 1970).

With regard to employment conditions, Astin (1972) and Joesting (1974) found that women psychologists are vastly underrepresented on the psychology faculties of the PhD-granting institutions despite the fact that, as Fidell (1970) showed, sex is unrelated to publication rate, presumably the factor that such institutions emphasize more than non-PhD-granting institutions. Astin and Bayer (1972) reported that when women in academia are matched with men on all criteria used for promotion (e.g., rate of publication and 32 other variables) a difference of $1,000 per year in salary and one fifth of a step in rank, favoring men, was found. These studies firmly established the fact that female professionals earn less than their male counterparts and are promoted at a slower rate even when achieving at an equal level. In the study reported here, the questions designed to assess differential reward structures in employment were open-ended. It was hoped that these questions would encourage respondents to supply researchers and policymakers with information concerning other, more subtle, but perhaps equally important areas of potential discrimination by sex, including reverse sex discrimination of all types.

With regard to opportunities for professional performance (e.g., invitations to give colloquiums or nominations to offices in professional organizations) evidence suggests that such opportunities can be viewed as similar to publishing rate. These opportunities function not only as contributions to one's profession but also as criteria for receiving rewards (e.g., peer recognition and pay increases).

Studies mentioned earlier, which controlled differences in academic position and prestige of institution of employment, found that, although female psychologists do not publish less than their male counterparts, as a group they hold lower positions, work in the less prestigious institutions, and receive lower salaries than male psychologists. These facts have been viewed by some as evidence that most women "choose" to be employed in less prestigious institutions, that they fail to exert the effort to advance as quickly as men because professional rewards are not as important to them, and that they would continue this behavior even if the professional reward structure were the same for women as for men. Some female psychologists, however, already contribute as much and in similar ways as their male counterparts under the current reward structure. In fact, the structure itself may function as a negative incentive for many other women psychologists who believe that a woman must achieve more professionally than a man in order to receive the same rewards.

The study reported here is a regional rather than a national analysis. A regional analysis has been shown to be a particularly useful approach to investigating the status of professional women when the research is intended to be a springboard for action (Kimmell, 1974; Mitchell & Starr, 1971). By reason of greater accessibility of meetings, lower membership fees, less formidable obstacles to action, etc., regional organizations, as compared to national associations, are strategic centers for men and women working toward reform within their profession.

Survey Methodology

The sample for the study was selected from the 1974 membership list of the Western Psychological Association (WPA). It consisted of all 689 female members of the WPA and 689 male members, who were selected at random from among the 2,069 male members. Seven ambiguities of sex of names were resolved by the flip of a coin.

One hundred questions were sent to each of the potential respondents on February 15, 1974. These questions were entitled "Western Psychological Association Training and Employment Questionnaire," and the introductory paragraph identified them as a project of the WPA's Committee on the Status of Women. (A self-addressed stamped envelope was not included with the questionnaire since the extent of financial support was uncertain at the time the questionnaires were mailed.) The questionnaire was divided into five sections of different lengths; all but the first section were titled. Section 1 (Questions 1–23) focused on the respondent's personal and educational background and current job-seeking status. Section 2 (Questions 24–36) inquired about the respondent's current primary paid employment, while Section 3 (Questions 37–41) consisted of similar questions concerning his or her current secondary paid employment. Section 4 (Questions 43–92) was entitled "Hiring and Employment Conditions." Questions 43–49 of this section asked whether various types of irrelevant criteria for hiring had been used against the respondent. Questions 50–69 of this section were concerned with the respondent's experiences in the job market during the two prior years. Questions 70–78 of Section 4 inquired about the respondent's employment preferences and sought information concerning factors related to employment, including child care. The remaining questions (79–92) dealt with experienced and perceived sex discrimination on the job and within the psychology profession as a whole. Section 5 (Questions 93–100) consisted of similar questions regarding graduate school. Every returned questionnaire was read by the principal investigator who also checked the work of three transcribers by sampling questionnaires and comparing them with transcriptions.

Results and Discussion

A total of 562 (40.7%) of the questionnaires were completed and returned by the deadline. The rates of completed returns were 33.8% and 47.6% for males and females, respectively. The data base was thus 562 questionnaires: 234 (41.6%) from males and 328 (58.4%) from females.

Personal, Educational, and Professional Background

More male respondents than female respondents indicated minority group membership (7.6% vs. 3.0%). (While this study concerns sex differences rather than race differences, these data compel the attention of all psychologists to direct immediate and forceful efforts to begin changes in graduate education and in the foundations of psychology to increase the proportion of minorities.) Likewise, more men than women reported being married (77.3% vs. 57.0%) and having children (70.4% vs. 51.8%). While men in the sample were equally likely to have children of any age, the likelihood of women having children increased with the age of the children. This could reflect a tendency for female respondents to suspend WPA membership during years when their children are younger.

The majority of respondents (84.5% of the men and 73.8% of the women) reported holding a doctoral degree. Men and women were equally likely to have received their degrees from prestigious institutions, as classified by the American Council on Education (Roose & Andersen, 1970); 21.0% of the males and 23.2% of the females reported receiving their degree from one of the institutions in the highest prestige category. The mean year for beginning the respondent's highest degree was 1958.00 for males and 1959.31 for females, while the mean year of attaining the respondent's highest degree was 1962.51 for males and 1964.06 for females. The proportion of clinical or counseling psychologists to those in nonclinical/ noncounseling fields was about 4 to 6, with little difference between the percentages of men and women within each field except for industrial psychology and developmental psychology. While 44.5% of the wives of male respondents were reported to be employed professionally and 33.0% of them to hold a master's degree or higher, 78.4% of the husbands of female respondents were reported to be occupied professionally and 74.0% of them to hold such degrees.

Inspection of the data concerning primary titles of male and female respondents revealed that similar percentages of male and female respondents were employed in the listed job categories with two notable exceptions: Proportionally over three and a half times as many males as females were full professors (22.5% vs. 8.5%) and fewer males than females held titles other than those listed (16.7% vs. 22.6%). None of the males and 1.5% of the females reported being unemployed. Results on the distribution of full professors can be compared with those of Bayer (1973), who found that among academics in general 30% of the males and only 11% of the females are full professors. Astin's (1972) figures showed 31% of academic males and 15% of academic females in universities are full professors. The discrepancy diminished in four-year colleges. Table 4-1 presents findings concerning the types of institutions in which respondents were employed. The greatest employment difference between sexes was found in the PhD-granting "University of" (e.g., California, Oregon, Washington) system (31.8% for males vs. 20.1% for females). In contrast, nearly equal percentages of males and females (18.9% and 17.7%, respectively) were employed in the state university system; however, most of these universities do not grant the PhD degree. Although 56.2% of the males and 43.0% of the females held positions in academia at least at the level of instructor or research associate, 35.6% of the males and 24.4% of the females reported having attained tenure.

TABLE 4-1   *Primary Employer of Respondents*

Primary employer	Sex of respondent	
	Male	Female
No response	1.3	7.3
"University of"	31.8	20.1
State university	18.9	17.7
Junior college	3.4	5.2
Private university	4.7	4.6
Private college	3.0	2.1
Research institute	2.6	1.5
Private consulting	.9	1.2
Government	12.4	12.2
Clinic	3.9	7.0
School district	5.6	6.4
Industry	.9	.3
Self-employed	7.7	7.6
Other	3.0	6.7

Note. Figures are expressed in percentages.

Female respondents were employed 1.7% less time than males (92.6% and 94.3%, respectively) at their primary jobs and earned an average of $3,278.18 less than males annually. At secondary jobs, males and females reported working 19.0% and 21.8% time, respectively, but males earned $1,235.17 per year more than females. While these data do not necessarily show that female respondents receive less pay for equal work, they do indicate that the female respondents receive less pay for equal percentage of time worked. The total salary discrepancy between the sexes was $4,513.35 per year, favoring males.

In summary, the data on the personal and educational background of the respondents revealed that the typical female psychologist in the sample was similar to the typical male in most respects but that she was somewhat less likely to hold the doctorate, began and received her degree about a year and a half later than the typical male, and was less likely to be married and have children. If she was married, her spouse was very likely to be professional. Despite her having received her degree from an institution of equal prestige as the typical male respondent, she was much less likely to be employed in one of the prestigious, PhD-granting public universities of the West and less than one third as likely to be a full professor if employed anywhere in academia. She earned $4,500 less per year than the typical male respondent even though she worked approximately the same percentage of time at her job.

Graduate School

When asked to indicate whether they received financial support while in graduate school, 59.5% of the males and 66.8% of the females reported having received a fellowship, alone or in combination with other forms of financial support.

Five questions concerned the respondent's experience while he or she was a graduate student. For the first four questions, respondents were asked to indicate on a scale of from 1 to 5 their beliefs concerning the treatment of male and female graduate students. The midpoint of the scale (3) was labeled "women equal to men," the low point (1) was labeled "women strongly favored," and the high point (5) was labeled "men strongly favored." Several summary statistics for each question in the series are reported in Table 4-2. The last question in this series asked the respondent if, while in graduate school, he or she believed that differential treatment existed in ways that had not been covered in the previous four questions. Affirmative responses were given by 23.2% of the males and 36.6% of the females. Of these respondents, 97.4% of the males and 100% of the females described the type of discrimination to which they referred. Table 4-3 shows the striking disagreement between the sexes concerning these other types of differential treatment in graduate school. Males tended to cite specific types of bias against females proportionately about one third as often as the females themselves did, but females cited bias against males proportionately less than one tenth as much as the males themselves did. The proportion of male and female respondents reporting specific types of differential treatment was quite similar for two categories of responses: both groups believed that females are treated as sex objects and that they are not as encouraged as males to pursue a career. The category of bias most frequently reported by females was that there was less respect for female graduate students and their opinions.

Several tentative conclusions may be drawn from the graduate school data. First, in light of the fact that females reported fellowship awards slightly more often than males, it appears that female respondents were at least as well qualified academically as male respondents upon entrance to graduate school. An alternative hypothesis is that males were discriminated against in fellowship awards. This hypothesis does not seem likely for a number of reasons, not the least of which is the agreement of a sizable minority of male and female respondents that females were discriminated

TABLE 4-2   *Respondents' Perception of Treatment of Male and Female Graduate Students*

Treatment	Male responses			Female responses		
	% responding	Mean response	% responding by scale points 4 or 5	% responding	Mean response	% responding by scale points 4 or 5
Criteria for graduate admission	92.7	3.32	29.6	92.7	3.70	44.5
Faculty judgments of students' commitment to career	89.7	3.66	51.0	93.9	4.11	68.0
Grades and evaluations for work of comparable quality	96.6	3.00	6.9	95.7	3.28	28.9
Faculty efforts to obtain professional placements for students	91.4	3.26	24.5	89.3	4.00	52.4

Note. Scale point 4 was labeled "men favored," scale point 5 was labeled "men strongly favored."

TABLE 4-3   *Respondents' Perception of "Other" Types of Differential Treatment by Sex in Graduate School*

Category of responses	Frequency from males	% of males responding thus	Frequency from females	% of females responding thus
Sexist comments degrading females	1	.4	9	2.7
Less respect for females	9	3.9	31	9.5
Females treated as sex objects	8	3.4	15	4.6
Females left out of decision making	0	0	0	0
Males have closer relationships with male professors	1	.4	9	2.7
Females must be better than males to receive equal reward (e.g., pay or grades)	3	1.3	23	7.0
Limited admission, financial, or other career preparation opportunities for women	7	3.0	23	7.0
Females not encouraged as much as males to pursue career	6	2.6	11	3.4
Other bias against females	3	1.3	18	5.5
Males treated as sex objects	8	3.4	1	.3
Other bias against males	7	3.0	1	.3
Responded affirmatively but failed to describe	6	2.6	0	0
Total respondents giving affirmative responses[a]	54	23.2	122	36.6

[a] A few respondents gave more than one comment, therefore these totals do not include more than one affirmative response.

against in criteria for graduate admission. Furthermore, the majority of respondents agreed that despite the high academic qualifications of the females, the faculty judged them to be less committed to their careers, and the majority of the female respondents believed that the faculty acted on this judgment by expending less effort to help the females obtain professional placement. If the facts are in correspondence with this last belief, they would be particularly debilitating to those women who were married to other professionals at the time of their first postgraduate training job hunt. It should be obvious that such two-career couples need as much help as nonmarried students of both sexes in obtaining suitable career placements, since they are restricted to positions within commuting distance of their spouses.

The picture that emerges is one of more frequent reports of bias against females relative to the amount of reported bias against males (2.5:1 among males and 70:1 among females). Even if one chooses not to believe in the factual basis of the reports, it is difficult to ignore the fact that a majority (52.4%) of female WPA respondents believed that they were subject to one or more forms of discriminatory treatment while in graduate school. What motivational and emotional toll these beliefs exacted from the female WPA respondents and their female classmates in terms of perseverance in their goals, self-confidence in their abilities, and belief in the quality of their accomplishments is not known. For some, it may have spurred them on to a more dedicated pursuit of their goals. For others, the belief that their status was less favorable than males may have caused them to perform less well and/or to abandon their original career goals. To the extent that there were females who, although intellectually qualified, could not motivate themselves to continue their studies for these reasons, the female dropout rate would rise, fulfilling the prophecy and providing more fodder for those wishing to support the notion that females lack career commitment. Their defection would also decrease the ranks of women who, armed with a well-earned, prestigious PhD, could be considered qualified for the high-status positions in the field.

At the institutions from which this sample obtained their degrees male graduate faculty and peers may have discriminated against women students; but apart from this question both male and female respondents would certainly have benefited from the exposure to more women graduate faculty as role models, mentors, and confidants. Ironically, the paucity of such faculty might have been due to actual and/or perceived discrimination against women at the graduate level. In the next section, data suggesting additional reasons for the paucity of female faculty at PhD-granting institutions are discussed.

Recruitment and Hiring

Success in the recruitment and hiring marketplace is closely tied to success in graduate school since it is the graduate schools that provide the "recruits" with their credentials. In this sense, discrimination in hiring and recruitment, where it exists, is in part due to the actual and/or perceived discrimination experienced at the graduate level. In addition, however, recruitment and hiring is fraught with its own types of sex bias. This section is concerned with recruitment and hiring criteria that are not based on qualifications but that differentiate by other, sex-related criteria. Levitin et al. (1971) termed this "access discrimination."

Some forms of access discrimination that affect the sexes differentially are imposed by institutions themselves, for example, institutional policies that forbid recruitment committees from considering spouses of current employees for job openings. This practice is especially prevalent in academia, where 90% of the faculty in psychology departments are male and most are married (Astin, 1972). In the present study, 31.3% of the males and 25.6% of the females reported that antinepotism rules existed in their place of employment, although in some cases respondents added that the rules merely required that spouses not be in direct line of authority of each other. Other forms of access discrimination appear, at least on the surface, to be self-imposed. Many of these forms, however, can be traced to societally rooted access discrimination. Career choice and job location constraints are especially prevalent among married women in a society where wives earn less than their husbands in spite of equal work (Astin & Bayer, 1972; Levitin et al., 1971) and where women are assumed to be the primary child rearers and homemakers (Bardwick, 1971). Data concerning both forms of potential access discrimination were gathered.

Respondents were asked if they had ever been offered a lesser job because a prospective employer knew they lacked geographic mobility, and, if so, when this had occurred. Results revealed that 3.9% of the men and 12.5% of the women reported this experience had occurred more than two years before the study, while 1.7% of the men and 4.3% of the women reported that it occurred within two years of the study. In the time interval of more than two years before the study, 9% of the men and 11.3% of the women reported being offered a job that was less than they were promised; the comparable figures for the more recent time interval were 4.3% and 7.0%, respectively.

Women reported the use of recruitment or hiring criteria irrelevant to job performance five times as often as men did; these data apply to discrimination that occurred more than two years before the study (20.7% for women vs. 4.7% for men). Nearly equal percentages of each sex reported having this experience within two years of the study, although women reported it slightly more often (5.8% for women and 4.3% for men). Sex of applicant was reported by 11.6% of the women and 1.3% of the men to have been used as a criterion by employers. Four percent of the women but none of the men reported employers citing children as an exclusionary factor. More than 11 times as many women as men indicated that employers had excluded them because their spouses were seeking a job (4.6% for females vs. .4% for males). Hiring criteria relating to ethnic factors or sex and ethnic group combined were reported 3.8 times more often by men than by women (3.4% for males vs. .9% for females).

The above data suggest that women are not likely to be considered for a job on an equal basis with men. After sex, the most frequently reported discriminatory hiring criteria are related to marriage and/or children. It is 6.5 times more likely that a female applicant will be excluded from consideration for a job on the basis of one or both of these criteria than a male applicant (11.0% vs. 1.7%). The decrease in reports of such incidents may be due either to a decrease in the proportion of applicants who are discriminated against, a decrease in the number of job openings, or both.

The questionnaire responses concerning "constraints when seeking present employment" are referred to as *past constraints* to distinguish them from questionnaire responses concerning "constraints in seeking new employment," which may be thought of as *present constraints*. Proportionately many more women than men (65.2% vs. 36.5%) reported having been under job-seeking constraints in the past; in fact, women comprised 71.6% of all persons who reported being under past constraints. Of all married women in the sample, 43.6% reported that their spouse's employment was a consideration when seeking their present employment, while the comparable figure for married men was 4.4% (9.9 to 1).

About equal percentages of men and women reported that they were currently seeking a job (18.9% and 19.8%, respectively). When asked the reason for currently seeking a job, proportionately six times as many women as men reported being unemployed (2.4% vs. .4%). Women constituted 88.9% of the unemployed job seekers.

Proportionately twice as many women as men in the entire sample (43.9% vs. 21.9%) reported being under present constraints in seeking a job. Sex differences also emerged among the reasons given for present constraints. Women reported spouse's employment as a present constraint proportionately almost nine times more often than men (14.9% vs. 1.7%). Of all married women in the sample, 26.1% reported that their spouse's employment was a consideration in seeking such employment, while the comparable percentage of married men in the sample was 2.2% (12 to 1).

Data presented in the first action of results suggest part of the reason for the discrepancy between rates of spouse-related job constraints by sex: 1.8 times as many married female respondents as married male respondents are married to a working professional (77.5% vs. 42.8%). Nevertheless, it must be concluded that a female psychologist married to a working professional is still many times more likely to consider her spouse as a constraint when seeking a job than is her male counterpart.

This finding could reflect a belief on the part of some of the professional couples in the sample that men's traditional cultural role is primary earner and that women's traditional cultural role is primary child rearer, regardless of the wife's educational level or career aspirations. For others, this finding might merely reflect an acknowledgement of the fact that, as reported in this and other studies, professional women make less money than professional men, so the husband should be free of constraints in seeking his best job, while the wife should seek her best job within these limits. Perhaps more male psychologists will be encouraged to take into account their wives' professional-level job opportunities when inequities in pay within and between professions are eliminated. But other biases peculiar to joint job-hunting couples also are waiting. The small percentage of the married males in the sample who, with their professional spouses, are attempting to "do the equalitarian thing" by jointly deciding where to apply for and/or accept positions, risk being viewed, along with married women applicants in general, as poor prospects for accepting a position if offered.

One solution may be to keep information to oneself concerning marital status and joint job seeking when writing a letter of application. But it is easy to see that this course of action too has its pitfalls. It precludes the potential employer from helping the couple in the search for jobs within commuting distance (a search substantially more difficult than finding only one suitable job) and leaves the potential employer feeling as if his or her recruitment money has been misused if the potential employee turns down a job offer for a spouse-related reason after coming for an interview. To the extent that potential employers assure inquirers that information concerning joint job hunting will not be used against them, job seekers will be encouraged to include such information in their letters of application.

From the data showing a much greater tendency for married females to be under spouse-related job-seeking constraints than married males, it should be clear that eliminating an applicant from consideration for a job because the applicant must take his or her spouse's job opportunities into consideration when deciding whether to accept a position will take its toll on women job seekers much more often than on men. To fail to acknowledge this as sex discrimination is to close one's eyes to the inequities in the society that account for the differential tendency in the first place.

A total of 54 males and 69 females reported that they had sent letters of inquiry concerning job openings to potential employers within two years of the time of the study. These respondents represent 23.2% and 21.8% of the total males and females in the sample, respectively. The males sent 19.7 letters each on average and received a response from 9.0% of the potential employers, while the females sent 23.8 letters on average and prompted a response rate of 7.6%. Of the males who sent letters of inquiry, 68.5% were offered a job by one or more of the potential employers and 54.1% of these males subsequently accepted one of the offers. Of the females who sent letters, 65.2% were offered a job and 80.3% of them accepted one of the offers.

Similar percentages of the males and females in the sample reported that potential employers had actively recruited them for jobs (39.1% of the males and 42.1% of the females). Among those actively recruited, 39.1% of the males and 42.1% of the females subsequently applied for the jobs for which they had been actively recruited and 100% of both groups were subsequently offered those jobs. Only 36.1% of the males and 52.9% of the females who had received such job offers actually accepted them, however.

Among respondents who reported the type of institution that had actively recruited them and offered them a job, a smaller percentage of the jobs offered to females than to males were academic (69.4% vs. 81.5%, respectively). Males and females did not differ with regard to the mean prestige rating of the academic institutions that had actively recruited and subsequently offered jobs to them. For all such job offers, the mean salary offered to males was $19,731.00 as compared to $14,421.00 offered to females.

The percentages of males and females in the entire sample who reported that they had been asked to terminate by their employers within two years of the time of the study were similar (6.0% vs. 6.1%). While 5.0% of these females reported that their employers had given a reason for termination based on sex discrimination, none of the males did so. Of the respondents, 50% of the terminated males and 35% of the terminated females agreed with their employers' reason for termination. Among the 35.7% of the terminated males and the 65.0% of the terminated females who did not agree with the employer's reason, none of the males reported sex and/or race to be the true reason for his termination, while 38.5% of the females did.

Within two years of the study, 12.4% of the males and 15.5% of the females in the sample reported having left one or more jobs voluntarily. Among those who left voluntarily, 39.7% of the males and 37.3% of the females did so because they had received a better job offer, while 10.3% of the males and 7.9% of the females left because of perceived race and/or sex discrimination. Family responsibility accounted for 9.8% of the females leaving and "different percentage time" accounted for 7.8%. No males reported reasons in these categories.

The picture that emerges from these data is one of similar percentages of males and females making inquiries in an attempt to change jobs and receiving offers, but more females than males ultimately accepting an offer. While similar percentages of males and females were actively recruited for a job, and while they subsequently applied and received an offer, more females ultimately accepted such a job offer even though the starting salary was 73% of that offered to males. Thus, regardless of which party initiates the process, a female who receives a job offer is more likely than a male to accept it. These data, taken together, lend additional support to the claim that women in the profession are not in a position to be as free agents as men in the job market. Furthermore, while nearly identical percentages of males and females were asked to terminate, a majority of females did not agree with the employer's stated reason, and 38.5% of these suspected sex or race discrimination on the part of their former employer; none of the males cited sex or race discrimination as the reason for termination. Apparently, not even the males who were terminated in the two years prior to the study believed the myth that they were being "fired" to make way for minorities and/or women. A final belief that these data failed to support was that of high female turnover employment rate. Females in this sample did not report changing jobs voluntarily much more frequently than males, despite the females' greater family responsibilities. Similar percentages of both sexes reported leaving their jobs to take better positions.

Employment Conditions

The third area in which differential treatment by sex might be found is in conditions of employment. This study investigated two such categories, both of which may have their roots in the different sex roles prevalent in our society. Several questions were asked concerning the first category— job attribute preferences. The first question revealed that 14.6% of the males and 27.4% of the females in the sample preferred part-time work. No difference by sex was found with regard to whether the respondents' present employer offered prorated but similar benefits for part-time employment as for full-time employment: 21.0% of the males and 23.5% of the females responded affirmatively.

Replies to questions concerning child care preferences revealed that the employers of 22.6% of the respondents provided day care and 27.8% of the day care centers were judged adequate by respondents. More males than females reported that they had children who would use a child care center provided by their employer if one were available (14.2% and 9.1%, respectively) and that they had one or more children presently enrolled in a day care center (7.7% and 3.0%, respectively). While less than one fourth of the respondents were employed by an institution that had a child care center, 71.2% of the respondents agreed that their employers should provide such a center (63.9% of the males and 76.2% of the females). When asked how such a center should be financed, 37.8% of the males and 52.7% of the females favored a combination of funds supplied by parents, government sources, and the employer.

The second category of conditions of employment involves differential treatment by sex on the part of the employer. Levitin et al. (1971) termed this "treatment discrimination." In Astin's (1969) study of women doctorates, 36% of these women reported experiencing employer discrimination in hiring, promotion considerations, or delegation of responsibilities. In the present study, the four questions that inquired about sex discrimination on the job revealed some large sex differences. Of the respondents, 3.4% of the males and 22.9% of the females reported the occurrence and the type of personal experiences of sex discrimination; 50% of the 8 males who responded to this question, compared to 26.7% of the 75 females who responded, reported sex differences in rank and/or promotion. While 17.3% of the females in this group reported discrimination in pay and 14.7% reported discrimination in the assignment of "higher level functions," none of the males reported these types of discrimination. When asked whether they were "afraid to disapprove of sexist comments," only 5.2% of the males and 2.7% of the females reported never having heard such comments, while 82.8% of the males and 72.2% of the females replied that they were not afraid to disapprove of them. Both males and females (28.3% and 30.8%, respectively) responded that they had knowledge of sex discrimination or reverse sex discrimination against persons in their place of employment other than themselves.

Table 4-4 shows that the reported frequency of discrimination against females is much larger than that of discrimination against males within every category of discrimination, with pay raises favoring males reported 10 times more often by both sexes than pay raises favoring females. From the data concerning employment conditions, it is clear that a substantial minority of female and, to a lesser extent, male respondents believed that females experience discrimination in their places of employment.

TABLE 4-4   *Knowledge of Sex Discrimination Against Others in Employment*

Discrimination	% males	% females	% combined
Knowledge of sex discrimination against another			
Yes	28.3	30.8	29.7
No	68.7	59.1	63.2
Types of sex discrimination against others			
Favoring Males			
Pay	6.1	5.9	6.0
Hiring, rank, promotion	13.6	30.7	24.0
Responsibilities	4.5	5.0	4.8
Higher level functions	3.0	8.9	6.6
Comments	7.6	15.8	12.6
Favoring Females			
Pay	0	1.0	.6
Hiring, rank, promotion	12.1	3.0	6.6
Responsibilities	0	2.0	1.2
Higher level functions	0	2.0	1.2
Comments	13.6	4.0	7.8
No Response	39.4	21.8	28.7

TABLE 4-5   *Respondents' Perception of Opportunities of Males and Females in the Profession*

Opportunity	Male responses			Female responses		
	% responding	Mean response	% responding by scale points 4 or 5	% responding	Mean response	% responding by scale points 4 or 5
Demonstration of competence in employment unit	92.7	3.02	11.5	90.9	3.69	25.0
Appointment to serve on editorial boards	70.0	3.32	24.9	71.3	3.95	47.5
Service on convention program review committees	74.2	3.08	13.8	74.1	3.63	36.9
Nomination for professional office	70.0	3.08	17.6	78.1	3.57	44.2
Service on grant review committees	73.8	3.15	20.2	76.2	3.89	50.3
Appointment to other professional boards	76.0	3.21	22.7	73.2	3.88	48.8

Opportunities for Professional Performance

The final area of potential discrimination investigated in this study concerns opportunities to demonstrate professional competence in one's place of employment and in the psychological profession in general. Six questions requested respondents to indicate on a scale of from 1 to 5 their beliefs in regard to this issue. The scale was labeled exactly as it had been for the questions regarding treatment in graduate school. The midpoint of the scale (3) was labeled "women equal to men," the lowpoint (1) was labeled "women strongly favored," and the highpoint (5) was labeled "men strongly favored." For each question in the series, the percentage of persons of each sex who perceived that males were favored over females is reported in Table 4-5. For any single question after the first one, from 21.4% to 29.2% of the persons in the sample did not respond. Often a failure to respond was accompanied by a notation indicating the person did not know enough about the category to form an opinion. Males and females failed to respond at approximately the same frequency. The last question in this series was designed to obtain examples of differential treatment that were not covered by the previous six questions. When respondents were asked if they believed that females were treated differently than males in their place of employment, or in the psychology profession in general, 44.3% of the males and 55.8% of the females responded affirmatively. Of these, 78.6% of the males and 98.4% of the females described the type of discrimination to which they referred. Categories of responses to this question and the percentages of responses of each type by sex appear in Table 4-6. As was true of responses concerning differential treatment in graduate school, responses differed with respect to the extent to which each sex agreed with the opposite sex concerning the amount of differential treatment. Males tended to cite specific types of bias against females proportionately about one half as often as the females themselves did, while females agreed that males were discriminated against pro-

TABLE 4-6   *Respondents' Perception of "Other" Types of Differential Treatment by Sex in the Profession*

Category of response	Frequency from males	% of males responding thus	Frequency from females	% of females responding thus
Sexist comments degrading females	2	.9	7	2.1
Less respect for females	9	3.9	41	12.5
Females treated as sex objects	4	1.7	6	1.8
Females left out of decision making	0	0	6	1.8
Females must be better than males to receive equal reward (e.g., pay)	7	3.0	19	5.8
Limited hiring, pay, or other career-related opportunities for women	36	15.4	81	24.7
Females not encouraged as much as males to pursue career	0	0	9	2.7
Other bias against females	8	3.4	22	6.7
(Recently) males must be better than females to receive equal reward	21	9.0	6	1.8
Other bias against males	7	3.0	1	.3
Responded affirmatively, but failed to describe	22	9.4	3	.9
Total respondents giving affirmative responses[a]	103	44.3	183	55.8

[a]A few respondents gave more than one comment, therefore these totals do not include more than one affirmative response.

portionately one fifth as much as the males themselves did. The largest category of differential treatment reported by both sexes was limited career-related opportunities available to women. Nearly 25% of the entire sample of female respondents cited this type of discrimination.

In summary, males and females within the psychological profession are viewed by half of the respondents to be treated differentially in one or more ways. With regard to opportunities to demonstrate professional competence, discrimination against women is viewed to be most severe in three areas, each of which elicited affirmative responses from approximately 38% of the sample: opportunities to serve on editorial boards, on grant review committees, and on "other professional boards." On the average, 4.3% of the sample felt that male psychologists are given fewer opportunities than female psychologists to demonstrate professional competence. A similar percentage (4.8%) felt that recently male psychologists had to be better than their female counterparts in order to receive equal rewards. Nevertheless, when given the opportunity to describe ways in which the sexes are treated differently, bias against females relative to bias against males was reported much more frequently by both sexes (1.8 to 1 by males and 24 to 1 by females).

Summary and Recommendations

Clearly, substantial percentages of female WPA members, and, to a lesser extent, male members, view women psychologists as a disadvantaged minority within their profession. Whether this awareness can motivate reform remains to be seen. The responsibility for elimination of barriers to equal opportunity by sex within the profession has traditionally been placed on women themselves, who have been variously encouraged to adjust to a predominately male profession by being told either to emulate male patterns or to use their "femininity" to advantage.

Traditionally the profession, for its part, has "accommodated" itself to women in a number of ways documented in this study. For example, the graduate admissions committees of its PhD-granting institutions have imposed higher admissions standards for females, often as a solution to alleged differential dropout rates by sex. Various legal restrictions now forbid this practice. Since the strictness of the admissions criteria themselves may be quite irrelevant to the reasons why women (or men) drop out, the basis of this practice can itself be questioned. While equalizing admissions criteria by sex is helpful, it will not assure that more women (or men) will finish their studies. Research is needed to ascertain the criteria that predict PhD attainment and to develop ways of making the academic environment more favorable to women.

Graduate education and the profession are themselves in need of radical reform to assure women an equal place and an opportunity for greater contribution. First, women's potential to bear children must no longer be used as a negative weight in considerations for admissions or employment. Childbearing is more incompatible with a woman's career than a man's only when it is assumed that the childbearer must pay for her privilege in lost wages and lost seniority and that the childbearer is the principal child rearer. The educational and employment institutions must recognize the right of women to childbearing and to careers by providing paid maternity leave, with no loss of seniority, for those women employees who elect to have children. In some circumstances men could be granted paternity leave. There are many reasons to recognize men's right to participate equally in child rearing, not the least of which is that male participation may be a prerequisite for women's equality of opportunity in employment.

This is a much more difficult problem for institutions to help solve. The data from this study reveal that child care centers and, to a lesser extent, part-time employment opportunities with prorated benefits are favored by many respondents. To these data the authors would like to add the suggestion that males be recruited to be child care givers and be included in part-time employment opportunities. Perhaps as a side benefit, an upgrading in the status and pay of both types of employment will occur. In addition, arrangement for part-time study to obtain the doctorate should be increased for both sexes. Marlowe (Note 1) pointed out that since the years immediately after the doctorate are, for academic women, the same years that women often must devote to child rearing, different rules for tenure should be established for such women. To the extent that they participate in child rearing, male and female parents should be given different rules for tenure and should be allowed leave for child rearing.

Independent job hunting of the kind practiced by most male psychologists in this study is not a reasonable solution for two-career couples because such job hunting usually necessitates separation of the couple as the price of the best job placement. Independent job hunting by the male is an example that employs traditional male behavior as the standard for female professionals to emulate. Its attractiveness to traditional males lies in the fact that it does not require them to change their behavior in any way. Guidelines for job applicants and potential employers are needed to ensure fair treatment for two-career couples in the job market.

Motherhood and/or marital status, however, while continuing to provide reasons for discriminating against women, do not account for all of the differential treatment by sex. It would be a mistake, therefore, to view parental leave benefits, child care centers, part-time employment opportunities, revised tenure rules, and guidelines for fair treatment of two-career couples as sufficient recommendations to effect equal opportunity by sex within the profession. Additional excellent recommendations for reform from within the profession have been made by Keiffer and Cullen (1970), who presented their recommendations at the American Psychological Association (APA) Convention in 1969, and by APA's Committee on Women in Psychology and its predecessor, the Task Force on the Status of Women in Psychology (APA, 1973).

The above recommendations are designed to overcome the near exclusion of women psychologists from positions of power in academic and nonacademic private and governmental institutions. But it is not enough for women to merely grab a larger slice of the professional pie. Hopkins (1975) argued that academia rewards those who do what men think is valuable. Some men and women, but especially women, in and out of academia are questioning traditional values. In many instances these challenges are coming from within the profession itself, from those who have already attained the prestigious credentials necessary for full participation in the profession. According to their view, not only must the profession work toward removing the inequalities that hamper women's opportunities in psychology but it must simultaneously begin to reexamine and perhaps change the rules by which success is achieved and the definition of accomplishment. Clearly, responsible and responsive teaching must become a legitimate criterion of promotion and tenure at all educational institutions. As this study has shown, women in psychology are found in the institutions that emphasize teaching over research, but academia generally rates research over teaching in the reward system. The argument is often used that teaching quality is difficult to measure, but this ignores the difficulty of measuring research quality. We suggest that ways be sought to improve the measure of both, rather than to use the difficulty of measuring one as the excuse to perpetuate the prevailing hierachy of values.

To continue this analysis, the following questions are being asked by those who are challenging the traditional professional values: Must accomplishment be defined in terms that disfavor, if not outright exclude, the ways in which women professionals have traditionally performed? Is alienation from their respective out groups the price women and other underrepresented groups in psychology must pay for their success? Is it possible for married women professionals to get their mostly professional male spouses to share the child care duties as an alternative to hiring less privileged women or men? If not, are professionals willing to pay the child care giver, whether male or female, a generous wage with the same fringe benefits that are received within their own profession? If it is necessary that some persons be in positions of power over others, are there ways to provide that the choice of such persons be made more democratically? How can women and other underrepresented groups in psychology help each other gain positions of power without merely replacing the "Old Boys' Club" with an "Old Girls' Club"? Is it possible to perform in an instrumental, entrepreneurial role effectively without exploiting those over whom we have power? To those of our colleagues who would dismiss these questions as examples of "typically female role conflict," we should like to add that we intend to seek new ways to resolve these conflicts and we hope they will join us.

REFERENCE NOTE

1. Marlowe, L. *Prejudice against women in the university.* Paper presented at the Conference on Women and the University, New York, N.Y., March 1973.

REFERENCES

American Psychological Association. Report of the Task Force on the Status of Women in Psychology. *American Psychologist,* 1973, *28,* 611–616.

Astin, H. S. *The woman doctorate in America.* New York: Russell Sage Foundation, 1969.

Astin, H. S. Employment and career status of women psychologists. *American Psychologist,* 1972, *27,* 371–381.

Astin, H. S., & Bayer, A. E. Sex discrimination in academe. *Educational Record,* 1972, *53,* 101–118.

Astin, H. S., El-Khawas, E., & Bisconti, A. S. *Beyond the college years.* Washington, D.C.: National Institutes of Health and National Science Foundation, 1973.

Bardwick, J. *Psychology of women.* New York: Harper & Row, 1971.

Bayer, A. E. Teaching faculty in academe: 1972–73. Washington, D.C.: American Council on Education, Office of Research Reports, 1973.

Boneau, C. A., & Cuca, J. M. An overview of psychology's human resources: Characteristics and salaries from the 1972 APA survey. *American Psychologist,* 1974, *11,* 821–840.

Colson, E., & Scott, E. *Report of the Subcommittee on the Status of Women on the Berkeley Campus.* Berkeley, Calif.: University of California Press, 1970.

Epstein, C. F. *Woman's place: Options and limits in professional careers.* Berkeley, Calif.: University of California Press, 1971.

Ferber, M. A., & Loeb, J. W. Performance, rewards, and perceptions of sex discrimination among male and female faculty. *American Journal of Sociology,* 1973, *78,* 995–1002.

Fidel, L. Empirical verification of sex discrimination in hiring practices in psychology. *American Psychologist,* 1970, *25,* 1094–1098.

Joesting, J. Women in academe. *American Psychologist,* 1974, *29,* 520–523.

Hopkins, E. B. Unemployed! An academic woman's saga. In G. E. Bonham (Ed.), *Women on campus.* New York: Change Magazine, 1975.

Keiffer, M. G., & Cullen, D. M. *Discrimination experienced by academic female psychologists.* Pittsburgh: KNOW Inc., 1970.

Kimmel, E. Status of women in the psychological community in the southeast: A case study. *American Psychologist,* 1974, *29,* 519–520.

Levitin, T., Quinn, R. P., & Staines, G. L. Sex discrimination against the American working woman. *American Behavioral Scientist,* 1971, *15,* 237–254.

Mitchell, J. M., & Starr, R. P. A regional approach for analyzing the recruitment of academic women. *American Behavioral Scientist,* 1971, *15,* 183–205.

Roose, K. D., & Andersen, C. J. *A rating of graduate programs.* Washington, D.C.: American Council on Education, 1970.

Scott, A. *The half-eaten apple.* Pittsburgh: KNOW Inc., 1970.

5

Kevin Hynes

Innovative Career Opportunities and Job Placement Mechanisms in Psychology

The increasing supply of psychology graduates has focused attention on the problem of a diminishing job market. This chapter proposes that solving the job placement problem requires the coordination of two areas —placement services and graduate training. Methods for coordinating these two areas are suggested and described in relation to innovative career opportunities in psychology.

A passive approach to the placement problem would be to curtail graduate admissions, thereby reducing the applicant/job ratio. But the producers and consumers of psychology graduates, as well as potential graduate students, would not benefit by this action. The wisdom of adopting such an approach therefore must be questioned.

Instead of curtailing graduate admissions, an active approach would be to increase the number of jobs available to psychology graduates. Any such increase would probably not occur in the academic employment setting. Boneau and Cuca (1974) reported that about 60% of APA members are already employed in academic settings. This fact, combined with projected decreases in college enrollments, suggests that any increase in the number of jobs available to psychology graduates will be more likely to occur in the nonacademic setting.

As a result of the 1972 American Psychological Association (APA) manpower survey, Boneau and Cuca (1974) reported the number and percentage of APA members (and eligible nonmembers) employed in such nonacademic settings as the following: hospitals, clinics, independent/ group practice, government agencies, private or quasi-government agencies, research establishments, private consulting firms, business or industry, associations or societies, religious institutions, military service, law enforcement agencies, judicial systems, and correctional systems. It is interesting that only 141 members (or .6%) were employed in military service job settings. This may be an area for potential job openings. The Navy Medical Service Corps, for example, has positions for clinical and

Kevin Hynes is a Graduate Research Assistant in the Department of Psychology, Purdue University.

Appreciation is expressed to John F. Feldhusen for his insightful comments on a draft of this chapter.

experimental research psychologists. Other interesting figures are that correctional systems employed 201 members (.8%), but business and industry employed only 789 members (3.2%). Business and industry may also be areas for potential job openings for psychologists.

Placement Services

If we assume that business, the military, or some other nonacademic employment setting has been identified as an area having innovative career opportunities for psychology, then the question is, How can placement services and graduate training be coordinated to maximize the potential of the job market? The answer to this question must begin with a reexamination of the potential of APA placement services.

Astin (1972) proposed a computerized manpower placement system for APA. He commented that "the Association will continue for some time to employ horse-and-buggy methods in carrying out its responsibilities in the area of job placement" (p. 479). The emphasis of Astin's suggestions was on improving the efficiency of the employee–employer interaction.

There are, however, ways that the existing APA placement services can be improved. First, APA could intensify advertisement of its placement services to prospective employers in the nonacademic setting. This is one way to explore what innovative career opportunities are available. If job listings in business and the military are few, it may be that these areas have not been encouraged sufficiently to list their job openings with the placement services. APA could therefore advertise the availability of placement services to these areas.

Examination of placement data for 1969 through 1972 (Cummings & Cates, 1973) provides an indication of the number of positions offered in various employment settings. The Cummings and Cates (1973) report documents the decrease in jobs offered in the academic setting and also indicates a decline in the number of jobs offered by state governments (234, 121, 92, and 64 jobs offered from 1969 to 1972, respectively). Placement data reported in the *American Psychologist*, and elsewhere, could be improved if more specific documentation for areas of specialization in psychology were made available to readers upon request. In writing to regional placement services, one finds that detailed information concerning last year's placement activities is no longer available. This suggests that more detailed recording, followed by better reporting, of the various APA placement service activities is a second area of improvement for the existing placement services.

A third improvement concerns the timing of the APA convention placement service. (Timing of the regional conventions and placement services is not a problem). Currently the APA convention, along with its placement service, is held at the beginning of the academic school year. This limits the usefulness of the placement service because most jobs have been filled by that time. Therefore, fewer applicants use the service, and the potential of the service is curtailed. In order to make the service more attractive and useful, a type of preconvention placement service would be

JOB PLACEMENT CHECKLIST

____1. As an undergraduate or beginning graduate student, examine the job market in psychology to identify areas of job potential that coincide with your aptitudes and interests. Examine such sources as the *APA Monitor, Employment Bulletin, Regional Placement Bulletin*, and placement reports in the *American Psychologist*.

____2. Seek counseling from professors and friends concerning the job market in psychology.

____3. Shape your graduate training to prepare you to compete for jobs in the areas of job potential that you prefer.

____4. Seek counseling by writing or by talking to persons associated with the APA placement services.

____5. Keep track of changes in the job market during your graduate training and adapt your plans as necessary.

____6. Prepare a vita describing your strengths in the area of job potential you prefer.

____7. When you begin to look for a job, make full use of the following techniques:

____*APA Monitor, Employment Bulletin*, and *Regional Placement Bulletin*

____APA convention placement services

____APA regional placement services

____Other convention placement services

____Leads from your major professor or other professors at your university

____University placement services

advantageous, a service that could possibly be handled through the mail. (This approach assumes that the APA convention cannot be held earlier in the year.)

Finally, a fourth improvement to the APA placement services concerns their feedback role. Feedback concerning the job market should be directed to both academic institutions and individuals so that training programs can reflect changes in the job market. "Placement counseling" could, for example, be established as part of the existing placement services. In this way, professors and *beginning* graduate students attending APA conventions could receive up-to-date information on the job market and adapt training programs, if necessary. Placement services and graduate training could thus be coordinated by this type of placement counseling.

Graduate Training

It is the thesis of this chapter that solving the job placement problem requires the coordination of placement services and graduate training. Attention has focused on the possible improvements in APA placement services. But even if the placement services were improved in the ways described, it would still be necessary for graduate training to adapt to the job market. Much of the responsibility for this adaptation rests with the individual graduate student. For example, if improved placement services were available and if the placement services indicated that industry had the greatest potential for career opportunities, then it would be the responsibility of the student to enroll in industrial psychology courses in order to establish a knowledge base in this area, assuming that the student found the area to his or her liking.

Ideally, placement services would provide beginning graduate students with placement counseling concerning job market trends, and graduate students would realistically adapt their preferences to the changing job market. Such an ideal situation does not exist. Therefore, suggestions on how beginning or job-seeking students in psychology can most effectively use the existing job placement mechanisms are summarized in the form of a checklist (see page 51). By using the checklist as a guide, the student should be better prepared for job opportunities in the psychological field. This approach should enable the student to deal in a rational way with a somewhat irrational job market.

REFERENCES

Astin, A. W. A manpower placement system for APA. *American Psychologist*, 1972, *27*, 479–481.

Boneau, C. A., & Cuca, J. M. An overview of psychology's human resources: Characteristics and salaries from the 1972 APA survey. *American Psychologist*, 1974, *29*, 821–839.

Cummings, T., & Cates, J. N. Placement report: 1972. *American Psychologist*, 1973, *28*, 930–932.

6

Edward K. Crossman and
J. Russell Nazzaro

The Vita

For many professionals, the first introduction to a potential employer is likely to come by way of a vita (also called curriculum vitae). Essentially the vita is a document, usually of two or more pages, that summarizes the personal information, academic history, and professional experience of a job applicant. In spite of the seeming importance of such a document, few, if any, published guidelines are available to assist the applicant in designing a vita that will present a complete and accurate picture of his or her qualifications. The current practice for someone who is preparing a vita for the first time, or even modifying the style of a previously used vita, appears to be requesting sample vitae from colleagues and using the best features. The problem with such a procedure, of course, is that the number of samples obtained is likely to be small, thereby reducing the probability of discovering more suitable models.

In view of this limitation, we conducted a survey to determine the style and content of those vitae most acceptable to various professional groups in psychology. The outcome of this survey will be of primary interest to recent graduates who are preparing a vita for the first time. With this audience in mind, we offer a few additional suggestions on the physical appearance of the vita and the materials that should accompany it. We hope that those individuals who have already prepared a vita will find at least a portion of the survey's outcome useful for their purposes.

In January 1975 we wrote to four different groups of psychologists: (a) directors of internship training programs, (b) directors of clinical, counseling, and school psychology doctoral training programs, (c) chief psychologists, and (d) chairpersons of graduate psychology programs in the United States and Canada. We requested them to send "one or more vitae that you feel to be exceptionally impressive in terms of layout and completeness." On the basis of this request, 254 vitae were received, representing a response from about 32% of those surveyed. It is important to note that several chairpersons resisted the request, stating that a second function of the vita, somewhat akin to a projective technique, is to indicate the

Edward K. Crossman is an Assistant Professor in the Department of Psychology, Utah State University; J. Russell Nazzaro is Administrative Officer for Educational Affairs, American Psychological Association, Washington, D.C.

The authors extend thanks to psychologists who responded to the survey and to Merrill Crosbie for his assistance in the survey analysis.

applicant's creativity and originality as revealed by the way in which his or her vita was structured; established guidelines, they argued, would destroy this function. Although the vita may indeed serve this function, we felt that offering suggestions for vita style is somewhat analogous to stating stylistic requirements for publishing a thesis, a dissertation, or a journal article. A more reasonable place to search for the creative aspects of an individual is in the content of the vita, not in its structure. Also, it should be emphasized that the models presented in this article are not restrictive in the same sense that the rules contained in the APA *Publication Manual* are restrictive; rather, they are recommendations to be drawn upon as the individual sees fit.

Before going further, it may be of interest to consider the meaning and suitability of various terms used to identify the subject of this chapter. *Vita* (pl. *vitae*) is the Latin word (nominative case) for "life" and is defined by Webster's *Second International Dictionary* as "an autobiographical sketch." Sometimes, the phrase *curriculum vitae* (pl. *curricula vitae*) is used to emphasize the educational aspects of the sketch because the word curriculum refers to a course or program of courses taken. Note that in the phrase curriculum vitae, vitae is the genitive singular form of the noun vita; the phrase is translated "course of life." Another term that appeared on a number of the autobiographical sketches was *resumé*. A resumé, however, is usually a short, one- or two-page statement, and the term more often refers to a summarized autobiographical sketch of someone who is applying for a position in business or industry. Although the term curriculum vitae headed 16% of the vitae received, the shorter term vita was used by a larger number (56%) and for this reason is used hereafter in this chapter.

The vitae that were received fell into two distinct categories: those that emphasized academic and research experience and those that emphasized clinical experience. Even so, considerable overlap occurred in the structure and content of these two types. It is worthwhile, however, to present both styles as sources of ideas in preparing the vita.

The categories contained in the two vitae presented in this chapter were selected on the basis of the frequency with which this information appeared in the samples. With one exception, all categories were found in at least 10% of the sample vitae. Surprisingly, very few of the vitae listed the name of the dissertation adviser. We felt that this information might be valuable to an employer and we suggest its inclusion. Students who terminate their formal education with the MA or MS degree might consider indicating their thesis title and adviser. Two categories that did exceed the 10% criterion but were not included were citizenship and manuscripts in preparation. It was felt that citizenship could be mentioned in the cover letter (discussed below) and that "manuscripts in preparation" represents information that may or may not reach public record, and hence would be of limited usefulness to an employer. In contrast, "manuscripts in press" is viable information, particularly from a recent graduate, and should be shown in the "Publications" section of the vita.

In general, the sequence of categories shown in the two model vitae represents the sequence followed in the majority of the sample vitae, but other details of the layout represent suggestions by the authors. Personal names and addresses used in the model vitae are intended to be fictional.

To be sure, the styles below are not to be considered exclusive of other methods of organization. They simply represent a distillation of the sample vitae received in this survey. One variation worth considering is to reserve the last page of the vita for publications, making it easy to add a new one without having to retype the entire vita (assuming that publications are listed in chronological order with the most recent one last). Individual creativity on vitae is encouraged, although one caution is offered. By far, the most serious shortcoming of many of the samples received was the inclusion of too much superfluous information, some of which gave the impression of a "padded" vita. The purpose of the vita, once again, is to give the employer a comprehensive and accurate picture of the capabilities of a professional or potential professional. A number of chairpersons in their informal correspondence regarding the survey stressed that high school attended, name of spouse, membership in community service groups, hobbies, and the like are irrelevant pieces of information and should be omitted.

Insofar as the physical preparation of the vita is concerned, the following suggestions are offered. The vita should be professionally typed, with a clean ribbon, on good quality 8½ × 11 inch bond paper. For reproduction, the best and cheapest method is offset printing if a large number (100–200) of vitae are desired. For small numbers (10 or less), xerographic duplication is satisfactory and may be cheaper. Because it is often necessary to distribute multiple copies of a vita to a research committee, avoid using wet-process methods (ditto, mimeograph) or thermal methods because both of these create copies that are hard to reproduce.

A cover letter should be submitted along with the vita. Although the design of a cover letter was not part of the survey, its importance should not be underestimated. Make it a personal cover letter; that is, address it to the chairperson or head administrator by name. Avoid those characteristics that give it a "form" appearance. State the position for which you are applying and where you learned of the opening. Indicate why you are interested in the position in terms of how you see your skills contributing to the program of the department or institution in question. (A knowledge of the department's interests and goals is helpful here.) You might also use the cover letter to describe specific skills—for example, your expertise as a computer programmer—that may have been omitted in the vita. Too much of this detail, however, will give the impression that the vita should have been revised. The central purposes of the cover letter are to introduce the candidate and his or her skills to the employer and to entice the employer to examine the vita. To this end, the cover letter should be well organized and limited to a single page.

Reprints of the candidate's outstanding articles may also be forwarded, although some candidates prefer to wait until these have been requested or, because of the cost, to send reprints only to those institutions where they feel they have the best chance for consideration.

Prior to submitting the cover letter and vita, it is common practice for eager candidates in today's difficult marketplace to blanket their territory with unsolicited letters of inquiry. An excellent guide for writing such letters appears in Chapter 7, by Robert Grinder.

[See vitae on following pages.]

VITA: TYPE A
(N = 75)

PERSONAL DATA   Spring 1973

Name	Albert Lucas Saxon		
Birthdate	April 3, 1939	*Home Address*	617 South Locust St.
Place of Birth	Omaha, Nebraska		Oxford, MS 38655
Social Security No.	413-72-0202	*Home Phone*	601-232-0657
Marital Status	Married	*Office Address*	Department of
Children	1		Psychology, University
Military Status	U.S. Army, 1959–1961;		of Mississippi, Oxford,
	Honorable Discharge,		MS 38655
	1961	*Office Phone*	601-232-7216
		Current Title	Assistant Professor

EDUCATION   *Predoctoral*

1959	BA	University of New Hampshire
		Durham, New Hampshire
1962	MA	University of Maine
		Orono, Maine
1964	PhD	University of Maine
		Orono, Maine
		Major: Clinical Psychology
		Dissertation: Effects of Early
		Experience on Later Behavior
		Adviser: Dr. Arthur K. Saran

Postdoctoral

1964	Clinical Internship, Veterans
	Administration Hospital,
	Hope, Indiana
1965	Postdoctoral Institute in Hypnosis,
	American Psychological Association,
	New Orleans, Louisiana

CERTIFICATES

1965   Certified Psychologist, Oregon State Board of Examiners.

1970   Diplomate (Clinical Psychologist), American Board of Examiners in
Professional Psychology.

AWARDS AND HONORS

1959   Phi Beta Kappa.

1969   Outstanding Teacher Award, University of Mississippi.

1971   Recipient of President's gold medal for outstanding achievement in test
development for mentally retarded 6-year-olds.

PROFESSIONAL EXPERIENCE

Clinical

1963   Supervised individual and group counseling practicum at Downtown Counseling Center, Orono, Maine.

1965   Staff psychologist at University of Oregon Child Guidance Clinic, Salem, Oregon.

Consulting

1967   Evaluation and development of clinical program; personnel selection; Alcoholic Rehabilitation Center, San Antonio, Texas.

1968   Supervised experience with behavior modification using paraprofessional therapists; Head Start Program, Four Counties in Kentucky (summer).

Teaching

1966   Instructor, Department of Psychiatry, University of Oregon Medical School, Salem, Oregon.

1968–Present   Assistant Professor, Department of Psychology, University of Mississippi, Oxford, Mississippi.

PROFESSIONAL AFFILIATIONS

1962   Sigma Xi

1964–Present   Member, American Psychological Association, Divisions 6 and 8

1965–1967   Member, Western Psychological Association

1968–Present   Member, Mississippi Society of Clinical Psychologists

SCHOLARLY ACTIVITY

Presentations

Saxon, A. L., & Broadbent, A.S. *The effects of posthypnotic suggestion on disruption of biofeedback.* Paper presented at the meeting of the Midwestern Applied Behavior Analysis Association, Des Moines, Iowa, April 1963.

Publications

Saxon, A. L. The Navajo Indian: A clinical perspective. *International Journal of Social Psychology,* 1965, *31,* 321–336.

Saxon, A. L., & Smart, J. K. Evaluation of help-line centers. *Journal of Crisis Therapy,* 1968, *12,* 112–119.

Saxon, A. L. *New directions in hypnosis.* Chicago: Aldine-Atherton, 1971.

REFERENCES

Dr. Karen L. Lamb   Dr. Ann K. Hadley   Dr. Paul S. Sorensen
Department of Psychology   Department of Psychology   Department of Psychology
University of Mississippi   University of Mississippi   Indiana University
Oxford, MS 38655   Oxford, MS 38655   Bloomington, IN 47401

VITA: TYPE B
(N = 179)

PERSONAL DATA   Fall 1975

Name	John David Hemp		
Title	Professor	*Home Address*	201 Manzanita Ave.
Birthdate	January 6, 1938		Palo Alto, CA 94306
Place of Birth	Dayton, Ohio	*Home Phone*	415-326-3795
Social Security No.	415-07-6212		
Marital Status	Married	*Office Address*	Department of
Children	2		Psychology,
Military Status	U.S. Navy, 1956–1958;		Stanford University,
	Honorable discharge,		Stanford, CA 94305
	1958	*Office Phone*	415-326-3100,
			Ext. 7236

EDUCATION

1956	BA	DePauw University
		Greencastle, Indiana
1960	MA	Kent State University
		Kent, Ohio
		Major: Experimental Psychology
1964	PhD	University of Arizona
		Tucson, Arizona
		Major: Social Psychology
		Dissertation: The Effects of Group
		Size on Interpersonal Distance
		Adviser: Dr. Stanley Bischoff

AWARDS AND HONORS

1958	Ford Foundation Scholarship, Kent State University, Kent, Ohio.
1962–Present	Member, Phi Kappa Phi.
1963	National Science Foundation Summer Traineeship for Graduate Teaching Assistants, University of California at Los Angeles.

PROFESSIONAL EXPERIENCE

1958	Research Assistant, Perception Laboratory (summer), Duke University, Durham, North Carolina. Director: Dr. Larry A. Barhuff.
1959	Teaching Assistant, Statistics, Kent State University, Kent, Ohio. Professor: Dr. Frank W. Hamm.
1965	U.S. Public Health Service Fellow, University of Alabama, University, Alabama.
1966	Senior Research Assistant, Small Groups Project, Washington University, St. Louis, Missouri. Director: Dr. Loren E. Beatle.

1967–1970   Assistant Professor, Department of Psychology, Arizona State University, Tempe, Arizona.

1970–1972   Associate Professor, Department of Psychology, Queens College of the City University of New York, Flushing, New York.

1973–Present Professor, Department of Psychology, Stanford University, Stanford, California.

GRANTS AND CONTRACTS

Date and Title		Agency	Amount
1968	Human Operant Chaining	Office of Scientific Research, U.S. Air Force	$25,000
1970–1972	Effects of Early Social Deprivations on Normal and Retarded Children	National Institute of Mental Health	$65,000

PROFESSIONAL AFFILIATIONS

1967–Present Member, American Psychological Association, Divisions 3 and 6; Fellow, Division 1.

1968–Present Member, International Society for Developmental Psychobiology.

1973–Present Member, California State Psychological Association.

CONSULTANTSHIPS

1970   Dr. Claude D. Chadwick, Alcohol and Drug Addiction Center, Beltsville, New York.

1971   Western State Hospital, Bowling Green, Kentucky.

EDITORIAL RESPONSIBILITIES

1970–1973   Member, Board of Editors, *Journal of Applied Behavior Analysis.*

1974–Present Guest Reviewer, *Psychological Bulletin.*

PAPERS READ AT MEETINGS

Hemp, J. D. *Short-term memory in second-grade children.* Paper presented at the meeting of the Southeastern Psychological Association, Nashville, Tennessee, May 1968.

Hemp, J. D., & Torrey, C. F. *Some factors influencing creativity in the infant rhesus monkey.* Paper presented at the meeting of the Western Psychological Association, San Francisco, April 1973.

PUBLICATIONS

Hemp, J. D. Rate and accuracy of assembly-line performance under ratio reinforcement. *Journal of Productivity,* 1967, *17,* 401–410.

Barbersall, O. B., & Hemp, J. D. Method of obtaining titration in seagulls. *Journal of Bird Behavior,* 1971, *60,* 10–17.

TEACHING INTERESTS

Introductory Psychology
Social Psychology
Personality
Behavior Modification

RESEARCH INTERESTS

Effects of Environmental Factors on Social Distance
Effects of Smoking on Verbal Behavior in Small Groups
Parameters Related to Space Flight and Small Group Interaction

REFERENCES

Dr. Harvey F. Smith
Department of Psychology
Stanford University
Stanford, CA 94305

Dr. Zing Tuo
Department of Pharmacology
Medical School
Stanford University
Stanford, CA 94305

Dr. Ashley P. Sabarov
Director of Clinical Internships
Veterans Administration Hospital
Palo Alto, CA 94304

Part 2

Academia

Robert E. Grinder

Unsolicited Letters
*(A Do-It-Yourself Prescription for
Coping with the Job Shortage When
You Are a Member of the PhD Surplus)*

Graduate students are usually uncertain of their future employment. While courses, professors, and research projects preoccupy interest, occupational matters arouse little concern. But at some moment in the twilight of doctoral study most students begin to consider job placement and aspire to a comfortable life-style and a rewarding career. Many students then distribute dozens of unsolicited letters to advertise their availability. The unsolicited letter has been popular with doctoral candidates generation after generation because it affords each candidate a measure of control over participation and destiny in the academic marketplace. Yet nearly every such letter, after being acknowledged perfunctorily by a pool secretary, finds its way into the circular file. The probability that unsolicited letters will attract the attention of the departmental heads and search committees is perhaps among the lowest of known probabilities.

Employment practices in higher education are governed by patronage. Job placement depends primarily on the contacts of the doctoral candidate's professor (Fletcher, Beagles, Dodd, & Wildman, 1974). The prestige of a university and the sociometric status of a professor determine the range and status of jobs available. During prosperous times, professors reward successful graduate students with better openings and guide less able students to lesser status jobs (Love, 1972). Times were so good during the 1960s that even candidates who possessed low levels of competence and attended undistinguished institutions could pick among choice opportunities. Today, in contrast, even the relatively undesirable positions have vanished. Deans and departmental chairpersons find themselves fettered by tightfisted administrators who deny them new positions and instead all too frequently demand that department faculty be reduced in number.

Patronage is faltering because (a) interaction is occuring less frequently among professors at different institutions and (b) openings are developing without forewarning. First, frequency of face-to-face contacts among pro-

---

Robert E. Grinder is Associate Dean, College of Education, Arizona State University. This chapter is derived from his experience as a recipient of unsolicited letters while serving as Chairperson, Department of Educational Psychology, University of Wisconsin, and as Dean, College of Education, University of Maine.
This chapter is reprinted with permission from the *AAUP Bulletin*, 1975, *61*, 274–278.

fessors is dwindling. Prestigious professors have been accustomed to attending several professional conventions every year; casual comments in hotel elevators and lobbies, during cocktail parties, or while awaiting taxis created a communications conduit to job openings for countless graduate students. But the trend toward heavily attended conventions is reversing itself in the face of budget restrictions. Financial resources are scarce and travel to professional meetings has been curtailed. Travel accounts are particularly sparse at two-year community colleges and small four-year colleges where funds are being pumped into teaching. Personal contacts for making known available positions may be wholly lacking among the faculty at these institutions. Second, patronage breaks down when openings are dependent on leaves, deaths, and retirements. The appearance of an unanticipated opening seldom coincides with the moment during which professors are in face-to-face contact at conventions. Patronage is slipping, consequently, as the primary mechanism of advertising doctoral candidates to prospective employers. How then is availability to be announced? Let us review a do-it-yourself prescription designed to improve the capacity of the unsolicited letter to fulfill this aim. An outline of seven blunders commonly committed in the process of composing an unsolicited letter concludes the essay. These witless blunders corrupt every unsolicited letter campaign. Their calamitous effects may be averted, however, by embedding them firmly in consciousness at the very outset of planning.

Prescription

Timing is the first consideration. An unsolicited letter is wasted that appears at moments tangential to departmental budget shuffles and critical staff changes. A letter distributed in September, for example, will have been buried in the files by the time applications are sought for an opening that arises in February or March. On the other hand, a search begun in November might ignore a letter arriving in February, when screening activity is underway. Further, consider the plight of the imaginary graduate student who sends a letter in October to both Northsouth University and Eastwest University. Northsouth, let us assume, has an opening; but in January prominent Professor Merit from Eastwest is appointed to the post. Now Eastwest has an opening, but the unsolicited letter arrived in October, long before Professor Merit resigned, and its impact has been eroded by poor timing. Most of the problems of timing can be overcome, however, by keeping prospective employers continuously attuned to one's availability, for example, by distributing not one but three sequenced letters—the first in the early fall, the second shortly after the first of the year, and the third about midspring. The activity must be kept low key, for initially impressed departmental heads may be swiftly disillusioned if they begin to believe that they are being imposed upon.

The graduate student also must face the task of convincing administrators that the student is uniquely suited to be employed at the particular institution. A great deal of fact finding and contemplation are necessary.

Such factors as institutional size, departmental size, programs, geographical region, and living conditions must be analyzed carefully, and the doctoral candidate must develop a realistic assessment of "fitting in" at each institution in which he or she seeks to establish availability. Thus, prior to actual composition of the first letter, the following four points must be attended to carefully.

1. Identify the schools that are appealing. Study either library reference texts on higher education or college and university catalogs. The materials are likely to be available in admissions offices and community libraries. If necessary, write colleges and universities for them. Disregard prestigeful schools like Harvard, Yale, and Stanford, where patronage continues to govern employment practices.

2. Study the programs of the colleges and universities in which one is qualified to participate. Note the characteristics of each institution—teaching emphases, service involvements, research commitments, traditional or innovative programs. Survey journals in one's area and read articles that have been written by the faculty.

3. Consider the locale: rural or urban, proximity to metropolitan areas, accessibility to colleagues at nearby institutions, convenience to conventions, etc.

4. Note the name of the individual who is likely to be responsible for screening candidates. This person may be a senior professor in one's area, a departmental chairperson, a coordinator, or a dean.

After thorough analysis of the programs, locales, and personnel of the institutions to which letters will be sent, the stage is set for composing the three letters. Each possesses distinctive characteristics.

Initial Letter (early in the fall)

Salutation. Write personally and directly to the administrator likely to be the prospective employer.

First paragraph. Indicate briefly one's status in the degree program, for example, "I will complete my doctoral degree requirements in June, 19___, and I would like to be considered for a position at _____ [name the institution] in _____[Educational Psychology, Counselor Education, etc.]."

Second paragraph. Indicate why in particular the prospective employer has been written. A letter to the University of Maine, for example, might point to its land grant status, its breadth of programs, and its appealing size, which is small enough to facilitate faculty discourse across disciplines and to offer frequent contact with students. Describe why the *specific* program for which one may be qualified is appealing (e.g., because the individual courses or the sequence of them is noteworthy and the prospects for either innovative or traditional teaching are good). Comment on the ideas expressed in articles written by the faculty. (Be wary here since the prospective employer may be unenthusiastic about the ideas of his or her colleagues.)

Third paragraph. Explain tactfully how one's strengths might complement those of the institution. Show briefly how one's experiences and dissertation are preparing oneself for the opportunity.

Fourth paragraph. State one's timetable for completing the degree requirements. And importantly, stress in conclusion that the purpose of the letter is to alert the prospective employer of one's interest in that institution; emphasize that no reply is necessary and that a subsequent letter will describe the progress that one will have made toward completing the timetable.

Second Letter (after the first of year)

Salutation. Same as in first letter.

First paragraph. Note the date of the first letter and summarize its four paragraphs in a few brief sentences. In the last sentence of this paragraph, indicate one's continuing interest in a post at the prospective employer's institution.

Second paragraph. Demonstrate that one's timetable is being fulfilled; mention that relevant experiences are being obtained, either as a teaching assistant, research assistant, or on one's own and that the theory and data in the dissertation are proving to be provocative.

Third paragraph. Acknowledge that it may be too early for the prospective employer to have definite knowledge of openings, but express hope that one's interests will be kept in mind. Indicate that one will write again in the spring with another report of availability and progress. Emphasize again that no reply on the part of the prospective employer is necessary. Enclose a brief resumé or vita that includes references (it is possible that between the second and third letter an opening will occur and the prospective employer may wish to develop one's file).

Third Letter (in the spring)

Salutation. Same as in first two letters.

First paragraph. Summarize the first two letters and indicate one's active interest in employment at the prospective employer's institution.

Second paragraph. Stress one's professional competencies and emphasize that one's timetable is assured of being fulfilled.

Third paragraph. Reveal explicitly that one is hopeful that an opening relative to one's qualifications has become available and how much careful consideration would be appreciated. As in the earlier letters, do not solicit a reply.

Blunders

The strategy for composing the three foregoing letters was derived partly from a review of 228 unsolicited letters distributed over a recent two-year period. Several of the letters were well constructed, but the majority contained blunders that demolished the intent of the writer to put his or her talents forward. The seven blunders that were committed in letter after letter are illustrated below. Each is a costly mistake, but, fortunately, foresight can be a ready and effective antidote.

1. Unpersonalized Salutation

The most common blunder (committed by nearly half of the solicitors) is that of distributing letters containing anonymous salutations such as "Dear Dean," "Dear Colleague," "Dear Mr. Chairman," and worst of all, "Dear Sir." Sometimes even when the author identifies the correct name, it is misspelled, which is in itself a major error. The unpersonalized salutation abases the credibility of the candidate and leads the administrator who receives it to wonder how much the author has extended himself or herself to learn about the institution.

2. Shotgun Attack

The same unsolicited letter is distributed to everyone in the administrative chain—chancellor, president, vice-president for academic affairs, dean, departmental chairpersons, and one or more professors. The administrator who is responsible for replying to unsolicited letters often is the particular victim of this blunder. After promptly acknowledging receipt of the letter, he or she may be forwarded the copies received by colleagues, all of whom request that it be acknowledged in their behalf. Occasionally an unsolicited letter is distributed fourth-class bulk mail, and, in such instances, the salutation may link together several members in the chain (e.g., "Dear President, Vice-President, or Dean"). Since each administrator assumes (hopes) that the other has acknowledged it, no one takes responsibility for it, and the sender is likely never to know whether his or her letter was even received.

3. Pressing for a Reply

Forty percent of the authors explicitly requested that their unsolicited letters be answered. Administrators whose interests are aroused obviously will reply. To insist that they respond only ensures immediate closure on one's candidacy. The receipt of a letter seldom coincides with the occurrence of an opening, and in the absence of any reason for doing otherwise, many administrators reply by form letter. Once the form letter is signed, the matter is closed, even when an opening occurs within a few months. It is imperative, therefore, that administrators be diverted from foreclosing on one's availability. The solution is to *emphasize* the unnecessity of a reply in each of the three letters. The following statements illustrate ways in which this principle is readily violated. The presumptuousness reflected by them negates whatever positive impact other portions of the letters might have:

"Please let me know if you are interested in someone with my qualifications."

"I do hope to hear from you at your earliest convenience and enclose an international reply coupon."

"Please advise me . . . and if you would like to give one of your courses an uplift with a western flavor, let me know immediately."

"I am looking forward to hearing from the respective administrators in the business and/or educational faculties of your institution at the earliest convenience."

"Please feel free to call if you have any questions as I look forward to hearing from you soon."

"I anticipate your reply."

4. *Pushing for a Face-to-Face Interview*

To beseech a prospective employer for an interview is even more damaging than pressing for a swift reply. Face-to-face contact is always desirable, especially as a candidacy becomes viable, but it should be initiated solely by the prospective employer. It is audacious to ask for interviews; it suggests that the authors hold themselves in such esteem that they believe administrators are compelled to create openings for them and that an interview is all that impedes consummation of a contract. In practice, it provokes a form letter, which suggests, in polite academic jargonese, "go to hell."

"I will be happy to hear from you. Please feel free to write or phone to arrange a meeting. . . ."

"I am available to travel to your institution for an interview, and would welcome the opportunity to do so."

"I would like to visit your campus and meet you at your convenience."

"If you prefer to talk with me personally regarding a position, I will make every effort to arrange a mutually satisfactory time for such an interview."

"I would welcome an opportunity to discuss my aspirations and future plans with you."

"I think that I can be an asset to your faculty and would be pleased to come to your campus for an interview."

"If I can answer any questions or come personally for an interview, I will be able to do so during our winter vacation period."

"I will travel any reasonable distance for an interview, but finances limit my being able to travel any great distances unless there is recompense for such travel."

"If my credentials are satisfactory, an interview would be appreciated."

5. *Pomposity*

Authors of unsolicited letters, perhaps in their ardor to project the best possible images of themselves, often stumble into the eviscerating blunder of self-adulation. Such praise usually reflects an irritating egoism. Maybe it also reveals compulsion to describe themselves as they know others are disinclined to do. In contrast to the examples below, sensitive authors of unsolicited letters will describe their strengths in terms of concrete experiences and accomplishments. They will permit others to identify their virtues and communicate them to prospective employers.

"My forte is the ability to organize complex programs, design them within limitations, and see them efficiently through to completion."

"I have broad experience in all levels of education which brings a realistic perspective to courses I teach."

"I believe that my classroom experience will be of value for the training of future science teachers, and in the conducting of educational research."

"I feel that my interest in college students, training, and experience will be invaluable to your campus community."

"With this broad, yet intensive preparation, I feel that I can be quite flexible in meeting the needs of your department while doing a quality job at the same time."

"I enjoy the classroom atmosphere a great deal and love the teaching profession enough to believe that I could put my rather comprehensive background to excellent use at the University of Maine at Orono."

"At age 26, I believe I can offer a unique perspective to the previously listed areas of education."

"I feel myself to be extremely energetic, progressive, and completely dedicated to enhancing the helping relationship, whether it be the facilitation of learning or the dynamics of the counseling relationship."

"Promotion of meaningful interactive relationships is what I feel to be the essence of life."

"I feel that I am creative, flexible, and get along with people from a variety of backgrounds and age groups."

6. *Regional Priority*

Expressing a regional preference based on nonprofessional criteria is ruinous in an unsolicited letter. Administrators are always seeking ways of strengthening the administrative unit for which they are responsible, and the letter must convince them that the author's career motivations will contribute effectively to *their* goals. Revelations based on self-interest downgrade the credibility of the author's professional intentions. The state of Maine, for example is an especially appealing state in which to live. It offers fishing, hunting, camping, boating, skiing, and hiking in abundance. Its lake and ocean shores are lined with cottages owned by out-of-staters who treble the population of the state during the summer months. The rural life-style and rugged landscape of Maine lend credence to the belief that the state is engulfed by a pinetree curtain, behind which an extraterrestrial serenity prevails. The University of Maine, nonetheless, is comprised of faculty and administrators who are committed to academic excellence. Thus at the University of Maine, as at dozens of institutions blessed with attractive environments, comments such as those below are interpreted to mean that the authors are primarily seeking early retirement:

"My wife and I are native New Englanders; we have lived elsewhere for a number of years and wish very much to return and settle down."

"The University of Maine at Orono is located in the type of community in which I would like to raise my sons. It would provide for them a number of experiences to which they are not presently exposed."

"Since my family and I are from the state of Maine we are interested in returning if there are any opportunities available."

"I love the East and would really like to hear from you in regard to any openings you may have."

"I am applying for the specific purpose of finding employment in an area of my competence in the state of Maine. My family and I have been coming to Maine for many years. We have owned a second home and summered in your state for the past five years. I have decided, hopefully, to consummate the romance; we want to permanently make the move."

"I look forward, in earnest, to this opportunity to make a contribution to my home state and to the educational future of Maine people."

7. *Compromising Professional Integrity*

This refers to stressing a range of competencies that one could not possibly possess. The academic world is highly competitive, but authors of unsolicited letters often inflate the breadth of their training and assume that they are qualified to teach in any area in which there may be an opening. Administrators, on the other hand, can readily find candidates with unique qualifications for every position that opens up. A generalist, who comes across as a master of nothing, seldom makes much impact. An unsolicited letter, therefore, should stress specific strengths in the area in which the author has chosen to prepare himself or herself. It is useless today to apply for jobs for which one is peripherally trained; indeed, blanket applications, such as illustrated below, serve mainly to obscure the qualifications of the authors.

"If there were to be a place for me at the University, even though it did not fall directly in line with the type of development I have done in the past, I would welcome an opportunity to discuss it."

"I am interested in securing a teaching position in the College of Education."

"Should you have a position open for a teacher in research methodology, school administration, or teacher preparation, your consideration of my credentials would be appreciated."

"You will note that my training encompasses educational research, evaluation and measurement, elementary and secondary teaching in music, and that I have had experience with education in several different cultural settings."

"After a careful assessment of both my experience and professional goals I feel qualified to engage in teaching and research in the Departments of Clinical Psychology–Psychiatry (psychodiagnostic, psychopathologic, and psychotherapeutic psychologies), Psychology (human sciences and developmental psychologies), and Education (learning and learning disabilities psychologies, educational psychology, measurement and related disciplines)."

"My experience has been successful and varied. I have taught at every level from elementary and junior high through high school, community college, university and graduate school. I am well versed in both education as a whole and in higher education in particular."

"I would appreciate your considering me for any position that seems appropriate."

"If you have a position open in elementary education, I would like to be considered."

Conclusion

Graduate students fail uniformly to anticipate the kind of impression that their unsolicited letters will make on prospective employers, and symptomatic of the extent to which they overestimate their qualifications, few seek the dispassionate counsel of peers, advisers, or professional letter writers. The utility of their unsolicited letters is thus victimized both by ineffectual distributive and composition strategies and by self-destructive content. This chapter, therefore, offers graduate students a prescription for rectifying their more callow errors and for projecting a favorable image of themselves in the unsolicited letters that they choose to put in the mail.

REFERENCES

Fletcher, H. J., Beagles, C. A., Dodd, H. T., & Wildman, T. M., Institutional participation in the 1974 AERA annual meeting. *Educational Researcher*, 1974, 3, 8–10.
Love, R. E. Getting your first job: A view from the bottom. *American Psychologist*, 1972, 27, 425–430.

8

Helen S. Astin

The Academic Labor Market

For a better understanding of the academic labor market, especially as this market relates to psychology, I would like to discuss recent employment patterns for new doctorates and compare them with patterns of the last decade. First, a set of tables compares employment patterns of new doctorates in psychology with those of new PhDs in all fields. Second, prospects for the future are highlighted and some of the factors that determine supply and demand for new doctorates are outlined.[1]

The data discussed here were collected by the National Research Council (NRC) of the National Academy of Sciences. The Office of Scientific Personnel of NRC has been collecting data from all doctorate recipients at United States universities for a number of years. As of 1974, responsibility for collecting and reporting these data has been assigned to the Board of Human Resource Data Collection and Analysis of the Commission of Human Resources (NRC).

Table 8-1 shows clearly that since 1970 the rate of growth in new doctorates in psychology has been greater than that of all fields combined. Although psychology accounted for less than 7% of the doctorates awarded in 1970, it accounted for nearly 20% of the growth between 1970 and 1974.

Looking at the employment prospects for new doctorates (Table 8-2), we find that between 1960 and 1970 men had more success in obtaining employment than did women. Men psychologists fared as well as men in all fields combined, whereas fewer women psychologists as compared to women in other fields had signed contracts by the time of the earned doctorates survey (late spring and early summer of the year in which the degree was awarded). Overall, doctorates in sociology fared better than psychologists for all three years examined.

Table 8-3 shows that a greater proportion of new psychology PhDs sought employment in educational institutions in 1970 than in 1960. However, psychologists in general are less likely to seek employment in educational institutions than doctorates in other fields. Psychologists are more likely than other doctorates to go to work for governmental or nonprofit organizations.

Helen S. Astin is a Professor of Higher Education, Graduate School of Education, University of California, Los Angeles.
1. Most of this latter information is based on the work of my colleague Allan M. Cartter, who has just completed a book on this subject (Cartter, in press).

TABLE 8-1   *Growth of Psychology Doctorates 1960–1974*

Year	Total psychology doctorates	Percentage growth	Total doctorates: all fields	Percentage growth
1960	772		9,734	
1965	954	23.6	16,341	67.9
1970	1,883	97.3	29,436	80.1
1972	2,262	20.1	33,001	12.1
1973	2,444	8.0	33,727	2.2
1974	2,587	5.8	33,000	−2.2

Source: For the years 1960 and 1965, National Research Council; for the years 1970, 1972, 1973, and 1974, National Research Council. *Summary report: Doctorate recipients from United States universities.* Washington, D.C.: Author, 1970, 1972, 1973, 1974.

More recent data for employment patterns of new doctorates (Table 8-4) show that psychologists still fare better than other doctorates with respect to having signed employment contracts and that both women psychologists and women in general still lag behind their male counterparts. This suggests that affirmative action efforts by institutions have still not equalized employment opportunities for new men and women doctorates, at least as of 1974.

Looking at the types of employers for the years 1972, 1973, and 1974 (Table 8-5), we see that compared to other new doctorates psychologists are still less inclined to seek employment in educational institutions. Proportionately, two and three times as many psychologists as doctorates in other fields seek employment in governmental or nonprofit organizations.

This brief review of the employment trends of psychologists during the last few years suggests that in spite of much current concern about over-supplies of PhDs, employment prospects and employers have shown a relatively stable pattern during recent years. Psychologists have been about as successful at locating employment as doctorates in other fields, and women have consistently been at a disadvantage compared to men. Whereas more than half (52%) of all new doctorates in 1974 sought employment in educational institutions, only 43% of psychologists did likewise. One can surmise that psychologists, compared to other social scientists, have more options for employment outside the academic sector.

What the Future Holds

From what we have all been told by the media and by colleagues and friends, the future of new doctorates appears to be quite bleak. The familiar scenario goes something like this. If we look at the 110 years between 1970

TABLE 8-2   *Trends in Employment 1960, 1965, and 1970*

Year	Psychology		Sociology		Total for all fields	
	Men	Women	Men	Women	Men	Women
1960	80	69	86	78	82	73
1965	79	71	89	83	80	72
1970	79	61	88	72	78	65

Note. Numbers are given in percentages. Numbers indicate the proportions who had signed a contract. Special tabulations were provided by the National Research Council.

TABLE 8-3   *Trends in Type of Postdoctoral Employer*

Type of employer	Psychology				Sociology				Total for all fields			
	1960		1970		1960		1970		1960		1970	
	Men	Women	Men	Women	Men	Women	Men	Women	Men	Women	Men	Women
Educational institution	46	54	64	59	77	77	91	88	60	73	68	82
Industry/business	11	3	6	5	5	0	1	0	18	3	16	3
Government	25	14	19	18	5	8	4	2	8	5	10	6
Nonprofit	8	12	9	11	5	4	3	5	3	3	3	4
Other	10	17	2	8	9	12	2	5	11	15	3	5

Note. Numbers are given in percentages. Special tabulations were provided by the National Research Council.

and the time the first doctorates were awarded, 1861, some 340,000 persons have earned doctorates. Half of these doctorates were awarded in just the last 10 years of that period (1961–1970). About 340,000 or more doctorates are expected to be awarded during the 1970s.

Even though new faculty positions will also be increased, their growth is not expected to be anywhere near the rate of new doctorates. According to projections, new doctorates will have to find alternates to the traditional academic careers pursued by doctorate holders in the past.

During the years 1950–1955, new job openings in academe were not sufficient to employ the number of new doctorates seeking employment in academic settings. From 1962 to 1968, however, there was a significant shortage in doctoral wo/manpower to meet available academic openings. In 1970 an imbalance again appeared in the direction of oversupply.

According to Cartter (in press), during the rest of the 1970s between 10,000 and 12,000 new doctorates will be employed as college teachers. This figure represents only about 30% of all doctorates to be awarded. In the 1980s the gap will increase unless there is a downward adjustment in the number of doctorates awarded.

There will be fewer new openings because of slower economic and population growth. The number of college-age youth will decline up to 1990, when growth is expected again because of the increase in birthrates

TABLE 8-4   *Employment Patterns of Doctorates 1973–1974*

Plans	Psychology				Sociology and anthropology				Total for all fields			
	1973		1974		1973		1974		1973		1974	
	T	Women only	T	Women only	T	Women only	T	Women only	T	Women only	T	Women only
Definite post-doctoral study	9	10	10	11	5	3	4	7	11	9	11	9
Seeking post-doctoral study	3	4	3	4	2	4	2	4	4	5	4	4
Definite employment	62	54	60	54	73	62	72	64	59	53	58	52
Seeking employment	20	26	21	26	15	24	15	19	19	26	20	26

Source: National Research Council. *Summary report: Doctorate recipients from United States universities.* Washington, D.C.: Author, 1975.
Note: Numbers are given in percentages; *T* represents the total men and women.

during the postwar years. Those births constitute the parents of the college-age youth of the 1990s.

In short, the predicted pattern will be as follows: Growth in new openings will be slow during the 1970s with a drastic reduction in openings in the 1980s and a possible recovery in the 1990s. These market fluctuations will have their greatest impact on those doing graduate work now and becoming available for employment in the 1980s.

Factors Affecting Demand for Teachers

All of these projections and discussions concern the new doctorates and the academic labor market that has in the past been the primary employer of doctorates. The demand for new college and university teachers generally depends on four factors: (a) college enrollments, (b) student/faculty ratios, (c) faculty retirement policies, and (d) net migration of experienced faculty. Let us consider each of these in turn.

College enrollments depend on actual birthrates; however, recent trends suggest that the demographic composition of the college-going population might change to include more adults as a result of greater interest in recurrent education and lifelong learning experiences sought by adults. Also, if financial aid packaging were to be altered—with possible inclusion of paid educational leaves—one might anticipate an even greater participation of adults in postsecondary educational activities.

Student/faculty ratios are not necessarily fixed. Administrators in higher education institutions can make adjustments to these ratios in order to provide better balance to the supply–demand question. However, one could predict that the ratios might increase because of limited finances and cuts in budgets in higher education institutions.

The replacement demand as reflected in faculty retirement policies and in net migration in experienced faculty has been on the order of $1\frac{1}{2}\%$–2% per year during the last 10–15 years. If salaries were to deteriorate in relative terms, more experienced faculty could be forced to leave academe and thus cause an increase in *out migration*. This, in turn, would provide more new openings. On the other hand, recent efforts at unionization and

TABLE 8-5   *Trends in Employers 1972, 1973, and 1974*

Employer	1972		1973		1974	
	Total for all fields (N=33,001)	Psychology (N=2,262)	Total for all fields (N=33,727)	Psychology (N=2,444)	Total for all fields (N=33,000)	Psychology (N=2,587)
Postdoctoral study	15.5	12.2	15.6	12.4	14.9	13.0
Total employment	77.6	80.8	78.2	82.1	77.6	81.1
Educational institution	55.3	46.6	53.7	44.4	51.6	43.4
Industry/business	7.7	3.8	9.0	5.0	9.8	5.5
Government	8.7	18.8	8.3	16.9	8.9	16.9
Nonprofit	2.7	7.3	3.3	9.7	3.3	11.1
Other and unknown	3.2	4.3	3.9	6.1	4.0	5.8

Source: National Research Council. *Summary report: Doctorate recipients from United States universities.* Washington, D.C.: Author, 1972, 1973, 1974.
Note. Numbers are given in percentages. Percentages do not add up to 100% because of "unknown postdoctoral plans."

collective bargaining on the part of faculty may prevent any significant deterioration in relative pay.

Some other recent trends suggest the possibility of increases in replacement demand, however. A number of institutions are providing early retirement incentives. This procedure is bound to produce new openings for junior faculty since institutions tend to replace experienced faculty with junior faculty in order to reduce budget deficits.

The PhD Supply

Two key variables that can alter the supply of PhDs are (a) student aspirations and (b) market conditions that affect these aspirations. Recent years have already witnessed significant changes in student aspirations for advanced degrees. For example, between 1966 and 1970, there was a 2% drop in PhD degree aspirations among entering freshmen men. However, this drop was paralleled by a comparable increase among women entering college. The PhD aspirants among entering freshmen men dropped from 14% to 12%, whereas PhD aspirants among entering freshmen women increased from 5% to 7%.

Market fluctuations affect the plans and aspirations of young people in a variety of ways. In some instances lack of job opportunities for BA or MA recipients forces new graduates to pursue the doctorate in the hope that future job opportunities will be improved. On the other hand, a shortage of jobs for new PhDs can influence graduate students to terminate their studies prior to degree completion. A third category controlling PhD output is institutional admissions and graduation standards. Institutions can control their PhD supplies simply by altering these standards.

An oversupply of doctorates is most likely to occur in fields where employment opportunities are mainly in the collegiate sector. These are primarily the humanities, but also include those fields in which there has been a decreased interest among undergraduates (e.g., foreign language and certain areas of the humanities). Fortunately for psychology, neither of these conditions applies. Psychologists have all along been sought after by a variety of employers other than academic institutions. Moreover, psychology as an undergraduate major has enjoyed substantial growth in recent years, and the interest in psychology among undergraduates is expected to remain high. Thus, even though the picture is bleak for doctorates in many fields, our discipline is in a relatively favorable position with respect to employment prospects in the near future. This situation should not be taken for granted. It is important, however, to recognize that our diversity and versatility are part of our strength as a field and that our students should be encouraged to think in terms of alternative careers. Moreover, graduate training programs would be well advised to continue preparing doctorates with an array of skills that are broader than those required for the teacher and scholar role.

REFERENCE

Cartter, A. M. *PhDs and the academic labor market.* New York: McGraw-Hill, in press.

Part 3 —————————————————
Human Services

9

George W. Albee

Innovative Roles for Psychologists

There are a number of innovative roles that psychologists can and should play in improving the quality of life, and some of these roles have definite implications for the employment picture. But before having the temerity to suggest how psychologists might improve it, we first need to know what is meant by "quality of life." Let me suggest some of the characteristics of quality of life that will have relevance for innovative roles psychologists might play in helping people move in a positive direction, quality-wise.

I will neglect for the most part a consideration of economic affluence and level of consumption on the quality of life. (This could invalidate the whole effort at definition, of course. Recently, I drove from Miami to Palm Beach along Route 1, nearly 100 miles. My senses were assaulted steadily by the roar of high-powered automobiles; the garish neon of a thousand franchise drive-in junk-food palaces of plastic, formica, and chrome, interspersed with roadside stands selling everything from pink plastic flamingos to oranges sprayed with poisonous coal-tar dye; alligator jungles with Indian villages; porno drive-in movies and shops; liquor stores; on and on. Most of these places were jammed with apparently affluent people, so obviously these services are in demand in an affluent society. To those like myself who are contemptuous of such offerings there is the worrisome knowledge that European teenagers apparently yearn for or imitate their American peers in the consumption of junk food and hard rock, of old jeans and Coca-Cola.) Sometime we must confront the curious positive correlation between rising indexes of economic affluence and an increase in alienation, crime, drug use, and disaffiliation. René Dubos has described at some length (without obvious romanticizing) the high level of satisfaction, joy, and longevity enjoyed by groups of people scattered throughout the world and throughout history who live on a small fraction of the calories, the energy, and the material possessions of "civilization." Despite wide variance in climate and geography, these groups, living on meager diets and working hard at primitive agriculture, enjoy their children, music and dancing, storytelling and ritual. They are very active sexually and socially throughout a very long life (in which the older people are expected, as a

George W. Albee is a Professor in the Department of Psychology, University of Vermont.
At the meeting of the American Association for the Advancement of Science in New York in 1975, a group of psychologists discussed psychologists' roles in improving the quality of life. Dr. Albee's paper was concerned with innovative roles. Because some of these roles have implications for employment, this edited version of the original paper has been included.

matter of course, to be full participants). Clearly, affluence and our potlatch-style consumption are not necessary conditions for a life of reported satisfaction.

Psychologists and the Quality of Life

More systematic data are needed about people's subjective perceptions of the quality of their lives and how they feel about their lives. The data we do have suggest that the answers we get from people will be determined in part by the kinds of questions we ask. When a cross section of Americans were asked how *happy* they felt, investigators found a decreasing score with increasing age. But when these people were asked how *satisfied* they were with their lives, an *increasing* score with increasing age was reported. Certainly there are some data on quality of life that are clear and relevant to our task. A certain amount of economic security is required for a person to report that he or she finds life to have a real measure of quality. Further, the more challenging and stimulating one's job, the more satisfaction one reports. Pleasant physical surroundings also are reported to be related to life satisfaction. Another study found an almost perfect correlation between where one lived on the rural–urban continuum and reported life satisfaction. The direction of the correlation need not be spelled out. The New Yorker, cowering behind locked doors with a trained Doberman pinscher watchdog, reports feeling a lower level of life quality than the farmer, from Vermont or elsewhere, despite the enormous discrepancy in certain cultural resources between the two.

This chapter suggests that felt *quality of life* is predictable from a multiple correlation whose predictor variables include (a) an emotionally stable and socially nurturant infancy and early childhood; (b) an interesting and challenging way of contributing to one's livelihood in the world of work; (c) a reasonable security from random or capricious blows of fate and from irrational handicaps and hurdles based on racial, sexual, and other prejudices; (d) a pleasant and nurturant physical and social surrounding; (e) a sense of identity; (f) a sense of self-respect; and (g) a feeling that one has reasonable control of one's life direction.

Now the question is, What modest contributions can psychologists make to foster more of these experiences and feelings in more people? Psychology is frequently defined as the scientific study of individual differences. Traditionally, psychologists have focused attention on individual behavior—they have researched how the behavior of individuals is affected by external and internal forces. In recent years, however, there has been an enormous increase in the number of service providers in psychology so that the definition of psychology must be broadened to include increasing numbers of therapists, helpers, consultants, social change agents, and others whose primary identification is more professional than scientific. The professionals will become more numerous in the future; the scientists seem destined to decrease both in numbers and resources in an increasingly anti-intellectual climate and a sluggish steady-state educational system.

Americans have developed a love–hate relationship with psychology. Part of this ambivalence derives from the fact that psychology and some of its related disciplines have made major contributions to the growing suspicion that God is dead, or at least that She is very different from the nineteenth century patriarch floating in the heavens in an imitation of Michelangelo's Jehovah sidestroking across the ceiling of the Sistine Chapel.

Psychology, of course, has not been alone in nurturing these seeds of doubt. The suspicion has been growing at least since Copernicus' discovery that we are warmed by a pale little star somewhere out on the periphery of an enormous, though relatively insignificant, galaxy, lost in the trackless void of space. More recently, Darwin added to our uncertainty when he shared the shattering insight that the human species was continuous with lower forms of animal life and was not created separately in the image of God. Latter-day Victorians, terrified with this information and with the upheavals occasioned by the perceptions of Karl Marx, then faced the implications of the works of Freud and Skinner.

Consider the implications of the Freudian message that the mind is like an iceberg, nine tenths of it unavailable to human consciousness; that human behavior follows the same lawful processes as do other natural phenomena; that people's behavior is determined by experiences and impulses over which they have little or no control. Add to this Skinner's message that behavior is largely controlled by external reinforcement and that behavior changes with changes in reinforcement. He implies that we invent attitudes and philosophies to explain or rationalize behavior that is largely an automatic response to external forces. Skinner (1975) stated it this way:

> I submit that what we call the behavior of the human organism is no more free than its digestion, gestation, immunization, or any other physiological process. Because it involves the environment in many subtle ways it is much more complex, and its lawfulness is, therefore, much harder to demonstrate. But a scientific analysis moves in that direction, and we can already throw some light on traditional topics, such as free will or creativity, which is more helpful than traditional accounts, and I believe that further progress is imminent.
>
> The issue is, of course, determinism. Slightly more than 100 years ago, in a famous paper, Claude Bernard raised with respect to physiology the issue which now stands before us in the behavioral sciences. The almost insurmountable obstacle to the application of scientific method in biology was, he said, the belief in "vital spontaneity." His contemporary, Louis Pasteur, was responsible for a dramatic test of the theory of spontaneous generation, and I suggest that the spontaneous generation of behavior in the guise of ideas and acts of will is now at the stage of the spontaneous generation of life in the form of maggots and microorganisms 100 years ago. (p. 47)

These messages undermine the comforting beliefs that sustained Western society for so long: that there is order, planning, reason, and justice in the universe. As the supports are removed, we must increasingly face the existential terror of ambiguity and meaninglessness. But the onion has many more layers, and most of us surmount the existential depression and struggle on, often with some joy and verve. What are some of the areas of this struggle where psychology has an influence?

Revolution often comes after a successful challenge of authority. Once authority has been challenged and has failed to destroy the challengers, there comes a time of ferment, of creativity, of anxiety, and of uncertainty, out of which evolves a whole set of new social structures and institutions. This intriguing subject is not explored here beyond reminding the reader of the wide-ranging social development in England following the Magna Carta, of the bursts of energy following the Protestant Reformation, of the dramatic developments in the Soviet Union and China in recent years (Albee, 1970).

Although the challenge to authority I want to mention is on a smaller scale and far less cataclysmic, the fact remains that psychology has challenged the official explanation of mental disturbance as being a result of defects or illnesses. The old medical model is simply no longer credible. As a consequence, the hold that psychiatry and medicine have had on the field of intervention with the mentally disturbed is perilously close to being lost.

The Future of Psychology

One consequence for the future will be the movement of large numbers of psychologists, and other new groups with new doctrines, into the field of personal counseling and psychotherapy at a time when demands for help are increasing. It is hard to anticipate what new and innovative kinds of therapies will develop because of the great variety that has sprung up over the past 20 years from the ashes of the sickness model. Encounter groups and nude marathons are competing with meditation and the religions of the East in the garden of psychotherapy, all striving for the nurturance of the warm sunlight of financial support. To mix a metaphor, psychology will be there with plenty of troops. Twelve thousand new, first-year graduate students are being selected annually from a huge pool of aspiring psychologists, many of whom are aspiring therapists. Undergraduates in astounding numbers are majoring in psychology and a large number of them are reporting themselves motivated by a burning desire to "help people." Psychology is selecting from its applicant pool recruits who are very bright and highly motivated, with whose demands we can just barely cope (Albee, 1973).

Psychotherapy

It is very difficult to see how there will be anything but a significant increase for the near future in the role of psychologists in the delivery of psychotherapy. One of the greatest hungers of the lonely person, or the person searching for meaning, is for a sympathetic listener, a guru to talk to. One of the greatest needs of the anxious person is for a voice of authority giving reassurance. A universal need among those who have lost their faith is a new faith, a system that explains life's mysteries with authorities to interpret the obscure places in the scripture. Also, the role of the psychotherapist is exceedingly rewarding in financial tokens as well as in personal reassurance and status. If national health insurance is passed and includes psychological services, speculation about other fields of employment in psychology may be wasted effort. Professions with a near monopoly and with controlled entry into the field cannot fail to prosper with any form of government-paid reimbursement for services in great demand. Psychotherapy is in great demand. (The cognitive dissonance created in the psychologist who knows emotional disturbance is not an *illness*, but who accepts money from a national health scheme for "treatment" of "patients," is not discussed here.)

Clearly, there is a large public that is willing and eager to pay for psychological services. In certain regions—New York, Chicago, most of California—psychologists in the private practice of individual and group psychotherapy find a ready market for their services. Indeed, the market seems so large that these psychologists are seriously going about establishing new professional schools to train more people like themselves, complaining bitterly of the lack of responsibility of traditional graduate programs for not providing more practitioners. If a demand for these sorts of personal psychological services exists or can be created in other regions of the country, it seems probable that a great many of our newly trained PhDs might find employment in such service activities. Obviously, there are other areas of applied psychology where employment opportunities are still promising. Despite the federal reduction in mental health funding the demand will continue strong for people to intervene with the mentally disordered poor and with the retarded and handicapped in state and local tax-supported facilities.

There is something enormously seductive about the combination of influence and affluence, perhaps because of the high reinforcement value of power. Influence over others develops a sense of power, and affluence purchases the trappings and artifacts of power. So long as there is a widespread demand for psychotherapy delivered by psychologists, a large number in the field may be lured away from those areas of service where more innovative developments might be expected. For example, the number of mentally retarded persons in our society will continue to increase for several reasons that have been detailed elsewhere (Albee, 1968). Psychology is the appropriate field for developing a rich range of training programs aimed at maximizing the limited abilities of the retarded in ways that would help them enjoy a life of reasonable quality. But the affluent life-style available to the psychotherapist is sufficiently seductive (reinforcing) that it lures away persons who might make contributions in the field of retardation. But more importantly, the visibility of this life-style is a significant factor in recruitment. Young people attracted to the field of psychology as a life profession are *self-selected*. No one forces anyone into this field. Young people are recruited as a result of their perceptions of those people already in the field. As we become more committed to the delivery of psychotherapy in suburbia (how many millions of teenagers watch the Bob Newhart Show?), we find our recruits from among those who have little motivation to work with the retarded.

Behavior Modification

Another trend bears careful watching. Despite setbacks and mistakes, both civil libertarians' and authoritarians' grumbling and hostility, the field of behavior modification marches ahead. The numbers of behavioral therapists increase, and their dedication to both basic and evaluative research sharpens the power of their methods (or leads them to abandon or change their ways). A number of the experimentally oriented young psychologists who will not find employment in academia may be diverted to this area of intervention.

The growth of behavior modification programs in both educational and clinical settings may offer one possible bridge for the experimental psychology graduate student who wants to improve his or her employment capability in an applied area. Indeed, this area of application could become a dominant force in applied psychology over the middle-range future.

Other Trends

There also seems to be in prospect some increase in societal demand for people trained in evaluation research. With the growing federal interest in the solution of urgent "applied" social problems (such as crime, alcoholism, and drug addiction), there is a concomitant demand for people who can evaluate the new approaches and new programs. As of now, the university graduate psychology programs seem to be highly committed to producing people in relatively pure scientific fields rather than in applied and evaluative research. Evaluation research appears to be another area deserving self-conscious study and possible change.

Industry and education are two areas that will continue to have a demand for psychologists. Fields like marketing, community counseling, organizational counseling, public program planning and assessment, and educational counseling show continuing growth. While the present number in some of these fields is small, the path has been blazed and large numbers could follow.

Many psychologists have decided that our field has knowledge that if combined with legal and political clout could change social institutions and could build a better, more egalitarian, higher quality society. It was the testimony of psychologists and other social scientists that led the Supreme Court to the 1954 decision opposing separate but equal school facilities. The evidence from psychological studies is clear. Separate housing and separate job assignments and educational opportunities simply destroy the quality of life for the people affected. It will be the research and the social effectiveness of psychologists that ultimately put an end to discrimination based on race, sex, and age. Psychologists are moving into collaborative efforts with environmentalists and futurologists; political people are asking for help in social indicators, in survey data, etc. Other chapters will deal with these areas in detail; they are mentioned here to identify them as part of the future employment picture.

While on the subject of social justice, it must be pointed out that the society of the future, if it is to have high quality, must solve the problems of sexism and racism. In some areas a kind of Hegelian dialectic operates to create a healthy force, counterforce, and synthesis. Psychology, more than any other field, has shown great interest in the women's movement. Psychotherapists, most of whom are male, have been caught and nailed to the wall for espousing a sexist double-standard view of mental health. The women psychologists have marched thrice around the arena with Freud's head on a pike, and psychoanalysis will never be the same again, fortunately. In terms of innovative activities by psychology to improve the quality of life, I would place the elimination of sexism and of racism very high on my list of priorities. The problem to be solved is, Who will pay to support this effort?

Psychologists, almost to a person, belong in the humanistic camp. This does not include those psychologists who call themselves humanists in order to rip off the freebies that are part of the open, egalitarian humanistic exchange. Rather, psychologists, including even the most hard-nosed, experimental, data-oriented laboratory researchers, tend to be strongly committed to the human enterprise. Most of them will need considerably less consciousness raising than, say, engineers, mathematicians, or astronomers to oppose subtle racism and to be acceptable to the feminist group. If the society of the future is to be higher quality than the society of today, we need to help prevent sexist and racist thinking and behavior, so that whatever improved quality of life exists, exists for everyone.

If we are to set a goal, consciously or otherwise, of the elimination of sexism and racism, we had better be prepared for strong and powerful opposition from forces in society that benefit economically from the perpetuation of these kinds of damaging ideologies and myths. If you are data oriented, then sentence yourself to watching an afternoon of television, where it will quickly be apparent, from the commercials particularly but also from all of the greed shows, that millions of women are brainwashed into being consumers of worthless products bringing enormous profits to manufacturers who thrive in a sexist, nuclear-family-oriented consumer society.

Future Environments

There will undoubtedly be demands for other innovative psychological services in the future steady-state society. If population growth levels off while production scales go down and the workweek is shortened; if in a hundred years we abandon our cities and people live 50 to 100 miles out in the country in planned communities, commuting to three-day-a-week jobs—if all of these and other changes proposed by the futurologists occur, what will be the psychological problems and what will be the kinds of intervention demanded of psychologists? Universities should consider revising curricula to include the psychological study of leisure, the effects of boredom, etc. We should be concerned, too, with changes in patterns of child rearing, in the future of the nuclear family, in group marriage, in commune living, etc.

Psychologists have paid too little attention to the effects of changing sexual morality and behavior. With the separation of sex from procreation and with the growing importance of sex as recreation, all sorts of psychological effects should be investigated. These areas are largely untouched but will demand social science input.

Conclusion

There are some things about the future of which we may be reasonably certain (if these assumptions are wrong it really doesn't matter): (a) There will be people; (b) people will be behaving; (c) the behavior will occur in environments that condition behavior; (d) there will be behavioral problems. Part of the futurology game is to try to anticipate the nature of these future environments and problems, extrapolating from current trends. This is a game that anyone can play. Some mind stretching and brainstorming should be occurring among those responsible for planning graduate programs in psychology. Clearly, we may have to cut back on our analytic style of research training. Psychologists skilled at manipulating clean-cut variables in clearly controlled environments are not going to be in great demand. Our human problems, now and for the near future, are far more diffuse and ambiguous. While there are those who would argue for the importance of transfer of training from the laboratory to the social problem arena, there is not much evidence that hard-nosed scientists enjoy working with "the big problems." (Note should be taken of the fact that not all students pursue their graduate studies with an eye on later job opportunities. Some, like the depression generation students, are attracted to psychological study out of zest for the subject matter. We suspect, however, that this group is small.)

The APA Council of Representatives has recently approved the establishment of a new Committee on Human Resources and Employment in Psychology. The Committee is asking that every psychology department appoint an employment counselor. The hope is that up-to-date information on wo/manpower and job opportunities can be made available in such a way that we can avoid the problems of oversupply that plague other fields.

REFERENCES

Albee, G. W. Needed—A revolution in caring for the retarded. *Trans-Action*, January/February 1968, pp. 37–42.
Albee, G. W. The uncertain future of clinical psychology. *American Psychologist*, 1970, *25*, 1071–1080.
Albee, G. W. The uncertain future of psychology. *APA Monitor*, May 1973, p. 6.
Skinner, B. F. The steep and thorny way to a science of behavior. *American Psychologist*, 1975, *30*, 42–49.

10

APA Task Force on Health Research

Contributions of Psychology to Health Research: Patterns, Problems, and Potentials

If asked to indicate the thing in life that they value most highly, most Americans, and probably most people anywhere, would surely list "good health" among the top two or three items. This concern for health is not misplaced. One's state of health may be fundamental to most other pleasures or values. Its economic impact is well documented. A recent report from the Carnegie Commission (Juster, 1975) suggests that individuals in poor health earn on the average about $7,000 per year less than those in good health with the same education (Taubman & Wales, 1975). The importance of health and the extent of health-seeking activity by Americans are clearly indicated by the fact that more than $100 billion was expended on health care services in the United States in 1972 (Burns, 1973). During fiscal year 1974, this level of expenditure represented almost 8% of the gross national product; that is, approximately $1 of every $14 for goods and services produced in this country is a health dollar. Thus, health care is the largest single service industry in the United States today. Yet, the health industry seems to be an unmanaged system. Research on the functioning of its component parts has been undertaken by few psychologists.

Health is rapidly emerging as one of the most crucial social problems facing our nation. Access to health care is increasingly recognized as a basic human right; no citizen should be denied such access because of inability to pay. Despite the huge expenditures on health care services in the past few years, it is widely recognized that large segments of our society do not have access to adequate care. Conventional methods of providing and financing health services are nearly exhausted. Our medical schools are so inadequate in terms of the quantity of physicians they produce that a very large proportion of our physicians are now being trained abroad. Approximately 20% of all physicians in this country are being "imported,"

The Task Force on Health Research of the Board of Scientific Affairs was established in June 1973 upon the recommendation of the Committee on Newly Emerging Areas of Research (NEAR). Members of the Task Force are Claus B. Bahnson, Edward J. Kelty, Miriam F. Kelty (APA staff liaison), John E. Rasmussen, William Schofield (Chair), Lee B. Sechrest, and Walter W. Wilkins.

This chapter is reprinted with permission from the *American Psychologist*, 1976, *31*, 263–274.

and 46% of the physicians licensed in 1972 were graduates of foreign medical schools (Association of American Medical Colleges, 1974). Moreover, the shortage of physicians, along with rapidly growing costs of their services, is encouraging more attention to the use of paraprofessionals and to other innovations in the delivery of traditional health care services. Changes in the service delivery system also have been brought about by an evolution over the years in fundamental medical concepts relating to health and illness.

In earlier times, illness was thought to result from the presence of a single pathogenic agent—germ, toxin, neoplasm, endocrine imbalance, vitamin or other nutritional deficiency, etc. New knowledge, however, has increased the recognition that the etiology of poor health is multifactorial. The virulence of infection interacts with the particular susceptibility of the host. Predisposition of the individual to succumb selectively to various assaults on physical integrity not only is related to particular early life experiences but also is associated with economic and social status, especially as reflected in living and working conditions.

The emergence of health as a social issue has been accompanied by a slow but evident shift in responsibility for coping with the problem. Health care delivery is no longer solely within the purview of medicine. The consumer is assuming a major role in shaping programs and policy, the economist rather than the physician is now leading the search for solutions to the problems of funding the delivery of care, and sociologists are conducting applied research focused upon the development and evaluation of health delivery systems. By contrast, psychology as a discipline has been surprisingly slow to recognize and accept research challenges in this problem area. Possibly the historical prominence of mental health as a focus for applied psychology has overshadowed other types of health-oriented psychological research.

It is time for an increased awareness of the research contributions that may be made in the broader fields of health and delivery of health services by organizational, educational, social, and experimental psychologists. It is obvious that the present crisis in health care delivery is not going to be resolved by psychology alone, or any other single discipline. Nevertheless, certain aspects of the problem call rather uniquely upon the body of knowledge and the methods that have been developed within psychology. This chapter highlights some of the contemporary issues in health care delivery and identifies research challenges for psychologists.

The American Health Care System

Is there a health care system in the United States? Or is there simply available a large and complex set of facilities and services? The term *system* implies organization and dynamic interaction of functional units; such organization and relationship are found only in limited degree in health services today. The lack of coordination of services that characterizes clinical medicine, general hospitals, optometrists, pharmacies, podiatrists, long-term care facilities, drug manufacturers, and the myriad other parts of our health goods-and-services grab bag is difficult to over-state. There is little evidence of an overall plan (Freymann, 1974; Illich, 1975).

Moreover, the dynamic character of the interrelationships is not always apparent. Each of the groups or institutions referred to above makes deci-sions as if the others did not exist, and in fact the decisions may have little outside impact. We have most of the elements of a system but without the functional interrelationships and the financial coordination of health ser-vices needed for a truly systematic endeavor.

In 1973, 182 million Americans had health insurance that covered part, and often nearly all, of their health expenditures (Health Insurance Insti-tute, 1975), and most of those persons had substantial freedom in picking the purveyors of the facilities or services they sought. Some of these insured Americans, a growing number it appears, belonged to "prepaid" health plans that provided them access to preventive services because it was in the interest of the provider to keep them well. Americans in the military services, along with many in other types of organizations, have health services provided as a condition of employment and can scarcely be distinguished from those persons receiving care under "socialized medi-cine" systems in other countries. There are, of course, Americans who do not have insurance and who pick and pay the physician of their own choice. Still others receive a medical subsidy under Medicare and Medicaid programs. There are many Americans, however, who lack personal re-sources and fail to meet requirements for any program of health care; they do not receive health services of any kind on any consistent basis. The services they receive are haphazard and more often than not are in response to some emergency or personal desperation.

We do not wish to gloss over the complexities alluded to above. What follows is an oversimplification to make another point; we realize that there are limitations to the concept of "system" when that concept is applied to health services in the United States.

Health care delivery involves more than the treatment of illness. The goal is to minimize the need for treatment of disease through positive and proactive programs of health maintenance. With the advances that have been made in modern medicine, infant mortality has been greatly reduced, and mass death from epidemics of highly fatal infectious disease has become almost nonexistent in North America. With the reduction in death from controllable disease and the consequent increase in life expec-tancy, clinical medicine might be characterized as expanding the tradi-tional concern for treating the sick to include increasing emphasis on prevention of illness and the extended treatment and rehabilitation of the chronically ill.

Health maintenance includes, but extends far beyond, the prevention of infectious disease. It includes the early detection and correction of defects, reduction in the severity of chronic disease processes through early diag-nosis and treatment, and education in positive health practices that reduce the need for subsequent treatment. Health care delivery begins with the consumer rather than the physician. If the system is to work, the consumer, rather than the medical team, makes the initial decision to participate. Moreover, initiative for sustained participation rests with the consumer. For many individuals, however, initiative rests with other persons who must detect and assess a problem, often of great complexity, and decide whether further help should be obtained. Children, the aged, the mentally incompetent, and the accident victim are dependent on the judgment of others who make the initial diagnosis and treatment decision. It should be recognized that many individuals, probably most persons potentially in need of a health service, consult at least one other lay person before making the decision to seek professional help (Friedson, 1970). Wives and husbands ask each other, children ask parents, friends ask neighbors, workers ask supervisors, and so on. An important link in the health care chain is the individual consumer and lay "consultant." It should be recognized also that more often than not when troubled by pain or some other symptom or problem, the consumer diagnoses the problem as a minor or familiar one and treats it himself or ignores it (Fry, 1966). For these reasons health education would be expected to have important payoffs.

The consumer plays yet another role in shaping the health care delivery system. The general consumer advocacy movement in the United States has had a profound impact on health care delivery. The consumer movement is playing a large part in bringing about the establishment of minimal quality standards of health care delivery. Lack of access to adequate health care by large segments of the American population, particularly the disadvantaged and minority groups, has stimulated consumer pressures, which in turn are bringing about the development of innovative change and increased government intervention in the financing and delivery of health care. Although all of the above factors have varying degrees of impact on contemporary health care delivery, it is clear that our present system not only is heavily shaped by consumers but also depends on their behavior as participants.

With the consumer as the first element, the second element in the health services delivery enterprise is that of the professional service provider, broadly defined. Many professionals in the health service system other than physicians may deliver primary health care or provide important diagnostic or preventive services. Although pharmacists may not "practice medicine," it is only in a fairly narrow technical sense that they are constrained from doing so. The victim of a toothache may be given a palliative, the sufferer from nasal congestion may be given a decongestant, and the person in pain from stomach cramps may be given a drug or may be referred to a "specialist," a physician. Optometrists may prescribe glasses for eye defects or may detect dangerous eye disorders (e.g., diabetic retinopathy), for which they will refer the person to a specialist, that is, a physician. Dentists may treat a wide variety of diseases and defects, and they may also detect conditions (e.g., early signs of cancer), for which they will refer the individual to a specialist, again a physician. For many persons, the first health professional to be seen is perhaps a public health or clinic nurse. Again, treatments may be prescribed and administered or referrals may take place. The important point is that the health services delivery system includes at the very first line of professional action many persons of varied training other than physicians.

The physician is, of course, a vital part of health care delivery. Especially at the level of the so-called "primary care" physician there are important issues of access to and cost of medical care. These may not loom large to most people who do not need or want to visit a physician more than once or twice a year, if that. For other persons with more frequent or more chronic illnesses, the availability of a physician at reasonable cost is critical. Clearly, given the central role and the virtual monopoly on certain aspects of medical care that have been granted to physicians, the public has a vital interest in their performance as a part of a total system of health care.

For people lacking access to an individual physician there are alternate subsystems to provide care. The hospital emergency room is important as a part of the system in its own right. It also provides a source of primary care for many persons, especially those lacking access to other parts of the system. It has been estimated that up to 80% of the cases appearing at the emergency room are not in fact medical emergencies at all (Gibson, Bugbee, & Anderson, 1970; Knowles, 1973). A great many of them are seeking help from the only source known to them. Hospitals, other outpatient departments, and clinics are also important as places of first professional contact with the health system for many people. Though it may make some people uncomfortable to acknowledge it, there are many equivalents of "native healers" who provide care for persons seeking help. At present, little is known about the structure and delivery of emergency services or about the factors that lead a person to define his or her situation as an emergency in the first place.

If the first professional contact does not prove adequate to deal with the health problem presented, our health resources present a virtually dazzling array of specialized facilities and professionals to carry on diagnostic and treatment efforts. There are renowned diagnostic centers, hospitals, specialized and superspecialized physicians, and ancillary professionals to provide whatever care can be paid for. The system even provides life-sustaining measures, somewhat undependably and arbitrarily, to individuals who, only a few short years ago, would have died; hemodialysis and kidney transplantation are notable examples. At this level of specialized professionals and the zenith of medical technology, expenses mount rapidly and can quickly become ruinous. Only relatively few persons need access to health care at its most advanced levels, but for those who do, the need is likely to be critical. To the extent that we may think of American health care as constituting a system, it is evident that it is highly complicated, that there is no smooth organization and working together of the parts, that it is often adventitious and even arbitrary in the way services are distributed, and that it can be very expensive at its extended best. Causing the system to operate more effectively, more fairly, and at lower cost is an objective worthy of the attention of all Americans, but especially of psychologists, who have a privileged opportunity to contribute to the attainment of that objective.

Psychological Aspects of Health and Disease

Few persons deny the importance of psychological factors in health and well-being. Educated lay persons as well as scientists express both colloquially and formally some of the interrelationships between good health and successful adjustment or between poor health and poor adjustment. There has been a considerable increase in the interest of social scientists in health and illness. One of the more productive branches of sociology is medical sociology; one of the more intriguing branches of anthropology is one that studies the beliefs and practices of our contemporary primitive and not-so-primitive cultures in the areas of illness, its prevention and treatment; economists and epidemiologists have gathered data that show relationships between social class poverty and illness. Simply to list the behaviors that affect health and its maintenance would be a difficult and tedious task.

One of the questions that psychologists, with their skills in educational technology, are beginning to address is why many people do not follow medical advice about their health and its maintenance. What are the determinants of specific but important acts of commission (brushing one's teeth) or omission (refraining from smoking)? When symptoms do appear, why do some persons avoid formal diagnosis and deny illness—a denial that may be self-destructive. Psychologists are investigating factors that motivate such health-related behaviors.

The area of health research is replete with topics suitable for predictive studies. Measurable constitutional factors that predispose to one or another illness may be the domain of anatomy and physiology, and measurable somatotypical factors have been a subject of physical anthropology. The assessment of life-styles and life crises as they affect near-future illness, however, is certainly a proper study for psychology. Similarly, how and why individuals vary in their responses to sickness are questions for psychological investigation. One sailor aboard ship, for instance, may turn up at sick call when medical evidence indicates that he has little physically wrong; another, apparently much sicker by objective tests, continues at his job and carries his work load. One housewife may keep things going when her temperature is high and her strength low; another, with fewer symptoms, may take to her bed. An elementary-school child, faced with scholastic and peer problems, may find health problems worsened, while another, whose social adjustment is proceeding smoothly, experiences fewer sicknesses. How are these response patterns to be understood?

The substantive areas for application of psychological method to the study of health and illness behaviors are many. Their potential yield of insights into psychobiosocial determinants of such behaviors is great and could provide the basis for improved prophylactic and therapeutic efforts. A few questions can illustrate the challenge: How are health care practices related to the amount and quality of the individual's health information? What are the determinants of more and less effective specific health education programs? How should such programs be evaluated? What are the primary sources of persisting health care attitudes? What are the relations of such attitudes to information and to care resources?

While a proportion of the research effort by psychologists interested in health has been directed toward persons who now, or who may in the future, suffer from some specific illnesses, a surprisingly large share has focused on studies of fairly healthy populations (Heath, 1965). In the 1940s there were many studies of background characteristics, personality factors, and life events that might be related to one or another form of illness. Examples include the many studies of how persons with a specific illness, presumed to be psychosomatic, behaved on a standard set of stimuli, like inkblots, or on an omnibus set of questions, like the MMPI or the Maudsley Personality Inventory. These continue today, as exemplified by the Jenkins (1971) questionnaire about Type A or Type B personality in the prediction of heart disease. Studies of this sort test normal populations, for example, members of an urban fire department or employees of a department store, and then attempt to identify those in the population who may succumb to the disability of interest. Other studies, like those of Gunderson and Rahe (1974), inquire about a person's recent life changes, assuming that situational crises can be weighted and cumulated, and then try to identify, in a healthy population, those who may become ill in any way at all. This adds a new dimension to susceptibility, a psychosocial one, that may create a modest but useful amount of unique variance to prediction of illness.

Some recent work deserves mention as a positive example of what can be done in the area of attitude research. In a series of studies, Richard I. Evans and his colleagues at the University of Houston have applied the tools of social psychology to one aspect of health maintenance, dental hygiene (Evans, Rozelle, Noblitt, & Williams, in press). Recent investigation by these workers on the effects of feedback in modifying health maintenance behavior and maintaining the changes has indicated that repeated contacts with the subject may themselves be more important in maintaining change than the particular method of persuasion or feedback involved. There are many areas of health besides dentistry in which attitudes influence behavior and are extremely important either in health maintenance or in treatment programs. Although some valuable work is currently being done, there is need for additional competent researchers to become involved in this area of endeavor.

The processes of rehabilitation provide another potentially major arena for basic and applied psychological research. The patient who has suffered a major debilitating illness or physical handicap is essentially faced with a variety of learning tasks—learning new patterns of activities, relearning lost aptitudes, or acquiring new skills. Basic fields of developmental, cognitive, learning, and motivational psychology have relevance, and their principles can direct research aimed at the discovery of more efficient rehabilitation programs. In the process, there is opportunity for testing hypotheses and discovering new principles.

Both collegiate and military populations participate in the study of the relationship of stress to disease. How humans adjust to unusual challenges, to perils, to isolation, to disappointments has been studied with health and illness as critical outcomes (Levi, 1971). The ergonomist's criterion of efficiency must be supplemented by the broadest criteria of health. A sizable amount of research on the health of the healthy is done on young populations because of their availability. Normative studies in Boston and Chicago (Heath, 1965) of healthy young college students can be matched by a variety of studies carried on by psychologists in the armed forces. Research centers like the Army Research Institute of Environmental Medicine at Natick, Massachusetts, or the Naval Health Research Center at San Diego, which specializes in cohort studies, have followed some service personnel for almost a decade (Gunderson & Rahe, 1974).

The way people cope when struck by ill health or accident is also an important area of study. Response to pain, to persistent discomfort, to physical handicap, and to debilitation can be assessed by a variety of psychological measures. It is not only the individual differences in coping ability that people show when attacked by illness or handicap that is of interest, however. These differences in adaptation need to be related to physical and psychological characteristics.

Illness can be thought of as the product of exposure interacting with resistance. Some germs are so potent that exposure alone can bring about death—no amount of stamina or determination can prevent the outcome. At another extreme, some illnesses seem to result from a minimum of potency of the invading agent and a maximum of stress.

Researchers into health and illness behaviors must attend to the criterion problem. Longevity is too crude a criterion of health. Definitions are beginning to reflect recognition of degrees of quality of life, as shown, for example, in extent of self-sufficiency, satisfaction, and personal fulfillment.

Illness as a research criterion also does not allow simple definition. The synoptic researchers who have reviewed the concept have seen it as including some role playing. Is illness at least partially a self-defined state? It would be helpful to arrange the array of diseases along an acute–chronic continuum and to investigate the degree to which chronicity is correlated with the extent of disturbed psychological factors.

Psychologists and researchers in related health fields have studied psychological correlates of a number of psychosomatic and somatic disease syndromes (entities) as well as illness in general (Gunderson & Rahe, 1974). Early studies were done of asthma, dermatoses, duodenal ulcer, colitis, and other diseases considered "psychosomatic." Later, interests focused on conditions that previously had been considered purely "somatic," such as hypertension, coronary heart disease, and arthritis. The relationship between hostility and repression of hostility and hypertension was outlined (Alexander, 1950), and a specific personality profile, the so-called coronary-prone Type A behavior pattern, was hypothesized for individuals vulnerable to myocardial infarction (Friedman & Rosenman, 1959, 1974; Jenkins, Rosenman, & Zyzansky, 1974; Rosenman et al., 1966). More recently, investigators have begun to study the role of psychological factors in the etiology of cancer.

The etiology of cancer, or more accurately, the cancers, still is not well understood. Hopes have repeatedly been shattered for finding a specific agent (e.g., a virus) that extends the principles of study that were important for the understanding and control of infectious diseases. The failure of the old approaches is probably related to the fact that cancer is a disease involving basic cell behavior apparently responsive to slight changes in the ribonucleic acid (RNA) and deoxyribonucleic acid (DNA) transmission of genetic coding. Within a systems-theoretical approach, RNA and DNA coding, in turn, are responsive not only to genetic conditions but also to changes in the endocrine, hematologic, immunologic, and neurologic systems and thus, indirectly, to behavioral variables. In the area of immune responses it has been shown (Rasmussen, 1969; Solomon, 1969; Solomon, Amkraut, & Kasper, 1974; Bahnson et al., Note 1) that stress and depression may reduce the antibody response and that adult immunologic responsivity may be a function of early infantile experiences. In animal models (Ader & Friedman, 1965; Ader, Friedman, & Glasgow, 1969; Newton, 1964) it has also been demonstrated that early life experiences and environmental manipulation modify responses to later cancer challenges. This and related research are summarized by Bahnson (1969a) and Bahnson and Kissen (1966).

Psychologic and psychosocial research has been concerned with long-term etiologic behavioral factors (e.g., personality, childhood stress) as well as with behavioral correlates to different types of response to cancer and to impending death. Studies of etiology have implicated three different but overlapping problem areas related to cancer: (a) a particular repressive personality pattern that is related to specific childhood experiences, (b) a tendency to respond with hopelessness-helplessness-despair to the loss of a significant person or life situation, and (c) a history of bereavement or loss of significant interpersonal relationships or life contexts. Traditional studies of personality in cancer patients, using control subjects who were both well and sick, have been done by a number of American and European psychologists including Tarlau and Smalheiser (1951), LeShan (1966; LeShan & Reznikoff, 1960; LeShan & Worthington, 1956), Cobb (1952, 1959), Reznikoff (1955), and Bahnson (1969a, 1969b; Bahnson & Bahnson, 1969). Psychiatrists and medical psychologists overseas have added to this research, including Kissen et al. in Britain (Kissen, Brown, & Kissen, 1969; Kissen & Eysenck, 1962; Kissen & Rao, 1969); Baltrusch (1975) in Germany; Oo (Note 2) in Hungary; and many others. A variety of objective and projective questionnaires and tests were used, and these several different groups arrived independently at a consistent description of the cancer patient as a rigid, authoritarian, inner-directed, and religious person, having ample conflict around sexual and hostile impulses, using excessive repression of affect, and having poor emotional outlets. Patients with slow- and fast-growing cancers have been compared. Blumberg, West, and Ellis (1956), using MMPI and Rorschach data, found that cancer patients with fast-developing diseases are more defensive and overcontrolled than patients with slow-developing diseases. Cobb (1959), using interview data, confirmed these impressions. The patient with rapidly progressing cancer shows a lack of ability to decrease anxiety and presents a polite, apologetic, almost painful acquiescence. This is contrasted with the more expressive and sometimes bizarre personalities of those who respond well to therapy with long remission and survival. Klopfer (1954) related investment in ego defense and ego strength to the differential development of fast- and slow-growing cancers. High investment correlated with fast-growing cancers.

Several psychologists have addressed themselves to the problem of adaptation to cancer and to impending death. Eissler (1955), Feifel (1959; Feifel, Freilich, & Hermann, 1973; Feifel, Hanson, Jones, & Edwards, 1967), Shneidman (1967, 1973), Murray (1962), and Shusterman (1973) are among those who have published in this area. Most have emphasized the importance of both interpersonal and intrapersonal communication for successful adaptation to disease. There is agreement that system approaches also are relevant here, because illness produces problem areas between patient and family, patient and medical staff, medical staff and family, and institution and medical staff. Not only the mental health and quality of life of the cancer patient and family but also the actual length of survival and response to treatment are correlated with the resolution of these several complex psychologic interactions.

Research is greatly needed to improve our understanding of psychological factors related to the onset of cancer. Psychologists can make significant contributions to the sophisticated rehabilitation and psychotherapeutic treatment of the complex emotional reactions of the patient to terminal disease and of the patient's family both to the disease and to death. Several studies have indicated that a new disease appears in a family particularly during the first year following an unresolved loss, indicating that prophylactic psychologic management of bereavement problems may yield significant gains for the survivors with regard to both their mental and their physical status in the years to come.

Current Patterns of Psychological Research on Health

The focus of the Task Force has been on research contributions by psychologists who are working on health and illness problems lying *outside* the traditional concerns with mental health and mental illness. It has been difficult to arrive at a secure estimate of the extent of such research activities. An appraisal of the general research literature and an examination of the roster of psychologists who have expressed interest in the work of the Task Force suggest that both the size and impact of our research on health-related behaviors are presently anemic, especially when viewed against the matrix of problems having potential for extensive contributions through psychological research.

The number of psychologists who have identified themselves to the Task Force as having definite interests in health research is quite small (fewer than 500), especially when contrasted to the memberships of those APA divisions (such as clinical, physiological and comparative, personality and social, rehabilitation, and psychopharmacology) in which one might expect health researchers to find their APA "home." The likelihood of sizable research contributions on health and illness factors may be further reduced in light of the fact that approximately one half of those who express health research interests have their major employment outside of medical or health settings. More significantly, their research reports frequently are published in non-APA journals, which not only are rarely seen by the average APA member but in some instances are not included in the *Psychological Abstracts* Search and Retrieval (PASAR) abstracting review process. Thus, the actual extent of research contributions by psychologists working in the general domain of health problems may be larger than is reflected by the more common modes of visibility.

One of the objectives of the Task Force has been to collect, organize, and disseminate information on the status of health behavior research. To accomplish this objective the Task Force used the PASAR system to identify literature cited in *Psychological Abstracts* on psychological aspects of (a) physical illness, (b) physical disability, or (c) health. In addition, the search included the role of psychologist and of psychological research in the delivery of health services. Mental health services were included only as they were more generally a part of health services.

The broad search resulted in approximately 3,500 abstracts or citations, covering the years 1966–1973. These abstracts were read and sorted into topical categories. The initial sorts were then reread, and those not relevant to the primary interest of the Task Force were eliminated, namely, all articles that were not research studies (i.e., reviews, anecdotal reports) and those that dealt primarily with mental health variables or psychiatric focuses. This second, more restricted categorization led to a disappointingly small literature sample of approximately 350 articles, scarcely more than 40 articles per year.

The literature search encountered some difficulties along the way. Ambiguity coupled with the limited amount of information available from an abstract impaired attempts to develop a useful classification schema. Abstracts often consisted mostly of the author's conclusions and were unclear as to the research methodology involved. Thus, in many cases it was difficult to distinguish anecdotal reports from more rigorous studies. Kahana (1972) experienced similar difficulties in his search for literature in the area of medical psychology, using the Medlars system of the National Library of Medicine. He reported that it was necessary to search under many terms to identify concepts and that the output was enormous. He too, however, reported that of 5,000 references selected from the computer search, 2,500 were judged directly relevant to the topic, and about 25% seemed useful.

In addition to problems in interpreting the abstracts themselves, the 3,500 abstracts retrieved from PASAR represented only a sample of the total literature in this broad interdisciplinary area. *Psychological Abstracts* is not designed to cover every journal in which a health-related article of interest to psychologists occasionally appears. In the interests of economy it is limited to publications that offer higher hit rates. Further, while a number of core journals are completely abstracted, most of the chosen list of journals is selectively scanned for articles judged likely to be of interest to the user of the system. Some loss of article abstracts in peripheral or less traditional areas such as health research may occur in this way. A final reason for the incomplete nature of the data base is that not all health-related research is reported in a journal format. Health researchers frequently work in nonuniversity settings and publish in-house reports, technical and progress reports, or other items not likely to be picked up by an abstracting system.

With these caveats in mind, the categories and current trends in health research revealed by the PASAR search are interesting. Several schema for breaking down the results of the scan were proposed. The abstracts gathered can be subsumed under three general categories: psychobiological aspects of health, health care delivery, and studies of health-related attitudes. Under the psychobiological category, accounting for 66% of the abstracts, fall such topics as the effects of stress, psychosomatics, social and environmental factors, and the effects of physical health and biological cycles on psychology and behavior.

Papers related to health care delivery (56 papers) accounted for 18% of the abstracts. Nearly half of these dealt with relatively specific aspects of treatment and rehabilitation rather than with larger issues or systems research. Needs and resources in health maintenance, health systems, and manpower, improvement of communication (e.g., between doctor and patient), and evaluation studies (including perceptions and impacts of health care) made up the remainder of this category. Studies of attitudes related to health and health care accounted for the remaining 16% of the abstracts. These ranged from surveys of attitudes held by various populations to attitude-change research.

Still another basis exists for the impression that psychology is neglecting the health area as a fertile field for research contributions. This is found in the topical concentration of our research endeavors, especially when appraised against health areas of major economic importance and public concern. Using "armchair" categories of health-related topics, *Psychological Abstracts* yielded a total of 4,719 entries for 1966–1967 (Schofield, 1969) inclusive, and 14,427 entries for 1971–1973 inclusive. This suggests considerable growth, but the absolute figures constitute an increment of only 5% in the proportion of total abstract entries. More significantly, the areas of research interest have not shifted. Topics neglected in the earlier PASAR survey continue to be relatively ignored, for example, population control, accidents, smoking, cancer, and pain. By contrast, the three topics of psychotherapy, mental retardation, and schizophrenia account for over 50% of the abstracts in both survey periods (see APA Task Force, 1974a).

This appraisal of the extent of health research contributions by psychologists may be unduly bleak. The Task Force has learned that many psychologists who are productive health researchers (e.g., in the field of dentistry) do not belong to APA. Some have resigned because they find no divisional affiliation that is effectively compatible with their research interests.[1]

To some extent, the restricted level of activity by psychologists in health and illness research may result from a lack of awareness of support funds from agencies other than the National Institute of Mental Health (NIMH). The Task Force has sought to alert psychologists to the behavioral science research programs presently supported by the National Heart and Lung Institute, the National Dental Institute, the National Institute of Neurological Diseases and Stroke, the National Institute of Alcohol Abuse and Alcoholism, and the National Institute of Occupational Safety and Health. Current planning for behavioral research programs is underway at the National Cancer Institute and the National Institute of General Medicine (see APA Task Force, 1974b).

Two conclusions are suggested. Up to the present time, American psychologists have not been attracted in large numbers to the problems of health and illness as fruitful areas for both basic and applied research activity; nor have these psychologists perceived the potentials for their work in effecting important improvements in health maintenance, illness prevention, and health care delivery. Some good work is being done. There is a need, however, for continuing effort of the sort initiated by the Task Force in stimulating and facilitating increased research contributions by psychologists.

Needs and Potentials

There is probably no more widespread deterrent to the achievement of a truly comprehensive system for health care than our dualistic conceptualization of health and illness. The obstruction to meaningful research and to optimal services resulting from a "practical" adherence to the mind–body dichotomy has been appreciated by persons as diverse as a state governor and a philosopher of science. Governor Evans (1975) of Washington observed, "Doctors, who once treated the human body as an entity, are so specialized that none seem to know any more that the head bone is still indirectly connected to the great toe" (p. 136). Theodore Roszak (1975) said it well when he wrote:

My position is that every such dichotomy is a symptom of disease in us: of fear, rigidity, compulsive distrust. The dichotomy is the problem, and choosing one or the other half of it is not a solution, because no healthy personality, no healthy culture, no healthy science can be built on less than the full and integrated range of human mentality. (p. 792)

---

1. A Section on Health Research has now been formed within Division 18.

No other discipline is better suited and equipped than psychology to discover, delineate, and demonstrate the organismic nature of humans and to encourage an ever-broadening realization that humanity's total functional health is threatened whenever either side of the interactive mind–body equation is neglected. Any program for health care and illness management can achieve comprehensiveness and integration only as there is respect for the functional unity of the individual. Psychologists can further the adoption of a usefully integrated concept of humans by applying their research methods to uncover the relationships between psychological factors and physical health.

If the current picture of psychological health research is not impressive, it must be recognized that psychology is probably in the earliest stage of a pioneering endeavor. There is no lack of opportunity. Rather, we need an educational endeavor within our profession. In particular, we need to blueprint programs for graduate education of researchers that will provide an early awareness of the needs and opportunities to apply psychological principles and methods to the understanding and improvement of health behaviors.

Psychological inquiry into factors determining health or illness can be pursued at more molecular or more molar levels. The psychophysiologist can track down the subtle physical responses to perception of threat and provide a basis for the physician to understand better the onset and course of illness in a patient. The personality researchers can explore attitudes (behavioral predispositions) that influence the individual toward responses that bring either immediate or later threat to health. The social psychologist can study the influence of group mores on the individual's accessibility or resistance to health education and health practices. The measurement expert can devise instruments to provide quantitative indexes of important qualitative variables, such as the "quality" of health services. The organizational psychologist may assist in bringing about change in health care delivery systems and in enhancing their effectiveness. The experimental psychologist may be of help in designing better monitoring equipment or in improving diagnostic algorithms. The educational psychologist can explore the variables that determine the extent to which health-related information is understood, stored, and acted upon. There is probably no speciality field within psychology that cannot contribute to the discovery of behavioral variables crucial to a full understanding of susceptibility to physical illness, adaptation to such illness, and prophylactically motivated behaviors. The areas open to psychological investigation range from health care practices and health care delivery systems to the management of acute and chronic illness and to the psychology of medication and pain.

If psychology's potentials for vital contributions to our nation's health are to be realized, certain needs must be met. First among these is the need for psychologists to be aware of the opportunity to contribute significantly to both the philosophy and the programs of our health care system. In this respect, psychologists should acknowledge that they are *life* scientists and consequently, no matter how tangentially, health scientists. The encouragement of such awareness has been one of the charges of the Task Force. This endeavor can be facilitated by recognition of and provision for still another need, the need for health researchers in our discipline to be directly aware of each other's work and of the research of health professionals in other disciplines.

With recognition of the new opportunities likely to arise because of the increasing public concern for better health care, with recognition of the presently very small number of psychologists who are health researchers (outside of the mental health area), and with recognition that these few have largely evolved and scratched out their own specialized training, there is a need to give serious thought to innovative programs of graduate training that will prepare psychologists to carry their expertise effectively into the general clinic, the hospital, the rehabilitation center, the community health center, and the group medical practice.

Finally, as a corollary to all of these needs, there is a need to find a suitable home within APA for what has now been identified as a core of health researchers, a distinct interest group that is likely to grow and has need for the basic organizational supports afforded by our major scientific and professional society.

REFERENCE NOTES

1. Bahnson, C. B., et al. *Relationship between emotion, repression of emotion, and immunity.* Manuscript in preparation.
2. Oo, M. *Personality examinations of cancer patients.* Paper presented at the Fourth International Conference on Psychosomatic Aspects of Neoplastic Disease, Turin, Italy, June 1965.

REFERENCES

Ader, R., & Friedman, S. B. Social factors affecting emotionality and resistance to disease in animals. V. Early separation from the mother and response to a transplanted tumor in the rat. *Psychosomatic Medicine,* 1965, *27,* 119–122.

Ader, R., Friedman, S., & Glasgow, L. Psychosocial factors modifying host resistance to experimental infections. *Annals of the New York Academy of Sciences,* 1969, *164,* 381–393.

Alexander, F. *Psychosomatic medicine.* New York: Norton, 1950.

American Psychological Association, Task Force on Health Research. Patterns of psychological study in health related areas. *Newsletter,* July 1974, pp. 6–7. (a)

American Psychological Association, Task Force on Health Research. Sources of funding. *Newsletter,* December 1974, pp. 5–10. (b)

Association of American Medical Colleges. Report of the Task Force on Foreign Medical Graduates. *Journal of Medical Education,* 1974, *49,* 811–822.

Bahnson, C. B. (Ed.). Second conference on psychophysiological aspects of cancer. *Annals of the New York Academy of Sciences,* 1969, *164,* 307–634. (a)

Bahnson, C. B. Psychophysiological complementarity in malignancies—Past work and future vistas. *Annals of the New York Academy of Sciences,* 1969, *164,* 319–334. (b)

Bahnson, C. B., & Bahnson, M. B. Role of the ego defenses: Denial and repression in the etiology of malignant neoplasm. *Annals of the New York Academy of Sciences,* 1966, *125,* 827–845.

Bahnson, C. B., & Kissen, D. M. (Eds.). Psychophysiological aspects of cancer. *Annals of the New York Academy of Sciences,* 1966, *125,* 773–1055.

Bahnson, M. B., & Bahnson, C. B. Ego defenses in cancer patients. *Annals of the New York Academy of Sciences,* 1969, *164,* 546–559.

Baltrusch, H. J. F. Ergebnisse Klinisch-Psychosomatischer Krebsforschung. *Psychoso-matische Medizin*, 1975, *5*, 175–208.

Blumberg, E. M., West, P. M., & Ellis, F. W. MMPI findings in human cancer. In *Basic readings on the MMPI in psychology and medicine*. Minneapolis: University of Minnesota Press, 1956.

Burns, E. M. *Health services for tomorrow: Trends and issues*. New York: Dunellen, 1973.

Cobb, B. *A socio-psychological study of the cancer patient*. Unpublished doctoral dissertation, University of Texas, Austin, 1952.

Cobb, B. Emotional problems of adult cancer patients. *Journal of the American Geriatrics Society*, 1959, *1*, 274–285.

Eissler, K. R. *The psychiatrist and the dying patient*. New York: International Universities Press, 1955.

Evans, D. J. The role of the state governments in educating the public about health. *Journal of Medical Education*, 1975, *50*, 130–137.

Evans, R. I., Rozelle, R. M., Noblitt, R., & Williams, D. L. Explicit and implicit persuasive communications over time to initiate and maintain behavior change: New perspective utilizing a real life dental hygiene situation. *Journal of Applied Social Psychology*, in press.

Feifel, H. (Ed). *The meaning of death*. New York: McGraw-Hill, 1959.

Feifel, H., Freilich, J., & Hermann, J. Death fear in dying heart and cancer patients. *Journal of Psychosomatic Research*, 1973, *17*, 161–166.

Feifel, H., Hanson, S., Jones, R., & Edwards, L. Physicians consider death. *Proceedings of the 75th Annual Convention of the American Psychological Association*, 1967, *2*, 201–202. (Summary)

Freymann, J. G. *The American health care system: Its genesis and trajectory*. New York: Medcom, 1974.

Friedman, M., & Rosenman, R. H. Association of a specific overt behavior pattern with blood and cardiovascular findings. *Journal of the American Medical Association*, 1959, *169*, 1286.

Friedman, M., & Rosenman, R. H. *Type 'A' behavior and your heart*. New York: Knopf, 1974.

Friedson, E. *The profession of medicine: A study of the sociology of applied knowledge*. New York: Dodd, Mead, 1970.

Fry, J. *Profiles of disease: A study in the natural history of common disease*. Baltimore, Md.: Williams & Wilkins, 1966.

Gibson, G., Bugbee, G., & Anderson, O. W. *Emergency medical services in the Chicago area*. Chicago, Ill.: Center for Health Administration Studies, University of Chicago, 1970.

Gunderson, E. K. E., & Rahe, R. H. (Eds.). *Life stress and illness*. Springfield, Ill.: Charles C Thomas, 1974.

Health Insurance Institute. *Source book of health insurance data: 1974–75*. New York: Author, 1975.

Heath, D. *Exploration of maturity*. New York: Appleton-Century-Crofts, 1965.

Illich, I. *Medical nemesis: The expropriation of health*, London: Calder & Boyars, 1975.

Jenkins, C. D. Psychologic and social precursors of coronary disease. *New England Journal of Medicine*, 1971, *284*, 244–255; 307–317.

Jenkins, C. D., Rosenman, R. H., & Zyzansky, S. J. Prediction of clinical coronary heart disease by a test for the coronary-prone behavior pattern. *New England Journal of Medicine*, 1974, *290*, 1271–1275.

Juster, F. T. (Ed.). *Education, income and human behavior*. New York: McGraw-Hill, 1975.

Kahana, R. J. Studies in medical psychology: A brief survey. *Psychiatry in Medicine*, 1972, *3*, 1–22.

Kissen, D. M., Brown, R. I. F., & Kissen, M. A further report on personality and psychosocial factors in lung cancer. *Annals of the New York Academy of Sciences*, 1969, *164*, 535–545.

Kissen, D. M., & Eysenck, H. J. Personality in male lung cancer patients. *Journal of Psychosomatic Research*, 1962, *6*, 123.

Kissen, D. M., & Rao, L. G. S. Steroid excretion patterns and personality in lung cancer. *Annals of the New York Academy of Sciences*, 1969, *164*, 476–481.

Klopfer, B. A. Results of psychologic testing in cancer. In J. A. Gengerelli & F. J. Kirkner (Eds.), *The psychological variables in human cancer*. Berkeley & Los Angeles: University of California Press, 1954.

Knowles, J. H. The hospital. *Scientific American*, 1973, *229*(3), 128–137.

LeShan, L. L. An emotional life-history pattern associated with neoplastic disease. *Annals of the New York Academy of Sciences*, 1966, *125*, 780–793.

LeShan, L. L., & Reznikoff, M. A psychological factor apparently associated with neoplastic disease. *Journal of Abnormal and Social Psychology*, 1960, *60*, 439–440.

LeShan, L. L., & Worthington, R. E. Some recurrent life history patterns observed in patients with malignant disease. *Journal of Nervous and Mental Diseases,* 1956, *124,* 460–465.

Levi, L. (Ed.). *Society, stress, and disease. I. The psychosocial environment and psychosomatic diseases.* London: Oxford University Press, 1971.

Murray, H. A. The personality and career of satan. *Journal of Social Issues,* 1962, *18,* 36–54.

Newton, G. Early experience and resistance to tumor growth. In D. M. Kissen & L. L. LeShan (Eds.), *Psychosomatic aspects of neoplastic disease.* London: Pitman, 1964.

Rasmussen, A. J., Jr. Emotions and immunity. *Annals of the New York Academy of Sciences,* 1969, *164,* 458–461.

Reznikoff, M. Psychological factors in breast cancer: A preliminary study of some personality trends in patients with cancer of the breast. *Psychosomatic Medicine,* 1955, *17,* 96–108.

Rosenman, R. H., Friedman, M., Straus, R., Wurm, M., Jenkins, C. D., & Messinger, H. B. Coronary heart disease in the western collaborative group study. *Journal of the American Medical Association,* 1966, *195,* 86–92.

Roszak, T. Gnosis and reductionism (Letter to the editor). *Science,* 1975, *187,* 790; 792.

Schofield, W. The role of psychology in the delivery of health services. *American Psychologist,* 1969, *24,* 565–584.

Shneidman, E. S. (Ed.). *Essays in self-destruction.* New York: Science House, 1967.

Shneidman, E. S. *The deaths of man.* New York: Quadrangle, 1973.

Shusterman, L. R. Death and dying: A critical review of the literature. *Nursing Outlook,* 1973, *21,* 465–471.

Solomon, G. F. Emotion, stress, and the central nervous system, and immunity. *Annals of the New York Academy of Sciences,* 1969, *164,* 335–343.

Solomon, G. F., Amkraut, A. A., & Kasper, P. Immunity, emotions and stress. With special reference to the mechanisms of stress effects on the immune system. In H. Musaph (Ed.), *Mechanisms in symptom formation.* Basel, Switzerland: S. Karger, 1974.

Tarlau, M., & Smalheiser, I. Personality patterns in patients with malignant tumors of the breast and cervix: An exploratory study. *Psychosomatic Medicine,* 1951, *13,* 117–121.

Taubman, P., & Wales, T. Education as an investment and a screening device. In F. T. Juster (Ed.), *Education, income and human behavior.* New York: McGraw-Hill, 1975.

11

Faye J. Goldberg

Opportunities for Psychologists in Drug and Alcohol Programs
(Why the Substance Abuse Field for Psychologists?)

With the reorganization of the major funding sources for mental health programs and training under the umbrella of the Alcohol, Drug Abuse, and Mental Health Administration (ADAMHA) it has become increasingly appropriate that psychologists examine opportunities in the substance abuse area. The equivalence of the status of alcoholism, of drug abuse, and of mental health at the federal level suggests that professional input should also be distributed equally into those three areas. Up to now psychologists have concentrated on the mental health segment almost exclusively while the other two areas have been the therapeutic province of self-help groups with ancillary medical treatment. Decisions at the national level have redefined mental health to include in its sphere a large number of areas previously considered to be social, rather than psychological. Psychologists are increasingly occupying roles previously held by the paraprofessional or the psychiatrist in the drug and alcohol field.

Additional impetus for expansion of these programs is coming from new legislation requiring states to provide treatment for alcoholics and from third-party payments for alcohol and drug abuse treatment. Although the expansion of facilities in the public sector for drug treatment has temporarily leveled off, more private sector activity is occurring. Large companies have shown their concern for alcohol and polydrug abusers by establishing treatment and early detection programs. Many general hospitals are incorporating detoxification programs for persons addicted to drugs and alcohol with longer term treatment on an outpatient basis, and private hospitals are developing facilities for patients with drug and alcohol problems. Financing for much of the individual treatment has come from industry's payments for its own employees and, in some cases, for dependents of these employees. The same is true in military and veterans' hospitals, both of which have had long-standing policies of hiring psychologists for such programs. Although publicly funded drug treatment programs are not

Faye J. Goldberg is Director of Treatment Research, Drug Abuse Rehabilitation Program, and Research Associate (Associate Professor), Department of Psychiatry, University of Chicago.

proliferating, public programs for alcoholics are. States that have passed legislation requiring that the alcoholic be treated rather than be funneled through the criminal justice system are developing therapeutic facilities that will attempt to rehabilitate rather than to simply detoxify alcoholics.

A third impetus for increasing public concern is the recent influx of heroin from Mexico. This increased supply is creating a market among groups that have not used opiates before, including middle-class Whites, and is contributing to an increase in the incidence of new cases in heavy heroin-using communities. Greater availability of cocaine and marijuana derivatives is also likely to cause a rise in the use of illicit drugs and associated problems. Licit drugs, such as tranquilizers and amphetamines, may constitute the greatest abuse potential in a group of consumers to whom little attention has been paid until the present. Both younger and older populations are now seen as having chemical abuse problems.

All of these areas are expanding and will require professionals who have specific knowledge and skills and who are able to work with different types of populations and with other professional and nonprofessional colleagues. This "professional" may hold a doctorate but is as likely to have a BA or MA with some mixture of clinical, community, and research skills, plus a knowledge of the properties of drugs and alcohol and of the public policy related to the prevention and treatment of their abuse.

In addition to pragmatic considerations, the use of drugs and alcohol throughout history and in all cultures raises challenging theoretical and practical questions for the understanding and alteration of behavior. Unlike other phenomena that we study in psychology, drug-seeking behavior represents a deliberate attempt to alter mood, behavior, perceptual and cognitive functioning, interpersonal behavior, intellectual performance, and perception of self and the environment. Frequently a high risk is involved in order to accomplish these ends. The behavior, in both humans and animals, is highly resistant to change despite severe social penalties and possibilities of self-destruction. Yet very little is known about the etiology of drug taking, how to change it, or how to provide less costly substitutes. Even less is known about the constructive elements of mood- and mind-altering substances and how their benefits could be increased. The experience of taking drugs remains a private subject, buried in myths and intergenerational and interclass misunderstanding. It is less well understood than the more taboo subject of sex, although drug use is certainly more destructive and probably more frequent. Deviance in regard to drug-taking behavior is arbitrarily defined and may result in consequences more deleterious than the drug taking itself. These many facets of chemical dependence and the increasing opportunities in the field should make the field an attractive career alternative for psychologists.

Available Training

There are few formal educational opportunities in the area of drug and alcohol abuse in psychology departments. There are at least two training programs funded by the National Institute on Drug Abuse (NIDA), one for undergraduates, at Morehouse College (Goldberg, in press; Note 1) and one at the University of California, Los Angeles (Carder, Note 2). Some departments are now offering drug-related courses and fieldwork experience. Courses on drugs can often be found in medical schools, in biology departments, or in schools of social work. Law school courses, although rare, may also be quite useful to the psychologist who plans to enter the field. Half of the sample of clinical graduate students questioned in a recent survey indicated that their curricula did not include drug and alcohol dependence. Of the half that reported that the subject was covered, half of those thought the coverage was inadequate (Zolik, Sirbu, & Hopkinson, in press). In another survey of clinical students completing their internships, 80% of the respondents had opportunities to participate in drug or alcohol programs although only about half took advantage of them. A third of the sample did not have such experience available or did not feel that the experience they had was adequate. The majority would have liked better coverage of drug and alcohol problems in their training (Zolik, Sirbu, Hopkinson, & Pozzi, Note 3).

Students who are interested in learning about this field might find it helpful to arrange their own experience through part-time employment, voluntary if necessary, or by visits to agencies that provide service to people with alcohol or drug problems. Research groups associated with universities, or state or federal agencies that are conducting research and prevention projects, would also be excellent places to receive training. For supervision, it is desirable to find a psychologist working in the area but often there are none. Paraprofessionals and professionals from other disciplines can provide excellent supervision, although this may not be acceptable for academic credit in some departments.

Sources of Ambivalence

The shortage of psychologists in the field of substance abuse is partly a function of the lack of academic emphasis in this area and the related ambivalence that many psychologists have toward the problems of drugs and alcohol. Many psychologists are now in the field by accident rather than by training or by choice, and many choose to return to more traditional pursuits when the opportunity arises. This ambivalence stems from several elements about the substance abuse field that are described elsewhere (Goldberg, Note 4). It might be helpful to summarize some of the major problems so that the prospective entrant to the field might be forearmed.

Psychologists, especially in the drug field, commonly complain of a lack of professional identify. This complaint stems largely from the success of self-help groups and the strong input of ex-addicts in the areas of administration and direct service. The skills of diagnosis or therapy in the traditional sense are not utilized to the extent they are in the mental health field. Nontraditional counseling approaches (e.g., Synanon, Alcoholics Anonymous) have been successful in these areas, and many psychologists feel that their skills in understanding and changing human behavior are not applicable with drug-dependent clients. However, behavior modification programs represent an innovative approach and involve a specific role for psychologists, as do other models where crisis intervention, family and group therapy skills, etc., can be utilized. Psychologists in this field are often confronted with unorthodox methods of changing behavior, and the fact that these methods are performed effectively by people without formal theoretical training is often threatening.

Another source of professional identity loss may come from the importance placed on medical intervention techniques and on the physiological problems that alcohol- and drug-dependent individuals experience. Methadone programs and detoxification regimens place a large emphasis on medication and physical symptoms that often may make the psychologist feel of secondary importance in the treatment team. Similar phenomena occur in the research area where physicians may be principal investigators in long-term research projects although psychologists may have more methodological expertise. Much like the mental health field a decade ago, administration of substance abuse programs also has an underrepresentation of psychologists, and this underrepresentation also stems from the physical problems involved in the addictive process. Once involved in the field, psychologists find themselves presenting papers at nonpsychology meetings and publishing in and reading nonpsychology journals, and the resultant loss of professional identity is likely to accelerate.

Negative feelings about the area also may stem from the traditional lack of success in the permanent rehabilitation of people who become dependent on drugs and alcohol. These are low-prognostic clients who frequently are motivated by forces extrinsic to their own desire to change, such as legal pressures, inability to support their drug habits, or pressure from employers and family. Additionally, there is some reluctance on the part of professionals to participate in many of the "cop" roles that are required, such as urine screening or tight security of inpatient drug units. Many professionals are reluctant to work in programs where paraprofessionals have large roles because they sense hostility and competition from people whose jobs are insecure and who may feel that they have a better idea about the problem than do professionals who lack direct experience. Many paraprofessionals in such programs pay little attention to record keeping, data collection, or formal aspects of program administration, and professionals may see the programs as badly managed and sloppy.

An additional source of concern for some psychologists, and this may be particularly true of minority group members, is that drug abuse programs are perceived as an extension of a "blaming the victim" philosophy, where the medical model is used to "cure" the patient but no attention is paid to the causes of the problem or to systems change. Many psychologists point this out as a difficulty not only in treatment programs but in research efforts that may be investigating medically oriented interventions or seeking the etiology of drug dependence in individual psychopathology without regard to economic or political factors.

Given the problems associated with the substance abuse field it is not surprising that relatively few psychologists have chosen to enter it or to provide training for students. There are many arguments that could be made to counter these negative characterizations. Briefly, they can be summarized as follows. Loss of professional identity will probably diminish when more psychologists enter the field and roles evolve that are specific to the psychologically trained individual. Many psychologists do not see their role diffusion as a problem. They enjoy the contact with nonprofessionals, feel that they can learn a great deal, and are comfortable with interdisciplinary input in research areas from pharmacologists, psychiatrists, sociologists, etc. Their increasing alienation from the profession of psychology may be more of an indictment of the closed viewpoint of traditional academic psychology than of substance abuse as a field. Psychology is becoming more aware of the area and is including it more in textbooks, journals, professional meetings, and curricula so that the isolation problem may not continue to be important. The issue of the lack of success in "curing" the drug user is also coming to be viewed with a degree of relativism. Rather than the expectation of complete abstinence or permanent cure, a policy of containment is becoming more accepted. The criteria for success that drug and alcohol programs have used have been more stringent and more visible than those of mental health programs, and the compounding of legal sanctions with behavioral problems produced by the drugs has been additionally complex. The mental health field frequently deals with self-limited, high-prognosis behavior that would improve without intervention, whereas continual drug or alcohol dependence produces a chain reaction of family loss, job loss, and physical deterioration that becomes increasingly difficult to interrupt.

The antagonism between the professional and the nonprofessional is often illusory and disappears when the professional can provide a useful service without appearing to be morally or intellectually superior. As for the blaming-the-victim approach, it can be argued that this exists in the mental health field as well as in substance abuse. Although these counterarguments may not be convincing to people who have serious reservations about the substance abuse field, they should be kept in mind and investigated on their merits if there is a reluctance to enter the area.

Areas for Psychologists

Most students who do not enter the substance abuse field do not do so out of ambivalence but primarily out of ignorance about available opportunities. The following categories are rough subdivisions of the field in which psychologists are active, are being hired, and are contributing.

Administration

It is not uncommon to have a psychologist as the director of an inpatient or outpatient private or public drug or alcohol program. This is particularly true in the Veterans Administration system and in many private programs.

In most cases the psychologist works closely with a medical director or consultant who may be part-time and who is responsible for prescribing medications. The prescribing habits of physicians and psychiatrists can be a source of contention. Psychologists in this position should try to clarify the role of physicians and their criteria for prescribing medication in relation to more psychologically oriented approaches.

Another administrative position may be in the area of program monitoring and supervising for regulatory or funding agencies such as the Food and Drug Administration (FDA), the Drug Enforcement Administration (DEA), or other federal or state agencies responsible for enforcing federal standards. These positions require people to evaluate treatment programs or grant proposals. Ideally, this would involve close cooperative work with treatment, prevention, and training programs to insure that they are meeting federal minimal standards and to help them achieve this objective. Or, the responsibility may be to visit sites of proposed or ongoing clinical or basic research and to make decisions about funding. Both NIDA and the National Institute on Alcohol Abuse and Alcoholism (NIAAA) employ people in this area. A background in the substance abuse area on the front lines increases one's credibility and makes work with staff more cooperative and less punitive.

Some agencies only peripherally involved in substance abuse issues, such as the Law Enforcement Assistance Administration (LEAA) and others working in the area of criminal justice, also need people with expertise in substance abuse to evaluate or administer studies or programs in which drug or alcohol use is a factor. State and federal prison systems are also eager to have college graduates with a background in drug abuse to work in special prerelease or diversion programs designed for criminals with drug histories.

Administrative duties may include personnel selection and evaluation, management, and budgetary skills. Knowledge of organizational behavior and its effect on the therapeutic process may also be an important asset as a director of or a consultant to a treatment program. Students who have the opportunity to take business, management, and organization courses may find themselves at an advantage not only in the substance abuse area but in mental health management generally.

Training and Education

Many psychologists train paraprofessional counselors or professionals from other disciplines such as pastoral counselors, medical students, psychiatric residents, or social workers. Training may be at treatment centers, at federally sponsored regional training programs, in junior colleges, or with state agencies or university-based alcohol or drug counselor training programs. The content area may vary from the behavioral effects of drugs to specific techniques in individual and group counseling, behavior modification, crisis intervention, or family therapy. Psychologists with clinical skills are employed in either part-time or full-time training capacities and are usually better equipped for this role than psychiatrists or paraprofessionals. Training may also be on an informal level working with counselors, reviewing records, listening to tapes of group or individual counseling sessions, conducting case conferences, and working with individual clients or groups to provide modeling opportunities for counselors. Although general, traditional clinical skills are required, psychologists will be more useful and have greater acceptance of their training efforts if they understand the orientation of the population and of the counselors. Professional consultants will be required to have both more familiarity with cultural and ethnic population differences and evidence that their traditional techniques are as effective as those with which the counselors have had personal experience during treatment.

Treatment

Psychologists working in public agencies usually see clients only in the course of their training or administrative work or if called in as a consultant on particularly difficult cases. Clinical judgments may often be required, however, even in the more remote roles of research, administration, and program evaluation.

Many psychologists in private practice see clients who have alcohol and drug problems. Since these patients may be more refractory to clinical intervention than the usual type of client, it is useful to know what techniques might be effective and to understand and detect the effects of the drug-taking compulsion.

Industrial programs and private hospitals may have psychologists providing direct treatment to a variety of drug-dependent individuals. Generally, then, the alteration of behavior of people whose problems involve the dependency on a mind- or mood-altering substance is an important new area for the clinical psychologist and one that may involve a reexamination of traditional clinical skills.

Prevention and Education

Traditional prevention programs that present information about drugs and alcohol to the community or to school children have fallen into decline since they have been shown to increase drug experimentation. A recent study undertaken by NIDA defined primary prevention in drug abuse as:

a Constructive Process designed to promote personal and social growth of the individual toward full human potential and thereby inhibit or reduce physical, mental, emotional or social impairment which results in or from the abuse of chemical substances. (NIDA, 1975, p. 16)

It is obvious from this broad categorization that any psychological technique that enhances personal growth, including the efforts of the community psychologist to create growth-producing environments and systems, would meet the criterion for a prevention program. More importantly, the psychologist's expertise might be in the area of evaluation, that is, arranging an intervention strategy and evaluating its effects on use and abuse of psychoactive substances. More traditional educational efforts that do present information to specific audiences are also still being offered to school and community groups. At the national level, psychologists are involved in designing advertising campaigns and community training packages focused on increasing the understanding of the public toward the abuse potential of licit and illicit substances and the cultural attitudes that facilitate their misuse.

A knowledge of (a) research design, (b) communities and their organization, (c) epidemiological techniques to understand the drug distribution systems and leadership patterns, (d) alternatives to the economics of the drug market, and (e) the lure of peer pressure to use drugs and alcohol are extremely useful tools in prevention and education. This is the ideal area for the student interested in community psychology to look at the problems of drug dependence from the point of view of the social system rather than of the individual and the individual's treatment.

Clinical Research and Evaluation

Psychologists trained in evaluation research are uniquely qualified to design and evaluate treatment programs, training efforts, new techniques, cost–benefit ratios of different intervention approaches, and general program effectiveness. Large amounts of public funds are being spent in the treatment of alcoholism and drug dependency but little is known about the efficacy of various approaches. It is important in evaluation of clinical studies not only to produce a methodologically sound design but to have an appreciation of (a) the implicit and explicit objectives of the program; (b) the sources of resistance to research on the part of the staff, clients, and community; (c) the safeguards for subjects; and (d) the perspectives of the physician and the ex-addict. Fieldwork in drug and alcohol programs, combined with a thorough background in methdology, a use of computers for data storage and analysis, and a statistical sophistication, would be a good prerequisite.

Basic Research

Students of behavioral pharmacology and physiological psychology are increasingly working with pharmacologists and psychiatrists to understand the effects of various drugs in animals and humans and to explore the circumstances that lead to dependency. Some psychopharmacologists work in the pharmaceutical industry or in medical schools either with animals or in clinical populations. Psychologists are working in the physiological area to determine if there are receptors for various drugs; other psychologists are studying the behavioral effects of antagonists— agents that block the drug's psychoactive and addictive qualities.

Other basic research might be done by social psychologists who could shed light on drug-taking and group behavior and the interpersonal processes that encourage the relapse of people who have been through treatment programs. Developmental psychologists could make contributions to the understanding of how drug taking is learned by children and the socialization process by which families who use drugs transmit their values. Little is known about the genetic effects on children of mothers who use psychoactive drugs, and few studies have traced the longitudinal patterns of drug users as parents and the evolution of their careers and attitudes. Psychologists in this area are very likely to work in interdisciplinary settings where more than one perspective is necessary to understand the context of the issue.

Measurement

Psychologists have made extensive contributions to the scaling and quantitative description of different aspects of the drug experience, from the "high" or intoxicated state to the withdrawal symptoms. A thorough knowledge of test construction and adequate norms and standardization are essential when traditional tests or new measures are used to describe drug-using populations. It is frequently necessary to explain concepts of reliability, validity, and standardization to people who are using the tests for diagnosis, classification, or research to insure that the instruments are not misused. A facility with tests and scale construction is useful in public and private treatment programs and in clinically oriented research programs.

Conclusion

The field of drug and alcohol use and abuse presents an exciting challenge to the psychologist both pragmatically, because of increased interest and funding in the area, and theoretically and conceptually, because of the unique questions raised by drug-taking behavior. Psychologists have traditionally been ambivalent about the area, and, although many negative aspects exist, these are changing and are balanced by the opportunities that differ in many respects from traditional areas in psychology. Training is limited but enterprising students can equip themselves with enough conceptual and practical knowledge by going outside of the usual channels to prepare for the unique challenges of the field. Opportunities, which could be expanded and developed, are present in the administrative, training, preventive, treatment, and research aspects of drugs and alcohol.

REFERENCE NOTES

1. Goldberg, F. *The Morehouse College certificate program in community psychology and drug abuse counseling.* Paper presented at the meeting of the Southeastern Psychological Association, Hollywood, Florida, May 1974.
2. Carder, B. *Reflections on training graduate students in drug abuse.* Paper presented at the meeting of the American Psychological Association, Chicago, Illinois, September 1975.
3. Zolik, E., Sirbu, W., Hopkinson, D., & Pozzi, M. Personal communication, November 19, 1975.
4. Goldberg, F. *Why so few psychologists in the drug abuse field?* Paper presented at the meeting of the American Psychological Association, Chicago, Illinois, September 1975.

REFERENCES

Goldberg, F. Bachelor's level training in community psychology in a black college. *American Journal of Community Psychology*, in press.

National Institute on Drug Abuse. *Toward a national strategy for primary drug abuse prevention* (Final Rep. Delphi II). Rockville, Md.: Author, 1975.

Zolik, E., Sirbu, W., & Hopkinson, D. Perspectives of clinical students on training in community mental health. *American Journal of Community Psychology*, in press.

12

John C. Wolfe

Psychologists In and Out of the Alcoholism Field

Psychologists traditionally have been neither more nor less reluctant to work with alcoholic people than have other degreed professionals. There are exceptions, of course, but in general psychologists must admit to sharing the same distorted perceptions and values that society at large has had about alcoholism and alcoholic people. Psychologists have certainly received little or no training in working with or understanding the problems of alcohol abuse. As a result, their deficiencies produced a multiplier effect that is detrimental to the field of psychology and certainly to the alcoholic person.

The difficulties that psychologists face in dealing effectively with the problems of alcohol abuse and alcoholism are rooted in their own feelings and values about the use of alcohol. Psychologists have not escaped the great American dilemma of denying their own potential to abuse alcohol or their own feelings that the alcoholic should be able to stop if he or she "really" wants to stop. Psychologists may even be the "neighborhood pusher" at the cocktail party, making sure everyone has a full glass of booze, wondering what is wrong with the person asking for a coke, and sending people home when they are intoxicated. As psychologists, we probably are guilty of conjuring up the stereotypic image of the skid row drunk when we think of alcoholic people. The psychologists' level of awareness must be heightened, especially as psychologists look inward and see that they too might be vulnerable to the problems of alcoholism.

This issue has been an impediment for many therapists (other than just psychologists) in working with alcoholic people, particularly when the drinking behavior of the therapist is very similar to that of the client. It is difficult to confront another person with regard to a problem area of life if one has difficulty confronting oneself on the same issue. The usual outcome has been to deny that a problem with alcohol exists, thereby relieving both the client and the therapist from having to confront the problem. Later therapists discover that their client has "become" an alcoholic; now they can reflect that they knew he or she was difficult to work with and that the alcoholism was just a residue or symptom of not solving the

John C. Wolfe is the Executive Director of the National Council of Community Mental Health Centers, Washington, D.C.

psychological problems that were manifested at the time of diagnosis and treatment. Balderdash!

As psychologists, we have examined, studied, and, at least intellectually, resolved the mind–body dualism visited upon us by Descartes. In practice, however, psychologists revert to more atavistic ways of thinking. Most psychologists perceive all alcoholic people as having a psychological problem as the base for their alcoholism. This may not be the case at all; in fact, as psychologists we have turned away and tuned out many alcoholic abusers and alcoholic people because of our preconceptions of what was wrong and what was needed. We did not know how to listen. We assumed that alcoholic people had a deep-seated psychological disorder and if they would only deal with that issue first, the alcohol problems would take care of themselves. And then we experienced frustrations with our "failures." Upon reflection, isn't it amazing what vicious circles we psychologists create for ourselves in our attempts to be of help to people! We did often fail, but in a more direct manner; we failed to make use of our training and education that indicated the interdependence of psychological, biological, and sociological factors in human behavior. Old myths and attitudes are hard to forget, and psychologists often foist them onto their clients. At this point in history, we can only say that alcoholism is indeed rooted in a complex interaction of psychological, biological, and sociological forces.

Alcoholics Anonymous

It should be of no surprise to psychologists that for many alcoholic people, after their experience with psychologists, Alcoholics Anonymous (AA) and/or service from other than degreed professionals has been the treatment of choice. William Madsen stated: "AA is a specifically American response to a problem that has proven to be beyond the solution of the family, police, church, medicine and psychotherapy" (p. 156). Whether psychologists can contribute to the solution is the essence of this chapter; but it is certain that to be part of the solution will require psychologists to approach alcoholism and alcoholic people from a very different attitude and perspective than they have formerly. AA, for example, firmly believes that alcoholism *can be* treated. Do psychologists share this belief? Or do they believe that the alcoholic person is really a hopeless case and that the best they can expect is to maintain some type of stabilization process?

AA also shares with the alcoholic person who is seeking help some values that often impact in a very meaningful way; for example, the value that life has meaning and is not merely chaos, that sobriety is the essential element in overcoming alcohol problems, and that belief in a power greater than oneself can assist a person in beating the battle of the bottle. There are more than these three values shared within AA, of course, but it is interesting to take these three and draw parallels to what psychologists often do, perhaps without recognizing what they are doing.

First, I do not know of a single practicing psychologist who does not, at some level, impart the value that there is some meaning to life. It is hard to imagine anyone expending the energy to even practice psychology who is devoid of believing or feeling something about life's meaningfulness. Second, if psychologists were to take a good hard look at the addiction process (without fixating on old values and feelings about the alcoholic), they would be forced to agree that it is necessary to change the pattern of drug use (in this case, alcohol use) before any other treatment will have much consequence. In fact, some researchers are now questioning the efficacy and/or effects of psychotherapy when a client is under the influence of medically prescribed drugs (Ostow, 1962). In short, psychologists may or may not disagree philosophically (or perhaps clinically or experimentally) with the abstinence model as the only method of altering the alcoholic person's destructive processes, but it is certain that some changes in the drinking behavior must occur. Finally, psychologists often become disturbed when they hear an AA member talking about "a power greater than oneself." It is almost as though psychologists interpret this statement in the same manner they learned to interpret (or not interpret) their parents' meaning of "God." Once again, in our infinite wisdom as psychologists, we leap over the structures of reason and understanding to fall flat on our faces in the morass of prejudice and prejudgment. And we fail to take a good hard look at ourselves and the fact that, whether we like it or not, many of our clients perceive us as "a power greater than themselves." Furthermore, many therapists firmly believe that such a phenomenon is necessary before therapy can even proceed to the next plateau. Yet how quickly therapists can discard the AA value as "too religious!"

The differences between the psychologists (perhaps the term "degreed professional" is better) and the alcoholism workers (the nondegreed professionals) have been the core of the conflict. Each has fought for its own territoriality, believing that the answers were within its respective domain of knowledge and/or experience. Each has damned the other for "not understanding" the dynamics and problems of the alcoholic person. Neither has had the success it would like to have. So what does this imply for psychologists who seek career opportunities in the general field of alcoholism?

The Psychologist's Role in Research

One implication is very clear, namely, that psychologists have an unlimited opportunity to conduct research in a field that has barely scratched the surface of knowledge and understanding. The etiology of alcoholism is not yet known; the interaction of genetic and psychosocial factors of alcoholism is just beginning to be discussed. The model that alcoholism is a disease is certainly open to scientific inquiry. The role of learning theory, its contribution and application to a better understanding of alcohol problems, is an area that needs considerably more research. There has been a great deal of study regarding the biochemical aspects of alcoholism, yet there needs to be more definitive work done in this area. Cross-cultural studies of drinking behavior can help in obtaining a better understanding of cause–effect relationships of responsible as well as abusive drinking. Alcohol and its relation to violence, crime, prison, driving, and other matters of legal concern certainly need more thorough investigation. The genetic aspects of alcoholism and the possible differences in tolerance levels for various racial groups are necessary and important areas of study. A study of the influence of values and attitudes toward alcohol and alcoholic people and the effect of these values on the health care system of this country would certainly be most revealing.

Since there has been far less clinical research in alcoholism than in the areas of neurotic and psychotic disorders, the whole area of clinical research is an open field. This raises some interesting research questions, such as, how effective is AA? If effective, why? If not, why not? Psychologists need to investigate and determine those variables that do indeed help alcoholic people make changes in their lives that result in less destructive behavior. Many therapists have not yet determined what appropriate outcome variables are for their alcoholic clients. Is it sobriety alone, or is it sobriety and something else? And how related or independent are various outcome results? In summary, the list of questions is almost unlimited and the research psychologist can provide valuable information and findings. The research psychologist who enjoys working with animals, people, social systems, or whatever can find a home in the field of alcoholism. There is a great opportunity and a great need for discovery.

The Psychologist's Role in Training

Psychologists also have a great deal to contribute to the field of alcoholism within the context of training. In training, the role of the psychologist is less clearly defined than in research. There may well be limits to what a psychologist can do. For example, can (or should) the psychologist train the recovering alcoholic how to be a psychotherapist? Or can the psychologist train the lay person how to counsel? Should the psychologist train the nondegreed individual to discriminate accurately the stages of alcoholism and/or psychopathology so the latter can make appropriate referrals to those with more in-depth skills in particular areas of behavior?

The field of psychology has had (and still has) its own difficulties deciding what is appropriate training for psychologists; it will be even more difficult for psychologists if they decide what kind of training is to be done for alcoholism counselors and others in the field of alcoholism. This does not mean that psychologists have nothing of importance to offer. They have many skills that can and should be shared with other fields of endeavor. Consequently, psychologists entertaining the idea of being training psychologists in the field of alcoholism have many new frontiers to shape and establish, not the least of which is new training concepts for psychologists themselves. The excitement of this field lies in the unexplored resources that have not been tapped in the human resources field in alcoholism. Many alcoholism workers are eager to improve their skills in order to work more effectively with alcoholic people. Yet problems such as territoriality have precluded most psychologists and alcoholism workers from training and working together.

Today, alcohol programs are growing by the hundreds, and yet there is a dearth of training efforts for skills for particular functions. For example, can psychologists help train alcoholism workers, doctors, labor people, management people, and others to recognize the early symptoms of alcohol problems; and can they train society or raise society's level of consciousness so that a person with an alcohol problem is not hidden but is encouraged to seek help for a problem (or disease, if you prefer) that can be dealt with effectively and treated? In short, the entire field of training in the area of alcoholism is only as limited as one wants to make it; the need for training in this particular endeavor will continue to grow and expand in the foreseeable future.

The Psychologist's Role in Treatment

The psychologist also has a role to play in the treatment process in both the private and public sector of clinical practice. In this aspect, perhaps more than in any other aspect of the field of alcoholism, psychologists need to discriminate what they can and cannot do for alcoholic people. In the treatment of alcoholics the greatest degree of self-change and self-awareness on the part of psychologists is necessary if they hope to be effective in their efforts. Psychologists must be aware of their own values about the use of alcohol and must change if they have abused the drug.

Clinical psychologists, if properly trained, can offer an invaluable service to the treatment continuum of alcoholic people; first, they can determine if there is a problem with alcohol, and then they can ascertain the severity of the problem. To repeat, to diagnose does not imply a foregone conclusion; in this case, clinicians should not conclude before investigation that if there is an alcohol problem, ergo, there is an underlying personality or character disorder. Clinical psychologists need to develop a keen ability to diagnose accurately in order to then make the referral that is in the best interest of the client. If psychologists are willing, they can learn a great deal in this area not only from academic and internship exposure but also from the recovering alcoholic person and the experienced alcoholism worker. The entire area of differential diagnosis and appropriate referral is in its infancy, and aspiring psychologists, if willing, can help develop new frontiers.

Provided an accurate diagnosis and referral have been made, clinical psychologists also have a very active role to play for many, but not all, alcoholic people. Where psychotherapy is appropriate for the alcoholic person, clinicians will need to discard old myths and prejudices. They will need to examine and understand a history of health care delivery to people who have been rejected, who have been abused, who have been considered stubborn and weak willed, and, most damning of all, who have not received what might be called adequate health care. The helping professions have often talked about how "difficult" alcoholic people are to work with; alcoholic people might say that the "healthniks" have been the "difficult" ones to work with. Clinical psychologists in both the public and private sectors are well advised to work with degreed and nondegreed professionals to supplement their own efforts in the treatment of the alcoholic person.

Clinical psychologists could also increase their own understanding of alcoholic people by attending AA meetings. This would be the equivalent of real-life field studies or ongoing practicums. Psychologists might even be able to draw some parallels between the process of group therapy and the process of AA meetings. The dynamics of these two groups might be found to have some commonalities that were unknown to the psychologist. Clinicians might find that the AA people are not so foreign and might see and perhaps experience some very moving and touching human experiences that can only be described as beautiful. But in some AA meetings clinicians will also experience the "low-bottom drunk" who has lost all appearance of dignity and feeling of self-worth. In essence, treatment in the field of alcoholism is an exciting growth experience that allows one to experience some of the highest highs as well as the lowest lows of human experience and emotion. This is an area in which psychologists have only limited experience and often little desire to become involved. But the challenge is there.

The Psychologist's Role in Administration

Psychologists who aspire to work in the field of alcoholism also have available to them at least two other general areas of endeavor, administration and community organization. Psychologists are seldom specifically trained for either area, but many of the theories and principles of psychology and experiences as a psychologist prepare them in an oblique way for either or both of these efforts. Alcoholism programs desperately need good, strong, qualified administrators who can deal with the complexities of planning, implementing, managing, evaluating, and financing an alcoholism program. Interested psychologists are well advised to take some course work in health services organization and management.

A similar situation exists for psychologists interested in what has traditionally been called "community organization." The volunteer groups in alcoholism have many experiences and much information to offer to psychologists involved in organizing their community. Many communities have untapped resources and/or problems associated with alcohol abuse and alcoholism. For example, the labor and management people in many communities have not yet addressed themselves to the problem of alcoholic people within industry. Many physicians do not know how to treat or relate to the alcoholic person or where to refer such a person within their community. The schools are experiencing an increased amount of alcohol abuse among students, and they are ill prepared to cope with this problem in a constructive, rational manner. The "hidden" alcoholic, usually the housewife, is a member of the population for whom no effective early identification procedure has been established. Such a procedure would provide help before addiction and before a whole life was acutely disrupted. The psychologist, working in concert with other community people, can organize new systems, supplement old systems, and help destroy ineffective and harmful systems in the field of alcoholism. As more alcoholism programs develop, such skills will be increasingly called for. But psychologists should always work with the alcoholism constituencies in their community. Planning and organizing in isolation from the alcohol constituency will result in bitter feelings among those who should be working together and in incomplete or competing systems of care that will be less effective for the alcoholic person.

Summary

Career opportunities for psychologists in the field of alcoholism are better now than ever before. The fulfillment of these opportunities will depend heavily on the training and experience psychologists receive. Psychologists must understand the history of alcohol abuse and alcoholism; must recognize the neglect of the health care system to treat alcoholic people; must appreciate the roles of volunteer organizations, AA, and alcoholism workers; and must initiate new conceptual models to deal with alcohol abuse and alcoholism.

Success will also depend on the ability of the psychologist to break away from old cultural myths and conceptions of the alcoholic person and to perceive how these old myths have impacted on their own use and abuse of alcohol (e.g., when it was required to drink as much as you could possibly hold in order to prove your adulthood). Success will depend on psychologists' ability to go outside of their own professional/disciplinary world into the world of alcoholic people and recovered alcoholic people. It is in that arena that the psychologist has much to learn from and much to offer to the field of alcohol abuse and alcoholism.

REFERENCES

Madsen, W. *The American alcoholic. The nature–nurture controversy in alcoholic research and therapy.* Springfield, Ill.: Charles C Thomas, 1974.
Ostow, M. *Drugs in psychoanalysis and psychotherapy.* New York: Basic Books, 1962.

13

C. Abraham Fenster, Gary Faltico, Jacob Goldstein,
Florence Kaslow, Bernard Locke, Harvey Musikoff,
Harvey Schlossberg, and Robert Wolk

Careers in Forensic Psychology

There is a strong need for the provision of professional psychological services within the criminal and civil justice systems. Psychologists who possess high levels of skill in diagnosis, consultation, social action research, organizational analysis, crisis intervention, treatment, and theory construction are vitally needed in all components of the legal system (Gottfredson, 1972; Twain, McGee, & Bennett, 1972). Forensic psychology involves distinct skills, background knowledge, and forms of practice, which in some ways are quite different from traditional functions of clinical, personality, and social psychology.

Forensic psychology is the application of psychological principles to the problems and administration of the legal-judicial system—both its criminal justice and civil justice components. Indeed, reformation and improvement of the civil justice system (e.g., the family court) will result in fewer criminal offenses and a smaller work load for the overburdened criminal justice system. In addition to needing well-rounded practitioners and researchers, forensic psychology needs a cadre of faculty to teach specialized skills in forensic psychology in academic and criminal justice institutions throughout the country. For example, increasing numbers of forensic psychologists are becoming police department psychologists and consultants. Innovative programs in this area have been quite effective (Bard, 1969, 1970; Barocas, 1971; Brodsky, 1972c).

The role of the psychologist in the criminal justice system is crucial. At present, psychologists are typically involved in the following aspects of the criminal justice system: (a) *pretrial phase*—psychodiagnostic test results are used as evidence in pretrial competency hearings; (b) *trial phase*—the

C. Abraham Fenster is a Professor of Psychology and Chairperson of the Department of Psychology, John Jay College of Criminal Justice, New York; Gary Faltico is Research Director of the New York City Police Department; Jacob Goldstein is a Psychologist working with the Mental Health Clinic of the Family Court of the State of New York; Florence Kaslow is a Clinical Associate Professor and Chief of Forensic Psychology and Psychiatry at Hahnemann Medical College, Philadelphia; Bernard Locke is a Professor of Psychology in the Department of Psychology, John Jay College of Criminal Justice, New York; Harvey Musikoff is Clinical Administrator of Court Psychiatric Programs, Bronx-Lebanon Hospital Center, New York; Harvey Schlossberg is Director of the Psychological Services Unit, Medical Section, New York City Police Department; and Robert Wolk is Principal Psychologist, Eastern New York Correctional Facility, Napanoch State Prison, New York.

claim of insanity is presented as a defense; (c) *sentencing*—presentence reports with psychological inputs are conveyed to the judge to help him or her choose from alternatives such as prison, suspended sentences, probation, or hospitalization; (d) *corrections*—the professional psychologist renders services such as individual psychotherapy, group psychotherapy, behavior modification, or vocational counseling. Indeed, in recent years there has been an emphasis (a) on the relationship between emotional factors, "mental illness," and personality problems and criminal activity and (b) on the implications of this relationship for treating and rehabilitating the offender (Abrahamson, 1967; Alexander & Staub, 1956; Brodsky, 1970, 1972a; Halleck, 1967; Lentz, 1966; Menninger, 1968; Schwitzgebel, 1964; Smith & Bassin, 1961; Smith, Bassin, & Froelich, 1960, 1962; Smith & Berlin, 1974; Smith, Berlin, & Bassin, 1963, 1965; Smith & Pollack, 1971, 1972; Sullivan, Grant, & Grant, 1956; Tharp & Wetzel, 1969; Warren, 1969; Shah, Note 1). Because psychologists have the expertise to identify and treat psychological disturbances, there has been a new demand for their services within the criminal justice system. Moreover, there has been an emphasis of late on the use of psychologists to train paraprofessionals and even ex-offenders to act as therapists in correctional settings (Nietzel & Moss, 1972; Twain et al., 1972).

But, it should be emphasized, our expectation is that in the future forensic psychologists will roam confidently and competently far beyond the traditional roles of the psychologist in forensic settings. The criminal justice system needs multifaceted and multitalented forensic psychologists, capable of performing at a high level of capacity *each* of a number of varied roles and functions within the criminal and civil justice systems.

Forensic psychologists should and often do play a prominent role in social action research and research evaluation; in clinical interviews and personality assessment in crisis situations and in forensic settings; in crisis intervention and short-term treatment, especially with delinquent adolescents and in correctional settings; in the socio- and psychodynamics of antisocial behavior, including white collar and corporate crime and what has been called the "criminal behavior of everyday life"; in group dynamics and organizational processes, particularly in criminal justice settings; in consultation with other criminal justice agencies; in techniques of primary prevention and the training of paraprofessionals; in the presentation of psychological and other social scientific data to the legal system, especially to the courts and to legislatures; in the nature and the organizational and interpersonal dynamics of the legal system itself; in the constitutional rights of those who are confronted with the coercive power of the state; and in the application of social psychology to legal issues and problems. Finally, forensic psychologists are trained in the utilization of relatively intensive, and relatively long-term, psychodynamic and behavior therapy techniques with delinquents and adult offenders. Unlike the past, this aspect need not be viewed as the primary function of the psychologist in the criminal justice system but, rather, as one among many "primary" functions of the forensic psychologist.

In addition to having more and better trained psychologists in the criminal justice field so that the above functions can be performed more adequately, we feel it especially important for psychologists to be active in *reforming* the criminal justice system. Areas suggested as being ripe for reform are (a) modifications of substantive criminal law; (b) modification of the police role; (c) bail reform; (d) development of community-based corrections; (e) prison reform; (f) training and employment of paraprofessionals, for example, line staff and ex-offenders, in corrections; (g) limitation of possible encroachments by psychology and psychiatry on civil liberties; (h) psychological and psychiatric testimony; (i) employee selection, job analysis and description, and performance evaluation; (j) aptitude and attitude measurement in the legal system; and (k) role of mental health professionals as consultants in the criminal justice system (American Friends Service Committee, 1971; Bard, 1969, 1970; Barocas, 1971; Brodsky, 1972d; Christie, 1971; Ennis & Litwack, 1974; Fenster, Litwack, & Symonds, 1975; Gottfredson, 1970; Kittrie, 1971; Litwack, 1974, Miller, 1972; Nietzel & Moss, 1972; Reiff, 1970; Silber, 1974; Spece, 1972; Szasz, 1963; Twain et al., 1972; Ziskin, 1975). While psychologists have shown diminished interest in the criminal justice system since 1950, the decline in psychological research in justice problems has begun to reverse itself (Brodsky, 1972b).

The criminal justice system characteristically maintains a policy of official silence in regard to disclosure of information. This wall of silence is particularly formidable to outsiders. Many forensic psychologists, however, are working members of the criminal justice system who, with training in basic research and analysis of data, are able to gather, interpret, and professionally publish material that ordinarily would not be accessible to the general researcher.

While limited opportunities currently exist for academic psychologists, society's ever-increasing demands for professional psychological services remain unsatisfied. Upper-class and middle-class individuals can readily obtain psychological treatment at the going rates; criminals, juvenile offenders, institutionalized citizens, minority-group members, and low-socioeconomic-class families usually cannot obtain appropriate psychological services (Groeschel, 1974; Twain et al., 1972). And when these groups are neglected in terms of treatment services, society suffers the consequences.

Recognition of the need for psychologists in correctional institutions in the criminal justice system has grown enormously (Task Force on Corrections, 1967; Twain et al., 1972), and the need for psychologists in primary prevention, consultative, and social action research roles is at least as great. Furthermore, now that the Supreme Court has ruled that non-dangerous mental patients cannot be confined in institutions against their will and without treatment (see *O'Connor v. Donaldson*, 1975), the need for psychological services to assist these individuals—many of whom will now return to the community for the first time in years—will increase dramatically. Even in places where competition for traditional clinical positions exists, jobs in criminal justice institutions, residential centers for delinquent youth, and the like often go begging (Piven & Alcabes, 1969; Task Force on Corrections, 1967). Currently there are job openings in many states even for individuals without the PhD, and a large healthy job market exists in correctional psychology (Bjorklund & Brodsky, Note 2). Yet it is not uncommon for forensic agencies to hire bachelor-degree graduates who lack basic skills and familiarity with the relevant literature to fill "psychologist" positions (Brodsky, 1972b). Indeed, the need for psychology personnel in this area is so great that wo/manpower needs in the field will never be adequately met by doctoral-level personnel (Speilberger, Megargee, & Ingram, 1972). Furthermore, even the doctoral-level personnel that are hired may not have appropriate training for forensic settings.

In the following sections of this chapter we outline the kinds of work that forensic psychologists engage in as police department psychologists, correctional psychologists, staff trainers and criminal justice consultants, drug addiction specialists, court psychologists, and family court psychologists. We end by pointing out relevant research areas in forensic psychology.

Police Department Psychologists

In today's society a police department is frequently called upon to intercede among the myriad of interest groups in a role that often reflects what one might call "social psychology therapy" rather than in a role that has traditionally been called "maintaining the peace." With the complexity of demands on police expanding, a considerable lag has resulted in evolution or adaptation of social science principles to handle these new pressures. As a result, police departments have desperately reached out to behavioral scientists for assistance. Unfortunately, the police have been slow to accept what seemed like radical change, and behavioral scientists have been ill equipped to apply or communicate in practical or understandable terms. The pressures have sharpened the awareness of a serious gap in both theory and practice that we have to bridge by research and by training psychologists in the many facets of police work that are in the realm of psychology. A survey of police departments across the nation reveals that there are growing ranks of psychologists working in various consultant capacities with police, a relationship that did not exist in the past. The past has been characterized both by police viewing psychologists as unrealistic dreamers and by psychologists viewing police as Neanderthals (Schlossberg, 1975). It is predicted that in the future police departments will employ psychologists to deal with internal stress and to improve the performance and the function of police work.

The New York City Police Department has one of the nation's full-time, full-service psychological units, which is a model for other units that are being created. The following represents a sample of the functions that psychologists currently serve in the New York City Police Department.

This sample only represents an introduction to the possibilities that could emerge (Schlossberg, 1974).

Psychological evaluation of police with emotional problems. The Psychological Unit is responsible for psychological tests, interviews, diagnosis, and prognosis. The testing procedure involves administering complete individual test batteries and a variety of projective tests. The problems that bring the officers into contact with the Psychological Unit are quite varied, as are the sources of referral. The referrals may be self-initiated or official inter- and intradepartmental recommendations. The psychologist in this role is charged with serious responsibilities, such as deciding the fitness of an individual to carry firearms or suggesting the types of assignments that best suit an individual. The psychologist may also refer the individual to a psychiatrist or an ancillary agency for treatment. Some therapy is in house, however. Complex compensation cases and malingering may lead to psychological evaluations by the Psychological Unit itself. Many police officers require marriage and family guidance and counseling. Also, the complex nature of police work and the changing role demands have caused on-the-job problems that often require group therapy. Therefore, several types of therapeutic groups are conducted as an ongoing procedure to deal with functional and administrative difficulties attributable to personality problems.

Application of psychological testing to candidate selection. The screening procedures for the selection of future police officers (e.g., Fenster & Locke, 1973a, 1973b, 1973c; Guller, 1972; Smith & Locke, 1968; Smith, Locke, & Fenster, 1970; Smith, Locke, & Walker, 1967) are still in their infancy and at this point they represent a two-pronged attack. The short-range approach is to eliminate psychologically unfit individuals; the long-range goal is to establish an adequate personality profile and to validate screening procedures against field performance. The present screening procedures involve a battery of group personality and intelligence tests coupled with an intensive clinical interview. Field performance is then continually monitored and evaluated against the psychometric prediction.

Human behavior and crime solving. Dramatic crimes such as murder and rape tend to elude traditional police solutions. Frequently, an analysis of the elements of the crime and the clues left behind by the criminal can lead to a personality profile of a suspect. When police are confronted by many suspects, the personality profile can help narrow the field. The fascinating element for the psychologist is to actually witness research efforts, which had been gathering dust on library shelves, come to life and assist police in solving crime. Further examples of the practical marriage between psychologists and police are the techniques developed through the principles of social psychology that can be applied by police to control crowds (by means other than brute force) and the hostage crisis intervention techniques, which have achieved worldwide acclaim for their effectiveness. These techniques have led to psychological interest in areas such as food and sleep deprivation, response to boredom, and more clinical aspects of personality interaction. Other crisis intervention techniques may be used to settle family disputes and to prevent suicides. By directing energies into more constructive channels, psychology can provide the police with techniques for facing and dealing with problems rather than avoiding them or confronting them with force. The psychologist can help the police orient themselves to the pressures that bear both on them and on criminals. The psychologist will help change the nature of police work and the image of the police.

Training. With the goal of changing the nature of police work and the image of the police in mind, the psychologist's role in training police becomes crucial. The psychologist can help devise curriculum and teach police officers. The training needed for successful police work involves an understanding of personality, reactions to stress, problem solving, techniques of interview or interrogation, as well as self-understanding.

In this brief space we only presented a superficial but exciting sampling of the many possibilities for careers for psychologists in police work. The types of work and their usefulness may only be limited by the imagination of the practitioner.

Correctional Psychologists

It has been estimated recently that approximately 10% of all inmates in any New York State correctional facility may be classified as latent, acute, or chronically psychotic in various states of remission. Actually, if we include neuroticism, character and behavior disorders, and other forms of psychopathology, the percentage would be approximately 50% or higher. Needless to say, the need for mental hygiene services in a correctional facility is vital.

Historically, mental hygiene has not been fully accepted in many correctional facilities. Psychologists and psychiatrists often pose a threat to archaic correctional practices. It was not until recently that a more progressive, open-window view was taken. Currently, most correctional facilities have one psychiatrist on their staff and at least one psychologist; in most instances these facilities have even larger staffs. The mental hygiene professionals themselves have been fully integrated into the correctional system and serve many functions and purposes. Fortunately, in today's correctional facility, with progressive thinking, the role of mental hygiene personnel is an essential one. The psychologist is a resource as well as an individual to whom referrals of patients with a specific pathology can be made.

At best, most people entering correctional facilities have been incarcerated because of acting-out behavior, self-destructive behavior, or victimless crimes. They often possess enough psychopathology to warrant intensive therapeutic intervention or, at the very least, exploration at some point during the incarceration to ascertain if they are prepared psychologically to take their place again in the community. Adjustment to a correctional facility is in no way related to the ultimate adjustment an individual must make to what the inmates refer to as "the street." Most correctional facilities, in themselves, serve as extensions of wombs. Inmates are protected, relieved of considerable external stress, and often are not suitably prepared for the environment to which they must return.

The correctional psychologist must function within areas for which he or she has been ill prepared by school, previous training, and even experience in community clinics, mental hospitals, research projects, or academia. When the fledgling correctional psychologist enters a facility, he or she is met by prisoners who spend their time cut off from society and who have few, if any, external or internal resources. The psychologist comes into conflict with an environment that violates, in many areas, the concept of good mental health. Yet it is impossible to manipulate that environment because to do so may very well violate the security and the necessary function of a correctional facility.

Within this social, environmental, and psychological conflict the psychologist is often called upon to provide solid theoretical and practical background in policymaking. To function in the inconsistent and, at times, inappropriate environment, however the psychologist must be nonthreatening and deal with authority figures of various levels. This task is rather difficult because most correctional facilities are semimilitaristic. This setting and the role of the psychologist have never been clearly defined.

To add insult to injury, the psychologist must deal with the incongruity of assisting inmates in adjusting to an institution to which, in many instances, they have been sent as punishment. In other words, a person is sent away as a punishment and then is actually expected to adjust to that punishment. When one then adjusts to the authoritative, and at times oppressive, environment of a correctional facility, it is often felt that he or she is "rehabilitated" and ready to take a place once again in society.

Within this framework, psychologists do serve a rather significant role. Prior to establishing mental hygiene services, psychologists must first establish solid relationships within the system. They usually have to demonstrate (if it has not been done by predecessors) that they can provide a service, can be part of "the team," can be nonthreatening, can function within the framework of the correctional facility, can contribute acceptable input to policymaking, and can be available to and trusted by the inmates.

Although these concepts are almost paradoxical, if suitable relationships and mutual trusts can be established with other members of the staff, the psychologist can perform and function in a most meritorious way. It is only when good relationships are established and communications are facilitated among personnel that further aspects of meaningful programming and treatment can be performed with the inmates.

In most facilities, all transferees to the institution are reviewed by the mental hygiene staff. Each inmate is evaluated for specific criteria, such as previous mental hospital history, previous suicide attempts, nature of offense, and amenability to treatment. Inmates are then offered the opportunity to be seen by the staff individually or in a group.

The psychologist plays a major role while the inmate is in this reception and orientation period. A member of the mental hygiene staff speaks with new inmates in a group and informs them of various programs offered by the mental hygiene unit. The psychologist's role, including confidentiality and availability of service, is established at that time. The psychologist is thus exposed to the new inmates and is recognized as being an individual who is not associated with either the correctional or the administrative staff of the institution.

In a correctional framework, the psychologist does not have an opportunity to know all the inmate population. Consequently, he or she must rely on first-line officers who deal with inmates and with treatment personnel. These other staff members are a prime source of referral to the psychologist. They suggest inmates who need psychological help, as observed by strange behavior or emotional or personal problems. It is essential in this framework that the psychologist give feedback to the staff member who makes the referral. All too often, although feedback may seem apparent and obvious, this communication is incomplete and should be done verbally and discretely so that the inmate's confidentiality is never violated.

The psychologist in the correctional facility also serves the more orthodox function of testing inmates. This function is frequently and justifiably minimized. Testing should be on a prescription basis, and IQs should be offered only when other test scores are "stale" or the tests were administered during "admission shock." Inmates may also require testing for vocational aptitude or interests, for preparation for school, or for very unique problems. Testing should be done on a need basis and should not be used as a casual, routine mechanism within the framework of psychological services.

The psychologist makes rounds throughout the correctional facility, spending time in academic, vocational, and recreational areas. He or she practices a form of informal referral service by answering questions immediately and accepting referrals from inmates about other inmates who are having problems.

Inmates are seen both individually and in groups. The psychologist chooses patients, and the patients have to voluntarily agree to treatment. Psychotherapeutic treatment includes orthodox forms as well as marathon groups, transactional group therapy, and other techniques, dependent upon the expertise of the therapist and the needs of the patients.

Treatment supervision is often provided by the psychologist both to junior members of the psychological staff and to staff members of other units, such as counselors, teachers, and correctional officers who are conducting group counseling sessions. The psychologist is seen as the mental hygiene expert and, as such, the person most capable and equipped to provide training and supervision.

In a progressive correctional facility, the psychologist leads weekly interdisciplinary clinical staff conferences. Staff members discuss various problem inmates. Parole officers, correctional counselors, teachers, and the correctional officers participate.

The psychologist also provides training for correctional staff within the facility. Courses are offered on the identification of mental illness, the care and management of the emotionally ill, the understanding of the mentally ill, the sociological factors leading to crime, the management of the depressed individual, etc. Training is usually well accepted by staff if the class discussions are pragmatic and helpful.

A portion of the psychologist's time is spent consulting with other professional departments such as the education department and service unit. Sometimes the psychologist participates in classification committee meetings and serves as a consultant to inmate groups. In certain correctional facilities, the psychologist trains and prepares the next generation of professional people planning to enter the correctional systems. The psychologist must orient, recruit, and encourage promising people to participate in meaningful correctional programs with proper ideologies. Usually these young people are graduates or undergraduates from colleges of criminal justice. Fieldwork for specific training is usually provided by the mental hygiene staff.

A unique but growing approach to providing psychological services to a correctional population is a mental health walk-in clinic. Several afternoons a week, an inmate can talk to a member of the mental hygiene staff. No record is made of the interview or contact. Usually, immediate short-term problems are discussed. If longer treatment is required, then an appointment is scheduled.

The psychologist working in a correctional facility also has a responsibility to the community at large. This role is essentially an educational one. The psychologist speaks to community groups and to the students in high schools. Often the psychologist is invited to address classes at the local colleges.

Another function of the psychologist within the correctional facility is to serve as a consultant for furlough and parole programs. In some instances, institutional personnel are uncertain whether to release an individual. The psychologist often either knows the inmate or will interview the inmate and offer recommendations.

Not to be minimized is the role of the psychologist in evaluation and research. All too often, programs are initiated with few evaluative techniques. The psychologist, with expertise in such techniques, is the logical person to evaluate a program.

Referrals to outside agencies are also within the purview of the psychologist. Psychologists involve themselves with agencies such as the Office of Vocational Rehabilitation, community Alcoholics Anonymous groups, drug treatment programs, and other facilities offering to help individuals on their return to the community.

Although this wide range of the psychologist's activities appears to be overwhelming to the individual considering work in corrections, these functions are not performed by one individual but rather by a treatment team of psychologists. Such work is distributed among the staff. Work within a correctional setting is exciting, is a fine learning experience for the study of psychopathology, and provides considerable gratification for the psychologist. Treatment results are easily measured in terms of success and failure on parole.

Working conditions and salaries are at least as good as in most other employment settings. The professionalism of the psychologist is fully utilized and exploited, and the need for psychologists in correctional facilities is great.

Staff Trainers and Consultants

In the past decade, as state and city bureaus or departments of corrections have begun adopting a philosophy of "socialized justice" (Werner, 1972) and moving in the direction of humanizing their correctional systems, a few pioneer commissioners of corrections have sought the services of psychologists as consultants in treatment and rehabilitative services, as staff trainers, and as organization development experts. These are roles that a few ingenious, well-trained clinical and industrial psychologists have assumed and have proved able to carry with consummate ability. They have made a substantial contribution to a field that needs and increasingly seeks to use both their humanistic and psychosocial perspectives for understanding and dealing with inmates and staff and their systems framework for comprehending the institutional network. It is anticipated that the demand for such input from psychologists will expand and that courageous innovators who combine clinical knowledge, organization development, change and consultative and training skills will be able to find full- or part-time positions in the challenging, complex world of corrections and its allied systems—the police and courts. Although this section is addressed specifically to work with the correctional system, by extension, the same principles and processes apply to serving in similar capacities with other wings of the criminal justice system.

Delinquency and crime now constitute one of the largest, most overwhelming and devastating social problems in America. Although society recognizes the dilemma of recidivism, society has never insisted upon or adequately financed sustained (re)habilitation services for offenders, services that would help offenders assume at least partial responsibility for their behavior, their whereabouts, or their future (Allport, 1955). Nor has the public, through the legislature, appropriated enough funds to see that the institutions are kept in decent physical condition; that the staff is properly qualified and compensated for its treatment, custodial, and managerial functions; and that the total experience of incarceration should not prove debilitating and destructive. Society has always held inconsistent views about the philosophy and psychology of punishment (Fenster & MacNamara, 1970). Society, perhaps with vigorous leadership from psychologists and other human service professionals, must be helped to view the loss of freedom that is experienced when one is "locked up" as horrendous punishment in and of itself.

The other task of these facilities, besides punishment of inmates and protection of society from its dangerous members, is "correction," helping the inmate toward law-abiding behavior and attitudes. This task is essential since the majority of prisoners are ultimately released and need to function civilly and productively in the outside world; in addition, these inmates have never lost the unalienable right to the pursuit of happiness. "Correction" cannot be accomplished by further demeaning and dehumanizing; rather, inmates need to gain some sense of confidence and self-worth to replace their "con-man" and/or failure life script. (Excellent material on life scripts and recidivism appears in articles in the *Transactional Analysis Journal;* see also James & Jongeward, 1971.) Inmates also need to acquire salable vocational and educational skills, to have some heightened degree of insight and self-awareness, to begin to have a sense of trust and optimism rather than pervasive despair and depression, and to think of themselves as creators rather than as victims. As Arthur Miller so aptly stated in *After the Fall:* "I think one must finally take one's life in one's arms."

For correctional personnel to comprehend the above and for them to make a commitment to wide-scale system changes to reduce crime is a large order indeed. Law-and-order panaceas that periodically come into vogue, such as longer sentences and harsher prison atmospheres, have proven false deterrents; some alternative must supersede such unworkable solutions. One possible pathway is socialized justice in a prison community with a therapeutic milieu. To pursue this route, the correctional system will need the revitalization, the provocation, and the fresh air that can be brought in by psychologists as consultants and staff trainers. As Werner (1972) stated:

The behavioral approach takes into account the whole man; the legalistic takes into account only his offending act. To become operative, socialized justice must provide the flexibility to allow for work with the individual's behavior. (pp. 52–53)

Since it is unlikely that there will ever be a plenitude of correctional psychologists, psychiatrists, or social workers to staff the penal system in direct treatment roles, and since the cost would likely be prohibitive, a more realistic staffing model would use highly trained professional personnel as directors of treatment services, as supervisors, and as staff trainers. In these capacities, they can teach a paraprofessional staff, comprised of bachelor's-level (and some master's-level) correctional counselors, ex-offenders recruited for staff, and correctional officers, the "how to" of individual and group treatment. In very progressive systems, marital and family counseling could be provided in the prerelease period (a) to help the inmate and relatives of the inmate make a healthy transition to living together again and (b) to help them cope with the problems that are almost certain to arise.

A careful training design must be drawn up to encompass what the counselors need to know, based on each particular staff and its level of education, experience, and competence. The curriculum will probably need to contain knowledge-based course content in such topical areas as growth and development, normal and abnormal behavior, social causes of deviant behavior, character and impulse disorders, neurosis and psychosis, alcoholism and addiction, and subcultural values and life-styles. In addition, neophyte therapists will need units on intervention strategies; probably the most useful techniques for correctional system clientele include crisis intervention, reality therapy, transactional analysis, and behavior modification. In all likelihood, counselors can learn to administer group tests like the MMPI, achievement tests for assessing educational levels and placement, and interest inventories. But more sophisticated psychodiagnostic tests, particularly projectives, and analytically oriented insight therapy should remain the purview of doctoral-level licensed psychologists.

If staff live in geographic areas near colleges, they should certainly be encouraged to pursue advanced studies. But whatever is not available at any other accessible resource should be offered on the premises in staff training series. This training should be supplemented by individual and small group clinical supervision by the director of treatment services and the professional psychologist staff. Certificates of completion of courses, raises, and promotions should be among the incentives for studying; however, intrinsic motivation to "do a better job" should surely be capitalized upon.

At the state level, psychologists serve as staff trainers as well as consultants to bureau chiefs and division heads, meeting with them weekly or, at a minimum, semimonthly. The modus operandi is similar to that elaborated above, with a few modifications. Since the staff trainer at the state level is likely to be external to the system and related to it only on a part-time basis (Kaslow, 1972), he or she must quickly learn a good deal about the system and the key persons and their personalities, the formal and informal channels of communication, the philosophy and objectives of the bureau, the level of staff morale and cooperation, the factions and power struggles, and the political climate in which the system operates. Much of this knowledge can be gained by conferring with individuals about why the trainer or consultant was hired, that is, what was the foremost problem of the organization. While collecting vital data in this manner, the psychologist simultaneously shows respect for the intelligence and ideas of the other staff, acquires a "feel" for the whole situation, and begins to establish collaborative, mutually trusting relationships. Meeting with several members informally over lunch or dinner can hasten gaining a sense of the organizational ethos and the administrative, managerial styles of the leaders. Based on the expressed needs of the staff plus the consultant's own organizational diagnosis, the consultant outlines the goals of the organization and the steps leading to their achievement. Likewise, the staff trainer evolves a training design and institutes sessions to "teach" the requisite content. For example, the trainer might be assigned to instruct, individually and in small groups, the directors of the various prisons and community treatment centers. This instruction could entail helping them with their supervisory practice, teaching them how to be staff trainers, and/or upgrading their diagnostic and treatment skills. But, since development of staff training curriculum has been discussed earlier in this chapter, the remainder of this section deals with the consultation process.

Let us assume that the expressed, if somewhat vague, purpose of hiring the consultant is (a) to improve, streamline, and humanize the administration and management of a mammoth state correctional enterprise and (b) to enable the staff team to function more cooperatively and productively. In Phase 1, an initial reading is taken to determine the underlying difficulties. Next, the group size and composition are judiciously decided, the schedule of meetings and duration of the consultation period are set and clearly announced, and the endorsement of the program from the top level through active involvement is affirmed. At this juncture, Phase 2 should rapidly commence. At the opening group session, one might use such a paper-and-pencil tool as the MacGregor Team Development Scale (MacGregor, 1960) to enlist the help of personnel in the assessment of the organization's current level of functioning. A compilation and analysis of the data can quickly be fed back so that the group members can compare their ratings, thus fostering awareness of differences in perception. Re-administering the MacGregor scale in the final session of the series will provide data on the change in organizational functioning.

At another point in time, if understanding leadership styles and their impact on staff morale and performance is a focal point, the consultant might turn to using the management grid for self-evaluation. The grid requires that persons rate themselves on two dimensions, concern for people and concern for production (Blake, Mouton, Barnes, & Greiner, 1964). Once the self-rating is performed, the group is subdivided and members are asked to rate each other. Each member then notes the differences and similarities in assessment by self and by others. It is often necessary to "differentiate between participatory management, in which contributions are valued and considered, but the ultimate decision rests with the person (or persons) who must be accountable and responsible for the decision and its implementation, and consensual management— where decisions are made by majority rule" (Kaslow, 1974, p. 47). All participants have the right to know which is the managerial philosophy of the organization's top executive.

Participants might acquire new information from a combination of interesting didactic lectures, pertinent reading materials, group debates and discussions, field trips to observe different bureaus, sensitivity or T-group laboratory experiences, and written analytic assignments. It is imperative that an open, vital learning environment be created so that long-time professionals remain receptive to new ideas and become "unfrozen" enough to risk experimenting with different methods. The cumulative effect of modifications in the perspectives and operating methods of each of the executives, individually and as a team, is often substantial and conscious enough to bring about major system improvements.

The psychologist must be certain that the staff training and consultation processes are evaluated periodically to determine if the stated aims are indeed being realized. The results of this evaluation should be shared with group members to underscore the commitment to continuous feedback as an ongoing part of a healthy organization.

Many clinical, interpersonal, and organizational problems confront correctional front-line personnel as well as executive and managerial officials at the city and state Bureau of Corrections. In seeking solutions to their daily crises and difficulties, and their long-range problems, some corrections officials are turning to psychologists for consultation and staff training services. Clinical and organizational development training combine to uniquely equip the psychologist to diagnose and treat individuals, families, groups, and organizations. Further, the model of stating problems, diagnosing, collecting data, seeking alternative viable solutions and action patterns, evaluating what has transpired, drawing conclusions, and solidifying gains is as applicable to organizations as it is to other kinds of client systems.

Psychologists in Drug Abuse Treatment Programs

The topic of drug abuse has attracted the interests and talents of psychologists for at least a generation. Clinical reports and research articles concerning addiction, alcoholism, and drug abuse have proliferated in recent years as concern about these problems has spread. Traditional roles for psychologists and boundaries for their professional responsibilities have blurred as the extent and complexity of the problem of drug abuse have become obvious.

It is clear from the authors' experience that traditional roles must be changed if psychology is to offer an effective response to drug abusers and drug abuse programs. The essential changes include a greater acceptance of the contribution to be made not only by other professionals (physicians, nurses, social workers, school counselors, police and probation officers, etc.) but by paraprofessionals as well. The ex-addict and reformed alcoholic often function as the primary therapists in drug-free therapeutic communities and many other drug abuse treatment facilities. Their roles can add stress and conflict to the role(s) played by the psychologist employed in the same programs (Bassin, 1973). The mutual goal of successful rehabilitation of the addict or alcoholic can be sabotaged quite easily if psychologists and other professionals do not recognize and deal with the overlapping responsibilities and risks of competitiveness and manipulation that can develop in their relationships with one another and with their allied paraprofessional teammates.

The psychologist may encounter an additional form of stress when attempting to establish credibility simultaneously in the community and in the drug abuse subcontext. Attitudes toward drug abusers within the larger community can put the well-intentioned psychologist "on the line" when the psychologist attempts to function as the agent or advocate of a client generally believed to be criminal, dangerous, or at least antisocial. Bratter (1973) presented a sensitive and sophisticated analysis of the resulting role conflicts that should be anticipated by anyone who expects to function effectively as a drug abuse counselor or drug program administrator.

The confusion of the psychologist's role has been a chronic problem in the field of drug abuse. The medical model continues to compete with behavioral and humanistic/existential, as well as legalistic, models in defining drug abuse and establishing social policy for drug treatment. The responsibilities of drug abuse counselors, physicians, psychologists, criminal justice professionals, and drug abusers themselves are defined largely in terms of which model of drug abuse is used as a basis for treatment and social policy. The resulting role conflicts have been illustrated and discussed in a growing number of recent publications on this topic (see, e.g., Brecher, 1972; Casriel & Bratter, 1974; Deitch, 1971; DeLeon, 1974; Devlin & Vamos, 1975; Glasser, 1973; Mandel, 1971; Szasz, 1974).

Therapy, counseling, and diagnostic testing are more traditional clinical functions that may be performed by psychologists in drug abuse treatment programs. The psychologist involved in providing clinical services to the drug abuser may wish for supplementary forensic training in addition to his or her typical graduate clinical training. The psychotherapist or psychodiagnostician in a drug treatment setting must be prepared to deal with the complex issues that result from the criminal status of the drug addict, the social stigma associated with drug abuse, and the vocational and educational limitations confronting most "graduates" of drug treatment programs. In addition, the psychotherapist must be prepared to face the unique challenge presented by the client who may resent professionals of all types'and who may have been diagnosed (and rejected as hopeless) as a psychopath by other psychotherapists. The authors have found it essential to deal with drug abusers as individuals rather than as representatives of stereotyped diagnostic categories. The reality therapy (Glasser, 1965) approach to behavior change has been valuable in attempts to deal with the complex combination of personal, emotional, and sociolegal problems that arise in the context of clinical involvement with drug abusers. The application of reality therapy to specific drug abuse clinical problems has been well described in papers by Bassin (1974) and Bratter (1973, 1974).

Nonclinical and New Roles for Psychologists

The psychologist involved in drug abuse treatment may find that the treatment setting is nontraditional but the role of the psychologist within the program is rather traditional, at least in terms of job title. Experience has indicated that even a conventional job description (e.g., director of research) can contain some rather unconventional unwritten expectations and requirements. It is clear that hidden agendas must be examined as such and conflicting assumptions about the role of the psychologist in the view of the employer, the client, and the psychologist should be resolved before the psychologist attempts to function effectively and fully within a particular agency or program. There are three broad areas in which psychologists can be identified in current drug abuse treatment programs that do not include more traditional clinical functions.

Administrators. Prior to the expansion of the concept of drug-free thera-peutic communities, most drug rehabilitation programs were directed by medical personnel. The medical model is still a controlling influence on most publicly supported, governmentally funded programs, and, as a con-sequence, physicians and registered nurses may have the most direct authority and control within such programs. Other staff members may include psychologists, recreation therapists, vocational counselors, and paraprofessional drug counselors in nonadministrative roles. This has been the case in the public methadone maintenance treatment programs. An increasing number of programs, however, have recruited psychologists (and other nonmedical personnel) to serve as administrators. These pro-grams are often advertised as prevention-oriented training programs or youth-oriented drug rehabilitation and "rap" centers. The educational and treatment objectives are generally fused in such programs. The possible role confusion for the administrator and planner of such programs has been noted (Faltico, 1973). It is essential for the psychologist/administrator of these programs to be aware of the community pressures as well as the program's objectives as he or she attempts to do the necessary team building.

Researchers. A psychologist may be employed as research director for a program that conducts research whose priorities may differ from those of the psychologist. Research may be an attempt to legitimize the activities of a program for funding purposes and may not even be a valid form of program evaluation. The ivory tower of basic research on drug effects or large sample surveys of attitudes about drug abuse may seem very remote to the psychologist at work on research projects within a drug treatment program. The problems for the psychologist as a researcher within drug programs have been well described and evaluated in a recent paper by DeLeon (1974). It is clear to the authors that the priorities of the program will generally dictate the nature and extent of the research director's role within a drug program. In general, the psychologist can expect to handle the following duties if selected to serve as a drug program research director: grant obtainment, program evaluation, in-service training, and (occasion-ally) basic research. The role of obtaining grants may be the real reason for hiring a research director. Many programs will expect the psychologist/ researcher to help publicize their activities and results. In this case, it can be a matter of "publish or perish" as the program demands a variety of reports of the positive findings about the program. The research director may also have an indirect impact on the program's policies if the research and program evaluation results are fed back to staff and if the research functions are truly integrated into other staff functions.

Teachers. Drug-free therapeutic communities and other drug rehabilita-tion programs frequently employ psychologists as trainers for their staff members. Subjects such as group dynamics, interviewing, psychodiagnos-tic procedures, crisis intervention, and theories of psychotherapy are all expected to fall within the competence of the psychologist/trainer. Experi-ence in dealing with such responsibilities has indicated that drug program personnel are highly motivated for the training offered but also highly resistant to suggestions about changing their own role definitions and techniques. It is generally better to operate such in-service training as a workshop rather than as a seminar or course. Experiential components such as role playing and case presentation can facilitate learning much more effectively than the well-chosen words of formal lectures or the slick content of most drug training films. It is essential, in other words, to teach the members of such workshops to be teachers both inside the workshop and in the drug treatment facility in general. The psychologist can also function as a teacher in innovative programs such as Daytop Village and Project RETURN in New York City, where residents of the program are offered college courses as a part of their treatment program. One author (Faltico, 1973) is currently teaching introductory psychology to 20 addicts in a drug-free therapeutic community. The course is sponsored by a private college (College of New Rochelle) but is taught within the drug facility. It is anticipated that students from the drug program will also enroll in courses taught on the home campus as they progress academically and therapeutically. Here, as well as in doing in-service training of staff, it is essential that the psychologist/teacher emphasize student involvement and experiential components in his or her teaching.

Summary

This section has emphasized changing patterns of involvement in drug rehabilitation programs for psychologists. Problems in defining new roles for psychologists have been discussed in relationship to conflicts among professionals and between professionals and paraprofessionals, as well as in relationship to the subtle demands placed on the psychologist as agent and advocate of drug abusers. In addition, the difficulty in defining drug abuse has been described as a factor in role confusion for psychologists attempting to function within drug programs. Three nonclinical roles were described for psychologists who wish to contribute to drug rehabilitation.

Court Psychologists

The Bronx-Lebanon Hospital is a voluntary agency that has a contract with the New York City Department of Mental Health and Retardation Services; as such it offers an array of psychological and psychiatric services to the Criminal and Supreme Courts of Bronx County, as well as to the Office of Probations of the Criminal and Supreme Courts. Using Bronx-Lebanon Hospital illustratively, this section describes the areas of professional activities of the forensic psychologist and the administrative as well as clinical aspects of forensic psychology.

There are five areas of service that are rendered to the judicial system by this court program: evaluation, consultation, training, treatment, and research. The psychologist is an integral member in the delivery of each of these services to the courts.

Evaluation

The role of the psychologist in the courts is more than one of a diagnostician; labeling and subsequent pigeonholing have little value to the courts. Consequently, psychologists have been asked, and are being asked, more substantive questions by the courts by order of a pre-sentence psychological examination. These questions usually focus on therapeutic alternatives to incarceration. If a treatment plan is to be recommended as an alternative to incarceration, the plan must be carefully and comprehensively delineated. The factors that lead to the recommendation should be stated precisely. The psychologist may draw upon standardized instruments to help with this assessment. The recommendation of a specific treatment plan usually involves more than an assessment of attitudes, values, and personality correlates. A knowledge of community resources, an understanding of cultural determinants, and a study of the psychodynamics of a family constellation are all essential in formulating a plan. Furthermore, the psychologist may be called upon to implement this plan. This may involve negotiating with a hospital for the admission of the patient (defendant); court-referred patients often carry a stigma that creates a formidable admission barrier.

Examinations to determine a defendant's competency to stand trial are performed by the forensic psychologist. Traditionally, these examinations have been the domain of the qualified psychiatrist. In New York State, however, the law permits a certified psychologist to assist in the examination when a defendant is thought to be mentally defective. Psychological testing (specifically, administering Wechsler-Bellevue Intelligence scales) is vital in this type of assessment.

On occasion, the court has asked psychologists to assist in the assessment of the mental status of a defendant at the time of arraignment. Clearly, the court may order a competency examination to determine whether a person is fit to proceed. This procedure, however, may result in a delay of up to 30 days, and, moreover, adequate treatment for a defendant may be postponed.

When an emergency call is received from the court, both the psychologist and the psychiatrist have gone into the courtroom to make their evaluation. The judge is immediately appraised of the findings and recommendation. Although this type of rapid intervention has not been widely used because of a shortage of human resources, its need has become clearly recognized. A program is now under study to service the court with a regular crisis intervention team.

Consultation

The forensic psychologist is often called upon to consult with probation officers, assistant district attorneys, and legal aid lawyers and judges. The psychologist may serve as a pivoting or central force in coordinating the work of these professional members of the judicial system. Consultations often involve problem-solving efforts with other professional members in devising and implementing the treatment plan. Quite often investigating probation officers, legal aid attorneys, and the prosecuting attorney are simultaneously seeking the assistance of the psychologist. The psychologist is called upon to coordinate the planning of the team so that a consensus is reached. A spin-off of this role has been the concept of the therapeutic team approach to the criminal justice system.

Judges have also called upon the forensic psychologist to explain the implications of psychiatric and psychological terminology. A judge can call the psychologist to the bench (off the record) to discuss a particular pre-sentence psychological evaluation. At this time the psychologist has the opportunity to educate the jurist to appreciate the psychological conflicts that have resulted in a patient's interfacing with the law. This technique often results in a sentence that is therapeutic and not punitive.

Training

The forensic psychologist has been involved in the training of the aforementioned law enforcement professionals. Training has been devoted to both affective issues (attitudes and motivation) and the more traditional cognitive components. Affective training sessions have focused on identifying attitudes and feelings associated with working with different types of psychopathologies.

The above approach has provided a springboard for teaching interpersonal counseling skills effective in speaking to different individuals; crisis intervention skills have been taught and guidelines for determining the limits of crisis intervention have been provided. A fundamental body of knowledge about a particular disease entity has been provided and participants have been taught to identify those persons who interface with the law because of their particular psychological problems.

As a result of this type of training more referrals are being made to the court clinic for psychological consultations. An additional benefit of this training is that the concept of a "criminal justice therapeutic team" has been more readily adopted.

Training has been extended to the community. The psychologist is often invited to speak to parent and religious groups, community mental health associations, and other professional associations. The goals are more than information sharing; support is often asked from the community to help devise and implement programs.

Treatment

The treatment plan recommended in the pre-sentence evaluation is often implemented within the component programs (partial and inpatient hospitalizations, as well as alcoholism programs) of the Department of Psychiatry at the Bronx-Lebanon Hospital Center. A team approach is in operation whereby all members of the staff (social workers, mental health workers, psychiatrists) treat the person who is on probation.

The forensic psychologist may serve as a primary therapist for the probationer and as a consultant to other professional members within the hospital setting. As a consultant he or she may work with the team in dispelling fears of working with a person convicted of a serious crime. Persons convicted of murder, for example, are often so stigmatized that the barriers for treatment are formidable. The psychologist may draw upon a variety of psychotherapeutic modalities. Individual and group psychotherapy is often employed. Group therapy has been an important therapeutic modality. Family therapy has also been vital in the treatment of the probationer.

Research

There is a great need for research in forensic psychology; research to generate theoretical knowledge as well as descriptive research leading to program design and evaluation is important. Recently, the relevance and value of competency-to-stand-trial examinations have been questioned. Alternative procedures for identifying those defendants who need and may benefit from treatment have been sought. Skills of the forensic psychologist may be of great value in the field of research.

Family Court Psychologists

In order to provide a meaningful context for a description of the role of the family court psychologist it is necessary to offer some introductory remarks concerning the functions of the family court.

The family court as it exists today represents a fusion of two types of judicial institutions that still maintain a separate existence in many jurisdictions in the United States and in other countries. One of these is the *juvenile* or *children's court*, which deals with cases of juvenile law violations as well as with a variety of other cases in which the court's intervention is sought for the benefit of the child or of the community, or both, even though no actual charges of law violation may be involved. The other is the *domestic relations court* or some equivalent body, which deals with such matters as child support payments, parental neglect, child custody, and visitation rights. Since in many cases parental neglect or other problems of parent–child interaction play a role in the emergence of the types of antisocial behavior and personality disturbances that typically come to the attention of the juvenile court, there is an obvious overlap in the functions of the two types of judicial institutions, and the emergence of the family court arises from a recognition that these functions can be more effectively handled by a unified body. (It should, however, be noted that a family court does not typically encompass *all* of the judicial functions pertaining to the family. Thus, in the case of New York State, where a merger of the Children's Court and the Domestic Relations Court took place in 1962, the Family Court does not have jurisdiction over divorces and annulments and has only partial jurisdiction over child custody.)

Although some of the laws providing for differential treatment of juvenile offenders are much older, the juvenile court as a distinct institution made its appearance in 1899, when two such courts were established (one in Denver and one in Chicago). The idea caught on rapidly, however, and by 1904 juvenile courts were already in operation in at least 11 large American cities (Barrows, 1904/1973).

The guiding philosophy underlying the establishment of these institutions was that the function of the juvenile court was not to punish but rather to plan for the juvenile's future in the best interests of the juvenile and of the community. One psychological assumption that was often involved, explicitly or otherwise, was that the child or adolescent offender did not have the degree of mature understanding to be held responsible for actions to the same extent as an adult. Another related assumption was that the personality of the young offender was not yet fully formed and that with proper handling the youth still stood a chance of being deflected from a criminal career. In line with this philosophy the juvenile court judge was seen in a quasi-parental role, and juvenile court proceedings tended to be characterized by an informality that stood in sharp contrast to the adversary character of criminal court trials. (While providing for differential treatment of juveniles, as compared to adults, the juvenile statutes typically also brought under court jurisdiction the delinquent acts of younger children who had not been previously considered legally responsible for their actions. According to the laws that existed in many of the states before the juvenile statutes were enacted, a child of less than 10 years could not be punished by a court at all, but a child of between 10 and 14 years was subject to the same penalties as an adult if found to have the degree of understanding presupposed in assigning criminal responsibility; see Sutherland & Cressey, 1974, p. 440.)

The concept of the juvenile court as a benevolent agency acting in the best interests of the child or adolescent ultimately laid part of the groundwork for the present-day functions of psychologists and mental health professionals in the family courts. In the early days of the juvenile courts, however, psychologists played apparently no role (or at most a minor role), and one gathers from the early reports that the personality and attitudes of the individual judge were the chief factors in determining how the cases were handled.

Apparently some of the early juvenile judges had personal qualities that made them highly effective in persuading juvenile offenders to steer away from a delinquent career. The paternalistic attitude of the court, however, while intended to serve a benevolent function, also lacked certain legal protections that were available to an adult defendant in a criminal trial. Since juvenile offenders were not technically charged with a "crime" and were often not represented by a lawyer, the charges against them were often taken for granted, and they could be placed in an institutional setting for a period much longer than the maximum term established by law for a comparable offense by an adult (e.g., a juvenile sent to an institution for an indefinite term before the age of 16 could be kept there until age 21).

Although there are still significant discrepancies between the procedural rights of an adult defendant and of an adolescent charged with a juvenile offense, some jurisdictions have made a substantial effort to reduce these discrepancies. Moreover, some degree of due process has been introduced into juvenile trials as a result of several United States Supreme Court decisions in the late 1960s. (For historical accounts and discussions of the current functioning of juvenile courts in the United States, see Barrows, 1904/1973; Emerson, 1969; Lemert, 1970; Levitt & Rubenstein, 1968; Murphy, 1974; Rubin, 1970; Sutherland & Cressey, 1974, pp. 440–461; for data on other countries see Cavanagh, 1959/1967; Reifen, 1972; Sanders, 1970; for a recent discussion of psychological and legal problems pertaining to child placement see Goldstein, Freud, & Solnit, 1973.)

Psychological Testing and Test Interpretation

One of the major functions of a family court psychologist is the administration of psychological tests to individuals referred by the court and the preparation of reports based on the test findings. As a rule the test battery includes an individual intelligence test, a test of reading skill, and whatever projective test or tests the examiner considers appropriate. In some family court clinics the Bender-Gestalt test is also regularly administered.

The psychological report usually includes an evaluation of the subject's intellectual level and reading skill, as well as a psychodiagnostic evaluation based on the test data and on clinical impressions. A recommendation concerning the disposition of the case is usually included, but may be withheld if the psychologist feels that further data, not available at the time (e.g., clinical data on other family members), need to be taken into account.

The intelligence test is usually either the Wechsler Adult Intelligence Scale, the 1974 revision of the Wechsler Intelligence Test for Children, or—much less frequently—the Wechsler Preschool and Primary Test of Intelligence. (The choice among these tests depends on the subject's age.) The psychologist, however, has the option of using one of the other recognized individual tests of intelligence.

The psychological report is normally expected to include an IQ score—or in the case of the Wechsler tests, a Verbal, a Performance, and a Full-Scale score. Apart from the fact that such information constitutes a conventionally accepted starting point for the analysis of intellectual performance, IQ scores may also be important for administrative reasons; for example, some agencies require a minimum IQ score for placement, and IQ scores of less than 70 fall into the mental defective category. It is questionable, however, whether some of the individuals in that IQ range are bona fide mental defectives; in the large majority of cases seen at the family court clinics, those with scores below 70 have clinical indications that preclude a diagnosis of mental deficiency.

The IQ scores provide only a starting point for the analysis of intellectual functioning, however. In the case of children and adolescents seen in family courts—many of whom come from families of low educational level and most of whom have a history of truancy and low achievement in school—the IQ score cannot often be taken as a face-value indication of the subject's potential. Apart from low achievement, there are also other factors that do not appear with the same regularity in the family court clinic population but that may also adversely affect the IQ scores in individual cases. Some of the more important of these include test anxiety, a tendency toward withdrawal of attention from the external environment, a negative attitude toward the testing procedure, a hyperactive tendency that sometimes results in responding too rapidly, or a tendency to give up too easily on items that are too difficult. A skilled examiner can often detect these factors and can make allowances for them in estimating the subject's potential.

The intelligence test data, particularly when taken in conjunction with the Bender-Gestalt, can also in some cases provide clues to possible organic problems. (Sometimes, when the evidence is ambiguous, additional tests may be needed to explore further the possibility of brain damage.)

The projective tests used by family court psychologists include the Rorschach, the figure-drawing tests (including the Draw-a-Person and the House-Tree-Person Tests as well as their various derivatives), the Thematic Apperception Test, Three Wishes, the Szondi, and the sentence completion test in its several forms. Among these the Rorschach and the figure-drawing tests appear to be the most popular. As a rule, the projective test materials—taken in conjunction with case history data and behavioral observations—are used to assess the overall personality dynamics. Sometimes, however, the psychologist might also be asked to answer a specific question that might bear on the disposition of a case. Thus, a psychologist might be asked whether projective tests indicate a level of aggression that may be dangerous to others or whether there is evidence of a latent or incipient psychosis or of a suicidal tendency that should be taken into account in case planning.

In the case of individuals who had been given psychological tests on some earlier occasion, a comparison of earlier and current projective test data may be of importance in indicating what kinds of personality changes, if any, have occurred, and such information might also be of importance in planning. Similarly, in cases where several members of a family have been tested, a comparison of the projective test data may be of value in providing light on the patterns of family interaction.

Other Activities of Family Court Psychologists

Family court psychologists have occasionally testified in court, conducted group psychotherapy, and participated in demonstration projects aimed at testing new approaches in dealing with problems of social pathology. Thus, several psychologists (as well as psychiatrists and others) at the New York State Family Court have recently participated in the Rapid Intervention Project, which explored techniques for dealing with problem families at the community level. Some psychologists have also been involved in research on problems related to their court functions. Family court psychologists are usually part of a team which includes psychiatrists and, in some cases, social workers.

Types of Cases Seen by the Family Court Psychologist

According to a popular stereotype, the family court is essentially a court for juveniles who have committed criminal acts. While it is indeed true that many of the juveniles brought before family courts are charged with acts that would be considered criminal if committed by an adult,[1] there are also many others who are charged with "status offenses"—offenses that would not be illegal if committed by individuals beyond a specified age bracket. Moreover, there are many instances in which a juvenile is brought to the attention of the court by parents (or other relatives or guardians) not because of any specific law violation but because of discipline problems at home, or, in a small proportion of cases, because the parents realize that the child needs psychological help. At least theoretically many of the cases in which the parent or guardian is the complainant do not constitute "delinquency petitions," but rather take the form of pleas for the court's help in the supervision of the child. Some of the most frequent complaints in such petitions are that the child or adolescent is "ungovernable," keeps late hours, stays away from home for days at a time, associates with undesirable companions, and does not attend school. In a smaller proportion of cases, however, the parent or guardian makes allegations of a more serious nature against the child or adolescent. These may include allegations of violence or threats of violence against the family, theft from family members or from others, gang membership, or drug abuse. (Some of the parents who make the more serious charges insist on placement of the child away from home, stating that they fear the threat of violence or that they cannot cope with the child's behavior. A few others, while taking a less openly rejecting attitude, nevertheless ask for placement on the grounds that as long as the child remains in the neighborhood he or she will continue to be unfavorably influenced by the local peer group. The large majority of the complaining parents, however, are willing to have the child remain at home but feel that their authority needs to be supplemented by the authority of the court.)

In addition to the broad categories already mentioned, there are still other cases that are much less frequent (not necessarily in terms of the overall court load but in terms of referrals for psychological examinations). In these cases the child is—even in a superficial sense—more of a victim than a wrongdoer; a parent, stepparent, or guardian is charged with neglect or child abuse or is characterized as being incompetent in the parental role because of mental illness or mental deficiency. Also included are cases in

---

1. It should be added that in some jurisdictions juveniles of 14 years or over who are charged with serious offenses can be turned over to the criminal court.

which there is a dispute with respect to the custody of the child or with respect to parents' visitation rights. Cases of child abuse as such are handled in a criminal court, but in cases where criminal guilt cannot clearly be established the family court still has the task of determining whether the child can be safely left in (or returned to) the custody of the parents and, if so, what additional steps can be taken to insure the child's safety. In typical cases of physical abuse (other than sexual abuse) the child is too young to be given psychological tests, but the testing of the parents is quite important for a sound disposition of the case. In cases of sexual abuse by a parent or stepparent, the child is often old enough to be tested. In such cases testing is important in order to evaluate the psychological effects of the experience and to obtain some indication of the kind of therapeutic aid that would be most helpful.

A different kind of custody conflict arises in cases involving separated or divorced parents. Among the very few cases of this kind that reach the family court psychologist, there are some which are extremely complicated because of the nature of the allegations and the counterallegations. Thus, in one such case not only the parents but also the grandparents on both sides were clinically studied in an effort to arrive at a sound recommendation.

The Future

The future usefulness of family court psychologists (and other mental health personnel) will depend to a substantial extent on the appropriations that the courts will receive for their mental health clinics. Larger appropriations not only will make it possible for the clinics to accept larger caseloads but will also enable them to intensify research activities oriented toward improvement of the clinics' functions.

Research in Forensic Psychology

The social-scientific research of forensic psychologists confronts the many open questions of the "psycholegal system" (Litwack, Note 3). Indeed, the legal system cries out for research into psycholegal issues beyond the concern of most psychologists and psychology graduate programs (Bazelon, 1974). This kind of research is often supported by universities and grants. Let us mention a few such research questions.

1. How valid are insanity determinations? (Perhaps a preliminary question should be, What are the criteria for the validity of an insanity determination?)

2. How accurate are expert predictions of violence, or "dangerousness" —whatever that means—and the like? Can "experts" make these judgments more validly than lay persons? (There is considerable evidence that psychiatrists are *less* accurate predictors of violent behavior than lay persons because of their great tendency to *overpredict* antisocial behavior.) Are there accurate means—actuarial or clinical—for predicting suicidal behavior?

3. What are the minimal acceptable standards of care and treatment that will give civilly committed individuals a reasonable chance of "improving" beyond the supposed need for involuntary hospitalization? (Court judgments regarding the constitutional right to treatment have maintained that if *no* standards exist—i.e., if there are no known means of care and treatment that are likely to significantly improve the condition of seriously disturbed individuals—then the civil commitment of at least nondangerous individuals is per se unconstitutional.)

4. What is the most appropriate form of institutionalization and psychotherapy for criminal offenders?

5. What are the effects of custody dispositions—and custody-awarding procedures—on the children who are the objects of such determinations? For example, what are the psychological consequences of enforced visitation rights? (Anna Freud and Joseph Goldstein have recently suggested that it would be better for the child if the parent taking custody had the sole authority to determine the visitation rights of the child's other parent.)

6. How do psychological factors contribute to the decisional processes of judicial and quasi-judicial personnel (e.g., parole officers)? For example, it is known that different judges vary markedly in the sentences they impose for crimes that appear very similar. Why is this so? How can it be corrected?

Finally, implicit in the above discussion is the fact that forensic psychology does not limit itself to a concern with the *criminal* justice system, but involves the *civil* commitment system and the family court system (which sorely needs increased psychological services). Indeed, significant research involving crisis intervention, family therapy, and the development of new treatment modalities could help meet the special needs of the prison population and the family courts. Finally, forensic psychologists need to be familiar with the role of social scientific evidence throughout the legal system and with the standards for its presentation.

REFERENCE NOTES

1. Shah, S. A. *A behavioral conceptualization of the development of criminal behavior, therapeutic principles, and applications: A report to the President's Commission on Law Enforcement and the Administration of Justice.* Chevy Chase, Md.: Center for Studies of Crime and Delinquency, National Institute of Mental Health, September 1966. (Mimeo)
2. Bjorklund, B., & Brodsky, S. *Employment opportunities in criminal justice and corrections psychology* (Rep. No. 16). Center for Correctional Psychology, University of Alabama, University, Alabama, May 1974. (Mimeo)
3. Litwack, T. R. *Legal and research aspects of the doctorate in forensic psychology.* Paper presented at the meeting of the American Psychology Law Society, San Francisco, June 1974.

REFERENCES

Abrahamson, D. *The psychology of crime.* New York: Columbia University Press, 1967.

Alexander, F., & Staub, H. *The criminal, the judge, and the public* (Rev. ed.). Glencoe, Ill.: Free Press, 1956.

Allport, G. *Becoming.* New Haven, Conn.: Yale University Press, 1955.

American Friends Service Committee. *Struggle for justice.* New York: Hill and Wang, 1971.

Bard, M. Family intervention police teams as a community mental health resource. *Journal of Criminal Law, Criminology, and Police Science,* 1969, *69,* 247–250.

Bard M. *Training police as specialists in family crisis intervention.* Washington, D.C.: U.S. Government Printing Office, 1970.

Barocas, H. A. A technique for training police in crisis intervention. *Psychotherapy: Theory, Research, and Practice,* 1971, *8,* 342–343.

Barrows, S. J. Children's courts in the United States, their origin, development, and results. New York: Abraham Magazine Service Press, 1973. (Originally published, 1904.)

Bassin, A. Taming the wild paraprofessional. *Journal of Drug Issues,* 1973, *3*(3), 333–340.

Bassin, A. Reality therapy at Daytop village. *Journal of Drug Issues,* 1974, *4*(4), 404–413.

Bazelon, D. L. Psychiatrists and the adversary process. *Scientific American,* 1974, *230*(6), 18–23.

Blake, R. R., Mouton, J. S., Barnes, L. B., & Greiner, L. E. Breakthrough in organization development. *Harvard Business Review,* 1964, *42*(6), 133–155.

Bratter, T. E. Advocate, activist, agitator: New roles for drug abuse program administrators. *Journal of Drug Issues,* 1973, *3*(2), 144–154.

Bratter, T. E. Helping affluent families help their acting-out, alienated, drug-abusing adolescent. *Journal of Family Counseling,* 1974, *2*(1) 22–31.

Brecher, E. M. (Ed.). *Licit and illicit drugs.* Boston: Little, Brown, 1972.

Brodsky, S. L. Mental disease and mental ability. In S. L. Brodsky & N. E. Eggleston (Eds.), *The military prison: Theory, practice, and research.* Carbondale, Ill.: Southern Illinois University Press, 1970.

Brodsky, S. L. Prisoners with promise. *Corrections Quarterly,* 1972, *2,* 16–26. (a)

Brodsky, S. L. Psychologists in criminal justice systems: Looking back and looking around. In S. L. Brodsky (Ed.), *Psychologists in the criminal justice system.* Marysville, Ohio: American Association of Correctional Psychologists, 1972. (b)

Brodsky, S. L. Special applications to law enforcement. In S. L. Brodsky (Ed.), *Psychologists in the criminal justice system.* Marysville, Ohio: American Association of Correctional Psychologists, 1972. (c)

Brodsky, S. L. Responsibilities, commitments and roles. In S. L. Brodsky (Ed.), *Psychologists in the criminal justice system.* Marysville, Ohio: American Association of Correctional Psychologists, 1972. (d)

Casriel, D. H., & Bratter, T. E. Methadone maintenance treatment: A questionable procedure. *Journal of Drug Issues,* 1974, *4*(4), 359–380.

Cavanagh, W. E. *Juvenile courts, the child, and the law.* Harmondsworth, England: Penguin Books, 1967. (Originally published, 1959, as *The child and the court.* London: Gollancz.)

Christie, N. Law and medicine: The case against role blurring. *Law and Society Review,* 1971, *5,* 357–366.

Deitch, D. Evolution of treatment roles in more recent responses to addiction problems. *Journal of Drug Issues,* 1971, *1*(2), 132–139.

DeLeon, G. Behavioral science in the therapeutic community: Some old issues revisited. *Journal of Drug Issues,* 1974, *4*(4), 435–442.

Devlin, J. J., & Vamos, P. The addiction worker: A crisis in identity. *The Addiction Therapist,* 1975, *1*(2), 20–24.

Emerson, R. M. *Judging delinquents: Content and process in juvenile court.* Chicago: Aldine, 1969.

Ennis, B., & Litwack, T. R. Psychiatry and the presumption of expertise: Flipping coins in the courtroom. *California Law Review,* 1974, *62,* 693–747.

Faltico, G. J. Planning community-based drug abuse treatment and training: An image and an actuality. *Journal of Drug Issues,* 1973, *3*(2), 155–170.

Fenster, C. A., Litwack, T. R., & Symonds, M. The making of a forensic psychologist: Needs and goals for doctoral training. *Professional Psychology,* 1975, *6,* 457–467.

Fenster, C. A., & Locke, B. The "dumb cop": Myth or reality? An examination of police intelligence. *Journal of Personality Assessment,* 1973, *37,* 276–281. (a)

Fenster, C. A., & Locke, B. Neuroticism among policemen: An examination of police personality. *Journal of Applied Psychology,* 1973, *57,* 358–359. (b)

Fenster, C. A., & Locke, B. Patterns of masculinity–femininity among college and noncollege oriented police officers: An empirical approach. *Journal of Clinical Psychology,* 1973, *29,* 27–28. (c)

Fenster, C. A., & MacNamara, D. E. J. Free will, determinism, and punishment. *Probation and Parole,* 1970, *2,* 36–48.

Glasser, W. *Reality therapy.* New York: Harper & Row, 1965.

Glasser, W. *The identity society.* New York: Harper & Row, 1973.

Goldstein, J., Freud, A., & Solnit, A. J. *Beyond the best interests of the child.* New York: Free Press, 1973.

Gottfredson, D. M. The base expectancy approach. In M. E. Wolfgang, L. Savitz, & N. Johnston (Eds.), *The sociology of punishment and corrections*. New York: Wiley, 1970.

Gottfredson, D. M. Five challenges. In S. L. Brodsky (Ed.), *Psychologists in the criminal justice system*. Marysville, Ohio: American Association of Correctional Psychologists, 1972.

Groeschel, B. J. Social adjustment after residential treatment. In D. Ricks, A. Thomas, & M. Roff (Eds.), *Life history research in psychopathology* (Vol. 3). Minneapolis: University of Minnesota Press, 1974.

Guller, I. B. Higher education and policemen: Attitudinal differences between freshmen and senior police college students. *Journal of Criminal Law, Criminology and Police Science*, 1972, *63*, 396–401.

Halleck, S. *Psychiatry and the dilemma of crime*. New York: Harper & Row, 1967.

James, M., & Jongeward, D. *Born to win*. Reading, Mass.: Addison-Wesley, 1971.

Kaslow, F. *Issues in human services: A sourcebook in supervision and staff development*. San Francisco: Jossey-Bass, 1972.

Kaslow, F. Adaptation of clinical skills to the solution of human relations problems and to team development in business firms. *Proceedings of the 13th Annual Conference for the Advancement of Private Practice*, 1974, p. 47.

Kittrie, N. *The right to be different*. Baltimore, Md.: Johns Hopkins University Press, 1971.

Lemert, E. M. *Social action and legal change: Revolution within the juvenile court*. Chicago: Aldine, 1970.

Lentz, W. P. Delinquency as a stable role. *Social Work*, 1966, *11*, 66–70.

Levitt, M., & Rubenstein, B. (Eds.). *Orthopsychiatry and the law, a symposium*. Detroit, Mich.: Wayne State University Press, 1968.

Litwack, T. R. The role of counsel in civil commitment proceedings: Emergent problems. *California Law Review*, 1974, *62*, 816–839.

MacGregor, D. *The human side of enterprise*. New York: McGraw-Hill, 1960.

Mandel, A. J. The sociology of a multimodality strategy in the treatment of narcotics addicts. *Journal of Psychedelic Drugs*, 1971, *4*, 132–133.

Menninger, K. *The crime of punishment*. New York: Viking, 1968.

Miller, D. K. Social reform and organized psychology. *Journal of Social Issues*, 1972, *28*, 217–231.

Murphy, P. T. *Our kindly parent . . . the state: The juvenile justice system and how it works*. New York: Viking, 1974.

Nietzel, M. T., & Moss, C. S. The psychologist in the criminal justice system. *Professional Psychology*, 1972, *3*, 259–269.

O'Connor v. Donaldson, 45 L. Ed. 2d 396 (U.S. Supreme Court, 1975).

Piven, H., & Alcabes, A. *The crisis of qualified manpower for criminal justice: An analytic assessment with guidelines for new policy*. Washington, D.C.: U.S. Department of Health, Education, and Welfare, 1969.

Reifen, D. *The juvenile court in a changing society: Young delinquents in Israel*. Philadelphia: University of Pennsylvania Press, 1972.

Reiff, R. Psychology and public policy. *Professional Psychology*, 1970, *1*, 315–324.

Rubin, S. *Juvenile delinquency: A rational approach to penal problems* (3rd ed.). Dobbs Ferry, N.Y.: Oceana Publications, 1970.

Sanders, W. B. (Ed.). *Juvenile offenders for a thousand years*. Chapel Hill, N.C.: University of North Carolina Press, 1970.

Schlossberg, H. *Psychologist with a gun*. New York: Coward, McCann & Geoghegan, 1974.

Schlossberg, H. Down at the station house: Police with psychologic training. *Modern Medicine*, February 1975, pp. 84–89.

Schwitzgebel, R. *Street corner research: An experimental approach to the juvenile delinquent*. Cambridge, Mass.: Harvard University Press, 1964.

Silber, D. E. Controversy concerning the criminal justice system and its implications for the role of mental health workers. *American Psychologist*, 1974, *29*, 239–244.

Smith, A. B., & Bassin, A. Application of small group theory to crime and delinquency. *Journal of Social Therapy*, 1961, *7*, 76–85.

Smith, A. B., Bassin, A., & Froelich, A. Change in attitudes and degree of verbal participation in group therapy with adult offenders. *Journal of Consulting Psychology*, 1960, *24*, 247–249.

Smith, A. B., Bassin, A., & Froelich, A. Interaction process and equilibrium in a therapy group of adult offenders. *Journal of Social Psychology*, 1962, *56*, 141–147.

Smith, A. B., & Berlin, L. *Treating the criminal offender*. Dobbs Ferry, N.Y.: Oceana Publications, 1974.

Smith, A. B., Berlin, L., & Bassin, A. Problems in client-centered group therapy with adult offenders. *American Journal of Orthopsychiatry,* 1963, *33,* 551–553.

Smith, A. B., Berlin, L., & Bassin, A. Hostility and silence in client-centered group therapy with adult offenders. *Group Psychotherapy,* 1965, *17,* 191–198.

Smith, A. B., & Locke, B. Authoritarianism in police college and non-police college students. *Journal of Criminal Law, Criminology and Police Science,* 1968, *59,* 440–443.

Smith, A. B., Locke, B., & Fenster, C. A. Authoritarianism in policemen who are college graduates and non-college police. *Journal of Criminal Law, Criminology and Police Science,* 1970, *61,* 313–315.

Smith, A. B., Locke, B., & Walker, W. Authorianism in college and non-college oriented police. *Journal of Criminal Law, Criminology and Police Science,* 1967, *58,* 128–132.

Smith, A. B., & Pollack, H. Crimes without victims. *Saturday Review,* December 1971, pp. 27–29.

Smith, A. B., & Pollack, H. Less, not more: Police, courts, prisons. *Federal Probation,* 1972, *36,* 12–18.

Spece, R. J. Conditioning and other technologies used to "treat?" "rehabilitate?" "demolish?" prisoners and mental patients. *Southern California Law Review,* 1972, *45,* 616–684.

Speilberger, C. D., Megargee, E. I., & Ingram, G. L. Graduate education. In S. L. Brodsky (Ed.), *Psychologists in the criminal justice system.* Marysville, Ohio: American Association of Correctional Psychologists, 1972.

Sullivan, C., Grant, J. D., & Grant, M. Q. The development of interpersonal maturity: Application to delinquency. *Psychiatry,* 1956, *20,* 373–385.

Sutherland, E. H., & Cressey, D. R. *Criminology* (9th ed.). New York: Lippincott, 1974.

Szasz, T. S. *Law, liberty and psychiatry.* New York: Macmillan, 1963.

Szasz, T. S. *Ceremonial chemistry.* Garden City, N.Y.: Anchor Books, 1974.

Task Force on Corrections. *President's Commission on Law Enforcement and Administration of Justice.* Washington, D.C.: U.S. Government Printing Office, 1967.

Tharp, R. G., & Wetzel R. J. *Behavior modification in the natural environment.* New York: Academic Press, 1969.

Twain, D., McGee, R., & Bennett, L. A. Functional areas of psychological activity. In S. L. Brodsky (Ed.), *Psychologists in the criminal justice system.* Marysville, Ohio: American Association of Correctional Psychologists, 1972.

Warren, M. W. The case for differential treatment of delinquents. *Proceedings of the Ninth Annual Research Meeting of the Department of Institutions, Division of Research,* 1969, *2* (2), 18–23.

Werner, S. To maximize the minimum. *Pennsylvania Prison Journal,* 1972, *2,* 50–55.

Ziskin, J. *Coping with psychiatric and psychological testimony* (2nd ed.). Beverly Hills, Calif.: Law and Psychology Press, 1975.

14

Stanley L. Brodsky

Psychology and Criminal Justice

What can psychologists do with problems of crime and delinquency? That question brought 20 psychologists and a sprinkling of lawyers and sociologists to the Mountain Lake Sanctuary in Lake Wales, Florida, in January 1972. A three-day conference was held on the topic of psychology's role and contributions in dealing with problems of crime, delinquency, and corrections.[1]

David Bazelon, Chief Judge of the United States Court of Appeals, addressed the conference. He challenged the functional usefulness of psychologists in corrections, asking if psychologists were doing good for their clients or well for themselves. With this concern very audible, the conferees struggled with the issues of loyalties, ethics, ills of justice agencies, research strategies, graduate education, and applications of professional and scientific psychology to criminal justice.

The conference eventually led to a book called *Psychologists in the Criminal Justice System* (Brodsky, 1973). This chapter, drawn from both the conference and the book, identifies the major issues and directions in psychology and justice.

Historical Note

At a time that emphases on both crime problems and psychology appear to be on the rise, one would expect a pattern of progressive increases in the amount of professional and scientific attention that psychology has directed toward justice settings and populations. However, until very recently, just the opposite seems to have been true. The percentage of psychological publications that concern crime and delinquency between 1927 and 1940 hovered around 2.0%. Percentages in the last decade have hovered around 1.5%, based on examination of crime and delinquency publications in *Psychological Abstracts*. When social science dissertations in law enforcement and corrections from 1938 to 1970 were examined, it was found that about 30% were psychological in nature and were

Stanley L. Brodsky is an Associate Professor in the Department of Psychology, University of Alabama.

An early draft of this chapter was presented at the Annual Congress of Corrections, Pittsburgh, Pennsylvania, in August 1972.

1. The conference was supported by a grant to the American Association of Correctional Psychologists awarded jointly by the National Institute of Mental Health, the Youth Development and Delinquency Prevention Administration, and the Law Enforcement Assistance Administration.

conducted in either psychology or educational psychology departments; 28% were apparently sociological; and 20% were of uncertain disciplinary origin. The remainder were distributed among social work, criminology, public administration, government, and other social or behavioral science disciplines. This finding differed considerably from the widely held belief that most criminological research is conducted by sociologists. Thus, a very small proportion of psychological research and writing is criminological in nature, but a large proportion of criminological writing and research is psychological in nature.

Psychological Centricity

Far too much emphasis exists on *clinical* psychological approaches to criminal justice problems, and, in turn, too much emphasis is placed on narrow psychological perspectives and ideas for psychologists participating in justice work. There are indeed some places and times when the psychologist's disciplinary theories and "handy-dandy" bag of techniques are useful and important. Many more times, however, the need is critical to incorporate wide perspectives beyond the one discipline in dealing with societal problems. A long-standing belief exists that psychologists look at criminality from an intrapsychic sickness model, and the conference examined the extent to which psychologists believe explicitly and operationally in these models of criminal behavior. The consensus was that this belief exits to some extent, but, in terms of where the profession is now and where it is going, this exclusively intrapsychic model is outdated and nonfunctional.

Responsibilities and Commitments

Let us direct our attention to the question, To whom is the psychologist in a justice agency responsible? Is he or she responsible and accountable to the client? To the agency? To society? To the profession? Or to himself or herself? There is a continuum along which one can conceptualize this problem. At one end of the continuum is the system challenger or skeptic and at the other end the system professional.

The system challenger is the kind of individual who challenges the assumptions and operating procedures of specific justice agencies. Such system challengers believe that most new correctional programs simply represent more of the existing inadequate, tired thinking and programming. The introduction of mental health personnel, as seen by these skeptics, simply serves to maintain inappropriate and often harmful agency procedures. The challengers believe that when a professional goes to work within a justice agency, he or she inevitably becomes co-opted by the agency. The person so co-opted can no longer maintain independent professional goals and is forced to adopt the agency objectives in order to survive. One way of surviving while maintaining integrity, according to this view, is to become a system saboteur, that is, to overtly accept the goals of the agency and covertly seek to sabotage and undermine the agency's functions and procedures.

At the other extreme of the continuum are those system professionals who suggest that to implement change and fulfill one's responsibilities within an agency, one first must attain high credibility. These professionals suggest that once they assume major responsibilities within an organization and do a job well, additional responsibilities and influence will result (much more than they might normally seek out on their own). They believe that if the professional works with the agency personnel, asking, "What is it you're trying to do?" and "How is it I can help you?" then he or she will have far more clout than anyone working outside the agency. The ideal combination is someone who would have the credibility and clout of the system professional and the skepticism, the questioning of objectives and goals, and the continuing critical facility of the system challenger.

Police and the Courts

Psychologists in justice agencies have directed too much attention to correctional concerns and settings. Psychologists' involvement with police departments and with courts is also of considerable importance. While the full-time court psychologist is a familiar phenomenon, the full-time police department psychologist is a new and rapidly expanding role. Martin Reiser (1972), and others taking a system professional view, have suggested that the only way for behavioral scientists to have an impact on police department functioning is to work from the inside.

In the psychologists' affiliation with the courts, the expert witness role, once exclusively in the realm of the clinical psychologist, is increasingly becoming a scene where contributions of experimental psychology can be made. Experimental psychologists have replicated situations similar to those in which criminal acts were committed and have studied accuracy of perception, acuity of vision, accuracy of recall, and other material well founded in the experimental method. Similarly, the study of eyewitness fallibility and the selective limitations on recollections are events mediated by both internal and external processes. To paraphrase Robert Levinson (who in turn paraphrased Santayana), "People believe what they see; the problem is they are better at believing than they are at seeing."

New Applications

Many new applications exist for mental health professionals within justice settings. The first priority is programs for the alleviation of acute distress in crime victims. Victims of traumatic or potentially traumatic crime should have free, readily available opportunities for crisis counseling or psychotherapeutic services as a way of alleviating suffering and aftereffects of a criminal act.

A second major recommendation is to make outpatient counseling and psychotherapy readily available for police. Runkel (1970), in his book *The*

Law unto Themselves, presented evidence that some police are especially in need of psychotherapy. Because of the enormous discretionary power that police have, they should be given routine access to services of mental health professionals without the likelihood of censure or of being seen as deviant by their fellow officers. To implement this routine, consultation with mental health professionals should be made mandatory, and mental health services should be accessible, confidential, free, and voluntary. A related question may be raised: What about all of the psychologists, psychiatrists, politicians, and others who also have enormous and potentially harmful impact on individuals' lives? Should they not be given the same routine consultation and extension of services? While that question is important, police have a specific mandate for legitimized violence, and, therefore, are particularly in need of this service and attention.

Another new function for psychologists is the development of cultural/racial tension-reduction programs. Almost every criminal justice agency has racial tension problems among either its clients or personnel. While some programs might be directed toward the immediate relief of the tension or difficulty, ultimately it is far more productive to aim at alleviating the roots of such tension and problems. One new application would be a program in riot prevention. After every prison riot, an investigating committee makes a series of good and thoughtful recommendations on future riot prevention. Out of these recommendations has emerged a body of information on prison and ghetto riot preventions. Looking at these recommendations, organizing them, and developing methodologies and strategies for putting them into effect before riots, rather than after, should be a high priority for psychologists.

Behavioral Sciences and Social Policies: Long-Range Goals

Behavioral scientists have a number of modalities for trying to influence their justice system clientele. Those of us participating in the Lake Wales conference opted for a model of social activism. Far more can be done by trying to influence broad social policies than by working exclusively on a one-to-one basis with clients. Efforts to change the policies that affect people, rather than to change the people themselves, are desirable in terms of long-range productivity and payoffs. These efforts include lobbying, working with legislators, filing class action suits, decriminalizing, and intervening. Wolfgang, Figlio, and Sellin (1972), in a study of Philadelphia youth, found that about 50% of the youths who were arrested once spontaneously desisted from any further criminal activity. The implication for those interested in early intervention programs is that they should avoid intervening at least with those youths likely to spontaneously stop and mature out of criminality problems. One of the dangers of early intervention is creating a state of clinical injustice in which individuals who are professionally touched suffer more punitive consequences than those who do not gain the presumed benefits of mental health services.

A Personal Statement

The emerging interdisciplinary future of psychology in the criminal justice system in encouraging. The breadth necessary to view and understand the processes, the social problems, and the potential solutions calls for gathering together the best knowledge from several disciplines, rather than for simply staying with psychological theories and techniques. And this seems to be happening.

The development of graduate programs in criminal justice psychology has been a related trend. The programs developed in the last few years at the University of Alabama, Florida State University, Hahnemann Medical College, and John Jay College of Criminal Justice all represent positive steps toward identifying a focus for interdisciplinary knowledge and psychological applications.

There has been a history of psychological disillusionment with work in the justice system, a feeling that psychologists have had no impact and have not been appreciated. Viewing this feeling, and the reciprocal feelings in the past by correctional administrators that many psychologists have minimal worth, recalls for me Ambrose Bierce's definition of the ostrich as a very large bird that has neither a hinder toe nor functional wings. The absence of a working pair of wings, however, has never represented a handicap, because the ostrich cannot fly anyway. Psychologists in justice work have been in a very similar situation to Bierce's ostrich, and we are just now at the point of giving flight to the role of the psychologist in criminal justice agencies.

REFERENCES

Brodsky, S. L. *Psychologists in the criminal justice system.* Urbana: University of Illinois Press, 1973.
Reiser, M. *The police department psychologist.* Springfield, Ill.: Charles C Thomas, 1972.
Runkel, P. *The law unto themselves.* Ann Arbor, Mich.: Planaria Press, 1971.
Wolfgang, M. E., Figlio, R. M., & Sellin, T. *Delinquency in a birth cohort.* Chicago: University of Chicago Press, 1972.

Part 4

Engineering, Human Factors, Industrial, Management

15

Erwin S. Stanton

Alternative Career Directions for the Industrial-Organizational Psychologist

In the past several years, many persons completing their professional education have, upon graduation, faced a rather disappointing job market when it came time to seek appropriate employment for their newly acquired skills and abilities. In the opinion of many observers, this difficulty, encountered by many graduates, is not likely to be of a mere transitory nature soon to be replaced by the relative abundance of job opportunities that prevailed during the 1960s and the very early 1970s. Indeed, labor economists and employment specialists foresee an "imbalanced" job market for many professional and scientific graduates, and this imbalance is likely to last for a number of years as the nation moves toward a mature economy. As a result, this situation will no doubt give rise to considerable disillusionment and disappointment on the part of many persons who will have completed years of prolonged and costly education only to find a paucity of suitable job openings awaiting them.

As always, the employment market is likely to vary significantly from profession to profession and occupation to occupation. As virtually everyone knows, university teaching positions are presently in short supply, while employment opportunities for business graduates in such highly specialized and much-in-demand fields as accounting and finance are more numerous. Other variations in employment opportunity will no doubt always prevail, based, for example, on the geographic location, on the prestige of the organization, and on the compensation and benefits offered by potential employers. Since it is anticipated that some graduating industrial-organizational psychologists may not find the job market to be quite as promising as they had hoped or expected, this chapter suggests some alternative career directions that graduates might wish to entertain that would still substantially utilize their training and education.

Traditional Employment Avenues

The customary employment avenues generally pursued by most graduating industrial-organizational psychologists are no doubt well known to the reader. These traditional settings have consisted primarily of the follow-

Erwin S. Stanton is associated with E. S. Stanton & Associates, Inc., and with the Graduate Division, College of Business Administration, St. John's University, New York.

ing: teaching at the college or university level, serving on the staff of a psychological consulting firm, working with a governmental agency, or working in the business and industrial sector—often but not exclusively in a research capacity. It might be useful to assess current and probable future employment prospects in those traditional settings, given the present and foreseeable job market.

Well-informed observers paint a generally disappointing picture of present and future academic opportunities at the college and university level. Some positions will obviously open up as the result of faculty retirement and normal personnel attrition. And openings will probably be more readily available in the less prestigious institutions as well as in the institutions in remote locations. Similarly, with the current emphasis on budgetary limitations in government service, employment opportunities at the governmental level—federal, state, and local—are not anticipated to be overly abundant.

Employment opportunities in the private sector will, of course, be highly subject to the overall state of the nation's economy. Much will depend upon such imponderable factors as economic and business consequences of another oil embargo, dislocations brought about by energy conservation programs, resumption of significant consumer buying, and inflationary pressures. Depending, then, upon how vigorous and robust the economy will be, the best opportunities for the graduating industrial-organizational psychologist may very well be in the private sector—in industry and business as well as with firms of consulting management psychologists. At the same time, however, if the economy should falter—or if the recent recession should resume—it is most unlikely that the job seeker will find this employment market particularly encouraging.

Alternative Career Directions

Counseling psychologists have long stressed to their vocational guidance clients the advisability of considering a variety of career alternatives should their first occupational choice not be readily attainable. The same recommendation might be suggested to the graduating industrial-organizational psychologist. Let us see, then, what alternative career directions might serve as appropriate settings for these graduates.

To this observer, the best possible career alternative to the traditional routes taken by the industrial-organizational psychologist probably lies in the area of personnel administration and human resources development.[1] Indeed, there is a considerable amount of accelerating interest within business and industry in designing and implementing more effective

---

1. The more enterprising and entrepreneurial job seeker might also attempt to establish a behavioral sciences division with one of the broader based firms of general management consultants, few of which have to date employed industrial-organizational psychologists to any great extent. Indeed, this is a relatively untapped area for the industrial-organizational psychology job applicant, although it may take a good deal of personal persuasiveness on the applicant's part to "carve out" an appropriate position in such a setting.

human resources utilization systems, for it is believed that the proper utilization of personnel is the very heart and essence of good business management (Mills, 1975).

A variety of job potentials exist within the range of activities carried out by traditional personnel departments or, as the departments are increasingly being referred to in some organizations, departments of human resources development. Notable among these are positions focusing on personnel staffing (specifically, recruiting, interviewing, and selecting) and its most rapidly growing subspecialization, employee training and management and executive development. Indeed, there appears to be a growing emphasis on the latter area that was not notably reduced, even in the wake of the recent economic recession. In fact, recognizing the rapidity of the change process—technological, social, and political—most well-managed and sophisticated business and industrial organizations appear to be committed to an expanded program of employee training and management development. The direction that these training programs often take includes the following: basic job skills training, training of the economically and educationally disadvantaged, management training programs, supervisory training programs, executive development training, client and customer training, organization development programs, and programs to upgrade the skills of minority and women personnel.

Some readers may voice the objection that they did not spend years of study in a graduate program in industrial-organizational psychology only to work under the title of "employment specialist" or "staff trainer." However, one might readily raise the question whether the industrial-organizational psychology graduate is not basically a human resources development specialist. More importantly, in such alternative settings as suggested would not the graduates basically be using many of the skills and knowledge to which they were exposed in their graduate programs? To extend the analogy somewhat, not every holder of a doctorate degree in history or sociology works as a historian or as a sociologist per se. Many of these graduates may be found in different employment settings—in a government agency or in a nonprofit institution—bearing such functional titles as "administrative specialist" or "intake interviewer." Yet, these individuals are still taking advantage of the professional training and education which they received.

Preparing for Alternative Career Directions

At this point the question might logically arise whether, in order to qualify for positions outside the traditional model, graduate students in industrial-organizational psychology should modify their educational curriculum. The answer would be decidedly in the affirmative. Indeed, if graduating industrial-organizational psychologists are to meet with significant success in securing employment in a company's personnel department or on the staff of a firm of general management consultants—and to make substantial job progress—they should have a solid grounding in basic business fundamentals. Actually, regardless of whether graduates find employment in the more traditional settings or secure positions in one of the alternative areas, a firm preparation in some basic business subjects is highly desirable, if not absolutely indispensable. Indeed, a frequent criticism aimed at industrial-organizational psychologists by many executives and managers in industry is that, while these psychologists may be well grounded in their particular area of specialization, they are often relatively unfamiliar with the basics of business.

If graduating industrial-organizational psychologists are enrolled in a program housed in a business school, they no doubt have already taken an assortment of basic business courses. On the other hand, if their industrial-organizational psychology program is being offered by a psychology department that is part of a graduate school of arts and sciences, they should supplement their educational curriculum with some solid business courses. Recommended courses are general management, principles of accounting, corporate finance, business law, marketing, and the conceptual foundations of business.

Lastly, it seems that it would be an excellent idea for prospective job seekers to do a good deal of reading, thinking, and planning as to the specific strategy and approach they will use in their search to find suitable employment. The reader might think that such a suggestion is surely superfluous, if not downright demeaning. However, it has always been surprising how inadequately prepared many otherwise well-qualified candidates can be in going into an employment interview and what an ineffective job is frequently done by these same individuals in presenting themselves to a prospective employer.

This chapter is obviously not the place to highlight the important and useful "tips for the job seeker." There are, however, many excellent books that can be readily consulted by the job seeker to assist in the mechanics and logistics of searching for a position and, more importantly, in the attainment of an appropriate opportunity. Indeed, on numerous college campuses today—particularly those that recognize the paucity of job offers extended by corporate recruiters in the wake of the recent recession—job clinics and practice interview sessions have been instituted to enhance the student's chances of finding employment.

Perhaps in the future, job opportunities will once again become so abundant that graduating industrial-organizational psychologists will be able—without any unusual difficulty—to select positions that best meet their requirements along the traditional employment models. However, indications are that such a situation is not likely to arise so readily. Therefore, it is hoped that the alternative career directions proposed in this chapter might nevertheless make full use of graduates' training and development and provide them with a high degree of personal job satisfaction and career fulfillment.

REFERENCE

Mills, T. Human resources—Why the new concern? *Harvard Business Review*, March–April 1975, 120–134.

16

Richard A. Kulp

New Directions in Engineering Psychology/Human Factors

Over the last decade several new directions have emerged in the field of engineering psychology, or human factors. There are numerous reasons for this evolution, but the primary ones are the following: (a) aerospace programs, where a substantial number of engineering psychology/human factors personnel worked, started to wane; (b) several technological advances occurred in the areas of the new directions; and (c) the creative engineering psychology/human factors practitioner was motivated to move into other areas by the uncertainty of government contractual work.

I define new directions as areas where an increasing number of engineering psychology/human factors technologists are working in research and development activities. It is these new directions that affect expanded career opportunities for future engineering psychology/human factors graduate students. Career opportunities in the new directions can be broadly categorized into the three areas of teaching, research, and application; however, the following discussion is restricted to the research and application areas, since these represent the greatest number of job opportunities.

Listed below are the new directions that have emerged over the last decade (evidence that these areas are active new directions comes from several sources: *Proceedings* of the Human Factors Society annual meetings from 1970 to 1975; workshops sponsored by the Society of Engineering Psychology from 1973 to 1975; a symposium [Human Factors, Note 1]; and an article by Kraft [1970]):

1. Health/medical care
2. Safety
3. Computer systems
4. Aerospace systems
5. Prosthetics
6. Environmental design
7. Oceanography
8. Architectural design
9. Recreation
10. Urban planning/problems

Richard A. Kulp is currently associated with the American Telephone & Telegraph Company, as Manager of the Training Research and Development Group, Basking Ridge, N.J.

11. Systems design (personnel subsystems design)
12. Work design/job design
13. Training
14. Communication
15. Consumer products
16. Maintenance
17. Transportation
18. Manufacturing and quality control
19. Biomechanics, work physiology
20. Handicapped
21. Legal/law enforcement
22. Gerontology
23. Welfare

The list of new directions may not be exhaustive, but it does represent the majority of new applications that have been reported in the literature. Obviously there is a certain amount of overlap among the 23 areas, and, therefore, they can be logically grouped into the following nine major categories (note that some areas are not aggregated with others but stand alone, for example, training, manufacturing, quality control, and consumer products). Klemmer, Parsons, McRuer, and Sheridan (1971) previously performed a similar interesting exercise and came up with eight categories, seven of which are identical to the ones listed below):

1. Environments: architectural design, oceanography, recreation, and urban planning/problems
2. Human operator dynamics: handicapped, prosthetics, and biomechanics, work physiology
3. Computer systems: communication
4. Systems design: maintenance, work design/job design
5. Health/medical care: safety, gerontology, welfare
6. Transportation: aerospace systems
7. Training
8. Manufacturing and quality control
9. Consumer products

Because of space constraints, only six of these new directions are discussed in detail. Coverage of these areas provides the reader with an overview of the activities engaged in by engineering psychologists and human factors technologists working in these areas. Detailed information on the areas not covered can be found in the *Proceedings* of the annual meetings of the Human Factors Society for the years 1972 and 1973.

Environments

Environmental issues are becoming important because of the increasing number of environmental factors we interface with on a daily basis, such as noise, pollution, vibration, overcrowding, and toxic agents. The engineering psychology/human factors technologist has been actively working in this area for several years, but lately the amount of activity has increased. For example, APA has recently formalized a task force ("APA Task Force Established," 1973) to investigate the burgeoning area of human–environment research and its application. Additionally, the Human Factors Society, because of substantial interest and activity in this area, has recently formed a Technical Interest Group on Environmental Design.

In studying human–environment relationships the engineering psychology/human factors technologist is basically concerned with the variety of ways in which the environment affects human behavior (Heimstra & McFarling, 1974; refer also to the *Proceedings* of the 1972 and 1973 annual meetings of the Human Factors Society), that is, how environmental factors impact perception, motor performance, motivation, crime, absenteeism, accident/errors, aesthetics, recreation, and values. The research and development activities of environmental design are occurring in three major areas. These three major categories and their subareas are as follows:

1. Special environments: oceanography, air/space, and underground
2. Stress environments: pollution/toxic agents, noise, vibration, heat/cold, radiation
3. Environmental planning: urban planning, architectural planning, overcrowding, personal space

With increasing concern over present-day changes in the quality of human life, and consequently with an increasing concern over the various relationships between the physical environment and human behavior, this area will continue to offer excellent career opportunities for future engineering psychology/human factors specialists.

Computer Systems

The past two decades have seen tremendous advances in computer systems, but those anticipated during the next 5 to 10 years should prove even more significant. As Madnick (1973) indicated, new developments can be divided into three categories: technological cost/performance breakthroughs in computer manufacturing, evolution of computer system architecture (both hardware and software), and major steps toward meeting user requirements and capabilities.

Advances in the first two categories will result in decreased hardware costs and increased flexibility, which will accelerate the use of computers for an extensive variety of applications, for example, the credit card economy, automated libraries, public information exchange systems, automated medical diagnosis, legal/law enforcement systems, traffic control systems, education (computer-assisted instruction), and language translators.

The engineering psychology/human factors technologist working in the computer systems area is concerned with meeting users' requirements and dealing with human capabilities and limitations. Specifically, the following are his or her primary areas of focus:

1. Design of input and output devices (Seibel, 1972)
2. Personnel subsystem design (Kulp, Note 2)
3. Human–logic interfaces (Grace, 1970; Schwartz, 1972)
4. Training considerations (Hunter, Kastner, Rubin, & Seidel, 1975): computer-assisted instruction and computer-managed instruction
5. Human operator characteristics

Each of the references noted above provides the detailed activities, problems, and concerns of engineering psychology/human factors personnel in the research, design, development, implementation, and operation of computer systems.

Within the next decade, we are going to see a substantial increase in communication and information revolutions. Taken together these trends mean that more people than ever before will have more information of the sort they want. Out of this will come automated medical diagnosis, the credit card economy, and several other applications that have been mentioned previously. With all of the future types of computer applications, as well as conventional applications, numerous career opportunities will open up for future engineering psychology/human factors technologists.

Systems Design

Goode and Machol (1957) described the emergence of "systems engineering" as resulting from the numerous failures of large-scale systems, where the components of the systems did not work when they were joined together. The technology of systems engineering over the last two decades has evolved into a total systems or integrated systems orientation, which utilizes a team development approach.

Some of the critical disciplines involved in the integrated systems approach are computer sciences, operations, research, engineering, and engineering psychology/human factors. The term used to describe engineering psychology/human factors activities in systems design is "personnel subsystems design."

In an integrated systems development approach, the personnel subsystems developers and the hardware–software developers work as a team, operating in parallel to develop their respective parts of the system. Throughout the total development, they interface on various design issues, and trade-offs are constantly being made. The trade-offs are typically made on the basis of the capabilities and limitations of the various subsystems. Important trade-offs are also made, however, on the basis of meeting system objectives and reducing operational costs.

The major activities involved in the personnel subsystems design process are as follows: system definition and requirements specification, function allocation, task analysis, preliminary estimates of personnel and training requirements, human–machine interface analyses and specifications (including design for maintainability), work module definition and documentation, training design and documentation, job design, testing and evaluation, system implementation and operation. Several excellent references provide more detail on the personnel subsystem design activities (De Greene, 1970; Gagne et al., 1963; Kirk, 1973; Kulp, Note 2).

The involvement of the engineering psychology/human factors technologist in the integrated systems development approach results in several operational and cost benefits. For example, human performance is improved, training costs are reduced, wo/manpower utilization is improved, and user acceptance is increased.

Because of the almost universal acceptance of the integrated systems approach, it is critically necessary for future engineering psychology/human factors technologists to have a firm foundation in this technology. Having this background will greatly expand one's career opportunities in several application areas.

Transportation

The demand for improved transportation, emphasized by the increasing environmental constraints and the oil crisis, has created challenging research and development activities. To answer a variety of engineering psychology/human factors questions related to transportation, several governmental agencies and industrial organizations are providing increasing support for research and development activities in this field.

There are several forms of transportation, some old and some new, for which engineering psychology/human factors considerations are necessary. Specifically, these forms of transportation are aircraft (hover, helicopter, subsonic, supersonic, etc.); automobiles and other motor vehicles, including an evolutionary highway vehicle; trains (subways, rapid transit systems); and ships and boats.

The basic objective of the engineering psychology/human factors specialist working on the various transportation vehicles is that of designing for efficiency, safety, and comfort. In research, design, development, and implementation activities, one is concerned with vehicle limitations (e.g., acceleration), access requirements, seating, operator requirements, storage, accessories, and operator–environment interface.

In addition to the design of safe, efficient, and comfortable forms of transportation, the engineering psychology/human factors specialist is involved in two other important transportation issues:

1. Patterns and needs: number and distribution of travelers, transportation information systems, evaluation of alternative forms of transportation
2. Transportation interface facilities: terminals, highways, and airfields

Construction of the Bay Area Rapid Transit (BART) System in the San Francisco area and the new rapid transit system in Washington, D.C., and the introduction of Metrolines in the Northeast are some examples of the new era of expanded transportation by train. Continued advances in this area and other forms of transportation will offer innovative and challenging career opportunities for engineering psychology/human factors technologists.

Training

Training is an area that has enjoyed a lengthy and active history, starting after the turn of the century in industrial and military settings. The engineering psychology/human factors technologist shares this area with another group referred to as instructional technologists, who receive their education in industrial technology/industrial systems programs.

Application of training technology is one of the areas that offers the greatest number of career opportunities for future engineering psychology/human factors technologists. It has been estimated that currently within the United States over 100,000 individuals are actively involved in training. The size of this discipline is attested to by the number of professional training organizations, for example, the National Society for Performance and Instruction (NSPI), the American Society of Training Directors (ASTD), the Society for Applied Learning Technology (SALT), the National Security Industrial Association (NSIA), the National Society of Sales Training Executives (NSSTE), and the Technical Interest Group on Training of the Human Factors Society.

Activities in training can be broadly categorized into three classes: research, training development, and training administration. Most of the engineering psychology/human factors technologist's efforts are concentrated in research and training development activities. The research activities cover the basic–applied continuum, for example, media research; transfer of training studies; research on mix of formal training and on-the-job training; studies investigating the effects of level of motivation, feedback, simulators, and fidelity of simulation.

Training development, also called instructional systems development, is a process that has been continually refined over time. However, most trainers would agree with the following sequence of development activities (Tracy, 1971): identifying training needs; performing job study/task analysis; developing training objectives and criterion items; selecting strategy, media, and mode of instruction; developing training material; evaluating and revising tests.

In summary, the instructional systems training area is quite active and will continue to be so in the future. It offers excellent career opportunities and is a challenging area for future engineering psychology/human factors technologists.

Consumer Products

In our everyday life, we are all consumers of products, from the alarm clock in the morning to the vehicles we use for transportation to eating utensils to bed at night. The great variety of consumer products we interface with can be categorized into the following major areas: transportation, heavy equipment, hand tools, business equipment, household appliances, household furnishings, recreational equipment, and medical equipment. With this vast array of products, the engineering psychology/human factors specialist has an excellent opportunity for work in the area of consumer product design. Specifically, the major concerns of the engineering psychology/human factors specialist in product design are (a) safety, (b) ease of use, (c) efficiency of use, and (d) use with minimal training. In addition to these design considerations, the engineering psychology/ human factors technologist is involved in determining consumer requirements, product reliability, product maintainability, and product advertising.

As the public attitude about consumer products becomes more sophisticated, this area will be an increasingly fertile application for the engineering psychology/human factors technologist. As Woodson (1972) indicated, the consumer products area is a "sleeping giant" with exciting and challenging opportunities. One indication of growth in this area is the fact that the Human Factors Society has recently formed a specialization subgroup on consumer products. Additionally, the Human Factors Society dedicated its 1973 annual meeting to the consumer factor. The *Proceedings* of this meeting provides an excellent overview of some of the activities involved in consumer product research and design.

Summary

It is clear that several new directions in engineering psychology/human factors have emerged over the last decade, and it is these areas that will offer exciting and challenging opportunities for future engineering psychology/human factors technologists.

Two significant points are in order in completing the new directions story: (a) engineering psychology/human factors graduate programs and (b) degree-level requirements. Pew and Small (1973) reported that there are currently 55 graduate programs offering engineering psychology/human factors education. Within these 55 graduate programs, Kulp (Note 3) reported that several new directions are being covered in courses, theses, and dissertations. With regard to the degree-level requirement, it is important to note that the greatest hiring preference for industrial, consulting, and governmental organizations is for engineering psychology/human factors specialists at the master's degree level (Kraft, 1970). In fact, Kraft found that the master's level was preferred to the PhD level by almost a two-to-one margin (approximately 58% to 30%). Summarizing these last two important points, then, there are a large number of graduate programs with fairly broad coverage of the new directions discussed previously, which will adequately prepare individuals for excellent careers in engineering psychology/human factors. Also, job opportunities seem to be as good or better for individuals at the master's level as they are for individuals at the doctoral level.

REFERENCE NOTES

1. *Human factors 1979–1980.* Symposium presented by the Human Factors Society and the University of Southern California Institute of Aerospace Safety and Management, Los Angeles, California, May 1970.
2. Kulp, R. A. *Designing telecommunication systems for effective utilization of human resources: Integrated systems development approach.* Paper presented at the Seventh International Symposium on Human Factors in Telecommunications, Montreal, Canada, September 1974.
3. Kulp, R. A. *New directions in engineering psychology: Implications for graduate training.* Paper presented at the annual meeting of the American Psychological Association, Chicago, September 1975.

REFERENCES

APA task force established to probe man–environment issues. *APA Monitor,* November 1973, p. 4.

De Greene, K. B. (Ed.). *Systems psychology.* New York: McGraw-Hill, 1970.

Gagne, R. M., et al. *Psychological principles in systems development.* New York: Holt, Rinehart & Winston, 1963.

Goode, H. H., & Machol, R. E. *Systems engineering: An introduction to the design of large-scale systems.* New York: McGraw-Hill, 1957.

Grace, G. L. Preface to special issue on human factors in information processing systems. *Human Factors,* 1970, *12,* 161–164.

Heimstra, N. W., & McFarling, L. H. *Environmental psychology.* Monterey, Calif.: Brooks/ Cole, 1974.

Hunter, B., Kastner, C. S., Rubin, M. L., & Seidel, R. *Learning alternatives in education: Where student and computer meet.* Englewood Cliffs, N.J.: Educational Technology Publications, 1975.

Kirk, F. G. *Total system development for information systems.* New York: Wiley, 1973.

Klemmer, E. T., Parsons, H. M., McRuer, D. T., & Sheridan, T. B. Technical interest groups within Human Factors Society. *Human Factors Bulletin,* April 1971, pp. 3–5.

Kraft, J. A. Status of human factors and biotechnology in 1968–1969. *Human Factors,* 1970, *12,* 113–151.

Madnick, S. E. Recent technical advances in computer industry and their future impact. *Sloan Management Review,* Spring 1973, pp. 67–84.

Pew, R. W., & Small, A. M. *Directory of graduate programs in human factors* (2nd ed.). Santa Monica, Calif.: Human Factors Society, 1973.

Schwartz, B. K. The man–logic interaction in information processing system. *Proceedings of the Sixteenth Annual Meeting of the Human Factors Society,* 1972, 391–394.

Seibel, R. Data entry devices and procedures. In H. P. Van Cott & R. G. Kinkade (Eds.), *Human engineering guide to equipment design* (Rev. ed.). Washington, D.C.: American Psychological Association, 1972.

Tracy, W. R. *Designing training and developing systems.* New York: American Management Association, 1971.

Woodson, W. E. Opportunity or oblivion. *Proceedings of the Sixteenth Annual Meeting of the Human Factors Society,* 1972, 1–3.

17

William F. Fox

Future Directions in Engineering Psychology: Business Information Systems

Although the topic to be discussed here is formally listed as business information systems, I believe that my remarks will have relevance for information systems in any setting. Further, while I recognize that there are several types of information systems, for example, purely manual (microfilm or microfiche) and computer based, I will be addressing only computer-based systems. Among the varieties of computer-based systems, the present discussion excludes applications such as process control, special purpose computer applications (e.g., minicomputers), and one-time applications (e.g., large defense systems).

Computer-Based Information Systems

An information system is a combination of software, hardware, people, and procedures assigned to receive, store, manipulate, summarize, and present data to a given organization. Once started, computer-based information systems are often critical to the ongoing existence of the sponsoring organization since they are completely embedded in day-to-day operations. Some have even begun to call such systems "operations" or "procedural" systems, reflecting their operational nature.

A look at the future of information systems must begin with a look at trends in computer technology. Over the next 10 years, hardware costs will decline significantly. Computer memory will be cheaper, larger in capacity, and more durable. This is likely to accelerate the trend to the use of "intelligent" or "smart" terminals such as point-of-sale devices now appearing in retail stores. The salesperson and the terminal will together be capable of forming a small information subsystem with infrequent need to communicate with the remainder of the system. Cheaper core also makes the household computer a viable concept, but it probably would not be for ordering the groceries or doing tax returns. Most likely it will serve a continuing, economically beneficial role such as controlling energy consumption by processing data from sensors on outside temperature, room occupancy, and traffic, and by responding by turning the heat up or down,

William F. Fox is Head of the Personnel Subsystems Department of Bell Laboratories, Piscataway, New Jersey.

or the lighting on or off. Other uses will depend on how much is left over from its main responsibility. There is little expectation of useful break-throughs in software or language development. Realists in the computer field expect instead that the same languages will be used, but programs will be developed more efficiently.

Most startling is the expected all-pervasive presence of data-processing systems 10 years hence. Whereas there were less than 100 medium-to-large computer systems 20 years ago, there are around 100,000 such sys-tems today and there will be nearly 400,000 in 10 years. A soon-to-be-published computer industry forecast predicts a *thousandfold* increase in stored information. By 1985, 75% of the United States work force will be involved with computers in their jobs, and another 20% will require some knowledge of computers to perform their jobs instead of the 25% and 10%, respectively, estimated for today. The United States expenditures on data-processing research and development will be around $2 billion.

It is my considered opinion that the field of data processing, specifically information systems, has the greatest need and offers the greatest chal-lenge for engineering psychology of any field since the early efforts on defense-related systems that began around 1940. But are we up to it? Can we adapt? Have we adapted?

Humans and Computers

Information systems are different. They are especially different from the systems engineering psychologists have been concerned with in the past. Information systems are generally under static, rather than dynamic, con-trol; no one "flys" them. Worse still, it is usually impossible to know the state of the system at any point in time. Even when a system is dying, those in charge usually know it only intuitively. The consequences of a dead information system are trivial when compared with loss of life resulting from the failure of an aircraft system, for example, but information system failure or death still results in a real loss, usually expressed in dollars.

The nature of human performance in information systems and the things that affect it are different also, at least in degree (Fox, 1974). Figure 1 is an attempt to place the role a system plays in shaping job-relevant behavior in context with all of the other factors impinging on that be-havior. Especially in civilian settings, organizational and personal vari-ables probably contribute nearly as much to job-relevant behavior as do system variables. Human performance in such a setting is a function of organizational goals and outcomes mediated not only by system design parameters but by organizational and personal factors as well. In fact, many variables are beyond the control of the system developer.

As Grace (1970) pointed out, the fundamental nature of humans' in-volvement in computer-based systems is markedly different from that in the traditional systems on which engineering psychologists have focused their attention. In noncomputer hardware systems, persons directly con-trol the operation of the hardware and provide the logic that guides that operation. Person and machine form a complete unit. This relationship has

Figure 17-1. Conceptual model of the variables affecting job-relevant behavior.

produced the emphasis on person–machine interface, both informational and manipulative. In contrast, computer hardware is incomplete without its own logic in the form of programs. The human involvement in a computer-based system consists of causing the hardware to operate through its attendant software. Thus human logic interfaces with program logic changing the nature of the interaction and the concerns of engineering psychologists. R. W. Bailey (Note 1) of Bell Laboratories has shown that at the character level of analysis over 100 times more errors are produced in *preparing* data for entry than at the actual data entry point (i.e., the person–machine interface). Our current working hypothesis about the relative importance of the several factors affecting human performance in civilian systems is shown in Figure 2. The relative weights of the factors have been derived from observations made in numerous simulations and several field studies. Although this representation must be viewed only as a working hypothesis, it is immediately apparent that the traditional areas of interest account for only a small portion of the total variance in human performance.

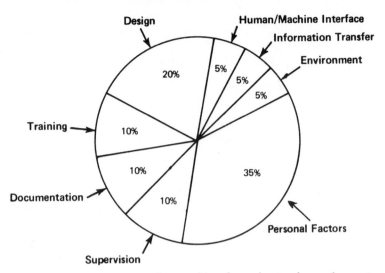

Figure 17-2. Representation of a working hypothesis about the variance accounted for by variables affecting job-relevant behavior.

Problems and Progress with Computers

One of the earliest attempts at describing the uniqueness of computer-based systems is a seminal article entitled "Man–Computer Symbiosis" (Licklider, 1960). In discussing the unique and complementary integration of person and computer, Licklider recognized several problem areas that would require investigation and development if the potential of human–computer integration is to be realized. Among these are logical data-base design or "memory organization" for problem solving, language, and input and output equipment.

Nine years later Shackel (1969) pointed out that roughly 70% of existing computer installations could be considered suboptimal, and either barely cost effective or not cost effective. Among others, he identified problem solving, language, and communication at the hardware and the software interfaces as key problem areas. Parsons (1970), a year later, also listed language, data entry and display, and procedures development (which I interpret to be similar to problem solving) as key problem areas. Thirteen years after the publication of the Licklider (1960) paper, Peace and Easterby (1973) pointed to the lack of progress in the human–computer field over the preceding decade. They attributed the lack of progress to two principal causes: first, a lack of understanding (among engineering psychologists and human factors people) of the basic nature of human–computer relationships, that is, the people–logic–machine relationship described by Grace (1970) and earlier by Licklider; and second, a tendency to view humans only as another system component with consequent failure to devote sufficient attention to the psychological aspects of human involvement in computer-based systems. Things are not very different today, over 15 years after Licklider's paper.

The picture is not completely dark, however. There has been a modicum of progress. Gould (1968) published a comprehensive review of the factors and parameters associated with the design of cathode ray tube (CRT) displays for terminal devices. Gould's review contained sufficent information for the design of terminal devices for nearly all general purpose applications. The Institute of Electrical and Electronics Engineers and the Society for Information Display through their journals have provided large amounts of data on the physical design of keyboards for general purpose use. Indeed, we recently conducted an evaluation of several CRT terminal devices from different suppliers against 58 human engineering criteria and failed to identify a single glaring or debilitating violation of good human engineering design practice. As one might expect, there has been a rather direct transfer of data from more traditional systems to the person–machine physical interface in computer-based systems.

Perhaps the most innovative development has been the initiation of fundamental work on human communication during problem solving by Chapanis (1971, 1973) and his colleagues (Chapanis & Overbey, 1974). This work begins with the premise that communication in computer-based systems often requires thought patterns and processes that are unfamiliar and even unnatural for most persons. An understanding of communication between humans in controlled problem-solving situations may then lead to an understanding of the most appropriate design approaches for communication requirements in future computer-based systems. It is creative and elegant work that goes directly to the differences between computer-based and traditional human–machine systems. Among the results of this work are the following: Communication via typewriter takes twice as long as face to face; 12 times as many messages were exchanged in face-to-face situations than when a typewriter was used; there were 6 times as many words in face-to-face messages than when a typewriter was used; an error rate of one per three to four words was found in typewritten messages; and problem-solving time did not vary as a function of typing skill.

To turn to other basic issues, one might ask, "Is there an audience for such research and technology outside of the engineering psychology community?" Several authors within the field have pointed out the problems and opportunities for engineering psychology in computer-based systems technology. Perhaps these are only self-serving commentaries; perhaps not.

Application of Computers

A brief examination of the data-processing industry literature shows clearly that there is a great concern with human involvement in computer-based systems. For example, Kling (1973) in the *Proceedings of the ACM* (Association for Computing Machinery) urged a person-centered computer technology in contrast to the present state of affairs in which the user is most often seen simply as a person who needs minimal response times. Some of the issues raised by Kling are in the province of engineering psychology and some are not. Among those that are probably not are the maxims that systems should increase personal competency and pride, that users can initiate or veto system design, and, to a lesser degree, that jobs be designed to be personally satisfying. Issues that are *squarely* in the domain of engineering psychology are tolerance for error, procedures designed to fit job needs, functional burdens placed on software/hardware, and clear communication of the design and its underlying assumptions. Lykos, Morgan, and Weingarten (1973) in the *Proceedings of the Association for Computing Machinery*, described a new section in the National Science Foundation Office of Computing Activities that has as one of its concerns improved interface systems using existing technology and focusing special attention on semitechnical or nontechnical users. Finally, projections within the data-processing industry show "user needs" as one of the three or four most important problems to be faced over the next 10 years. Alas, persons in the data-processing business are largely unaware of our discipline and its potential contribution to solving their problems (perhaps the lack of awareness is because much of our contribution *is still potential*).

Should we and can we rise to meet the challenge? The answer to the first part of the question is a resounding yes. If current projections are anywhere near accurate, in 10 years virtually every working person in the United States will be touched in his or her job by computers in some way. The very existence and stability of society will depend on the operation of computer-based systems. The answer to the second part of the question is also yes, but perhaps there is little reason for optimism that this is an accurate answer. Meister (1973), in a recent paper looking back over many years of military systems development, concluded that basic (or what Garner, 1972, preferred to call general) research has contributed little to problem solution in military human–machine systems. Whether this will be true in civilian computer-based systems is uncertain.

Future Directions

If we are to meet the challenge, I believe that the following broad directions are in order. First, we must become more interested and involved in design and development activities. The 1973 profile of doctoral scientists and engineers in the United States published by the National Academy of Sciences (Commission on Human Resources, 1974) shows that of the 24,365 1930–1972 doctorates in psychology *only* seven-tenths of one percent (.7%), or 170, are engaged in design and development as a primary work activity. This may be contrasted to the 14.6%, or 5,020, for engineering PhDs and even 2.3%, or 251, for nonscience PhDs. In fact, psychology exceeds only social science (history, sociology, anthropology, etc.) PhDs (129) in the number engaged primarily in design and development.

Second, we must begin to make better use of the storehouse of knowledge available to us. Data from the National Research Council show that approximately $7 billion has been spent on behavioral and social science research over the past decade. Indeed, Edward Walker (1970) asserted that there is as much or more real knowledge in the behavioral and social sciences than in the physical sciences. What is different is the effort expended in putting that knowledge to work.

Military systems are often characterized as exotic in terms of environment and demands on human performance, and this is cited as the barrier to using the results of general laboratory research in their design. Most computer-based information systems operate and will continue to operate in a normal environment and demand performance well within the repertoire of normal behavior. This fact alone significantly increases our opportunity to use the knowledge we have. Manley (Note 2), for example, reported the very effective use of the verbal learning, short-term memory, and information-processing literature to establish human-performance-based principles of code construction for use in computer-based information systems.

Finally, but not least important, we must direct our research efforts toward the important issues concerning human involvement in computer-based systems. These issues generally relate to the so-called "end user" rather than programmers and console operators. There are two classes of problems to be attacked: general research concerned with the fundamental parameters of system-relevant behavior and specific research leading to technological advances. In the first class are the behavioral effects of variation in system response time, the human problem-solving characteristics important for logical data-base design, the trade-offs among variables found to affect the use of codes, and the response tendencies that produce error in human performance. Among the items in the second class are documentation modes, training requirements, analysis and modes of training, methods for system diagnosis and evaluation, and methods for establishing end-user needs.

End-User Training

Virtually every list of problems facing the data-processing industry includes end-user reaction to system response time. Unfortunately, precious little is known about this behavior. The published literature is either anecdotal (Miller, Note 3) or deals with subjective reactions (Williams, Note 4). Little is known about the effects of variations in response time on performance. If response time is important it raises new and intriguing questions about time perception. What are the basic parameters of response time? What are the threshold values for noticeable change in mean response time or the consistency of response time? What is the role of expectancies in relation to response time and how do they develop? What is the effect of response time on errors and user efficiency?

Very little is known about behavioral characteristics that might affect logical data-base design. Studies done with the ingenuity and openness of Chapanis' (1971, 1973; Chapanis & Overbey, 1974) work on communication would be invaluable in beginning to understand this area.

Even though it is possible to construct principles of code design from present knowledge, the relationship among the principles is unknown. Examining the literature leads immediately to the conclusion that short codes are less error prone than long codes, that meaningful codes are better than those without meaning, and that grouped codes are less error prone than ungrouped codes. There is little guidance, however, with regard to the interactions of these principles, for example, whether a larger meaningful code is better than a shorter code without meaning.

When errors do occur are they random or predictable? Do they have a consistent direction? If they do, they can likely be not only directed by program logic but also corrected. R. W. Bailey (Note 1) of Bell Laboratories has recently shown that over 70% of transcription errors could be prevented by elimination of only 11 of the 36 characters in the alphanumeric set. If meaningfulness is important, what happens when the 11 are removed?

In the realm of specific technological advances, documentation appears on nearly every list of problems confronting the data-processing industry. If we are to impact this area we must first deal with the chaos in our own house. About a year ago we counted over 30 different documentation methods developed in the last 25 years. All had been compared with "conventional" documentation and found to be superior. However, we can find no published reports of cross-comparisons among the different "superior" methods. Worse still, there is no underlying set of agreed-to principles for guiding documentation design.

End-user training is also often cited as a key problem, and yet we still cannot say for sure when whole-task learning is superior to part-task learning. There are many anecdotal reports on individual differences in the ability to learn under computer-aided instruction but little systematic research to show whether this is factual or not.

What are the criteria of system success from a human viewpoint? How are they to be measured and what do they mean? And finally, how do we ascertain user needs, for sure? I believe that a future direction of engineering psychology can be the study of the dimensions of human involvement in computer-based information systems. I also believe that it is clear that it *should* be.

REFERENCE NOTES

1. Bailey, R. W. *Human error in computer-based data processing systems.* Unpublished manuscript, 1973. (Available from Bell Laboratories, Piscataway, N.J. 08854.)
2. Manley, C. W. *Research and methodological considerations for human coding behavior.* Paper presented at the 81st annual meeting of the American Psychological Association, Montreal, Canada, August 1973.
3. Miller, R. B. *Response time in man–computer conversational transaction* (IBM Technical Report TR00, 1660-1). Poughkeepsie, N.Y.: IBM, 1968.
4. Williams, C. M. *System response time: A study of users' tolerance* (IBM Technical Report 17–272). Yorktown Heights, N.Y.: IBM, 1973.

REFERENCES

Chapanis, A. Prelude to 2001: Explorations in human communication. *American Psychologist*, 1971, *26*, 949–961.

Chapanis, A. The communication of factual information through various channels. *Information Storage and Retrieval*, 1973, *9*, 215–231.

Chapanis, A., & Overbey, Ç. Studies in interactive communication: III. Effects of similar and dissimilar communication channels and two interchange options on team problem solving. *Perceptual & Motor Skills*, 1974, *38*, 343–374.

Commission on Human Resources. *Doctoral scientists and engineers in the United States 1973 profile.* Washington, D.C.: National Academy of Sciences, 1974.

Fox, W. F. An overview of the factors affecting human performance in telecommunication systems. *Proceedings of the Seventh International Symposium on Human Factors in Telecommunications*, 1974, Session XII.

Garner, W. R. The acquisition and application of knowledge: A symbiotic relation. *American Psychologist*, 1972, *27*, 941–946.

Gould, J. D. Visual factors in the design of computer-controlled CRT displays. *Human Factors*, 1968, *10*, 359–376.

Grace, G. L. Preface to special issue on human factors in information processing systems. *Human Factors*, 1970, *12*, 161–164.

Kling, R. Towards a person-centered computer technology. *Proceedings of the Association for Computing Machinery*, 1973, 387–391.

Licklider, J. C. R. Man–computer symbiosis. *Institute of Radio Engineers Transactions on Human Factors in Electronics*, 1960, *1*, 4–10.

Lykos, P. G., Morgan, M. G., & Weingarten, F. W. Computer impact on society. *Proceedings of the Association for Computing Machinery*, 1973, 374–380.

Meister, D. The future of ergonomics as a system discipline. *Ergonomics*, 1973, *16*, 167–280.

Parsons, H. M. The scope of human factors in computer-based data processing systems. *Human Factors*, 1970, *12*, 165–175.

Peace, D. M. S., & Easterby, R. S. The evaluation of user interaction with computer-based management information systems. *Human Factors*, 1973, *15*(2), 163–177.

Shackel, B. Man–computer interaction: The contribution of the human sciences. *Ergonomics*, 1969, *12*, 485–499.

Walker, E. T. Relevant psychology is a snark. *American Psychologist*, 1970, *25*, 456–463.

18

H. McIlvaine Parsons

Psychology for Engineering and Technology

We live in a world of technology. Proper though it may be to denounce its excesses, technology shapes our lives just as surely as earth and air, sun and rain sustain them. What would life be today without the printed word? Without the electric light? Without the telephone? Indeed, without automobiles and aircraft, machine tools and energy production, radar and computers? Without the complex structures and systems that characterize our times?

But technological innovations typically outrun the capacities of people to use them to their full advantage, much less to get all the enjoyment they might out of them. As a result, in recent decades some psychologists have become concerned with the physical world that people design and build for people. This chapter describes those psychologists.

Language and Technology

If printing was the first great technological development in the last 1,000 years, it should not be surprising that after experimental psychology began to accelerate in the twentieth century some psychologists sought, through the scientific method, to improve the printed word for its readers. Early research was summarized in *How to Make Type Readable* (Paterson & Tinker, 1940; see also Tinker, 1963). Research in legibility and readability of prose continues today. Other written language, required by new technology, includes highway signs, license plates, equipment instructions, computer programs, and symbols on cathode ray tubes in radar-based air traffic control systems; psychologists study all of these. The time lag between technological innovation and its psychological examination has dropped from about 500 years to only a few.

How should a display of language elements be designed so users can understand them? What is the best way to combine such elements to put the message across? To answer such questions, psychologists conduct empirical research or generalize from current knowledge about how human beings process such inputs. They also consider how individuals differ and how they can be trained to improve their processing.

H. McIlvaine Parsons is the Executive Director of the Institute for Behavioral Research, Inc., Silver Spring, Maryland, and President (1975–1976) of the Society of Engineering Psychologists, Division 21 of the American Psychological Association.

We find out indirectly about the world external to ourselves not only through the printed word but also through all kinds of visual signals, symbols, and patterns that some device presents to our view. Human beings have to process information from aircraft altimeters, radar blips, and reconnaissance photographs. Often such inputs have to be categorized and coded. How well can human beings comprehend such transformations? To find out, psychologists study discrimination and memory either with the particular device or with inputs abstracted from such devices. Although in the latter instance psychological research resembles experimental psychology in general, such inquiry arises from the technological world and should be applicable to it.

Since language enters our brains through our ears as well as our eyes, the telephone understandably also gave rise to psychological investigation. The Bell Telephone Laboratories were among the earliest employers of psychologists interested in adapting the design of new technology to its users, and remain one of the largest. Again, the investigation of technological problems embraces both specific devices and more general questions, such as auditory discrimination and memory. Psychologists study how noise affects reception of speech or other sounds and how it impairs other kinds of human performance. Noise exists in the "natural" world but its investigation has resulted largely from its impact within the technological world.

Human Performance

In much of human performance, a person's output—his or her motor activity—and its relation to input are of prime importance in the design of new technology or improvement of the old. A simple example is telephone dialing or key pressing. How should the mechanism be designed? Perhaps the most familiar instance of complex psychomotor performance is driving an automobile. The first laboratory to investigate how this new technology affects performance, and vice versa, was opened in 1928 (Lauer, 1960), and research and application have mushroomed in more recent years (Forbes, 1972). Psychologists involved in engineering and technology have tackled problems of making vehicles and highways safer through design and have examined driving skills, driver education, driver selection, and effects of alcohol, age, and other factors on driving performance.

Steering a car is "tracking" the highway. Tracking, which is involved in nonautomatic control of all vehicles, including aircraft, has been extensively studied by psychologists (a) to improve particular tracking devices and related displays, (b) to get information about tracking performance in general, and (c) to investigate the effects of such variables as stress, practice, fatigue, and motivation on human performance.

During and after World War II tremendous technological developments occurred in vehicles such as aircraft and submarines. Because of the demands these imposed on information processing and psychomotor skills, psychology for engineering and technology received substantial support within the military establishment. The new vehicles, in turn, led to new technology for detecting and identifying them, notably radar and sonar, which further fostered the growth of this new field of psychology. As vehicles and surveillance technology proliferated in both the military and civilian domains, team-operated control centers were developed to coordinate vehicular operations. Air traffic control is an outstanding example. These new centers, their networks, and the vehicles themselves and their supporting equipment became known as "systems." Unmanned intercontinental missile systems and manned space flight systems were additional vehicle-control center complexes that psychologists, through both specific research and advice to the design engineers, tried to make as effective as possible. More generalizable research accompanied the growth of the field, which recently has been shifting its preponderant involvement to civilian from military technology.

Because space vehicles, high-altitude aircraft, and undersea habitats operate in environments hostile or unnatural to human beings, psychologists have investigated how such factors as diminished and increased acceleration (gravity), reduced and increased atmospheric pressure, and other environmental stresses affected the performance of the operators, while medical researchers and psychophysiologists examined biological effects. Thus, specialists were able to indicate how immediate environments should be designed to maintain effective performance and physical well-being. Through simulation, effects of confinement and various work–rest schedules were also studied. More recently, psychologists of the same type have directed their attention to less exotic settings, asking how business offices, residences, and other constructed environments affect the people who use them.

New Directions

This field of psychology has grown and will continue to grow out of new technology. The course it takes depends partly on the course new technology takes, especially new technology that directly affects the performance of its immediate users. These include those who maintain as well as those who operate equipment. Indeed, problems of maintenance extend into all technological innovations, greatly expanding the need for psychological research and practice. Automated equipment and systems still need human maintenance, often of a highly sophisticated variety. Although increasing automation would seem to eliminate psychological consideration of people, mechanization rarely eliminates human operators completely. Instead, it gives some of them different tasks. Psychologists study how these new tasks, such as monitoring and dealing with emergencies, should be associated with automaticity, and they can advise how far to automate in view of the effects on the individual as well as the system.

In addition to what new technology inspires, this field of psychology still has a long way to go in both specific and generalized research to supply the answers for present technology. One must also ask whether it will limit itself to the study of what has been called human performance or how liberally this term may be interpreted. In the past, human performance has largely referred to work activities. But new technology creates or supports other activities, such as leisure-time play and recreation, social and sexual activities, and such basic functions as sleep and exercise. In addition, both old and new technology generates not only actions but feelings, some of which have been studied as stress effects, discomfort, inconvenience, and annoyance. It is becoming increasingly important to examine what satisfies or dissatisfies users of technology and what increases or diminishes their enjoyment of it, regardless of its effects on their performance. Motivational variables involving technological innovations also offer new opportunities for research and application.

In the light of these considerations, it seems reasonable to predict expansion of this field of psychology in urban transportation (which motivational variables should be studied to help determine whether people will ride a bus or drive a car) and in environmental design (where feelings and nonwork activities are significant). The field's emphasis on human information processing should lead to greater involvement in computer data processing (where what the computer does should be compared with what the person does and where improvements can be made in computer terminals, computer languages, and programming). Possibly the field will extend into such major human information systems as daily newspapers, weekly magazines, and radio and television broadcasting. It may widen its participation in crime prevention and health delivery programs, which need its help, and in industrial plants, where it has already begun to benefit quality control. This field of psychology has hardly touched on water and air pollution, perhaps because these seems so unrelated to individual human performance. It will have little impact on most consumer product design until consumers are more concerned about product effectiveness than sales appeal. However, it will be involved in consumer product safety and accident prevention in general (e.g., in nuclear power plants).

In its generalizable research on human behavior, this field of psychology will have to consider future systems, environments, and equipment so that research undertaken today will yield results applicable many years from now. Thus, those who are now in psychology for engineering and technology not only must regard it as an outcome of past, current, and new technology but also must continually project technology's future. We can assume that human nature will continue to constrain what technology can do, just as technology will continue to influence what people do; and we can conclude that the study of human behavior in a technological context not only is here to stay but will interest more and more psychologists and potential psychologists as they become aware of its challenges and opportunities.

Identification of the Field

We have said technology has produced a growing and exciting field of psychology concerned with equipment, systems, and environments, and with human behavior in such a context. It is a hybrid field of great variety. No label or simple definition pleases all of the people in it. Its very strength lies in its pluralism and opportunities for growth and diversification. We shall try to identify it further by specifying (a) who the people in it are, (b) what they do, (c) where they are, (d) how they are trained, (e) their substantive interest areas, (f) their techniques, (g) how the field can be distinguished from other disciplinary areas, inside and outside psychology, and (h) some of the field's significant characteristics.

Who

Some years ago, Grether (1968) estimated there might be as many as 2,000 American psychologists engaged in the field this chapter describes. It seems reasonable to assume that the number has grown since then, though not at the same explosive rate as from 1950 to 1960. Any estimate depends on the boundaries one places on the field. Grether's estimate can be approximated by combining an estimate of the total number of persons in the larger, interdisciplinary field of human factors (extrapolated from the membership of the Human Factors Society) with the proportion of that membership consisting of psychologists and by adding psychologists in closely related areas of psychology but not in the human factors domain. Although it would be misleading to suggest that psychologists in their field constitute more than a small fraction of American psychologists, they include two of the few psychologists who are members of the National Academy of Sciences.

Similar psychologists can be found in Canada, Scandinavia, England, Germany, France, and other industrialized countries including the Soviet Union and Japan, where they are held perhaps in higher regard than in the United States. They will be found also in developing nations as these adopt new technology, since psychologists must emphasize the human part of the human–machine combination and forestall the introduction of machines inappropriate to the new users.

What

These scientists engage in teaching, research, and application. Their research tries to derive new knowledge about people that is applicable to them as users of technology. Such knowledge ranges from the highly specific to the generalizable, from reactions to the design of a particular dial to responses to signals in noise broadly indicating human detection capacities and limitations. It is difficult to distinguish between applied and basic research in this field. Psychologists in industry are willing to tackle limited situations to solve a design problem. Those in academia prefer more general knowledge.

Some psychologists in this field conduct research not so much on people as on human–machine combinations and even on systems or subsystems. They compare systems or evaluate their performance under various workloads and circumstances. Psychologists ought to take part in this demanding and complex research as long as there are humans operating the equipment or human participants in the system. Although psychologists can contribute their research skills and make certain the human elements are suitably considered in research design, many believe it is improper to label as "psychology" those investigations where the system itself is the focus of inquiry. On the other hand, some make reference to "system psychology" —perhaps on the basis of an operational definition that psychology is what psychologists do.

Research in this field often examines human tasks and human–machine interactions *within* a system. It asks how well—how quickly, how completely, how accurately—a human being performs in a given context of inputs, environmental effects, required outputs, and feedback. Either the displays that provide the inputs, the constraining environment, and the controls that mediate the outputs take into account the users' level of capability or they can be designed to do so. Other research within a system may investigate procedures associated with performance, techniques for improving capabilities through training, individual differences in executing skilled tasks, and what a person feels about a task or how his or her performance affects what he or she feels.

Since such research occurs in system contexts, those psychologists who conduct it can be called "system psychologists" even if they do not focus on the system as a whole. Psychologists often do the same kind of research with equipment or environments outside of a system context. In either situation, the more a particular piece of equipment or a special environment dominates the task, the more the performance is jointly attributable to both human and machine and the less it can be described as purely human performance, especially if the criterion measure reflects what the total entity does rather than just what the person does. It is often uncertain when to call something human performance and when to call it joint performance. Some kind of equipment and some physical environment always figure in technology-oriented research (and in most experimental psychology). The more the equipment and the environment are specialized, the less generalizable are the results. In seeking general knowledge about human performance, psychologists try to conduct research in a context that seems as broadly representative as possible.

In their applicational work, technology-oriented psychologists work with system/equipment/environment developers and designers and specify who the users are, how well these users can operate proposed equipment or function in proposed environments, what procedures they can master, how they might be trained, or what skills are required of them. But psychologists can go further. They can actually propose a design thought to be best for the user, specify the environment, formulate a preferred procedure, develop a training program, or set forth personnel requirements. In fact, psychologists often perform these activities and do them well, but then they are psychologists who are also developers/designers and what they are doing does not fall precisely under the heading "psychology." When psychologists describe all the human performance required in a system, as they often do, they are practicing psychology. When they become managers of system development or make decisions about what machines should do and what people should do (as happens too rarely), they function on a broader base. This field offers opportunities to practice both psychology and design or management.

Where

Technology-oriented psychologists can be found in various settings: (a) government laboratories and agencies, (b) not-for-profit institutions, (c) consulting firms, (d) industry, and (e) universities. The university occupational locations are the same as those where this kind of psychology is taught (see "Training" section). Some specific locations in the other four categories are indicated below for illustrative purposes, and not as a comprehensive listing. These data are derived from the larger field of human factors, in which psychologists constitute a majority.

GOVERNMENT LABORATORIES AND AGENCIES

Drug Enforcement Administration
National Highway Traffic Safety Administration
National Bureau of Standards
U.S. Postal Service
Office of Naval Research
Army Research Institute of the Behavioral and Social Sciences
Army Human Engineering Laboratory
National Aeronautics and Space Administration
Naval Personnel Research and Development Center
Naval Training Equipment Center
Department of Transportation Systems Center
Air Force Aerospace Medical Research Laboratory
Air Force Human Resources Laboratory
Federal Aviation Administration
National Institute for Occupational Safety and Health
Law Enforcement Assistance Administration
National Oceanic and Atmospheric Administration
Smithsonian Institution

NOT-FOR-PROFIT INSTITUTIONS

Human Resources Research Organization
American Institutes for Research
MITRE Corp.
Institute for Behavioral Research
Stanford Research Institute
Institute for Defense Analyses

CONSULTING FIRMS

Anacapa Sciences
Applied Science Associates
BioTechnology Inc.

Dunlap and Associates
Essex Corp.
Lawrence Johnson and Associates
Bolt, Beranek and Newman
Applied Psychological Services
Life Sciences
Century Research Corp.
Human Factors Research
Human Sciences Research
Rowland and Co.

INDUSTRY

Bell Telephone Laboratories
Boeing Co.
Honeywell Inc.
Hughes Aircraft Co.
International Business Machines Corp.
McDonnell Douglas Corp.
Rockwell International
General Motors Corp.
American Telephone and Telegraph Co.
System Development Corp.
Litton Industries
Lockheed Missiles and Space Co.
Northrop Corp.
TRW Systems
Martin Marietta Corp.

Training

Information about locations where technology-oriented psychology is taught has also been drawn from the human factors field. In most of these locations the curriculum is cross-disciplinary, as human factors is. Although in recent years there has been a trend to place such programs in engineering departments, many are still in psychology departments.

The following universities in the United States have graduate programs in engineering psychology or human factors, as listed in Pew and Small (1973):

University of Alabama in Huntsville
University of Arizona
Arizona State University
Auburn University
University of California, Berkeley
University of California, Los Angeles
California State University, Long Beach
California State University, Los Angeles
California State University, Northridge
Carnegie-Mellon University
Catholic University of America
University of Florida

Georgia Institute of Technology
Harvard School of Public Health
University of Houston
University of Illinois at Urbana-Champaign
University of Iowa
Johns Hopkins University
Kansas State University
University of Maryland
University of Massachusetts
Massachusetts Institute of Technology
University of Miami
University of Michigan
Montana State University
U.S. Naval Postgraduate School
Newark College of Engineering
New Mexico State University
New York University
State University of New York at Buffalo
North Carolina State University
Northwestern University
Ohio State University
University of Oklahoma
Oklahoma State University
Pennsylvania State University
Purdue University
Rensselaer Polytechnic Institute
University of South Dakota
University of Southern California
Stevens Institute of Technology
University of Texas at Arlington
Texas A&M University
Texas Tech University
Tufts University
Virginia Polytechnic Institute and State University
Wayne State University
West Virginia University
University of Wisconsin

Whether to provide cross-disciplinary human factors training or training only in psychology has been a topic of considerable discussion. Aspiring psychologists can enter either type of program, including programs in engineering schools. It has been argued that schooling in "human performance" will best fit a psychologist to engage in psychology. Conversely, it has been urged that anyone entering the field of human factors, psychologist or engineer, should be trained more broadly so he or she (a) can be involved in system design or management as well as psychological research and application and (b) can understand the language and viewpoints of all the disciplines involved. In either case it seems essential to master the methods of psychological science.

Wherever psychologists in this field do graduate work, and whether they finish with a master's or a doctoral degree, they must expect to continue with training on the job. As in other fields of psychology, one learns by doing.

Interest Areas

As already indicated, most interest in the field of psychology for engineering and technology has been directed toward research in human performance—capabilities and limitations in information processing and psychomotor skills—and the guidance this can provide for equipment/system/environment design. Such design has often been called "human engineering." But the field has also involved the assessment of subjective reactions, development of procedures, research in techniques of training, skills analysis (and individual differences), and methodological aspects of research and performance evaluation. Headings of those articles[1] prepared for the *International Encyclopedia of Neurology, Psychiatry, Psychoanalysis, and Psychology* (Wolman, in press) that pertain to this field of psychology are listed below to illustrate the gamut of interests in both research and application:

Accident prevention and safety
Aircraft and aviation
Auditory communication
Comfort and convenience
Controls and control devices
Decision making
Displays
Engineering psychology
Environmental design
Environmental effects
Equipment and tool design
Error and reliability
Fatigue and motor performance
Group tasks
Health care delivery
Highway transportation
Hijacking
Human factors
Illumination and glare
Information and quality control
Inspection and quality control
Job analysis
Knowledge of results and feedback
Law enforcement
Legibility

---

1. Most of the encyclopedia articles were prepared by invitation of the section editors for applied psychology, others by editors for psychomotor learning and performance, sensation and perception, and applied social psychology.

Lie detection
Maintenance: design, procedures,
    and aids
Human–computer interaction
Human–machine systems
Methodology in motor skill
    learning and performance
Military psychology
Monitoring and vigilance
Personnel and management
    training and development
Personnel selection and placement
Personnel testing
Postal operations
Radar
Reaction time and choice
Readability
Recreation and sports
Short-term memory
Signal detection
Simulation
Sonar
Space missions
Systems theory and analysis
Tasks and task taxonomies
Techniques of training
Tracking behavior
Training for skills and knowledge
Transfer of training
Translating and interpreting
Undersea habitats
Urban transportation
Work environments and
    habitability
Work–rest cycles and fatigue

In addition to the above, major headings in chapters about "engineering psychology" in the *Annual Review of Psychology* (Alluisi & Morgan, 1976; Chapanis, 1963; Fitts, 1958; Melton & Briggs, 1960; Poulton, 1966) and in Howell and Goldstein (1971), McCormick (1976), and Van Cott and Kinkade (1972) reveal interests in this field. These can be further surveyed by inspecting the contents of the journals *Human Factors* and *Ergonomics* (and to some extent the *Journal of Applied Psychology* and *Organizational Behavior and Human Performance*) and the proceedings of annual meetings of the Human Factors Society and the Ergonomics Research Society and congresses of the International Ergonomics Association. This field enjoys a fare as rich as any in psychology.

For descriptions of this field as "engineering psychology" (and historical insights), the reader should consult Fitts (1951, 1963), Taylor (1957, 1963), Christensen (1971), Grether (1968), and Chapanis (in press), and for descriptions of human factors, Kraft (1970) and Chapanis (1971). Hunt, Howell, and Roscoe (1972) have discussed graduate education.

Techniques

The field of psychology for engineering and technology is essentially empirical and behavioral. It tends to abjure theory and hypothetical constructs and emphasize what can be observed and measured, though its information-processing conceptualization does include decision making and memory, and when it deals with feelings it speaks of comfort and convenience. Its principal research technique is experimentation, which includes experiments with multiple variables that have multiple states. It also makes use of systematic observation and correlational methods including multiple regression analysis. Factor analysis is less favored. Although the field relies essentially on objective measurement, it exploits self-report and observers' accounts for exploratory research, as in the exposition of critical incidents. In analysis, it systematically asks who does what, and its task descriptions are based on an input–output feedback model. It fully exploits simulation, both iconic (mock-up) and symbolic (computerized). In short, its techniques are quantitative and rigorous, as those of a science should be.

Other Fields

The other areas of psychology to which this field is related are primarily experimental and industrial. At times this field has been called applied experimental psychology because it grew out of experimental psychology. It overlaps that field's subdivisions of psychomotor performance, psychophysics, vision, audition, perception, and memory. It shares with industrial psychology interests in training techniques, job design, and personnel requirements. It has an emerging affinity with operant conditioning (behavior modification); they complement each other, one dealing with human performance, the other with motivational variables. Because of its emphasis on relationships between people and the contrived physical world rather than between people and people, it has had little association with social psychology—though it should have more. It has even less with clinical psychology.

This field of psychology is so closely related to engineering that it has been widely labeled engineering psychology. It has been particularly close to aeronautical engineering and electrical and electronic engineering, though it also shares interests with industrial and mechanical engineering as well as illumination and acoustical engineering. Its connections with civil engineering are more tenuous; highways have users but dams and other major civil engineering projects do not. In industry, engineering psychologists typically work in engineering departments. Engineers need psychologists to represent the users of what they design and make sure their designs fit what the users can do.

But engineers are not the only producers of modern technology. Architects design environments. Planners develop transportation systems. Programmers create the software for computers. Training specialists conduct training programs. Psychologists in the field we have been describing must work with these disciplines too. Other specialists with whom they interact include physiologists and medical researchers, physical anthropologists, and applied mathematicians in operations research.

We have already alluded to the multidisciplinary field of human factors, which across the Atlantic is called ergonomics and in which psychology is the largest component discipline. Human factors encompasses other fields mentioned above. It deals with human–machine–environment combinations and systems as entities in their own right whose design and performance are proper objects of research and application, though the contributions of the machine and its user can be assessed separately by engineer and psychologist, respectively. Like the psychology within it, human factors is concerned with human limitations and design (human engineering), procedures, training, personnel requirements, and test and evaluation. Since so much psychological research is conducted under the label "human factors," such research cannot be identified solely as "psychology," though it should be realized that psychology is what it is. Nor is it possible to restrict the label "human factors" to applicational work. Though because of its multidisciplinary nature and equipment/system/environment orientation human factors includes more of this work than does psychology, much research is conducted as human factors research. This chapter limits itself to saying how the various terms are used in fact; it is not our purpose to share in the debate as to how they ought to be used.

Characteristics

Psychology for engineering and technology enjoys a great diversity. Its pluralistic nature leads to disagreement within it about its definition and objectives. It includes divergent approaches to the relationships between people and the products of technology they use. The dominant approach is to adapt the product to the user through a design based on research into human performance (and feelings). Another is to adapt users to the product by training or selecting them. Systematic studies of trade-offs between these approaches are desirable, and more psychologists are needed who are competent or interested in both.

The field's diversity is shown in its involvement in both research and application and in the variety of other disciplines with which it interacts. The field has relevance to real-world problems, which either are the direct origin of its research and applications or serve as a purpose toward which research is oriented. The field also has utility. It seeks to make technology function better and, we hope, enhance benefits to its users. It is youthful, although its origins antedate World War II. Emphasis on nonmilitary systems, environments, and equipment is growing. Although it has concentrated on the world of work outside industry, it is extending itself into industrial operations and nonwork activities. It resides not just in universities but in other research and application milieus.

Among the subdisciplines of psychology, this one is relatively obscure. It encompasses only a small proportion of psychologists. Many psychologists know little about it, and the rest of the world less. But those in it are enthusiastic. They think what they do meets high standards of quality. Theirs is the field of psychology that relates modern technology to human behavior, and that is why it is called psychology for engineering and technology.

REFERENCES

Alluisi, E. A., & Morgan, B. B., Jr. Engineering psychology and human performance. *Annual Review of Psychology*, 1976, *27*, in press.

Chapanis, A. Engineering psychology. *Annual Review of Psychology*, 1963, *14*, 285–318.

Chapanis, A. Human factors in systems engineering. In K. B. De Greene (Ed.), *Systems psychology*. New York: McGraw-Hill, 1971.

Chapanis, A. Engineering psychology. In B. B. Wolman (Ed.), *International encyclopedia of neurology, psychiatry, psychoanalysis, and psychology*. New York: Van Nostrand Reinhold, 1976, in press.

Christensen, J. M. The emerging role of engineering psychology. In W. C. Howell & I. L. Goldstein (Eds.), *Engineering psychology. Current perspectives in research*. New York: Appleton-Century-Crofts, 1971.

Fitts, P. M. Engineering psychology and equipment design. In S. S. Stevens (Ed.), *Handbook of experimental psychology*. New York: Wiley, 1951.

Fitts, P. M. Engineering psychology. *Annual Review of Psychology*, 1958, *9*, 267–294.

Fitts, P. M. Engineering psychology. In S. Koch (Ed.), *Psychology: A study of a science* (Vol. 5). *The process areas, the person, and some applied fields: Their place in psychology and in science*. New York: McGraw-Hill, 1963.

Forbes, T. W. (Ed.). *Human factors in highway traffic safety research*. New York: Wiley-Interscience, 1972.

Grether, W. F. Engineering psychology in the United States. *American Psychologist*, 1968, *23*, 743–751.

Howell, W. C., & Goldstein, I. L. (Eds.). *Engineering psychology. Current perspectives in research*. New York: Appleton-Century-Crofts, 1971.

Hunt, D. P., Howell, W. C., & Roscoe, S. N. Educational programs for engineering psychologists: That depends a good deal on where you want to get to. *Human Factors*, 1972, *14*, 77–87.

Kraft, J. A. Status of human factors and biotechnology in 1968–1969. *Human Factors*, 1970, *12*, 113–151.

Lauer, A. R. *The psychology of driving. Factors of traffic enforcement*. Springfield, Ill.: Charles C Thomas, 1960.

McCormick, E. J. *Human factors in engineering and design*. New York: McGraw-Hill, 1976.

Melton, A. W., & Briggs, G. E. Engineering psychology. *Annual Review of Psychology*, 1960, *11*, 71–98.

Paterson, D. G., & Tinker, M. A. *How to make type readable*. New York: Harpers, 1940.

Pew, R. W., & Small, A. M. (Eds.). *Directory of graduate programs in human factors* (2nd ed.). Santa Monica, Calif.: Human Factors Society, 1973.

Poulton, E. C. Engineering psychology. *Annual Review of Psychology*, 1966, *17*, 177–200.

Taylor, F. V. Psychology and the design of machines. *American Psychologist*, 1957, *12*, 249–258.

Taylor, F. V. Human engineering and psychology. In S. Koch (Ed.), *Psychology: A study of a science* (Vol. 5). *The process areas, the person, and some applied fields: Their place in psychology and in science*. New York: McGraw-Hill, 1963.

Tinker, M. A. *Legibility of print*. Ames: Iowa State University Press, 1963.

Van Cott, H. P., & Kinkade, R. G. *Human engineering guide to equipment design* (Rev. ed.). Washington, D.C.: U.S. Government Printing Office, 1972.

Wolman, B. B. (Ed.). *International encyclopedia of neurology, psychiatry, psychoanalysis, and psychology*. New York: Van Nostrand Reinhold, 1976, in press.

Part 5
Ecology, Environment, Population

19

Bernard M. Bass and Ruth Bass

Concern for the Environment: Implications for Industrial and Organizational Psychology

Humanity, in its migrations, has been searching for an optimum environment for a million years. We often stopped for periods of time, first as hunters who designed increasingly effective spears and bows and succeeded in wiping out the animal supplies in one area after another; then as pastoralists who domesticated the goat and sheep, only to have them nibble away the seedlings of forests; then as agriculturalists whose slash-and-burn techniques leached out the soil until it became infertile; and now as industrialists whose application of power and machinery have polluted the air, water, and land, again threatening our extinction. Population pressures, war, and persecution have added much to our movement and have often sped up the process of waste and destruction of the natural resources available.

Our effectiveness in designing tools to exploit each current environment has also accelerated. We have refused to take into account in the production equation the real cost of waste and irreplaceable depletion. The hydraulic mining that yielded millions of dollars in gold could leave the river banks a billion-dollar wasteland for long centuries afterward. Health hazards associated with production have crippled and killed. Our mental health has suffered from anxieties, insecurities, the neurosis-generating schedules of payoff, and monotonous machine-paced work.

In the same way, we have failed to take into account the *positive* value to production and to the world of work of maintaining and enhancing the environment for its influence on attracting and retaining personnel. We must consider the social and geographical surroundings when thinking about the location of a new plant. It is easier to attract professionals to work in Monterey, California, than in Pierre, South Dakota. Similarly, it is easier to hire secretarial help for work in an office in an attractive central-city location convenient to shopping and transportation than in an office in a dingy factory district. In just three years, from 1969 to 1971, as many as 50 major firms moved their offices out of New York City ('Fun City,' 1971), and the rate of leaving accelerated in the following years.

Bernard M. Bass is at the Graduate School of Management, University of Rochester; Ruth Bass is in Rochester, New York.

This article is reprinted with permission from the *American Psychologist*, 1976, 31, 158–166.

In some instances, however, we have learned to give recognition to environmental surroundings when seeking new plant sites. The flight of the white population to the suburbs coincided with the development of the suburban industrial park: Workers now can live closer to plant sites, city congestion can be avoided, and suburban land and taxes are less expensive.

During the sweatshop era, improving pay, security, and working conditions was paramount in improving worker motivation and morale. Similarly, during the Great Depression of the 1930s and the recession of the mid-1970s, pay and employment security became central in importance to many. But as more satisfactory levels of pay, security, and working conditions were reached, behavioral scientists began to ignore these topics in favor of the workers' search for recognition and achievement. The behavioral scientists were "acting out" Maslow's (1954) hierarchy of needs. Given worker satisfaction with the basic economic and physiological needs, the scientists' concern was focused on the workers' higher-level ego strivings. As possible limits on world economic growth appear, such concern will become increasingly important because nonmaterial rewards for work will have to be substituted for material incentives (Bass, in press). Nevertheless, it may be that workers will be looking for more than recognition and achievement at the work place. If it takes commuting 1½ hours each way to work to achieve and gain recognition, some workers, probably a minority, will decide to forgo some of the higher-level needs to be able to walk around the corner to work. A full life may be more important than a completed career of achievement.[1]

Occupational Level and Work Satisfaction

Again, many sectors of the work force—the unskilled, temporary workers, and many women workers in particular—never were as impressed with ego involvement and self-actualization at work as our middle-class social scientists felt they ought to be. These workers expressed their feelings by their migrations, by the kinds of places in which they were willing to work, and by the strong need to be close to opportunities to hunt and fish or to have a few acres of land for part-time farming. Clear evidence exists that only at higher occupational levels are intrinsic job components (opportunities for self-expression, interest in the work) more valued. At lower levels, extrinsic factors (pay, security, good co-workers) may be more important. A cross-sectional sample by Centers and Bugental (1966), who interviewed 692 workers, was one of several studies supporting this proposition. Hulin and Blood (1968) concluded from a review of survey studies of satisfaction and level of job that whether a worker is seeking job challenge depends on the degree to which he or she accepts middle-class work norms and believes in the value of hard work (Blood & Hulin, 1967).

---

1. Bennis (1970) saw a shift in interest valuing independence to valuing interdependence, a shift from the endurance of stress to a capacity for joy, and a shift from full employment to full lives.

We sense that workers with rising affluence at lower skill levels are attaching an increasing importance to recreation and avocational opportunities. Kendall (1963) uncovered such an avocational factor among those who are satisfied with life in general but not with their work. Hulin (1969) noted an avocational orientation associated with attractive community characteristics. That is, people with high satisfaction with life in general but low satisfaction with their jobs in general tend to live in a community with few older people and few people in poor health, a community with a reasonable cost of living, a community with relatively little urban growth and little unemployment. At the same time we should not ignore the potential influence of the existing occupational structure in a community on the character of that community.

Occupational Structure and the Environment

A community made up mainly of day laborers with minimal education is obviously likely to be much different from a community in which a large percentage of the heads of households are professionals with advanced degrees. The occupational–educational structure is likely to affect satisfaction with the environment just as the environment is likely to have effects on the occupational structure.

The relationship between environment and occupational structure was revealed by Thorndike (1939) in a study involving the quality of 310 cities in the United States. The general goodness of life within each of the 310 cities was indexed by a composite of various mortality rates; per capita public expenditures for education, libraries, and museums; wages and poverty figures; value of public compared to private property; and per capita ownership of autos, telephones, radios, gas, and electric installations. Estimated per capita private income in each city was strongly associated with goodness of life, but occupational patterns accounted considerably for city quality after ruling out the effect of income. Partialing income, goodness of life correlated with the per capita number of dentists (.55), designers (.51), artists (.44), engineers (.41), musicians (.37), architects (.33), lawyers (.13), physicians (.05), clergymen (−.33), and illiterates (−.45).

As environmental quality becomes increasingly important in our postindustrial society, the need for accomplishment is being augmented by a concern for good living. Self-actualization may be achieved by some only if it includes enjoyment of a satisfying environment.

Ecology and Psychology

Ecology is the complement of psychology. Both study the interaction of people and their environment. Psychology concentrates on how we adapt and respond to our environment. Ecology concentrates on how our environment adapts and responds to us.

At the interface of ecology and psychology is the environment, which altered by our work in turn affects our work. For instance, our achievement of a highly industrialized society has led to increasing concentrations of carbon monoxide in the urban atmosphere (Russell, 1970). We have increased the amount of carbon monoxide in our blood through cigarette smoking, motor vehicle exhaust, industrial sources, and home heating and cooking (Goldsmith & Landow, 1968). And the main effect—even at low concentration levels—seems to be the impairment of complex psychomotor performance, although simpler performance remains unaffected. Increased motor vehicle accidents may partially be a specific outgrowth of this impairment (Ury, 1968).

A Systems Viewpoint

The work place and the working organization can be seen as open systems with permeable boundaries. According to the systems theory, the environment outside a work place influences what happens inside it. Employee safety and absenteeism reinforce the systems theory of the impact of outside happenings on inside occurrences, as shown by the greater numbers of accidents that occur while driving to work than on the job and by the higher absenteeism associated with the hunting season than with illness.

In a study of 161 men from various communities, Kendall (1963) found higher absenteeism in workers from slum communities, that is, areas characterized by a high nonwhite population or by much in-migration and consequent crowding ($r=.39$). Rapid change in environment rather than simple urbanization or population density stimulated absenteeism ($r=.33$ and .30, respectively), and sound housing and higher median income lowered absenteeism ($r=-.36$).

Increasing Interest in Environmental Quality

Concern for the environment and psychological research in the area are not new. For example, psychologists have made and continue to make contributions to our understanding of the impact of noise and the potability of water. But, as environmental quality becomes a "scarce commodity," more attention is paid to it, although often the attention is misdirected. Environmental degradation has curtailed recreational activities at a time when more leisure opportunities are desired. Yet some communities are seeking a total pattern of living and working that includes beautiful, harmonious, and attractive surroundings. Some factories are now designed with reference to the landscape. But sometimes sums are spent (or rather misspent) on the creation of architecturally handsome offices with interior designs that may even contribute to a loss of efficiency. (If workers must keep their desk tops clean and uncluttered at all times, it may become more difficult for them to complete assignments expeditiously.) Also, open, landscaped offices, although attractive to the eye, may mean a loss of privacy and considerable distraction to those who must work in them.

Willingness to Spend on the Environment

In 1969, surveys found 75% of the public willing to pay increased taxes to further conservation. Over 70% of those surveyed were willing to add an additional 25¢ or more per month to their utility bills to finance environmental cleanup (Kimball, 1970). And 63% of the surveyed families with incomes under $5,000 a year were willing to pay higher taxes for pollution control. Such public support continues despite pressures for relaxation of conservation efforts as a consequence of the energy crisis and the downturn in the business cycle. In 1975, 77% of a national sample expressed willingness to reduce their own consumption in the interests of conservation and a healthier economy (Harris, 1975).

Among management groups from various countries, Americans seem more ready to spend on the environment. In a simulated budgeting problem, entitled Exercise Objectives, managers were asked to make a series of budgeting decisions as part of a middle-management training effort. One concern was whether to spend $125,000 to prevent polluting a stream or to risk a $25,000 fine. When 3,385 managers from 12 countries (Bass & Eldridge, 1973) were surveyed on this question, 64.8% of those from the United States opted to spend the $125,000. Managers from other countries concurred as follows: Switzerland, 61.3%; Denmark, 49.1%; Italy, 48.4%; Netherlands, 45.7%; West Germany, 45.6%; Belgium, 39.1%; Norway, 38.3%; France, 33.2%; United Kingdom, 32.5%.

Institutional attention to ecological aspects of production has increased. For instance, Exxon has modified various exploration and production practices to reduce the harmfulness of these activities to marine life. Nevertheless, firms seem to spend more money advertising about their ecological efforts than they spend on actually solving ecological problems (Anonymous, 1971).

Financing the New Emphasis
on Ecology

In the 1970s we are devoting more money, time, and energy to conserving our resources, particularly those that are considered common property. By 1971, such expenditures began to rival the space program allocation of $3.5 billion. These expenditures are reflected in new jobs and new careers centered around ecology. Thus, for example, a mass retreading of aerospace engineers into environmental specialists was required.

The new emphasis on ecology is seen not only in increased expenditures and new career opportunities but also in increased research efforts in industrial psychology and organizational psychology that take cognizance of environmental factors. Engineering psychology, as such, has been directly involved since its inception in the systematic examination of how we at work are affected by temperature, noise, ventilation, etc. What is or will be new is the involvement of personnel, organizational, and consumer psychology as well.

Ecology and Organizational Psychology

Ecology and organizational psychology examine two separate questions: (a) What environmental factors attract us to a particular job? and (b) Which of these environmental considerations holds us to the job thereafter?

Environment and Attraction to Work

Prior to the Industrial Revolution, migration was a consequence of population pressures resulting from human fertility, climatic changes, wars, and persecutions as well as depletion of local land and animal resources (Huntington, 1945). The Industrial Revolution brought mass migration from rural to urban areas. In Britain the rural poor were literally forced off the land. More often, migration, whether from northeastern Brazil to São Paulo or from Puerto Rico to New York City, was for economic reasons, to obtain income above a starvation or subsistence level. The migration of the rural southerner, black or white, to the northern cities was certainly not in search of better weather. But, in the postindustrial scene, income is sometimes traded off for better surroundings. When plants do not need to be located near sources of supply or markets, sites are often selected in Florida, Arizona, or California, the same states that have attracted the masses of retirees.

As more of the white population of the United States move into a postindustrial society, these people say with their feet the importance they attach to their immediate environment. During the decade following 1950, whites aged 20–44 fled from Appalachia and the Great Plains. But was their flight only for economic reasons, reflecting the abandonment of small farms, the mechanization of agriculture, and coal mining? Or were those outmigrants also escaping rural isolation, the long, cold Dakota winters, and so on? And did they migrate toward the more attractive economic or more attractive environmental conditions?

During the 1950s nonwhites fled from the Jim Crow agrarian South. But were they also rural poor seeking better economic conditions? Bass and Alexander (1972) correlated with selected climatic variables the percentages of migration of white men and women, aged 20–44, into (rather than out of) each of the 48 continental states between 1950 and 1960. Selected measures of economic opportunities were held constant. A separate analysis was completed for nonwhites.

Climate was an equally important migration predictor for whites and nonwhites, but the direction of migration was opposite: whites moved toward sunny, warm, dry, snow-free weather; nonwhites, toward colder weather with more snow.[2] At the same time, economic factors were more predictive of nonwhite than white in-migration.[3] Here the direction of prediction was the same for both, but employment opportunities and

---

2. The multiple correlation of five climate variables with three economic variables held constant was .55 for whites and .51 for nonwhites.

3. The multiple correlation of three economic variables with five climate variables was .52 for whites and .69 for nonwhites.

welfare assistance were relatively more potent attractants to nonwhites than to whites.

It is comforting for hard-working social scientists with middle-class values to accept surveys of worker opinion that consistently point to the importance of self-actualization, job challenge, and recognition. But such surveys fail to reflect some of the major decisions of workers in our mobile society about what attracts them to the work place. What the workers actually reflect by migrating is not what they say in surveys. Our argument is that as long as America remains reasonably affluent, when given a choice between two jobs that are equally attractive according to what is ordinarily assessed, white workers (now mainly members of a postindustrial world) will gravitate toward more physically attractive environments. Contrarily, those who have not entered this plush postindustrial society, namely the nonwhites, will gravitate toward economically more enticing environments featuring better employment opportunities, higher wages, and bigger welfare payments.

Turner and Lawrence (1965) found that rural and small-town workers reacted more favorably to challenging, complex work than did urban workers. Strauss (1970) saw this and other related studies as evidence that some workers are more interested in finding a rich social life or better earnings than self-actualizing jobs. We suggest that the list of attractions be broadened to include more satisfying physical environments.

When we ask the white worker about satisfactions and dissatisfactions, we need to keep in mind that the worker may have already eliminated one of the main dissatisfactions by migrating, so such after-the-fact questionnaires may fail to reveal the importance attached to the physical environment. Further, those workers who selectively do not migrate are the very ones who do not find their current physical environment sufficiently dissatisfying to migrate.

Environment and Job Satisfaction

Although climate is an *attraction* to work, environmental factors generate considerable *satisfaction*. For example, Stedman (1945) found that samples of 100 residents and factory workers in each of 12 cities ranging from 100,000 to 3,500,000 in population were much more likely to report that they felt good about their place of work if they lived in smaller cities. Thus, 92% of factory workers felt good about Evansville, Indiana, while only 44% felt the same about Chicago. Consistent with Stedman's results, Katzell, Barrett, and Parker (1961), in a study of 72 warehouses of a pharmaceutical firm, found that warehouses in more urban settings not only were less satisfying places to work but were also less productive and less profitable. They exhibited more turnover and were more likely to be unionized.

In a study of 390 male and 80 female white-collar workers employed by the same company and living in two company towns in Canada, Hulin (1969) found systematic relations among job satisfaction, life satisfaction, and community satisfaction. For the men, community satisfaction variables most highly associated with job satisfaction and life satisfaction were weather, housing, adult recreational facilities, shopping facilities, cost of living, location, and attractiveness of town. Job satisfaction for women was positively associated with favorable housing, shopping, and cost of living conditions. Life satisfaction for women was associated with favorable weather conditions, child recreation facilities, and location of the town.

Different results emerged in a survey by Hulin (1966) of 300 female clerical workers in various mail-order establishments in numerous small communities. Worker satisfaction was negatively related to various measures of actual community prosperity, actual quality of housing, etc. Hulin concluded that workers' degree of satisfaction is relative to the actual conditions existing in a community. Thus, workers were likely to be more satisfied with their own pay when the actual income of others in the community was lower. Being "well off" is a relative matter.

Based on the preceding brief discourse and what would seem to be reasonable extensions, we offer the following as testable propositions worth further study concerning the effects of environment on attraction and satisfaction with work:

1. In the American culture, it is relatively undesirable to place preference for an attractive environment over preference for personal achievement or success. Questionnaires are less likely to reveal the importance of environment to workers relative to the importance of pay, recognition, or accomplishment.

2. Relative opportunities are paramount. Workers are more satisfied with their jobs if they live in an area with high rates of unemployment. But if alternatives *elsewhere,* such as an open frontier, are available, workers require more job satisfaction and/or pay to remain on the job.

3. Workers trade off unpleasant environment against pay, security, advancement, etc. If New York City is seen as a hardship post, employers there must pay a bonus to attract and hold personnel. Work under severe isolated Arctic conditions becomes attractive to the blue-collar worker if the pay is high enough, and to the professional worker if it offers opportunities for achievement and recognition. Nevertheless, there are limits to what can be traded. According to General Telephone and Electronics, in 1968, 1 in 20 executives refused to transfer to New York City. In 1969, 1 in 3 refused. In 1970, 1 in 2 refused such transfers. The company began planning to move its offices out of New York City soon after ('Fun City,' 1971).

Ecology and Personnel Psychology

Two issues in personnel psychology that stand out are (a) new jobs, tasks, and careers appearing as a consequence of our effects on our environment and (b) the physical environment possibly affecting aptitude and interest development.

New Jobs, Careers, and Tasks

As our societal objectives shift toward increased quality of living, large numbers of personnel will shift out of employment in production of goods and toward control of waste. New services will appear that involve semitechnical and professional workers. Various kinds of sanitation and health workers, testers, inspectors, environment educators, research personnel, demonstration agents, and change agents will be needed. A doubling of jobs in environmental management is expected during the 1970s, so that by 1980 well over one million people could be employed in this field. The expected growth of personnel in the separate disciplines concerned with the environment is forecast as shown in Table 19-1. Unless the environmental boom is followed by an environmental bust, industrial psychologists are likely to find themselves as occupied in the 1970s and 1980s with environmental manpower research as they were in the 1950s and 1960s with space manpower research.

Conservation careers. Needed work on conservation problems offers entry jobs at many levels and in multifarious areas such as air, water, and soil pollution; waste treatments; management of wildlife, forest, river, and mountain areas; and protection of resources.

Jobs dealing with water conservation problems can be developed over a wide range of activities: improvement of wildlife habitat; physical improvement and maintenance of water bodies; and enforcement of game, fishing, and other environmental protection laws.

As pressures grow on outdoor areas, there is an increasing need for trained professional-level conservationists and naturalists as well as for ecologically trained subprofessionals. The unemployed and the disadvan-

TABLE 19-1   *Expected Growth of Manpower Needs in the Environmental Disciplines*

Discipline	Practitioners in 1970	Practitioners needed in 1980
Ecology	4,300	12,000
Geology	22,800	33,400
Geophysics	6,800	10,400
Meteorology	4,000	12,000
Oceanography	5,800	40,000
Forestry	25,000	37,000
Forestry aids	13,000	23,800
Range management	6,000	8,000
Soil conservation	26,000	30,000
Wildlife conservation	15,000	20,000
Fisheries conservation	4,500	7,500
Recreation and parks	215,790	220,000
Architecture	34,000	61,600
Engineering (construction and consulting)	40,000	70,000
Landscape architecture	8,500	14,500
Urban planning	7,000	16,600
Environmental protection	217,500	565,000
Total	655,990	1,181,800

Note. From "The Environmental Boom" by D. Fanning, *Saturday Review*, May 1, 1971, p. 60. Copyright 1971 by *Saturday Review*. Reprinted by permission.

taged youth could be trained to fill these positions. People living in mining areas who are unemployed or underemployed and who prefer not to relocate could be trained for various jobs associated with mines, for example, surveying and testing to establish tallies of both surface damage and the acid content of water, observing safety factors, and recording conditions as found. Work on reclamation, rehabilitation, and development and use of surface-mined areas is also a possible source of new careers.

The field of recreational service provides stimulating activities covering all phases of human living—educational, social, cultural, and physical— and many new jobs are created each year. Total employment in the management of public and private recreation areas is expected to reach 1.4 million by 1980. In rural areas, 350,000 full-time jobs are expected to be added as the result of farm and rural recreational enterprises.

Careers for the unemployed. As we become capable of producing more goods and services with fewer people, and with slowing economic growth, it becomes essential to shift some people from production into ecologically relevant jobs such as those enumerated earlier. Jobs in related areas can be a solution both to environmental problems and to the problem of creating meaningful jobs that can provide the unemployed with a sense of pride, satisfaction, and status. Increasing demands by various segments of the population for improved environmental quality and for participation in decisions affecting their lives can lend a real sense of importance to the jobs developed to meet environmental needs.

Special public works programs can be developed to provide supplementary employment for those who are seasonally unemployed, hard to employ, or unemployed for reasons such as declining industries, obsolete training, and technological changes. The untrained or uneducated, the ex-supervisors, skilled personnel, and white-collar workers who may be unemployed as the result of cutbacks or advanced age, as well as the displaced farm workers and farmers can acquire new, meaningful jobs. To accommodate such a variety of needs, jobs and job categories must be developed that will themselves foster self-interest and, ultimately, an awareness of the importance of involvement with the maintenance and improvement of ecological balances. Jobs with environmental objectives can be designed to accomplish necessary goals that otherwise would be delayed or unachieved. Unemployed professional and technical workers could perform needed public service projects such as charting or mapping water, sewage, and other systems; performing distribution studies; making surveys of buildings for tax purposes; and following other pursuits that would use existing skills and have valid work goals. A sense of accomplishment and increased job status would result. What must be avoided is the sense of "make work" that served to reduce the perceived worth of WPA (Works Progress Administration) jobs.

Personnel and industrial careers. Of consequence to personnel and industrial psychology is the appearance of new tasks, new selection objectives, new job site designs, and new tools and equipment. For example, personnel psychologists will increasingly focus attention on how congestion affects job performance. Thus, Rawls et al. (1970) systematically examined individual differences with respect to preference for the amount of space between oneself and others and the deterioration in performance among those who want more space but must work under crowded conditions. It may be that humans can learn to tolerate more crowding if social structures are developed for doing so.

Consider what is being done or can be done to control noise: recruiting and selecting deaf personnel for noisy situations; evaluating the effects of muffling compressors, motors and blast; designing earplugs and earmuffs; determining maximum tolerable "dosage" levels for work scheduling; and establishing community guidelines for noise abatement.

Ecological inventories. One necessary strategy in establishing priorities and developing purposeful jobs for the future is to create ecological inventories that can provide the factual basis for rational decisions in the environmental area. Resource inventories that identify potential areas for reservoirs, future parks, and utility and transportation corridors will be required along with inventories to protect features such as park areas, landscapes, and even certain types of urban areas. Coupled with such inventories, a rehabilitation index needs to be developed to cover such potential conversions as dumps to parks and slums to open space. We need an antipollution index itemizing requirements for rehabilitating water, air, and soil, as well as areas that have been adversely affected by loud noises and offensive unusual effects. There should also be behavioral inputs into these efforts. Although economics might be viewed as the study of production and consumption without people, as Boulding has quipped, it is to be hoped that the human elements in such ecological inventories will be recognized early.

Planners. At higher executive levels, ecological planners are needed. Priorities must be established for the development and implementation of action programs aimed at controlling different forms of pollution and designed to enhance environmental quality. Because prevention is usually less expensive than restoration after degradation, it is essential that balanced programs be developed in both areas. The costs involved in restoration of such areas as water bodies can be enormous.[4] Psychologists can contribute by identifying the socioemotional elements, evaluating programs, and establishing priorities to help the administrator-planner make final decisions. The administrator-planner with an engineering background needs to avoid seeing a water pollution problem only in terms of its engineering solutions.[5] To assist in the education of such decision makers,

---

4. The estimated cost of remedying the water pollution problem of Lake Erie is around $4.5 billion.

5. Lest the reader think this is a trivial psychological problem, consider what happened when Thorndike (1939) asked 268 leading authorities to rate 117 cities in quality of "government, schools, morals, culture, public spirit and humanity." The most accurate in correlating opinion with fact, that is, in accurately estimating the quality of living in a city, were 97 educators ($r=.59$); less accurate were 31 "reformers" ($r=.51$), 72 clergymen and social workers ($r=.36$), and 99 businessmen ($r=.27$). The lattermost tended to overestimate the significance of recent growth and income.

the writers have designed a simulation of the negotiations among utilities managers and concerned citizens involved in deciding on a coastal zone nuclear plant site (Bass, Bass, & Shapira, 1975).

Influence of Ecological Factors

From Homer and Herodotus to Huntington, scholars have speculated on the subject of ecological factors associated with the differential development of aptitudes and interests. Criticism of such attempts to account for human behavior has been valid usually because cultural, ethnic, sociological, and historical factors have been uncontrolled.

Regional differences in interests and abilities are nothing new to social scientists, and we are usually ready to attribute such differences to social and cultural factors such as educational opportunities, racial composition, or degree of urbanization. There is a wealth of literature on the subject, ranging from the vast amount of data on intelligence test differences to studies of the distribution of eminence as reflected in "Who's Who." National surveys of talent provide more detailed representative samples for study. As a consequence of Project Talent (American Institutes for Research, 1960), we have available samples of tested abilities and interests sufficiently representative of the country as a whole to allow us to examine gross differences across geographical areas in which cultural, ethnic, and individual factors can be controlled statistically.[6]

Among the many aptitudes tested, some that seem most likely to be associated with climate and, particularly, terrain include spatial visualization, object inspection, form perception, and creativity. Self-concepts or personality traits from this national inventory likely to show modest geographical influences include vigor, productivity, tidiness, sociability, cheerfulness, culture, impulsiveness, persistence, calmness, and intellectual preferences. Even more obvious is the likelihood of environmental effects on inventoried knowledge about games, sports, outdoor activities, farming, and mechanics.

The following additional hypotheses could be tested:

1. Climates that are highly variable from season to season will produce greater differences in behavior than climates that are less variable.

2. Areas where weather is highly erratic and unpredictable within seasons will produce individual behavior different from that in areas where weather is reasonably predictable within seasons.

---

6. About 440,000 students in over 1,350 high schools took part in Project Talent to provide the first National Aptitude and Ability Census—a 5% representation of all U.S. high school students in 1960. Each student took a 2-day battery of tests and provided information about his or her background, interests, and aptitudes. The existence of such a census makes it possible to correlate ecological and behavioral variables. Cultural, economic, ethnic, sociological, and other contaminating variables can be controlled statistically. Moreover, the dampening of effects as a result of standardized television fare available everywhere presumably was of much less import during the 1950s for the population that would be studied.

3. Areas where one season is dominant (long winter, short summer, or vice versa) will produce more specialized behavior than that in more moderate areas.

4. Highly variable land surfaces will produce human perceptual skill development that is different from that found in flat surfaces.

The first focus of attention could be on how geographical variability and uncertainty affect aptitudes and interests, although the effects of various environmental factors such as soils, temperatures, humidities, vegetation, and topography can be considered along with such areal factors as nearness to metropolitan centers, density of population, and the like.

REFERENCES

American Institutes for Research. *Project Talent.* Pittsburgh, Pa.: Author, 1960.

Anonymous. Quote without comment. (From *The Sciences*) *Consumer's Reports,* 1971, 36, 194.

Bass, B. M. Self-managing systems, Z.E.G. and other unthinkables. In H. Meltzer (Ed.), *Humanizing the organization.* Springfield, Ill.: Charles C Thomas, in press.

Bass, B. M., & Alexander, R. A. Climate, economy, and the differential migration of white and nonwhite workers. *Journal of Applied Psychology,* 1972, 56, 518–521.

Bass, B. M., & Eldridge, L. D. Accelerated managers' objectives in twelve countries. *Industrial Relations,* 1973, 12, 158–171.

Bass, R., Bass, B. M., & Shapira, Z. *Nuclear site negotiation.* Scottsville, N.Y.: Transnational Programs Corporation, 1975.

Bennis, W. A funny thing happened on the way to the future. *American Psychologist,* 1970, 25, 595–608.

Blood, M. R., & Hulin, C. L. Alienation, environmental characteristics, and worker responses. *Journal of Applied Psychology,* 1967, 51, 284–290.

Centers, R., & Bugental, D. E. Intrinsic and extrinsic job motivations among different segments of the working population. *Journal of Applied Psychology,* 1966, 50, 193–197.

Fanning, D. The environmental boom. *Saturday Review,* May 1, 1971, p. 60.

'Fun city' no fun to business. *Democrat & Chronicle,* Rochester, New York, April 11, 1971, p. C1.

Goldsmith, J. R., & Landow, S. A. Carbon monoxide and human health. *Science,* 1968, 162, 1352–1359.

Harris, L. Shall we do without? *Democrat & Chronicle,* Rochester, New York, December 4, 1975, p. C1.

Hulin, C. L. The effects of community characteristics on measures of job satisfaction. *Journal of Applied Psychology,* 1966, 50, 185–192.

Hulin, C. L. Sources of variation in job and life satisfaction: The role of community and job-related variables. *Journal of Applied Psychology,* 1969, 53, 279–291.

Hulin, C. L., & Blood, M. R. Job enlargement, individual differences, and worker responses. *Psychological Bulletin,* 1968, 69, 41–55.

Huntington, E. *Mainsprings of civilization.* New York: Wiley, 1945.

Katzell, R. A., Barrett, R. S., & Parker, T. C. Job satisfaction, job performance, and situational characteristics. *Journal of Applied Psychology,* 1961, 45, 65–72.

Kendall, L. M. *Communal analysis of job satisfaction and behavioral personal background and instructional data.* Unpublished doctoral dissertation, Cornell University, 1963.

Kimball, T. L. *The environmental decade. Action proposals for the 1970's* (Hearings before a Subcommittee of the Committee on Governmental Operations, House of Representatives, Ninety-First Congress, Second Session, 10-29). Washington, D.C.: U.S. Government Printing Office, 1970.

Maslow, A. H. *Motivation and personality.* New York: Harper, 1954.

Rawls, J. R., et al. Personal space and its effect upon the performance of arithmetic tests under different degrees of closeness. *Experimental Publication System,* 1970, 6, No. 204.

Russell, R. W. "Psychology": Noun or adjective? *American Psychologist,* 1970, 25, 211–218.

Stedman, G. E. An appreciation index. *Personnel Journal,* 1945, 24, 64–72.

Strauss, G. Organization behavior and personnel relations. In W. L. Ginsburg (Ed.), *A review of industrial relations research* (Vol. 1). Madison, Wisc.: Industrial Relations Research Association, 1970.

Thorndike, E. L. *Your city.* New York: Harcourt, Brace, 1939.

Turner, A. N., & Lawrence, P. *Industrial jobs and the worker.* Cambridge, Mass.: Harvard University, Graduate School of Business Administration, 1965.

Ury, H. K. Photochemical air pollution and automobile accidents in Los Angeles. *Archives of Environmental Health,* 1968, *17,* 334–342.

20

Willo P. White

Alternate Job Settings in Environment and Behavior

The field of environment and behavior is a newly emerging area of research in psychology. In recognition of this fact a Task Force on Environment and Behavior was established in January 1974 by the American Psychological Association (APA) under the aegis of the Board of Scientific Affairs' Ad Hoc Committee on Newly Emerging Areas of Research (NEAR). The Task Force set forth the following goals: (a) to bring to the attention of APA members the research and scholarly potential in the area of environment and behavior, (b) to provide information about alternative educational models and courses of instruction in environment and behavior, (c) to develop interdisciplinary contacts, and (d) to promote application and policy-oriented research.

From the inception of the Task Force there was recognition that the field of environment and behavior was interdisciplinary and that the research conducted in the field would have a myriad of applications and implications for policy. The importance of this will become evident as we discuss the area of environment and behavior as one that is ripe for both job development and research.

This chapter specifically is based on an examination of the 100-word statements requested by and submitted to the newsletter of the Task Force on Environment and Behavior by persons in the field stating their research, training, and consulting interests. It also summarizes the mandates of federal agencies presented in the *United States Government Manual 1975/1976* (Office of the Federal Register, 1975).

Trends in Public Policy

There is a direct interaction among public policy, the availability of resources, and the development of science. Occupational opportunities are a negotiation between what a field is prepared to contribute and the perceived need of society for certain kinds of information and activity. The continued development of science requires an adequate level of support for those investigations and an ultimate benefit to society for that support.

Some converging trends in public policy highlight the richness of the area of environment and behavior for continued research and employment.

Willo P. White is Administrative Associate for Scientific Affairs, American Psychological Association, Washington, D.C.

First, as we change to an economy that is dominated by services, the human being figures as a larger part of the equation. Understanding the interaction between the human being and the environment becomes a critical factor in policy decisions. Second, there is widespread recognition that many of our past attempts to implement public policy have failed. A superficial examination of our problems with public housing points to only one painful example. There are multiple reasons for these failures. More often than not, all available knowledge was not brought to bear in the planning and implementation. Additionally, the need to include the consumer or the ultimate user of a product in the decision-making and evaluation process is being recognized by decision makers. Another trend is the increasing interest in constructing models to anticipate and examine all permutations of a given set of policies. Otherwise, the solution to one problem may provide the genesis for many more. As part of this planning for the future, alternatives need to be laid out so that the choice points are clearly articulated and the cost/benefit ratio is computed in advance. As Toffler remarked in *Future Shock*, finding the non-zero-sum solutions to society's pressing problems requires infinite imagination. A collective imagination of an interdisciplinary team, with each member providing a distinct but interlocking viewpoint, would result in the best possible effort. Finally, questions of environmental quality and quality-of-life issues are looming larger in public policy decisions. The National Environmental Protection Act (NEPA) requires that an environmental impact assessment be prepared prior to any major project that is federally financed. The NEPA specifically mandates that social science input should be included in these statements.

Persons in the Field of Environment and Behavior

The first generation entering a new area of research often consists of broad-gauged persons who have a facility for synthesizing concepts. Although they were trained in a particular discipline, they see the broad implications of the theoretical and methodological basis of the field. The second generation is trained in the new area by persons whose primary allegiance is to the parent discipline. This second generation, however, is not as constrained and borrows freely from other disciplines. It is this approach that infuses the area with a "hybrid vigor" that the second generation passes along to the third. The third generation may be theoretical mavericks whose position is startling to some members of the first generation who only sought to apply some of the technology of their discipline to new conceptual problem areas.

Although all three generations will think of themselves as psychologists, the labels that they might use in describing themselves are another way of understanding this conceptual evolution. The first generation might call themselves social psychologists doing research in environment and behavior while the second might use the term "environmental psychologists." The third generation might drop the label "psychologist" altogether and opt for "social or human ecologists."

Academic institutions are still able to absorb many of the persons from the second generation who seek employment. It may be the third generation, currently in school, who will be entering many of the jobs mentioned in this chapter.

Alternate Settings in Academic Institutions

The newly emerging area of environment and behavior is building on previous work in traditional areas of psychology. Jobs for persons trained in environment and behavior are similarly building on careers in traditional settings for psychologists—academic institutions and government. Persons in this hybrid field are breaking new ground by using both new techniques to work on old problems and old techniques to work on new problems.

Currently, many of the jobs for which persons trained in this field may be qualified are not advertised in such a way to stimulate application by psychologists. The job announcements may not be appropriately written and/or may not be advertised in places where psychologists are likely to see them. Active job development is necessary because the agency or organization may not be aware that a psychologist is qualified or needed for the job.

The field of environment and behavior is multidisciplinary, and this has been felt strongly in academic institutions. Psychologists in this hybrid field interested in pursuing research and teaching interests have felt free to move out of the traditional departments of psychology and education. For example, psychologists who are interested in extending theories, concepts, and methodologies have moved into allied departments such as anthropology, economics, geography, political science, and sociology. Others are deliberately working in departments or divisions that are multidisciplinary, such as social ecology, and human–environment relations.

Many psychologists whose primary interest is in the built environment have moved into schools of architecture, landscape architecture, civil engineering, interior design, or urban planning. Departments of forestry and geology have provided interesting working environments for psychologists concerned with problems of the person and the natural environment. Institutes and centers have been established to deal with specific issues in technology assessments and with alternate futures that have attracted psychologists who want to address futuristic concerns such as resource allocation and control.

Alternate Settings in Government

Because there is not a cohesive theory in the field of environment and behavior, the field is currently defined by what persons who purport to work in the field do and by the problems they seek to solve (Craik, 1973; Wohlwill, 1970). The next section of this chapter contains a listing of some of the problem areas that psychologists are currently working in and suggestions of some of the alternate settings in which they might fruitfully work. This is not intended to be an exhaustive listing but rather a suggestion of the many possibilities that need to be developed.

These problem areas should not be construed as conceptual areas of the field of environment and behavior but rather as labels that can be conveniently linked to government departments and agencies. The research problems listed under the sections concerning work by psychologists are samples of the work in progress as reported in the 100-word statements submitted to the newsletter of the Task Force on Environment and Behavior. The fact that more examples may appear in one section than another does not necessarily mean that more substantive work is being undertaken in that area. In many instances, there is considerable overlap among the problem areas that government departments might be interested in. Rather than be repetitive, departments or agencies are listed in only one place and an attempt is made to spread these among the problem areas. Some of the government departments and agencies might directly employ psychologists to formulate policy and to implement programs or to undertake research. In addition, these government departments might support extramural research. This federal government activity will also have derivative benefit in opening up similar jobs at the state and local government level and in industry.

Housing and the Built Environment

Psychologists' Approach to the Problem

Psychologists who work on aspects of housing and the built environment are addressing some of the following areas.

1. Public housing is being studied as a special management environment, including tenant perceptions of management, factors affecting rent delinquency, and effects of social programs on tenants' lives.

2. Situational determinants of the intensity and persistence of crowding experiences are being investigated.

3. Research on the effects of physical environment (especially ambient temperature on aggression, attraction, and personal space) is being conducted.

4. General data base and formal languages for computer-aided building design and the psychology of design are being developed.

5. Design criteria are being established to make limited space more habitable on ships.

6. Behavioral effects of different types of residential environments, particularly high-density, high-rise buildings, are being studied.

7. Autistic children and the special environmental needs of these children are being investigated.

8. Personal space and territoriality are being investigated for their affect on behavior in a built environment.

9. Techniques to help architects become better predictors of user responses to buildings are being developed.

Government's Approach to the Problem

Department of Housing and Urban Development
451 Seventh Street, S.W.
Washington, D.C. 20410

Community planning and development. The Community Development Block Grant Assistance program is designed to develop viable urban communities by providing decent housing and expanding economic opportunities through eliminating slum and blight and increasing the supply of low- and moderate-income housing. Conservation of existing housing, improvement of public services, improvement in the use of land, and preservation of property with special values are also activities pursued by the program.

State and local management assistance. The Department of Housing and Urban Development (HUD), through this program, provides technical assistance to states, area-wide agencies, and communities in management and comprehensive planning, including transportation planning.

Urban design. The NEPA directs the utilization of systematic, interdisciplinary approaches to environment, with particular emphasis on the built environment. HUD develops and promulgates urban design criteria, which include, among the bases for planning and decision making, the integrated consideration of the natural and social sciences and environmental design arts.

Environment. The environmental functions of HUD include the development of environmental standards, policies, and procedures for energy conservation; code modernization and administration; and strategies for the amelioration of environmental problems such as natural hazards and air and noise pollution.

General Services Administration
General Services Building
Eighteenth and F Streets, N.W.
Washington, D.C. 20405

Public buildings service. The service is responsible for the complex and difficult task of designing buildings that meet highest standards of excellence and economy of operation. It utilizes regional advisory panels to assure an architectural program of variety, vigor, and adaptability and to ensure that buildings constructed are compatible with the character and cultural heritage of a particular locale.

Department of Commerce
14th Street between Constitution Avenue and E Street, N.W.
Washington, D.C. 20230

National Bureau of Standards, Washington, D.C. 20234. The overall goal of the National Bureau of Standards (NBS) is to strengthen and advance the nation's science and technology and facilitate its effective application for public benefit. The Institute for Applied Technology provides technical services to promote the use of available technology and to facilitate technological innovation. Programs of special interest to psychologists include building technology and fire technology.

Office of Experimental Technology of the National Bureau of Standards. The Office of Experimental Technology conducts, analyzes, experiments with, and evaluates technology inventions and innovations. It helps shape the use of scientific and technological capabilities in the solution of national problems.

National Fire Prevention and Control Administration. The primary mission of the National Fire Prevention and Control Administration is to reduce the loss of life and property through better fire prevention and control. It develops national programs to educate the public about specific fire hazards and the importance of prevention.

Work and Leisure

Psychologists' Approach to the Problem

Psychologists who study aspects of work and leisure are addressing some of the following areas.

1. Research is being performed on habitability and on designs for work and leisure, especially during space flights. The effect of environment on performance, behavior, and social systems is also being investigated.

2. Attitude–behavior relationships in recreational settings are being studied.

3. Behavioral outcomes are being studied as a function of various components of shipboard living and working conditions.

4. Studies are being done of postindustrial psychology, of influence of environmental factors on educational and occupational achievement and satisfaction, of stress and coronary heart disease in industrial settings, and of social context of leisure roles.

5. The relationship between organized work environments and human behavior is being investigated.

Government's Approach to the Problem

Department of Labor
Third Street and Constitution Avenue, N.W.
Washington, D.C. 20210

Wo/manpower development programs. Emergency job programs: Under the Manpower Administration, the emergency job programs provide temporary public service employment for unemployed persons who can receive training in such fields as environmental quality, health care, education, recreation, pollution control, conservation, and other community services and improvement.

National Older Worker Program. This Program provides work experience and training for adults with poor employment prospects. Designed for rural areas and towns, projects concentrate on work experience and training activities that will improve and beautify communities and those low-income areas where the projects take place.

Community Services Administration
1200 Nineteenth Street, N.W.
Washington, D.C. 20506

Community action programs. These programs within the Community Services Administration seek to find effective solutions to basic social and economic problems related to povery.

Economic development program. This program encourages development of special programs by which residents of urban and rural low-income areas may, through self-help and mobilization of the community at large, improve the quality of their economic and social participation in community life.

Education

Psychologists' Approach to the Problem

Psychologists who work in the problem area of education have focused on the following topics.

1. The spaces of teachers and students are being redesigned to fit the definitions of their functions.

2. Traditional schools offering one learning environment for all students are compared with pluralistic schools offering a choice.

3. Physical characteristics of learning environments and their effect on human comfort and performance are being studied.

4. Longitudinal studies are being made of new schools, with particular emphasis on the degree to which the planner's intentions are realized in the social system of the school.

5. Learned helplessness is a current topic of reseach.

6. Physical environment is being evaluated in implementing educational philosophy and practice.

7. Social behavior is being studied in unique settings such as museums.

Government's Approach to the Problem

Department of Health, Education, and Welfare
330 Independence Avenue, S.W.
Washington, D.C. 20201

National Institute of Education, 1200 Nineteenth Street, N.W., Washington, D.C. 20208. The Institute was created to provide leadership in the conduct and support of scientific inquiry into the educational process, to provide more dependable knowledge about education quality, and to improve education. It provides for dissemination and use of knowledge for solving educational problems, studying, evaluating, and improving the capabilities of institutions.

Smithsonian Institution
1000 Jefferson Drive, S.W.
Washington, D.C. 20560

The Smithsonian Institution was created by an act of Congress in 1846 to carry out the terms of a will bequeathing an estate "to found at Washington, under the name of the Smithsonian Institution, an establishment for the increase and diffusion of knowledge among men."

Chesapeake Bay Center for Environmental Studies, RR4, Box 622, Edgewater, Maryland 21037. Projects are undertaken to determine the environmental issues of most concern to local environmental organizations and to determine what interface has occurred with state officials and legislators. The Center sponsors intensive courses and workshops on environmental education.

Health

Psychologists' Approach to the Problem

Psychologists who study aspects of health are considering the following problem areas.

1. The ecology of accidents, hazards, and safety in new town environments is being studied.

2. The ecology of health and illness and techniques of environmental adaptation in the area of drug use (perceived need for medicines, accessibility to and utilization of drug products, and epidemiological consequences of use) are being investigated.

3. Longitudinal studies are being made of children's psychiatric hospitals in reference to the architect's intent, the therapeutic philosophy, the use of space, and their interrelationship.

4. Planning aid kits were developed to enable community groups to plan their community's mental health program.

5. Research was performed on behavioral patterns prevailing in health care facilities and their translation to architecture.

6. Psychobiological factors relating to sickness were investigated.

Government's Approach to the Problem

Department of Health, Education, and Welfare
330 Independence Avenue, S.W.
Washington, D.C. 20201

Center for Disease Control, Public Health Service, 5600 Fishers Lane, Rockville, Maryland 20852. The Center administers the National Institute for Occupational Safety and Health, which carries out research to assure safe and healthful working conditions for all working people. The Institute also develops occupational safety and health standards.

National Center for Health Services Research, Public Health Service—Health Resources Administration, 5600 Fishers Lane, Rockville, Maryland 20852. The Center plans, develops, and administers a program of health services research, demonstration, evaluation, and research training. It makes grants and contracts to health service providers, coordinates health services research within the Public Health Service, disseminates research findings, and provides assistance to other federal programs and health services.

National Institutes of Health, 9000 Rockville Pike, Bethesda, Maryland 20014. National Institute of Environmental Health Sciences: This Institute conducts and supports fundamental research concerned with defining, measuring, and understanding the effects of chemical, biological, and physical factors in the environment on the health and well-being of human beings. National Institute on Aging: This Institute conducts and supports biomedical and behavioral research to increase the knowledge of the aging process and associated physical, psychological, and social factors resulting from advanced age.

Communications

Psychologists' Approach to the Problem

Psychologists working in the area of communication are addressing the following problems.

1. Psychosocial impact of interactive information technologies and services on present and future urban forms, on land use, and on life-styles is being investigated.

2. Face-to-face conferencing behavior versus electronically mediated communication is being compared.

3. Behavioral aspects of designing effective communication centers are being researched.

4. How information is perceived, stored, and retrieved is being studied.

5. Complex environmental stimuli are being examined in terms of information extraction and processing theories.

Government's Approach to the Problem

Office of Telecommunications Policy
1800 G Street, N.W.
Washington, D.C. 20504

The Office of Telecommunications Policy is the executive agency responsible for overall supervision of national communications matters.

Crime Prevention

Psychologists' Approach to the Problem

1. Residential design techniques are being studied to reduce crime rates.

2. Environmental impact studies are being made in the area of criminal justice and corrections (i.e., effect of closed circuit television on inmate behavior, program effectiveness, and maintenance of security in correctional institutions).

3. Environmental impact is being assessed in selection of sites for new prisons.

4. The effect of crowding in correctional institutions and the sociological and psychological impact of various residential accommodations in such facilities are being investigated.

5. Physical design as an approach to control social behavior, specifically crime prevention, is being studied.

Government's Approach to the Problem

Department of Justice
Constitution Avenue and Tenth Street, N.W.
Washington, D.C. 20530

Law Enforcement Assistance Administration, 633 Indiana Avenue, N.W., Washington, D.C. 20530. Research and development and technical assistance activities are operated by the National Institute of Law Enforcement and Criminal Justice, which also acts as a clearinghouse for the exchange of criminal justice information. The National Criminal Justice Information and Statistics Service collects, evaluates, publishes, and disseminates statistics on criminal justice and coordinates the development of information systems and communications, including the security and privacy needed for the criminal justice system. The Office of National Priority Programs has been created to develop and manage priority programs that express national leadership in contributing to the reduction of crime and improvement of criminal justice.

Transportation and Safety

Psychologists' Approach to the Problem

Psychologists interested in transportation and safety are investigating the following areas.

1. Pedestrial behavior (i.e., study of personal space as a function of different settings, gravitation toward walls and objects, response to incidental lines) is being studied.

2. The behavioral components of safety on stairs are being studied rather than simply computing the coefficients of friction of the materials used in building stairs.

3. Photoperiodic loading and circadian rhythms (jet lag) are being researched.

4. Methods of specifying lighting levels in terms of motorist's visibility needs are being developed.

5. The field of highway planning and the public involvement procedures being used by the nation's highway departments are being examined.

6. Studies are being made of urban travel behavior and the attitudes of individuals toward alternative innovative urban transportation systems (i.e., scaling of preferences for performance attributes of a dial-a-bus system, linking of preference patterns to socioeconomic characteristics of the individual).

7. The contingencies that can be arranged to motivate people to ride buses and form car pools are being studied.

8. The effect of major urban roads on residential communities is being measured.

9. The identity/ownership complex surrounding the automobile is being studied in relation to the needs for large-scale use of public rapid transit.

Government's Approach to the Problem

Department of Transportation
400 Seventh Street, S.W.
Washington, D.C. 20590

Environment, Safety, and Consumer Affairs, Office of the Secretary of Transportation. The Assistant Secretary of Environment, Safety, and Consumer Affairs is responsible for the implementation of the National Environmental Policy Act assuring that the department programs will protect and enhance the nation's environment and that those programs will enhance safety and security of passengers.

Systems Development and Technology. The Assistant Secretary for Systems Development and Technology is responsible for performing or arranging for the performance of research and development on technically advanced systems and for technological and socioeconomic research and development in all transportation disciplines.

Federal Highway Administration, 400 Seventh Street, S.W., Washington, D.C. 20590. The function of the Federal Highway Administration (FHWA) is carried out in encompassing highway transportation in its broadest scope and in seeking to coordinate highways with other modes of transportation to achieve the most effective balance of transportation systems and facilities under cohesive federal transportation policies. The FHWA is concerned with total operation and environment of the highway systems with particular emphasis on improvement of highway-oriented aspects of highway safety and social, economic, and environmental impacts of highway transportation.

Federal Railroad Administration, 400 Seventh Street, S.W., Washington, D.C. 20590. The Federal Railroad Administration supports research and development in advanced and conventional railroad systems and conducts research on techniques to enable this country to make a large step forward in ground transportation.

National Highway Traffic Safety Administration. Areas of primary emphasis in the traffic safety programs are the implementation of countermeasures to reduce accidents attributable to use of alcohol and drugs.

Urban Mass Transportation Administration. The mission of the Urban Mass Transportation Administration is to assist in the development of improved mass transportation, facilities, equipment, techniques, and methods; to encourage the planning and establishment of area-wide urban mass transportation systems; to provide assistance to state and local governments in financing such systems. Its research and development mission includes improving efficiency of systems and easing transportation problems of the elderly, the poor, and the handicapped.

Consumer Product Safety Commission
1750 K Street, N.W.
Washington, D.C. 20207

The Commission has primary responsibility to reduce unreasonable risk of injury to consumers from consumer products. It establishes mandatory product safety standards where appropriate and bans hazardous consumer products, if necessary. The Commission conducts extensive research on consumer product standards and engages in broad consumer and industry information and education programs.

Air Pollution

Psychologists' Approach to the Problem

Psychologists interested in the problem of air pollution are examining the following areas.

1. Irritation produced by airborne chemical agents is being investigated.

2. Costs of physical activity in neutral and hot environments are being researched.

3. Effects of environmental pollutants on behavior of nonhuman animals and on the developing organism and behavior are being studied; in addition, the effect of microwaves on human behavior is also an area of concern.

4. Studies are examining the biochemical, psychological, and behavioral correlates of stress factors (e.g., heat and cold, changes in air ionization levels, disturbances in weather conditions, and solar and lunar activity).

5. Research is addressing the behavioral problems underlying the misuse and overuse of pesticides.

Government's Approach to the Problem

Environmental Protection Agency
401 M Street, S.W.
Washington, D.C. 20460

The Environmental Protection Agency permits coordinated, effective governmental action on behalf of the environment. It endeavors to abate and control pollution systematically by proper integration of research, monitoring, standard setting, and enforcement. The Agency coordinates and supports research and antipollution activities by state and local governments and private and public groups, prepares regulations for air and water pollution control, and conducts evaluations of regional water activities.

Noise Pollution

Psychologists' Approach to the Problem

Psychologists who wish to solve noise pollution problems are addressing themselves to the following areas.

1. Methods for incorporating the human response to noise into measurement systems for use in noise abatement and control are being investigated.

2. Experiments are being conducted in human aversion to noise; human noise tolerance; human preference relations among various acoustic stimuli; and classical loudness, noisiness, and annoyance comparisons among sounds.

3. The impact of environmental noise and crowding on human memory and information processing is being studied.

4. The effects of environmental noise on human performance are being measured.

Government's Approach to the Problem

Department of Transportation
400 Seventh Street, S.W.
Washington, D.C. 20590

Systems Development and Technology. This branch conducts programs of research into the causes and effects of transportation noise, noise abatement, and automotive energy efficiency.

Water Resources

Psychologists' Approach to the Problem

Psychologists interested in water resources are focusing on the following issues.

1. The attitudes and perceptions of decision makers toward the adoption of renovated waste-water for potable use are being examined.

2. Methodology is being developed for the assessment of aesthetic criteria in relation to land–water interface as perceived by individuals.

3. Impacts of water resource development are being assessed.

4. Quality-of-life and social well-being concepts that are coordinated with economic development and environmental quality goals in water resource development are being assessed.

Government's Approach to the Problem

Department of the Interior
C Street between Eighteenth and Nineteenth Streets, N.W.
Washington, D.C. 20240

Geological survey. The survey determines the source, quantity, quality, distribution, movement, and availability of both surface and ground water; investigates floods and shortages of water supply; and evaluates available waters in river basins.

Energy Development and Utilization

Psychologists' Approach to the Problem

Psychologists interested in energy development and utilization are addressing the following problem areas.

1. Longitudinal studies are being made on the social impact of coal-related industrial development on lives of members of the community.

2. Energy development and social change connected with oil shale development are being studied.

3. Attitudes concerning the energy crisis and actual indexes of energy conservation behaviors are being examined.

4. Energy conservation and energy rationing as a social and psychological problem are being conceptualized.

5. Environmental values and attitudes are being measured in relation to the siting of power plants and the perceived risks associated with the storage and disposal of nuclear waste materials.

Government's Approach to the Problem

Federal Energy Administration
12th Street and Pennsylvania Avenue, N.W.
Washington, D.C. 20461

The purpose of the Federal Energy Administration (FEA) is to ensure that the supply of energy available to the United States will continue to be sufficient to meet the total energy demand. The FEA also assures that in case of energy shortages the burden is borne with equity. The Office of Conservation and Environment is concerned with easing the energy shortage by reducing the rate of growth of energy demand through the development of energy conservation programs and promotion of efficiencies in the use of energy resources.

Energy Research and Development Administration
20 Massachusetts Avenue, N.W.
Washington, D.C. 20545

The Energy Reorganization Act of 1974 brought together into the Energy Research and Development Administration (ERDA) functions of the Department of the Interior related to coal research, energy research centers, and underground electric power transmission research; functions of the National Science Foundation related to solar heating and cooling development and geothermal power development; functions of the Environmental Protection Agency related to research, development, and demonstration of alternative automotive power systems; and the military and production activities and nuclear research and development activities of the Atomic Energy Commission. The ERDA is required to encourage and conduct research and development, including demonstration of commercial feasibility and practical applications of the numerous activities related to the development and use of energy from fossil, nuclear, solar, geothermal, and other energy sources.

Resource Allocation and Conservation

Psychologists' Approach to the Problem

Psychologists who wish to promote resource allocation and conservation are focusing on the following issues.

1. The effects of behavior on natural recreation areas and the role of attitudes, values, and habits in relation to environmental problems are being conceptualized.

2. People's perceptions of the aesthetics of environmental stimuli are being scaled, using multidimensional scaling and signal detection theoretic techniques on diverse stimuli such as rivers, timber management practices, and strip mine reclamation practices.

3. The role of norms and norm activation on behavior that impacts on environment (e.g., littering, purchase of lead-free gasoline, and energy conservation) is being examined.

4. Farmers' perception of atmospheric environment and behavioral response are being studied.

5. The adequacy of multiple use doctrines with respect to national parks is being investigated.

6. The behavioral influence of various types of antilitter messages included on disposable items is being evaluated.

7. The differential effects of "clean" and "littered" environments on individual's compliance to litter instructions are being measured.

8. The efficacy of different behavioral methodologies designed to motivate individuals to bring paper to community recycling centers is being examined.

9. Fire prevention techniques and programs are being developed and evaluated.

Government's Approach to the Problem

Department of Agriculture
14th Street and Independence Avenue, S.W.
Washington, D.C. 20250

Rural Development Service. The Service is responsible for coordinating a nationwide rural development program utilizing the services of the executive branch departments and agencies in support of state and local rural development programs. The service establishes national rural development goals and evaluates the nation's progress in attaining these goals. It also provides research information on rural development to government agencies at all levels and works to initiate and expand research efforts related to human and natural resources and on community and economic aspects of development in rural areas.

Resource conservation programs. The program provides cost sharing with farmers to carry out needed conservation and environmental measures under annual and long-term agreement. Program emphasis is on practices that will provide substantial benefits to the public at the least possible public cost. The program is concerned with providing more open space and recreational areas for urban areas.

Extension Service. The Extension Service is the educational agency of the Department of Agriculture established to help the public learn about and apply to everyday activities the latest technology developed through research by the land-grant universities, the Department of Agriculture, and other sources.

Forest Service. The Forest Service has the responsibility to promote a pattern of natural resource use that will best meet the needs of people now and in the future, protecting and improving the quality of air, water, soil, and natural beauty; protecting and improving the quality of the open space environment in urban and community areas; encouraging the growth and development of forestry-based enterprises that readily respond to consumer's changing needs; and expanding public understanding of environmental conservation development.

Department of the Interior
C Street between Eighteenth and Nineteenth Streets, N.W.
Washington, D.C. 20240

Program Development and Budget, Office of the Secretary. The Assistant Secretary of Program Development and Budget has responsibility for department-wide programs concerning natural resources management and environmental quality.

Fish and Wildlife Service, Assistant Secretary, Fish and Wildlife and Parks. The Service guides the conservation, development, and management of the nation's fish and wildlife resources and administers a national program that provides opportunities to the American public to understand, appreciate, and wisely use these resources.

National Park Service, Assistant Secretary, Fish and Wildlife and Parks. The Park Service administers properties under its jurisdiction for the enjoyment and education of citizens, protects the natural environment of the areas, and assists state and local governments, and citizens groups in the development of park areas, the protection of natural environments, and the preservation of historic properties. It also cooperates with local schools in administration of environmental education programs.

Land Use

Psychologists' Approach to the Problem

Psychologists focusing on land use are studying these topics.

1. The relationship between value orientations and land use planning is being analyzed.

2. The differential perceptions related to population growth are being interpreted.

3. The behavioral and perceptual aspects of urban and regional structure and process are being studied with emphasis on planning, specifically analysis of corporate behavior related to retail location strategy.

4. Scientifically based performance standards to guide land use and environmental preservation decisions are being established.

Government's Approach to the Problem

Department of the Interior
C Street between Eighteenth and Nineteenth Streets, N.W.
Washington, D.C. 20240

Geological Survey, National Center, 12201 Sunrise Valley Drive, Reston, Virginia 22092. The Survey conducts highly diversified research programs to increase understanding and to aid in management of the mineral and energy potential of the land area of the United States. The survey collects information to provide a basis for many critical decisions and actions relating to land use, urban planning and development, construction practices, environmental and health problems, and natural disasters.

Bureau of Land Management. The Bureau provides for the protection, orderly development, and use of the national resource lands and resources under principles of multiple use and sustained yield, while maintaining and enhancing the quality of the environment; it also develops recreational opportunities.

Bureau of Outdoor Recreation. The Bureau of Outdoor Recreation serves as the federal focal point to assure prompt and coordinated action at all levels of government for coordinating, planning, and financing public outdoor recreation; encourages and assists all governmental and private interests to conserve, develop, and utilize outdoor recreation resources for the benefit and enjoyment of present and future generations.

Bureau of Reclamation. The function of the Bureau of Reclamation is to assist states, local governments, and other federal agencies to stabilize and stimulate local and regional economies, enhance and protect the environment, and improve the quality of life through development of water and related land resources.

Land and Water Resources, Office of the Secretary. The Assistant Secretary of Land and Water Resources has direct responsibility for programs associated with land use and water planning.

Natural Hazards

Psychologists' Approach to the Problem

Psychologists who are concerned with natural hazards are addressing the following topics.

1. Individual and community behavior in response to extreme events (e.g., floods, droughts, and earthquakes) is being recorded.

2. The acceptability of differing flood protection and prairie preservation schemes is being studied.

3. Community decision-making processes are being examined with respect to adoption of alternative adjustment policies to the earthquake hazard.

Government's Approach to the Problem

Department of Housing and Urban Development
451 Seventh Street, S.W.
Washington, D.C. 20410

Federal Disaster Assistance Administration. The Administration provides direction and overall policy coordination for disaster programs delegated to the Secretary by the President. This involves management of programs concerned with disaster research, preparedness, readiness evaluation, disaster relief, and recovery.

Public Policy and Decision Making

Psychologists' Approach to the Problem

Psychologists interested in the areas of public policy and decision making are considering the following problems.

1. The decision-making processes in industrial and public sector organizations pertaining to environmental policy are being studied.

2. Psychology, utility theory, and systems theory are being observed as they interface with environment and behavior.

3. The role of perceptions and attitudes in environmental decision making, particularly as it relates to the functions of specialists and interest groups involved in that process, is being examined.

4. Seminal theories combining American cultural beliefs and practices with existing environmental problems and potential solutions are being developed.

5. The effect of environmental policy on social well-being and the quality of life is being studied.

6. Perceptions and responses to natural hazards (earthquakes) are being studied with emphasis on reciprocal effects of public policy.

7. The impact of community social systems on the citizens of the community is being measured, especially the study of institutions and how they can be humanized to better serve the needs of citizens.

8. Individual differences in environmental preference and satisfaction are being noted.

9. Models for alternative behavior change procedures are being developed.

10. The effects of environmental variables on prejudice reduction between low-income (black) residential projects and adjacent mid-income (white) neighbors are being measured.

11. Mathematical modeling of resource allocation and wo/manpower planning decisions is being developed.

12. The psychological evaluation of social policy alternatives has been initiated.

Government's Approach to the Problem

Council on Environmental Quality
722 Jackson Place, N.W.
Washington, D.C. 20006

The Council on Environmental Quality develops and recommends to the President national policies that promote environmental quality; provides analyses of changes or trends in national environment; and assists the President in the preparation of the annual environmental quality report to the Congress.

Environment Impact Assessment

Psychologists' Approach to the Problem

Psychologists who assess environmental impact are studying the following areas.

1. Thresholds at which environmental impacts are perceived and assessed critically are being studied.

2. The impact of technologies on environment is being assessed.

3. Criteria for social impact assessment are being developed.

4. Environmental assessment techniques to measure systematically social and physical characteristics of various types of environment are being developed. Techniques for neighborhood-level analyses are being developed.

5. Existing environments are being evaluated in terms of contribution to human satisfaction.

6. Methodology for aesthetic impact assessment, covering the full range of environmental attributes of aesthetic value along with characteristics of human perception, is being developed.

Government's Approach to the Problem

The National Environmental Protection Act mandates all governmental departments and agencies to be concerned about the environmental impact of their activities.

Technology and the Future

Psychologists' Approach to the Problem

Psychologists who concentrate on technology and the future are studying the life-styles in a postindustrial economy; the impact of total credit card, cashless, and checkless system of exchange; and the interaction of technology and society.

Government's Approach to the Problem

Office of Technology Assessment
119 D Street, N.E.
Washington, D.C. 20510

The Office of Technology Assessment provides an independent and objective source of information about impacts of technological applications and identifies policy alternatives for technological-related issues. The basic function of the Office is to provide congressional committees with assessments or studies of the broad range of social and physical consequences that might emanate from various policy choices. There are eight broad program areas: energy, food, health, materials, oceans, transportation, technology, and world trade.

Some Closing Comments

The National Science Foundation in its publication *Basic Research, Applied Research, and Development in Industry 1965* (NSF, 1967) defined basic research as "original investigations for the advancement of scientific knowledge that do not have specific objectives to answer problems of sponsoring agencies or companies, although these investigations may be in the field of present or potential interest to the sponsoring organizations" (p. 101). In contrast, "applied research" is viewed as "research activities on problems posed by sponsoring agencies or companies for the purpose of contributing to the solution of these problems (p. 101). As noted by Vollmer (1972), the labeling of the research in this instance is based on the motivation of the group providing the monetary support. These definitions do not, however, address the intent of the individual researcher who might be asking the same questions whether or not the group sponsoring his or her research had posed the problem.

The real-dollar budgets of government agencies that have traditionally provided the monetary support for basic research in psychology are shrinking dramatically. Most government agencies have tighter budgets and feel the pressure to expend public dollars in a way that will have the most salubrious effect on society. Consequently, they will be awarding more money to particular researchers for work on a particular problem. Many of these government agencies are currently mandated to deal with questions of the environment and quality of life. Physical scientists, engineers, and economists have vigorously attacked these problems and have advanced their own fields. Psychologists will need to be equally active in extending the definition of environment to its logical parameters so that social science input is included. As the research literature builds up and undergoes selection, it is imperative that it appears in a form that is accessible and useful to policymakers so that input from psychologists is recognized as legitimate.

Because of the way that a problem is originally framed in legislation, an agency set up to solve a given problem may be traditionally linked with one particular discipline. The solution to the problem, however, is not discrete and often lends itself to multidisciplinary perspectives. Section 102(2)(A) of the National Environmental Protection Act provides the legislative mandate in environmental impact statements by requiring that agencies "utilize a systematic, interdisciplinary approach which will ensure the integrated use of the natural and social sciences and the environmental design area in planning and decision making." Psychologists, as well as biologists, engineers, sociologists, and architects, should be increasingly addressing the problems of air and water pollution, land use, technology assessment, and urban design, to name only a few. This chapter provides an initial outline for a strategy to make officials in governmental departments and agencies aware of the potential contributions that psychologists are prepared to make to solutions of their problems.

REFERENCES

Craik, K. H. Environmental psychology. *Annual Review of Psychology*, 1973, *24*, 403–422.
National Science Foundation. *Basic research, applied research, and development in industry* (NSF Report No. 67-12). Washington, D.C.: Author, 1967.
Office of the Federal Register. *United States Government Manual 1975/1976* (Rev. ed.). Washington, D.C.: National Archives and Records Service, General Services Administration, 1975.
Vollmer, H. Basic and applied research. In S. Z. Nagi & R. G. Corwin (Eds.), *The social contexts of research.* New York: Wiley, 1972.
Wohwill, J. F. The emerging discipline of environmental psychology. *American Psychologist*, 1970, *25*, 303–312.

21

Vaida D. Thompson and Sidney H. Newman

Training and Research Opportunities in Population Psychology

The goal of this chapter is to convey to young psychologists—and to those planning to become psychologists—the need for research that will contribute more fully to an understanding of population and population-related behaviors, which pertain to some of the most important problems in the world. To accomplish this goal, we discuss a number of significant population issues in need of psychological research, intending to stimulate graduate students and psychologists to consider doing such research. In addition, we delineate ways in which interested students and psychologists can educate and develop themselves for working in the population field, still a relatively new field for psychologists.

It is no doubt a most unusual researcher who has started a career from anything other than the launching pad of a faculty's interests. Students trained in sophisticated laboratory techniques pertaining to the study of reinforcement schedules are expected (nay, "shaped") to direct their own research, and that of their students and the students after them, to similar problems. Thus, the most advantageous first step in becoming a population psychologist is to find a mentor whose own research interests are in population. There is an ever-increasing number of such persons, and their counsel may be sought when the individual develops an interest in population, at any point in a career. Even a student currently being trained with no focus on population issues or related research can learn about the issues, can ultimately focus on these issues in research, and can possibly find postdoctoral training and research support to further these goals.

This chapter is thus directed toward three major topics: What are the areas and issues of research in population psychology? How can psychology trainees—even those in a "pure" research setting—prepare themselves for work in this area? What postdoctoral training and research support opportunities may assist them toward their goals? The faculty member who is interested in developing skills in population research and in assuring population training for current and future students, yet who senses a lack of preparation, may also find the suggestions for students of benefit.

Vaida D. Thompson is currently with the Department of Psychology and the Carolina Population Center, University of North Carolina at Chapel Hill; Sidney H. Newman is with the Center for Population Research, National Institute for Child Health and Human Development, Bethesda, Maryland.

Population Issues[1]

Many persons in the scientific community who were, in the past, concerned with developing teaching and research in population were lulled into thinking that current decreases in fertility rates portended the end of the population problem and obviated a high priority for population research. These are not valid conclusions. In the first place, current fertility rates do not necessarily predict to future or completed fertility of individuals or cohorts. Reasons for changes in period fertility rates are not well understood, and current rates may not be maintained. For example, during the Depression, much concern was focused on markedly decreased fertility rates and implications for the future; such concern contributed largely to the initiation of psychological research attempting to explain contraceptive and fertility behaviors. Certainly, nothing in the aggregate behaviors at that time would have led to predictions concerning the post-World-War-II baby boom. Currently, college students express intentions to have two children and give as their reasons the economic hardships that would be encountered with larger families. When interviewed, however, they state preferences for larger families and suggest that they might have more children if their own economic situation is better than they now anticipate or—an interesting point—if birthrates remain so low that they would no longer have to be concerned about population growth. Surely, if such thinking were prevalent, increased aggregate fertility could easily result.

A second population concern even in this period of decreasing fertility is that there remain subgroups in which there is still-increasing unwanted fertility. For example, among unmarried females under age 20 a 50% rate increase in births has occurred over the past decade. In this group, very inadequate contraceptive use is also prevalent. Kantner and Zelnik (1972, 1973) reported that only 19% of teenagers from their study stated that they "always" used contraception, although 62.9% reported using it "sometimes," and 15.7% reported "never" using it.

Even given some means of reducing unwanted fertility and in the presence of continued low fertility rates, several reasons exist why population should remain a high-priority research area. First, the population field is concerned not only with growth and overpopulation but also with problems of stationary and declining populations. In such populations, age distributions produce unique and perhaps frequently changing societal problems; for example, labor force potential may be markedly affected, and the number of older persons in the population may increase, resulting in altered needs for psychological, medical, and other services. Whatever trends exist in population growth and change, phenomena and processes involved remain poorly understood. A second issue of importance in the population area, without regard for the population growth status, is population policy. A need exists for informed population policy on diverse societal matters: transportation, taxation, medical care, and others. Such

---

1. This section is adapted from a report prepared by the Executive Committee, APA Division 34, and presented to the President's Biomedical Panel by Vaida D. Thompson.

policy, whether national or regional, requires guidance from accurate, empirical research directed at the multiple and complex problems associated with population growth, change, and distribution.

The study of population issues clearly indicates that interdisciplinary and complementary research is required and that psychologists must contribute to such efforts. Biomedical scientists may develop effective, safe, and inexpensive contraceptive techniques; however, if such techniques are not acceptable, or not used, behavioral scientists can provide an understanding of the nonacceptance and suggest guidelines for acceptance. Similarly, demographers may accurately report changes and trends in aggregate fertility, but the reasons for individual and couple behavior must be more fully understood. It is within the realm of psychology to explore the individual and couple processes that may explain such behaviors. Psychologists do have particular competencies for conceptualizing and conducting research on such issues. They are concerned with motives, attitudes, values, personal orientations, decision processes, and dyadic interactions that underlie or are associated with behavior and behavioral change. They are also trained in special research and methodological and analytical skills. Such competencies and skills should be directed at the study of problems such as individual and couple contraceptive and migratory behaviors.

Certain population issues may be of peripheral concern to psychologists, except for those who have been trained in aggregate quantitative techniques. These issues include population change, population characteristics, and mortality. Studies of population change have generally been historical in nature or have focused on projections from current data; interest has generally been directed at aggregate societal variables, such as economic and political situations, natural resources, and societal well-being. In studying population characteristics, the focus has generally been on aspects such as rural–urban, ethnic–racial differentials in fertility and migration. Cultural, historical, and economic development have often been incorporated, as has the association of population characteristics with such factors as social behavior, human territoriality, and economic situations. Issues of possible concern to psychologists have received little research attention; for example, the impact of population characteristics such as race, sex, or socioeconomic status on mental health and psychological stress has not received sufficient research attention. Also, little study has focused on the impacts of fertility and migration on demands for societal service. In the area of mortality, research has also been largely of a demographic nature, dealing with collection, tabulation, and analysis of aggregate data on deaths in the society and its subgroups (e.g., sex and race groups).

In all of the above areas, the research has been principally in the domain of sociological demographers, with demographic and mathematical specialists contributing the bulk of the work. Some ethnographic and political studies are beginning to emerge. Research of a psychosocial nature, however, as on health-related issues in population subgroups, is sparse. Thus, while quantitative psychologists might provide some increased sophistication in methods of data analysis, research on such issues is not beyond the purview of other psychologists.

There are many other population issues with which psychologists might deal more comfortably, because individual and couple processes are more central to the behaviors of concern. These include issues pertaining to (a) migration; (b) fertility, contraception, and sterilization; (c) marriage, divorce, and the family; and (d) population policy.

Migration

Migration has also been largely a focus of demographers, with research generally using census tabulations in the study of such issues as rural–urban migration. While some attention has been given recently to the study of adjustment and assimilation problems of migrants and the associated psychological and economic costs, there has been much neglect of individual, dyadic, and family processes associated with migration and of the interrelationships among mobility, family formation, and childbearing. Also largely ignored have been possible benefits to migrants (such as occupational mobility and income equalization) and the rewards and costs in nonmigration. Of particular concern to psychologists should be the individual and couple characteristics and decision processes that underlie migration or nonmigration. Interpersonal factors, such as intelligence and efficiency in seeking and evaluating information, motivations, and goals and aspirations, have been recognized but rarely explored. Interpersonal processes, such as information dependence and conformity pressures, have also been recognized but rarely examined empirically. Psychological models of migration decisions and behavior (Wolpert, 1965) reflect the individual and psychosocial nature of migration that must be understood if aggregate behaviors are to be explained and if effective policies are to be developed.

Fertility, Contraception, and Sterilization

The issues of fertility, contraception, and sterilization present perhaps the largest area of potential psychological research. Subsumed under this broad category are such issues as counseling in contraceptive and abortion decisions and teenage contraception and pregnancy. Demographic and epidemiological research has dealt with fertility issues in general. Many microlevel processes, however, have received inadequate research attention. Couple decision-making processes (particularly repeated and continuous decision making) pertaining to contraception and family planning are only beginning to be explored, as are the individual characteristics, couple interaction factors, life situations, and social factors that influence these processes. While many studies pertaining to contraceptive and biological knowledge have been completed, attitudes, motives, personality characteristics, and social factors that affect multiple population behaviors (including early marriage, sexual activity, contraceptive use, fertility planning, abortion, and sterilization) remain insufficiently understood. We do not know why techniques of family planning are accepted or rejected; nor do we know the psychosocial consequences of fertility regulation or nonregulation.

Researchers have commented on increasing sexual activity and inefficient contraception among teenagers (Presser, 1974). Such unprotected sexual activity has led to increased out-of-wedlock pregnancy and abortions in this group. Teenagers are reported to constitute the highest proportion of late aborters, the group in which risk is highest (Tietze & Dawson, 1973); teenage out-of-wedlock births doubled in the 1960s and increased the danger of infant and maternal mortality (Wright, 1972). Those concerned with such problems have reviewed the traumas potentially associated with an unwed teenager carrying a child to term: The female must generally leave school early; the couple may rush into marriage; early divorce may ensue; and, more tragically than all of this, the female's entire personal and productive life may be permanently disrupted (Russo & Brackbill, 1973). The consequences for all concerned—the mother, the father, the child if born, and the society—are inestimable (David, 1972). Because little is known about determinants and consequences of contraceptive use, of abortion, or of term-delivery decisions in this important teenage group, it is not possible to delineate fully the means of behavioral change or the handling of behavioral outcomes, nor can adequate contraceptive and reproductive education be developed.

Marriage, Divorce, and the Family

This third population area encompasses subareas that should be of great concern to psychologists. Two of the subareas are the complex and interrelated factors of (a) women's roles, labor force, and fertility and (b) family size and spacing.

With regard to the first set of factors, current fertility rates are low, and women's societal roles and labor force participation are changing concomitantly. As noted earlier, predicting future fertility is difficult; predicting the impact of changing sex roles and working behaviors on fertility and family formation patterns is equally difficult. Little understanding exists of such issues as trade-offs between working or careers for women and fertility. Much of the relevant research on such issues has used aggregate data to test hypotheses pertaining to household behavior (cf. Easterlin, 1969). Behavioral social scientists are currently engaged in research on the microlevel (using individual and couple data) to assess perceived rewards and costs in childbearing and the psychoeconomic rewards and costs of children, particularly in relation to alternative roles. Some theorizing (but little research) has been concerned with possible impacts of policies that assure women rights to careers and also to childbearing through guaranteed maternity leaves, fully adequate day care centers, and affirmative action guidelines. Genuine choices between careers and childbearing or both have just recently been fully assured; therefore, possible outcomes and consequences can only be speculated upon at present. Similarly, rapidly changing patterns of divorce and remarriage and their effects on population growth and distribution are currently only matters of speculation.

While many of the issues cited above have received little research attention, research pertaining to family size and, to some degree, family spacing has been somewhat more popular among psychologists. For example, interest in family size ideals is longstanding; since the 1930s, the two-to-four-child range has been desired (Blake, 1966). As noted earlier, data from current college students (Thompson, 1974) would suggest (as would European data reported by Blake, 1965) that current desires remain consistent with this range and that the prevalently stated desire for two-child families may reflect concern with economic conditions rather than a genuine change. Certainly we know that the one-child family is not highly valued in this culture (cf. Thompson, 1974). Although research on the only child and on family size has often had a number of methodological problems, distaste for the only child would appear to reflect more of a "cultural truism" than knowledge of facts based on empirical evidence. For example, only children (and children from widely spaced families) tend to be superior in intellectual development and in the acquisition of autonomy and independence. Such apparent superiority could be attributable to socioeconomic, genetic, or maternal factors or to the differential attention and differential opportunities for nurturance of desirable qualities for such children. Confirmation of any of these factors might result in very untoward policy outcomes (particularly if hereditary factors were demonstrated unequivocally as causal) or in individual—not policy inflicted—changes in family formation (if environmental factors were determined to be of primary importance). Without knowledge of reliable empirical evidence on such issues to influence change, and because of both continued negative attitudes toward only children and preferences for at least two children, family building patterns are not likely to verge toward optimal aggregate population growth; that is, the Commission on Population Growth and the American Future has recommended a two-child family average. Unless intentional childlessness and one-child families become more socially desirable, preferences for two or more children, and the economic situations to permit realization of these preferences, might preclude optimal growth patterns.

Population Policy

Much of the above has suggested at least implicit policies concerning population behaviors. Population policy itself is, however, an area requiring much research. "Population policy" is rarely defined; it tends to have different meanings to academicians of various disciplines and to politicians and policy planners. Generally it is thought of as policy for other countries that have excessive population growth, and suggestions generally relate to fertility reduction. Policies proposed are, in the main, on the societal level, pertaining to improved education, higher income and other socioeconomic benefits, and changing roles for women. Incentives and disincentives for family planning are also discussed. The Bucharest World Population Conference, convened in August of World Population Year (1974) by the United Nations, included representatives of 135 nations and adopted a World Plan of Action that was subsequently approved by the United Nations General Assembly. Among the propositions contained in the plan were the following: (a) Number and spacing of one's children is a decision that is a basic human right; (b) governments should provide individuals the information and the means to exercise this right; (c) population policies and programs should be part of development planning; (d) quantitative goals and timetables for reducing population growth and mortality are desirable; (e) improvement of the status of women will help to reduce population growth; and (f) population reduction and promotion of socioeconomic development are mutually reinforcing and together lead to a higher quality of life (World Population Conference, 1974). Both explicitly and implicitly, the conference thus yielded recommendations for population policy. Governmental policies intended to influence population behaviors will necessarily influence large numbers of people, by means of whatever mechanisms exist to produce change. As McGreevey (1974) noted, however, "the overarching problem in population policy is how to turn public objectives into private actions" (p. 69). Thus, societal programs will produce a change only if they directly or indirectly influence change in individuals or couples. In the realm of fertility, only if marriages are delayed, pregnancies avoided, and family size reduced will anything other than external force produce change. The Bucharest Conference certainly produced valuable interactions between behavioral social scientists, government planners, and population policymakers. It also suggested, relative to population policy research, that scientists are not sufficiently involved in research that provides immediate and genuinely useful guidelines to policymakers: What policies can be instrumented and why and how people can be influenced in accord with governmental and individual goals are poorly understood. Thus, policy generally evolves from nonempirical speculation on ways of expediting a country's goals, which may be inconsistent with the needs and goals of individuals.

The above review of population areas and issues requiring research attention by psychologists and other behavioral social scientists should surely suffice to alert both graduate students and psychologists to the breadth and depth of population psychology. How, though, does the psychology student prepare for a career in this area, particularly if there is no specific substantive or research focus on population within the student's graduate (or undergraduate) program?

Training for the Population Field

As noted earlier, all psychologists can provide unique competencies in the study of population issues. Psychologists acquire special skills and methods in their theoretical and empirical approaches to an understanding of individuals, dyads, small groups, and larger aggregates. Certain emphases in the education of psychologists, while not unique to psychology, are central to, and are those much required in, population research and service. These include developing precise and testable theories; testing of these theories by accurate, quantitative, empirical methods; using sophisticated, quantitative methodologies and techniques; using highly developed statistical and mathematical methods of data analyses and syntheses; making parsimonious and logical interpretations of data; and developing services and administration based on the analysis, synthesis, and interpretation of relevant data. These skills are initially acquired in graduate school where, to contribute effectively to the population field, the graduate student must receive the basic education that assures opportunities to acquire necessary psychological expertise.

Beyond the basic psychological training within a subprogram consistent with the trainee's interests (e.g., social, clinical, experimental), the most useful course of study for a student interested in applying skills to population issues would be that of a minor outside the discipline. Across universities, whether or not there is a cross-disciplinary population emphasis within a university, numerous courses are available that should provide content and expertise related to population. Following are a few of the kinds of courses that might provide this emphasis.

Since the major issues in population are fertility, mortality, and migration, and the effect of these interrelated issues is on growth, composition, distribution, and change in population, the largest focus on such issues would probably be in sociology departments, particularly in explicit demographic courses. Although the huge body of literature that exists has been amassed principally by sociologist-demographers and concerns numerical aggregate data (as from censuses), such data are by no means the sole focus in sociology courses. Not only have sociologists increasingly expressed concern about the individual and dyadic behaviors and decision processes that relate to population (cf. Price & Sikes, 1974), but many of the models of population behavior that suggest social psychological processes are sociological in nature; for example, (a) Davis' (1963) model of the demographic transition—a fall in deaths, followed, after a lag, by a fall in births—from which it can be inferred that the fall in births represents individual and/or dyadic decisions, essentially due to perceived rewards or benefits in small families and perceived costs of large families; or (b) Lee's (1966) social demographic theory of migratory behavior, which involves similar social psychological mechanisms.

Other aspects of sociology, particularly in family sociology, complement the concerns of clinical, counseling, and child/developmental psychologists. For example, interrelationships of family size, structure, and type of natality and of alternative roles for women and fertility are concerns dealt with in such courses.

In most universities, basic anthropology courses focus on issues similar to those cited above. Since population behaviors, including family structures, must be considered in the cultural (and subcultural) context, and because there is a commonality of interest in child developmental and child-rearing techniques, anthropology courses, even if not specifically population related, could be very useful to psychologists concerned with such issues.

Similarly, courses in microeconomics (as well as in macroeconomics) should provide valuable concepts and techniques for psychologists. One of the most useful theories of fertility is a social economic model developed by Easterlin (1969). The model has been tested principally with aggregate data. Conceptually, however, an individual/dyadic framework focuses explicitly on reward–cost components (in cost–benefit analysis terms) of fertility decisions. The model bears some similarity to social psychological conceptualizations of exchange (cf. Thibaut & Kelley, 1959), and thus any educational emphasis on microeconomic models might seem most relevant for persons in this subspecialty. The heavy emphasis on computer simulations and tests using large data bases, however, may make such a focus particularly useful for quantitative students (as would demography and biostatistics courses using demographic data).

The previous reference to population policy should suggest that basic political science courses, particularly those with policy focuses, would provide some useful training in the consideration of political impacts of individual and group population behaviors and, in turn, the resulting political and legislative effects on individual behaviors. Many political science courses that focus on the developing countries (the Third World) would seem particularly well suited to population implications.

Particularly useful, it would seem, for experimental and social psychologists interested in societal change would be courses in city planning and geography. Again, with judicious selection, the psychologist can find courses in these disciplines that would provide insights into societal structure and potential societal change pertaining to units larger than the dyad or family.

Finally, physiological and biological psychologists should find complementary interests in reproductive biology. With a focus on contraception, abortion, and sterilization techniques, researchers in these areas are concerned with the same physiological and hormonal mechanisms—and their interaction with behavior—as the psychological subspecialties noted. The behavioral issues relating to physiological concerns of reproductive biologists—that is, the use of contraception or the seeking of abortion or sterilization—represent a shared concern of clinical, counseling, personality, and social psychology in their common search for attitudinal and personality correlates and predictors of such behaviors.

In all the examples cited, methods of research may be similar to or highly discrepant from those used by psychologists. Surely physiological and computer analysis methods across disciplines are similar; on the other hand, ethnographic methods of anthropologists, descriptive methods of political scientists, and, in large measure, survey methods and census data analyses of demographers may differ markedly from psychological approaches. Nevertheless, much is to be gained by psychologists in learning new methods or in applying common techniques to different problems.

In the above examples, the kinds of courses that might serve as minors within one discipline or across several were chosen to provide complementary focuses to those of the various subdisciplines in psychology. They should also provide some guidelines for the student who seeks an intrapsychology minor that might be of use in approaching population issues. Judicious selection of courses that relate to motivation, developmental processes, attitudes, interpersonal processes, personality, and quantitative methods should provide a good basis for the kinds of research problems encountered in population. Some universities also have explicit population courses (such as psychological perspectives on population) and courses that relate to explicit population issues (such as crowding or sex roles). Also, many universities have courses in which population issues provide a "referent in residence," that is, a real-life topic or data set that is used to apply basic concepts. The student should be urged to select such courses in a minor (given that no more explicit courses are available) because such courses provide a strong basis for conceptualizing population issues: The instructor who examines the application of basic concepts to population has no doubt given a good deal of thought to such concerns.

One note on courses and programs: The above discussion of related disciplines would pertain on the graduate or the undergraduate level. If the student is properly counseled (which includes the student's own analysis and input), courses within and outside the discipline can be selected that will provide a strong base for population research, teaching, and service. Perhaps undergraduate students are more fortunate in that more psychology–environment or interdisciplinary undergraduate programs are emerging where students may find the kinds of courses described above. Such undergraduate majors may provide the broad background upon which graduate training in any discipline can be both overlaid and directed toward ultimate research goals in population; that is, the student who has broad knowledge of population should be able to tailor graduate training toward the study of more relevant issues.

Finally, it should be emphasized that students, even in the most traditional graduate program, can direct their own research, especially the dissertation, toward population issues. Some of the best research by psychologists on population behaviors has been developed as MA or doctoral theses by students who have either been fortunate enough to have had contact with faculty with commitment to a study of such issues or to have entered graduate school with—or themselves developed—a comprehensive, generally interdisciplinary background in population.

Psychologists, like other behavioral social scientists, have demonstrated increased interest and activity in the population area. The interests and activities of psychologists, however, are not nearly commensurate with the potential contributions that they can make to the scientific and practical solutions of population problems. One of the reasons why psychologists have not been more involved in the scientific study of population issues is that training programs with a population emphasis have not been sufficiently developed within graduate or undergraduate programs in psychology. Researchers who have developed interest and expertise in this area do involve graduate students in their work, and many of these students go on to do their own dissertations on population issues. Almost no psychology program in the United States, however, has clearly identifiable course tracks or well-delineated ouside minors specified for training in population. The latter course (of gaining expertise in population solely through outside minors in other disciplines—as sociology or economics) presents hazards as well as benefits; without codirection of interests from within psychology programs, psychology majors can fail to develop psychological perspectives on the major issues, yet establish research focuses and breadth in population as dealt with in these other disciplines.

Postdoctoral Opportunities

The person who has already completed graduate school and wishes to begin population research does, of course, have the possibility of self-instruction. In a paper prepared for the spring/summer 1975 Population Psychology Newsletter (Division 34, APA) Newman and Thompson (1975) cited a number of useful references that should provide some background concerning what psychologists and other behavioral social scientists are doing, or can do, in population.[2] These references include the following: *Psychology*—Fawcett (1970, 1973), Pohlman (1969), Chung, Palmore, Lee, and Lee (1972), and Newman and Thompson (in press); *Sociology-Demography*—Freedman (1975), U.S. Commission on Population Growth (1972a), Bogue (1969), Price and Sikes (1974), and Hawthorn (1970); *Anthropology*—Nag (1973), Polgar (1971), and Matras (1973); *Economics*—U.S. Commission on Population Growth (1972b), Easterlin (1969; in press), and Schultz (1971); *Political Science*—Clinton and Godwin (1972), Clinton (1973), and Weiner (1971); *Geography*—Zelinski, Kosinski, and Prothero (1970); *General*—U.S. Commission on Population Growth (1972a, 1972b, 1972c). The *Inventory of Federal Population Research* (Interagency Committee, 1974) lists all the behavioral social population research funded by the federal government each fiscal year under the following classifications: population change; population characteristics; fertility; mortality; migration and population distribution; marriage, divorce, and the family; population policy; general or multiple.

The Center for Population Research has issued brochures for each of the six behavioral social disciplines noted above.[3] It may be worthwhile to list here the research needs in psychology specified in a recent brochure:

1. Psychosocial factors involved in fertility and pregnancy, including motivations, personality, psychological or emotional disturbances, ability, knowledge, minority or subcultural differentials, spouse or other familial interrelationships, family size, alienation, social isolation, etc.

---

2. The recently formed Division of Population Psychology (Division 34) of the American Psychological Association is the focal point for population psychology in the APA and issues a newsletter and other relevant materials.

3. The brochure and inventories of federal funded research can be obtained from the Center for Population Research, NICHD, Landow Building, Room C737, Bethesda, Maryland 20014.

2. Psychosocial factors in the use of various contraceptive techniques, including choice of contraceptives; psychological characteristics of contraceptive accepters, dropouts, and rejecters; emotional resistance to contraceptives; factors involved in the "careless" use of contraceptives; psychological reactions of spouses when contraceptives are used; roles of men and women in making decisions concerning the use of contraceptives in birth planning; psychological factors in the delivery of contraceptives to prospective users; sources of information about contraceptives; attitudes of physicians, psychiatrists, clergymen, and other kinds of personal advisers that affect contraceptive practices; sociopsychological impact of contraceptive programs on individuals, youth, status of women, abortion, illegitimacy, etc.

3. Psychological and socioeconomic factors in the formation and determination of choices or preferences involved in making decisions about childbearing and spacing.

4. Origin and development of attitudes toward family planning; reproductive norms, fertility desires or expectations, birth spacing.

5. Origin and development of attitudes toward sex, especially as these attitudes relate to nonmarital sexual behavior and illegitimacy, as well as to marital sexual behavior and family planning.

6. Antecedent and consequent psychosocial factors in abortion and sterilization.

7. Antecedent and consequent psychosocial factors in internal migration (i.e., rural to urban); relation to fertility and population changes.

8. Psychosocial factors and considerations in the design and evaluation of population policy and action programs; development of attitudes of leaders toward population problems and effect of such attitudes on policy formation.

9. Psychosocial consequences of population changes and growth, as produced by such factors as increased size, density, and heterogeneity; experimental testing of methods for dealing with such consequences.

10. Methodological studies; measurement of attitudes, choices, preferences, opinions, values, and other psychological characteristics; developing methods for relating such measurements to fertility rates, family planning, contraceptive practices, sexual behavior, population change, etc.

11. Psychobiological factors—physiological, neurological, endocrinological—in reproduction and sexual behavior.

Quite clearly, these are all patent psychological issues and include those with which many researchers are already concerned, whether or not they consider themselves population trained or population researchers. The list also suggests those areas in which individuals may attempt self-development should this be the only likely alternative for training.

Postdoctoral Training

While the self-development approach can certainly familiarize a person with the areas of concern, and agencies such as the Center for Population Research, National Institute of Child Health and Human Development

(NICHD) can also consult with individuals about current research needs and directions, the fact that psychologists have had few population training opportunities in their graduate career may make it necessary for the person seeking career opportunities in population to seek advanced training on the postdoctoral level. Such training can be sought for varying lengths of time.

Short-Term Training

For short-term, and necessarily limited, training in population, psychologists can attend training and workshop programs when these are available. Short-term workshops and conferences are primarily concerned with aspects, issues, and problems of research. The workshops and conferences usually focus on a developing and significant research problem or area, building a program around such aspects as background; gaps in knowledge; theoretical and methodological approaches; and possibilities, ways, and means of achieving scientific advances. Generally, workshops and conferences are funded for a brief period of a few days. In the past, however, various institutions have received funding for purposes of more extended —and more explicit—training purposes. For example, in the summer of 1973 and again in 1974, the Center for Population Research, NICHD, supported four-week institutes at the Carolina Population Center for training of behavioral social scientists from five disciplines, including psychology. Participants were selected for their clearly identifiable interests in population research and their promise in this area, as based on past professional accomplishments, references, and so on. Similarly, the University of Hawaii has held frequent institutes on population topics. While these are generally developed for training international researchers, United States' researchers can attend those with announced openings.

Since there are no established annual institutes, those persons interested should remain alert for relevant workshops, conferences, and institutes. These short-term training experiences are generally advertised through population centers and population organizations; relevant departments and known population researchers in the areas of concern are generally informed of proposed activities so that they may inform possible candidates. Interested persons may also inquire of the agencies most likely to fund such activities.

Fellowships

Because there is no assurance that institutes and other short-term programs will be available, it is possible that persons seeking training in population would be best advised to explore individual postdoctoral training fellowships that may be in the program of the Center for Population Research, NICHD. A person applying for such fellowships must have a sponsor with recognized expertise in the population area; such persons are generally associated with larger population centers, such as those at the University of Michigan, the University of North Carolina, Harvard University, Cornell University, the University of Hawaii, Princeton University, the University of Chicago, Johns Hopkins University, the University of Texas, and the University of Wisconsin. In making application, the individual must also delineate a proposed training program, which will vary in accordance with the applicant's needs. For example, proposals may include, to varying degrees, descriptions of courses the students wish to take, specific research to be completed within the training period, and general research skills which the students plan to obtain. Fellowship support may be requested for periods of from one to three years. It bears noting that relatively few psychologists have ever applied for these fellowships, despite the fact that this opportunity may be the most expeditious for those interested in developing research proficiency and expertise and will surely contribute greatly to career development.

The above fellowship program is generally intended for new PhD applicants. It is also possible for more advanced scientists to obtain research career development awards. These awards are intended to enhance the research career of scientists with outstanding research productivity and potential. For these awards, the applicant is required to have at least three years of relevant postdoctoral experience and to be less than 40 years old. These awards are for five-year periods (with the possibility of renewal for not more than three years). Successful applicants devote most of their efforts to performing significant research, but they may give or receive research training and engage in teaching.

Currently, the Center for Population Research also provides support for postdoctoral research training at several major population centers. Applicants for these fellowships generally have research interests compatible with researchers associated with the population program at these institutions. However, given compatibility of interests and applicant potential, these fellowships provide essentially the same training opportunities as do the individual fellowships.[4]

Persons who have already developed research interests may further their research through grants and/or contracts available to individuals or groups of individuals as part of the program of the Center for Population Research. The 11 areas cited earlier as needed research areas comprise the major categories in which individual psychologists (or groups with which a psychologist is related) may have some research background. Of course, research grants are not by any means limited to this comprehensive list of topics. Proposals must be specific to population, however, and, of course, must meet criteria of scientific merit, as evaluated by an interdisciplinary peer review panel of which psychologists are a part. Research of a pilot or preliminary nature is considered, given that it meets the criteria employed by the review panel.

Program project grant proposals, which are also within the Center for Population Research program, attempt to integrate the research of a

---

4. Persons interested in more information concerning training opportunities for psychologists in the population field should direct their inquiries to Center for Population Research, NICHD, Landow Building, Bethesda, Maryland 20014.

number of investigators in order to study a multifaceted theory, problem, or issue. A multidisciplinary approach is taken, and a unifying view, theory, and/or methodology builds the research into a coherent structure. These projects are certainly available to teams in which psychologists are represented; however, few proposals have been received from teams including psychologists or other behavioral social scientists. Program projects are not likely to be headed by a relative novice in population, but any meritorious proposal can be funded. Those interested would be well advised to explore early in planning the program research with the Center for Population Research, NICHD.

Teaching Opportunities

At this time, relatively few available academic positions exist that are specifically allocated to population psychology. This lack, however, should not discourage persons with population interests; as noted earlier, population psychologists have principally contributed to the development of this field through research that uses the theories, methods, and analytical techniques of their own psychological specialty. In addition, persons interested in advancing their own careers in population psychology and furthering the potential for upcoming generations of scientists in this area can introduce specific population courses and incorporate population into more traditional courses. Thompson and Newman (1974) provided a report of a workshop in which leading population psychologists and chairpersons of psychology programs who are seeking to advance population education and training in their departments examined ways of introducing new courses and enhancing existing courses on the undergraduate and graduate levels (a more complete report of the workshop can be found in Newman and Thompson, in press). Any course content that facilitates understanding of the individual, dyadic, small group, and larger (e.g., societal) systems—understanding that is central to population research and services—could (or should) concomitantly facilitate understanding of population processes and behaviors. Among the very transferable skills are those pertaining to developing precise and testable theories of these processes and behaviors; testing these theories by accurate, quantitative, empirical methods; using sophisticated, quantitative methodologies and techniques in the study of these processes; using highly developed statistical and mathematical methods of data analyses and syntheses; making parsimonious and logical interpretations of data; and recommending the development and administration of services based on the analysis, synthesis, and interpretation of relevant data.

Placement Opportunities

Opportunities are emerging for population psychologists in public and private institutions and agencies. In fact, some of the more promising research in this area is being conducted in association with both national and international agencies. For example, one of the leading social psychologists involved in population is associated with Battelle Institute in Seattle, Washington; and some of the leading theory development by clinical, experimental, and quantitative psychologists has emerged under the auspices of the Transnational Family Research Institute and the World Health Organization. It should also be emphasized that a psychologist who has developed in the area of population by virtue of graduate training and/or participation in population research and other activities could be competent to fulfill teaching, administrative, counseling, or other functions in a department of psychology or another unit in a university or college. Population training, interests, and background add a significant dimension, with meaningful, real-life concerns that may enhance the psychologist's other professional and academic attributes. Psychologists with clinical or administrative interests might find satisfying work activities in family planning programs and clinics.

Conclusion

It is hoped that this chapter has opened new and attractive occupational vistas for psychologists who want to work in areas that can be not only scientifically productive but also socially meaningful. Population research, teaching, and administration provide work on important, meaningful problems and require all of the scientific sophistication and acumen that a competent psychologist can bring to the field.

REFERENCES

Blake, J. Demographic science and the redirection of population policy. *Journal of Chronic Disease*, 1965, *18*, 1181–1200.

Blake, J. Ideal family size among white Americans: A quarter of a century's evidence. *Demography*, 1966, *3*, 154–173.

Bogue, D. J. *Principles of demography*. New York: Wiley, 1969.

Chung, B. M., Palmore, J. A., Lee, J., & Lee, S. J. *Psychological perspectives: Family planning in Korea*. Seoul, Korea: Hollym, 1972.

Clinton, R. L. (Ed.). *Population and politics: New directions in political science research*. Lexington, Ky.: Heath, 1973.

Clinton, R. L., & Godwin, R. K. (Eds.). *Research in the politics of population*. Lexington, Ky.: Heath, 1972.

David, H. P. Unwanted pregnancies: Costs and alternatives. In C. F. Westoff & R. Parke, Jr. (Eds.), *Demographic and social aspects of population growth* (Vol. 1 of the Commission on Population Growth and the American Future Research Report). Washington, D.C.: U.S. Government Printing Office, 1972.

Davis, K. The theory of change and response in modern demographic history. *Population Index*, 1963, *29*, 345–366.

Easterlin, R. A. Toward a socio-economic theory of fertility: A survey of recent research on economic factors in American fertility. In S. J. Behrman, L. Corsa, & R. Freedman, (Eds.), *Fertility and family planning: A world view*. Ann Arbor: University of Michigan Press, 1969.

Easterlin, R. A. The economics and sociology of fertility: A synthesis. In *Early industrialization, shifts in fertility, and changes in family structure*. Princeton, N.J.: Princeton University Press, in press.

Fawcett, J. T. *Psychology and population: Behavioral research issues in fertility and family planning*. New York: The Population Council, 1970.

Fawcett, J. T. (Ed.). *Psychological perspectives on population*. New York: Basic Books, 1973.

Freedman, R. *The sociology of human fertility: An annotated bibliography*. New York: Halsted Press, 1975.

Hawthorn, G. *The sociology of fertility*. London: Collier-Macmillan, 1970.

Interagency Committee on Population Research. *Inventory of federal population research, fiscal year 1974* (DHEW Publ. NIH 74-133). Washington, D.C.: U.S. Government Printing Office, 1974.

Kantner, J. F., & Zelnik, M. Sexual experience of young unmarried women in the United States. *Family Planning Perspectives*, 1972, *4* (4), 9–18.

Kantner, J. F., & Zelnik, M. Contraception and pregnancy: Experiences of young unmarried women in the United States. *Family Planning Perspectives*, 1973, *5* (1), 21–35.

Lee, E. A theory of migration. *Demography*, 1966, *3*, 47–57.

Matras, J. *Population and societies.* New York: Prentice-Hall, 1973.

McGreevey, W. P. (Ed.). *The policy relevance of recent social research on fertility* (Occasional Monograph Series No. 2). Washington, D.C.: Smithsonian Institution, Interdisciplinary Communications Program, 1974.

Nag, M. Anthropology and population. Problems and perspectives. *Population Studies*, 1973, *27*, 59–68.

Newman, S. H., & Thompson, V. D. Needed population research and teaching: Challenges and opportunities for psychologists. *Population Psychology Newsletter*, 1975, *2*, 7–16.

Newman, S. H., & Thompson, V. D. (Eds.). *Population psychology: Research and educational issues.* Washington, D.C.: U.S. Government Printing Office, 1976, in press.

Pohlman, E. W. *The psychology of birth planning.* Cambridge, Mass.: Schenkman, 1969.

Polgar, S. (Ed.). *Culture and population: A collection of current studies* (Monograph No. 9). Chapel Hill, N.C.: Carolina Population Center, 1971.

Presser, M. Early motherhood: Ignorance or bliss? *Family Planning Perspectives*, 1974, *6* (1), 8–14.

Price, D. O., & Sikes, M. M. *Rural–urban migration research in the United States.* Washington, D.C.: U.S. Government Printing Office, 1974.

Russo, N., & Brackbill, Y. Population and youth. In J. Fawcett (Ed.), *Psychological perspectives on population.* New York: Basic Books, 1973.

Schultz, T. P. An economic perspective on population growth. In Study Committee of the National Academy of Sciences, *Rapid population growth: Consequences and policy implications.* Baltimore, Md.: Johns Hopkins University Press, 1971.

Thibaut, J., & Kelley, H. H. *The social psychology of groups.* New York: Wiley, 1959.

Thompson, V. Family size: Implicit policies and assumed outcomes. *Journal of Social Issues*, 1974, *30*, 93–124.

Thompson, V. D., & Newman, S. H. Education psychologists to work in the population field. *Professional Psychology*, 1974, *5*, 320–324.

Thompson, V. D., & Newman, S. H. Developing psychologists for work in the population field: Workshop report. In S. H. Newman & V. D. Thompson (Eds.), *Population psychology: Research and educational issues.* Washington, D.C.: U.S. Government Printing Office, 1976, in press.

Tietze, C., & Dawson, D. Induced abortion: A factbook. *Report on Population/Family Planning*, December 1973, pp. 1-56.

U.S. Commission on Population Growth and the American Future. *Demographic and social aspects of population growth* (Rep. No. 1). Edited by C. F. Westoff & R. Parke, Jr. Washington, D.C.: U.S. Government Printing Office, 1972. (a)

U.S. Commission on Population Growth and the American Future. *Economic aspects of population change* (Rep. No. 2). Edited by E. R. Morss & R. H. Reed. Washington, D.C.: U.S. Government Printing Office, 1972. (b)

U.S. Commission on Population Growth and the American Future. *Population and the American future* (Final Report). Washington, D.C.: U.S. Government Printing Office, 1972. (c)

Weiner, M. Political demography: An inquiry into the political consequences of population change. In Study Committee of the National Academy of Sciences, *Rapid population growth: Consequences and policy implications.* Baltimore, Md.: Johns Hopkins University Press, 1971.

Wolpert, J. Behavioral aspects of the decision to migrate. *Papers of the Regional Science Association*, 1965, *15*, 159–169.

World Population Conference. World population plan of action. *Studies in Family Planning*, 1974, *5*, 381–392.

Wright, N. Some estimates of the potential reduction in U.S. infant mortality rate by family planning. *American Journal of Public Health*, 1972, *62*, 1130–1134.

Zelinski, W., Kosinski, L. A., & Prothero, R. M. (Eds.). *Geography and a crowding world.* New York: Oxford University Press, 1970.

Part 6

Miscellaneous

22

Lee Sechrest

The Psychologist as Program Evaluator

At every level of organization within society, as problems are experienced, proposals for solving the problems are put forth and debated. For most of the problems some solution or set of solutions is selected to be implemented, usually with the at least implicit expectation that the solution will be successful. Often, in fact, solution is explicitly promised. In the usual course of events, programs are implemented in ways that make it impossible to tell whether they conform to the plan, and they remain in force until either funds have expired or the recurrence or persistence of the original problem makes it obvious that the programs are not working. In some cases programs, however effective or ineffective they may be, persist indefinitely because of a lack of any firm information concerning their success or failure. In order to facilitate the solution to important social problems and to make a wise allocation of resources, it has been suggested by numerous writers that social programs should be carefully evaluated with respect to the goals they are intended to achieve. This chapter points to some of the special qualifications of psychologists for program evaluation that may suggest a particular and important role for psychologists in program evaluation.

Research Methodology

The appropriateness of at least considering the contributions that psychologists might make to program evaluation is clearly supported by the fact that as much as any one man, Donald T. Campbell, a psychologist, has been responsible for the strong currents, both volitional and methodological, that are pushing government and other agencies so strongly toward program evaluation. In what was truly a seminal paper entitled "Reforms as Experiments" Campbell (1969) set forth a philosophy presenting a basis both for the development of social interventions and for their careful evaluation. He proposed that ameliorative social programs should be presented not as panaceas of obvious worth but as tentative hypotheses to be tested by the same methodologies as scientific hypotheses are tested in laboratories. He suggested that socially ameliorative programs should be adopted only tentatively and that explicit provision should be made for providing evidence on the basis of which they might ultimately be made permanent features of society. While there are many factors, for example,

Lee Sechrest is currently a Professor in the Department of Psychology, Florida State University.

251

economics or political pressures, that enter into the ultimate decision to adopt a social program, the psychologist has potentially an important contribution to make to the extent that the adoption of social programs depends upon the development of evidence of effectiveness based upon sound research.

If we are to make a case for the psychologist as program evaluator, it would seem desirable that the case should be made as strongly as possible and that we should be able to suggest that compared with many types of scientists the psychologist might have something more to offer. We believe, in fact, that psychologists, if not unique among behavioral scientists in their potential contributions to program evaluation, at least have a background and an orientation to research that puts them in a generally stronger position than members of other social and behavioral science disciplines. That is not to say that economists, political scientists, sociologists, and the like have less to offer, but rather that their contributions to social reform are of a different nature and probably come at different points in the entire process of creating, implementing, and testing a socially ameliorative program.

For a variety of historical reasons, psychology began as a laboratory science with a strong commitment to carefully devised and controlled experiments. While subsequent developments in psychology have fully illustrated the values of careful naturalistic observation and other like methodologies, it remains the case that the primary methodological orientation imparted in most psychology graduate training programs is that of the experiment with associated control groups and with treatments having been allocated randomly to cases. While it is widely recognized that there are many instances in the real world in which experiments are difficult, and perhaps even impossible, to carry out, the fact remains that the randomized true experiment represents the bench mark against which other methodologies are judged by psychologists. In fact, the insistence upon the primacy of the true experiment has not impeded the development of alternate methodologies, but rather has forced upon those methodologies a continuous attention to their weaknesses and provided impetus for improvement. Campbell and Stanley (1963) were responsible for the first careful comparison of various alternative methods to the true experiment. While they clearly tolerated, and on occasion even advocated, what they call quasi-experiments, Campbell and Stanley clearly regarded the true experiment as a measure for which the quasi-experiment is only a relatively weak and often costly substitute. Psychologists have been in the extreme forefront of the movement to develop the best possible alternative research methodologies to the true experiment. While it certainly cannot be alleged that all, or perhaps even most, psychologists are really good research methodologists, a larger absolute number and proportion of psychologists will probably be found among the higher ranking individuals in research methodology in the social and behavioral sciences.

The preceding claim is, fortunately, not merely professional vanity but is buttressed by some evidence. Bernstein and Freeman (1975) studied the methodological adequacy of a large number of government-sponsored grants and contracts for program evaluation and found that one of the most sharply distinguishing predictors of the overall quality of research methodology was the involvement of a psychologist in some important role in the project. Whether the psychologist was involved as principal investigator, project director, or some other similar position of responsibility, the rated quality of the research methodology was higher than if the same position were occupied by an economist, a sociologist, a psychiatrist, etc. Inasmuch as Bernstein and Freeman are sociologists, it may be supposed that they had no particular axe to grind in showing the substantial contributions of psychologists to good research methodology. Bernstein and Freeman's results are properly a source of pride, but also should serve as a stimulus to psychologists to continue whetting their research skills.

Quantitative Research and Measures

A second major contribution that psychologists can make to a wide variety of program evaluations stems from their interest and background in quantitative research and measures. Some social science disciplines such as sociology and political science developed either without a tradition for objective measurement or else with a rather narrow, circumscribed view of the problem. Survey methodologists from either sociology or political science are certainly oriented toward measurement, but their primary concerns have been with errors of sampling rather than with the properties of the instruments they used. It is rare, for example, to find a survey research project that pays any attention at all to either the reliability or validity of the measures that are employed.

Economists have been considerably more concerned with quantitative problems in their field, but their major orientation has been more in the direction of development of theories and models, and they have paid scant attention to the sources and quality of their data. Perhaps it is characteristic of model builders, for it has been noted to be so in psychology, that they have little regard for the source of the numbers that are the grist for their mill. What they are primarily concerned with is the grinding of those numbers. While Morgenstern (1950) was pointing out some 25 years ago that many of the sets of data on which economists rely are quite untrustworthy, his objection seems either not to have been heard, or simply to have been pushed aside as an interesting but trivial caveat.

Out of their early experiences in laboratory studies with human beings and their attempts to measure intelligence, psychologists became very much aware of the differences between the highly precise, although certainly not error free, measures possible in the physical sciences and the much less precise and often highly indirect measures required in behavioral science. It became apparent very early that one could not necessarily depend upon the stability of even the simplest of measures, and a very important and long-lasting psychometric tradition developed out of the desire of psychologists to establish reliable, dependable measures or, in more current terms, those having a high degree of generalizability (Cronbach, Gleser, Nanda, & Rajaratnam, 1972). At the same time, psychologists had very practical interests in measurement of intelligence and personality characteristics to predict such things as performance in school and military units, and they became painfully aware at a rather early date that the relationships between the measures they were developing and the criteria they wished to predict were far from perfect. Consequently, it became necessary to consider the validity of measures, and with no trouble at all it was discovered that validity was not easily attained. Questions of validity still pervade the design and conduct of evaluation projects of all kinds. Intervention programs have such nebulous aims as improving "social skills" or "quality of medical care," enhancing "work motivation," and increasing "health status." Characteristics such as those are not to be measured directly, and one must ask and answer the question not only whether the measures that are chosen are reliable but whether they in fact do reflect the characteristics that are intended as program goals. Psychologists are often in a considerably better position to contribute to the answering of such questions than are individuals from disciplines lacking the psychometric tradition of psychology. Psychologists have been and are making valuable contributions to measurement in such areas as indexes of health status (Kaplan, Bush, & Berry, Note 1), quality of medical care (Payne & Lyons, Note 2), outcomes of compensatory early childhood educational and nutritional programs (McKay, McKay, & Sinisterra, Note 3), police performance (Bloch, Anderson, & Gerrais, 1973), and college teacher evaluation (Frey, 1973).

Emphasis on Observable Behaviors

A third general way in which psychologists can contribute somewhat uniquely to program evaluation efforts arises out of the emphasis in psychology on observable behaviors and the consequent inclination of most psychologists to attempt to specify in operational terms the major constructs that enter into their theory and research. While some of the early enthusiasm for and rigidity about operationism in psychology have abated, the development of the philosophy of multiple operationism (Campbell, 1960), that is, the recognition that no single measure is likely to exhaust the meaning of a construct, has made the behavioral orientation of the psychologist consistently useful. While it has been widely recognized that dependent measures need to be carefully specified and measured, and that any subject variables that enter into research must similarly be carefully measured, it is also being realized that the measurement of independent variables is equally important (Riecken & Boruch, 1974). Indeed, the first step in the measurement of independent variables is the careful specification of them. Probably one of the major causes for failure of evaluations is the fact that the independent variable, that is, the program to be evaluated, is often very poorly specified, if at all, and there is no way of knowing after the evaluation has been accomplished how well the program was actually implemented. There is a now well-entrenched tradition in social psychology to attempt to measure the strength of experimental manipulations as a way of casting light on interpretations of experimental findings, particularly negative results. It is likely, for example, that in the evaluation of Head Start programs, if the nature of each program were to be carefully specified and the strength of the program implementation were to be measured, expectations about outcomes for Head Start programs would be sharply altered. It is also improbable that any investigator would, with the available information about specific Head Start programs, choose to lump them all together for evaluation purposes. Such a lump clearly would not constitute a homogeneous set in any sense.

Quality of Life

Assuming that the psychologist can contribute to program evaluation, one may ask in what sense such a contribution might result in improvement in quality of life. There are both obvious and less obvious consequences of adequate as opposed to inadequate program evaluation. At an obvious level, the careful evaluation and demonstration of effectiveness of social programs can result in the promotion of effective and eventually efficient solutions to important social and human problems. Such problems as inadequate housing and medical care, unemployment, waste of energy, and despoiling of the environment may yield to the development of interventions that can be adequately tested and implemented. At a still obvious level, effective evaluation of social programs can eliminate waste of resources. The monetary or human energy pool from which resources are drawn for social interventions is not by any means infinite. When money is soaked up for ineffective nonsolutions to problems, it is not available for more productive approaches to the same problems, nor for investment in solutions to different problems. Our society can ill afford to be wasting tax dollars for efforts of professionals such as physicians, lawyers, and energy specialists on programs that are not going to be effective. At a less obvious level there is a potentially great human cost in the alleviation of concern about human and social problems by implementing interventions that are palliative but not curative. Whether it is effective or not, a newly mounted program to deal with the problems of minority unemployment in a community may so successfully reduce concern about the problem that it blocks the development of more effective measures for a considerable period of time. One of the risks with programs such as Head Start and "Sesame Street" is that they may persuade people that something very useful and helpful is being done about the problem of unequal educational opportunity when in fact very little, or perhaps nothing at all, is being done. In fact, in the case of "Sesame Street," recent evidence suggests that far from reducing social class disparities in educational opportunities, the program may in fact be increasing those disparities (Cook, Appleton, Conner, Shaffer, Tamkin, & Weber, 1975). Another instance of the need for careful evaluation is provided by the "911" all-purpose emergency telephone number that is rapidly being installed in cities across the country at what will eventually be an enormous total cost. As yet almost nothing is known about how emergency calls are made, how the 911 number will affect them, how the public will react to 911, what efforts will be needed to produce proper and effective use of the number, and so on. About the best justification for 911 that is now available is that "it seemed like a good idea at the time."

To the extent that social programs are well planned and well evaluated, psychologists may rest assured that their efforts can contribute in important ways to improving the quality of life of their fellow citizens and hopefully of all humanity in the long run.

It should be made clear that it is not proposed here that psychologists, nor other program evaluators for that matter, should become the arbiters of what is good and desirable in our lives or in the solution of our problems. The solution of important social problems and the improvement of quality of life are a complex business that clearly involves economic, political, ethicomoral, and other concerns. However, we would firmly insist that to the extent that *evidence* is to become a part of the total decision process directed toward the improvement of equality of our lives the evidence should be as complete, as high quality, and as clear-cut as possible.

The role of psychologists in program evaluation is certainly not viewed here as a replacement for participants from other social science disciplines. While it has been suggested in various places that a rigorous experimental design necessitates the rejection of other types of evidence, often of a less objective nature, that is in fact not the case, as has been made abundantly clear by Campbell (Note 4). We are of the firm belief that anthropologists, sociologists, economists, political scientists, and others have much to contribute to the evaluation of social programs. Psychologists may *complement* the efforts of colleagues from other disciplines, however, by their somewhat more substantial contribution to the methodological and quantitative rigor of the evaluations in which they are involved.

Training Limitations

It should also be pointed out that the psychologist suffers from certain limitations in approaching the task of program evaluation, limitations that are not inevitable but that reflect in part the types of training and the orientation that psychologists have received. In the first place, we would have to confess that many psychologists are trained quite narrowly, even within the discipline of psychology, let alone in terms of relationships with other disciplines. The narrowness of the training of psychologists extends not only to the realm of substance, of subject matter, but also to methodology. Many psychologists trained for research in laboratories where high levels of control and precision are possible are virtually useless in the more demanding, broader field investigations that are involved in program evaluation. Similarly, psychologists trained in some of the looser corners of our discipline, where experimental methods are largely ignored, if not derided, are not well equipped to contribute to rigorous program evaluation. We believe that program evaluation probably requires some special training and experience beyond that usually given in graduate training programs in order to make the psychologist maximally useful.

Another limitation in the training of psychologists for program evaluation is that relatively few graduate students have very good models for the behavior being expected of them. Participation in program evaluation has been rather limited among psychologists to the present time, and most of what has occurred has been within rather narrow segments of the field. A good case in point is educational evaluation, most of which has been done by a very few educational and measurement psychologists, not all of whom were trained in psychology departments. Evaluation in research in the health care field has been largely in the hands of sociologists and specialists in public health, and there are still very few psychologists with expertise in that area. We have heard a number of suggestions recently about the desirability of involving psychologists in program evaluation coming from departments that have no competent specialists in that area. We doubt that it is very effective to try to train graduate students in areas in which the faculty has no commitment nor any considerable competence.

While it is reasonably true to say that the methodology of program evaluation is sufficiently content free that it can be readily transported from one type of program evaluation to another, there are, nonetheless, differences between fields that require that psychologists involved in program evaluation specialize somewhat, and probably also that they commit themselves to a program of continuing education. Psychologists who want to work in the health field, for example, must learn something about the language and problems of medicine, of hospitals, of health delivery systems. To be useful they must learn something about economics and systems analysis. They must learn the taboos of medicine and how to communicate with a variety of health care professionals. Similar requirements are exacted upon the psychologists who wish to work in education, or in law and criminal justice, or in welfare planning, or whatever. While the present writer is quite convinced of the contributions that psychologists can make, he is also painfully aware of their many limitations. It is possible for psychologists to presume too much about their knowledge, to be arrogant. Psychologists who wish to contribute to program evaluation must learn to work as part of a team of individuals and cannot expect that the evaluation of their own contributions will at any point be greater than they have been able to demonstrate. Probably one of the most hopeful indicators of the eventual smooth working of an evaluation team is when its members can all sit down at the table and eat humble pie together. If that satisfies their appetites they may not later have to dine on crow.

REFERENCE NOTES

1. Kaplan, R., Bush, J. W., & Berry, C. *Studies of the validity of the health status index.* Paper presented at the meeting of the American Association for the Advancement of Science, Boston, Massachusetts, 1976.

2. Payne, B. C., & Lyons, T. F. *Method of evaluating and improving personal medical care quality: Episode of illness study* (Contract No. HSM 110-70-69). Washington, D.C.: Department of Health, Education, and Welfare, National Center for Health Services Research, 1972.
3. McKay, H., McKay, A., & Sinisterra, L. *Stimulation of intellectual and social competence in Colombian preschool children affected by multiple deprivations of depressed urban environments* (Progress Report 2). Cali, Colombia: Universidad del Valle, Human Ecology Research Station, 1973.
4. Campbell, D. T. *Qualitative evaluation in action research.* Paper presented at the 82nd Annual Meeting of the American Psychological Association, New Orleans, August 1974.

REFERENCES

Bernstein, I. N., & Freeman, H. E. *Academic and entrepreneurial research: The consequences of diversity in federal evaluation studies.* New York: Russell Sage Foundation, 1975.

Bloch, P., Anderson, D., & Gerrais, P. *Policewomen on patrol* (Vol. 1). Washington, D.C.: The Police Foundation, 1973.

Campbell, D. T. Recommendations for APA test standards regarding construct, trait, or discriminant validity. *American Psychologist*, 1960, *15*, 546–553.

Campbell, D. T. Reforms as experiments. *American Psychologist*, 1969, *24*, 409–429.

Campbell, D. T., & Stanley, J. C. *Experimental and quasi-experimental designs for research.* Chicago: Rand-McNally, 1963.

Cook, T. D., Appleton, H., Conner, R., Shaffer, A., Tamkin, G., & Weber, S. T. *Sesame Street revisited: A case study in evaluation research.* New York: Russell Sage Foundation, 1975.

Cronbach, L. J., Gleser, G. C., Nanda, H., & Rajaratnam, N. *The dependability of behavioral measurements: Theory of generalizability for scores and profiles.* New York: Wiley, 1972.

Frey, P. W. Comparative judgment scaling of student course ratings. *American Educational Research Journal*, 1973, *10*, 149–154.

Morgenstern, O. *On the accuracy of economic observations.* Princeton, N.J.: Princeton University Press, 1950.

Riecken, H. W., & Boruch, R. F. (Eds.). *Social experimentation: A method for planning and evaluating social intervention.* New York: Academic Press, 1974.

23

Arthur H. Brayfield and Mark W. Lipsey

Public Affairs Psychology

This chapter describes and discusses briefly the emergence of a new professional specialty—public affairs psychology. In the interest of achieving some common understandings, we will begin with a couple of clarifying definitions.

First, when we say "professional specialty," we follow the usage of the sociologist Wilbert E. Moore, who defined a profession as "an occupation whose occupants create and explicitly utilize systematically accumulated general knowledge in the solution of problems posed by a clientele (either individuals or collectivities)" (Moore, 1970, pp. 53-54). We use the phrase "public affairs" to refer to all those human affairs in which the public interest is such that some governmental body, national or local, may contemplate, propose, or take some action. This preliminary definition does indeed cast a wide net. We are then dealing with public policy, especially as it may be proposed or expressed in the form of legislation, defined or clarified through administrative regulations, implemented through government agency actions or operations, or assessed or interpreted by judicial review.

Our interest in public affairs psychology is somewhat at variance with academic psychology's history as a laboratory science. In the course of our exploration of this concept we have developed some measure of empathy for an observation that Florian Znaniecki (1940/1968) made in his classic book *The Social Role of the Man of Knowledge:* "All new developments in the history of knowledge have been due to those scientists who did more in their social roles than their circles wanted and expected them to do" (p. 164). Our own growing pains aside, we will see that public affairs psychologists must do more in their roles than the precedents in the discipline ask them to do. We turn now to some of the various aspects of this concept of public affairs psychology.

Functions and Roles

A profession has, of course, distinctive functions to perform and roles to assume. The core functions of public affairs psychology are to conceptualize, understand, and investigate a public policy issue in its psychologi-

Arthur H. Brayfield is Chairperson of the Graduate Faculty in Psychology, Claremont Graduate School; Mark W. Lipsey is an Assistant Professor of Psychology, Claremont Graduate School.

cal dimensions and to translate that analysis and research into terms and information that a "consumer" of such knowledge can readily understand and act upon. These core functions embrace at least three major areas of activity.

One key activity is the creation of new knowledge relevant to various public issues. This research activity may investigate the psychological nature of a particular social problem such as the effects of air pollution, alienation on the assembly line, or discrimination in housing. Some public policy research, however, must attend to matters broader than any single social problem, for example, the nature of prejudice, the roots of violence, and the impact of technological changes.

Public affairs psychologists may also investigate the nature of present public policy—its operation and consequences, as in an examination of school desegregation, drug rehabilitation programs, or capital punishment. In other cases the focus of inquiry will be on *alternative* policies, for example, income maintenance, decriminalization of victimless crimes, and gun control. The process of formulating policy and making decisions will itself come under scrutiny sometimes, for it too is a significant component of public policy.

A second key function of public affairs psychology is the application of existing psychological knowledge to public issues. Existing psychological knowledge might thus be translated directly into useful policies, programs, or products (hardware as well as software). We see examples of this activity in the application of behavioristic learning theory to teaching machines and the use of results from psycholinguistic research for training language skills.

A third important area of activity for public affairs psychology involves not so much knowledge as techniques and methods. Chief among these are procedures for evaluating and monitoring both the implementation and the outcome of public policy. The development of social indicators, the use of survey research for assessing public reaction to policy, and the methodology of evaluation research represent promising instances of this sort.

Perhaps it sounds like we are simply describing an "applied" psychology or social engineering to complement or contrast with traditional "basic" science. We think the basic–applied distinction is not very appropriate for psychology. It is difficult to conceive of valid knowledge about psychological functioning that would not have almost immediate implications for "application," irrespective of the intent of the investigator. Much more important for public affairs psychology than the basic–applied issue is the distinction between representative research and unrepresentative research. Psychological research that reflects the full complexity of human behavior in the natural, social, political, and ecological context will

---

This chapter was originally presented as an invited address at a symposium entitled "Innovative Roles for Psychologists in Improving the Quality of Life," held at the annual meeting of the American Association for the Advancement of Science, New York, New York, January 30, 1975.

necessarily be useful to the formulation of public policy. Public affairs psychology will be most distinguished for its efforts to develop knowledge in that real world context and to bring that knowledge to bear on the presenting problems of the society. Much of the resulting research will indeed be mission oriented and directed toward particular social problems. The applied or engineering function, however, must be coupled with research of broad theoretical implications for a range of public issues, research which in scope and depth will most resemble what we have traditionally called "basic" research. Not only do we want to know how to develop an effective community relations program for the local police station but we want to understand the roots of criminal behavior well enough to dream of its eradication.

Career Settings

The opportunities for public affairs psychologists occur in a wide variety of career settings. Potentially the most influential, of course, is service in the federal government. This may take the form of various positions in the executive and legislative branches. Most frequently, public affairs psychologists will serve in staff rather than line positions where the emphasis is upon data gathering, description, analysis, formulation of policy alternatives, and assessment of operational or procedural contingencies. Approximately the same pattern exists in state, county, and city units of government.

Similar services may be required in nongovernmental, nonprofit organizational settings of a specialized nature such as the social subsystems devoted to health care, education, population control, or conservation. Cultural organizations such as art museums may also be appropriate settings, and, in fact, environmental psychologists have already been invited into museums on a consulting basis.

Discussions with policy and planning officials of business and industrial organizations convince us that the skills and methodologies of public affairs psychologists may be readily transferred to the profit-seeking private sector. As the crisis of human survival deepens and the rationale for corporate self-interest begins to waver under the impact of public opinion, it seems likely that acceptance of a corporate philosophy of social responsibility will accelerate. Public affairs psychologists may well find a place in corporate chambers where the public interest is more broadly conceived than in the past.

Whatever the institutional base, however, public affairs psychologists have an ethical obligation to exercise influence on behalf of a broad constituency of the society in which they function. We reject the notion that, by aspiring to contribute directly to policy and decision making, the public affairs psychologist necessarily becomes an elitist in the social hierarchy, manipulating others or assisting the powers-that-be to impose their will on those who are subject to their power.

On the contrary, we believe public affairs psychology's intellectual endeavors are as likely to offer a profound critique of existing policy as to confirm it. Moreover, we see public affairs psychologists laboring as diligently with local and grass-roots organizations as with government or corporate policymakers. Nader's Raiders, the National Center for Voluntary Action, the local PTA, and the United Farm Workers may find as much use for the talents of the public affairs psychologist as the Department of Health, Education, and Welfare, the Rand Corporation, the Congress, the Pentagon, or the General Motors Corporation.

Intellectual Foundations

Some years ago, Harold Lasswell (1951) proposed that the social sciences be examined and redefined as the *policy sciences.* Under this broad rubric we would include anthropology, sociology, economics, political science, and, of course, the social aspects of psychology. Public affairs psychologists make their contribution by drawing upon the substantive content of much of psychology, but perhaps especially upon the broad domains of social, cognitive, and personality psychology. Other, more specialized domains also contribute, as, for example, when the findings of sensory psychology bear upon the formulation of public policy concerned with noise pollution. In addition, public affairs psychologists must acquaint themselves through formal and informal means with concepts and data from all of the policy sciences and, indeed, in the pursuit of value orientations, relevant cultural history, and inspiration, they may turn to the humanities for insight.

The breadth of preparation required is illustrated by the mere enumeration of some of the pivotal concepts that public affairs psychologists find of likely relevance to the performance of their role. Among these we list the following:

Power
Leadership
Conflict
Accommodation process
Bargaining and decision making
Communication and persuasion
Cooperation and trust
Cost–benefit relationships
Resource allocation
Problem solving
Social change processes
Conformity and deviance
Social and organizational structure
Social roles and social stratification
Social norms and values

Some of these concepts originated outside of psychology and have been more fully explored within the other policy sciences. All, however, have a psychological cast, and in calling attention to them we are, in part, inviting exploration, investigation, and theory building by psychologists.

Perhaps more important than the concepts current in the policy sciences is the methodological armamentarium that the public affairs psychologist brings to the role. Again, we would argue that an expanded view must be taken of the relevant tools of the trade. Public affairs psychologists must range across disciplines for useful and significant methodological contributions. We identify as likely candidates the following:

Statistical methods and experimental design
Observational and quasi-experimental techniques
Survey research methods
Social indicators and program evaluation
Computer programming and simulation techniques
Demographic analysis
Archival and historical analysis
Systems analysis and operations research

Public Policy Issues

Everyone finds it easy today to draw up a laundry list of contemporary public policy issues that might appropriately concern the public affairs psychologist. For illustrative purposes, we suggest that the following constitute a minimal list of deserving social problem areas:

Employment
Social welfare and income maintenance
Human resource development
Energy resource allocation
Environmental degradation
Crime, administration of justice
Transportation
Housing
Education
Urban life
Technology assessment
Minorities and prejudice
Health services
Old age and retirement
Population and crowding
Violence and social unrest
Militarism and war

The skeptic may feel that this is an unrealistic, or at least an overly ambitious, list of policy issues for public affairs psychologists. In response, permit us to become provincial for a moment. In our own small graduate department of psychology, which, we should add, is unrepresentative because we focus on the contribution of psychology to public policy, we have during the past four years had faculty members and graduate students engaged in research, sometimes as consultants, in the following public policy areas: employment, social welfare, waste disposal, transportation, air pollution, housing, education, criminal justice, technology assessment, recreation, discrimination, health services, population control, drug abuse, and alcoholism rehabilitation. We might add that we have not solved all of these problems, but we have found that there is external funding available for much of this activity.

Entry into Public Affairs Career Settings

For the young psychologist who aspires to a career in public affairs psychology, a crucial question is how to get started. Such a person cannot simply run through the list of position openings in the *APA Monitor* and expect to come up with something labeled "public affairs psychologist." Many employers who might need a public affairs psychologist may not even realize it or at least not recognize it by that name.

Our experience with graduate students, which is somewhat limited with our new program, has emphasized the importance of significant contact with potential employers and employment settings well in advance of the point when actual employment is desired. Students must first have some idea of the public affairs area they wish to pursue, for example, the criminal justice system, development of legislation, health care. They must then make some entry into a relevant setting. Our program assigns each student to a "field placement" for a semester or more at an appropriate agency. Other students simply make their own contact, perhaps by offering to do some research of interest to the organization or volunteering other services, even quite routine ones, simply to build up some experience. In several instances, these experiences have resulted in employment in the agency of initial contact. In any event, the student gains an insider's view of relevant organizations, learns the channels for seeking employment, and develops a personal relationship with people who can be helpful in using those channels.

Another strategy we plan to explore more systematically is placement of advanced graduate students and postdoctoral students in full-time, year-long internships. The *Directory of Public Service Internships*, published by the National Center for Public Service Internship Programs, lists hundreds of such opportunities, many with pay, in fields as diverse as legislation, environment, and urban problems. For the potential public affairs psychologist, such internships might function like traditional postdoctoral appointments in more conventional psychological specialties. It would give them an opportunity to sharpen their skills and learn a great deal more about the public affairs setting of their choice while at the same time providing them with contact, information, and experience that would facilitate moving into a full-time professional role in an appropriate setting.

Outlook for the Future

What is the outlook for this new professional specialty? Here we briefly assess the supportive elements that contribute to the development of public affairs psychology as a distinct profession. Perhaps the most important supportive element resides in the fact that psychology is already primarily a *public interest* profession in its traditions and in its career settings. Approximately 85% of all psychologists earn their livelihood in nonprofit settings. Thus in some sense the tradition of service is well established and provides an appropriate foundation for performance in new public service roles.

Historically and currently many psychologists have pursued full-time careers in government service. At present, for example, almost one fifth of the psychologists in the United States are employed in federal, state, or local units of government, filling roles in service, research, and administration. Most serve in positions obviously appropriate to such conventional psychological specialties as clinical, personnel, and experimental psychology. A few, however, have been more directly involved in the process of policy formulation. These pioneers in public service and policy have helped create a climate of acceptance for psychologists in governmental settings.

Another less well recognized group of psychologists has been increasingly active in the culture-building process of gaining recognition for psychology at the level of policy formation. This group is comprised of psychologists who have served in part-time capacities on various panels, councils, commissions, and boards, and as individual consultants on policy issues. This group includes those psychologists who have testified before congressional committees—as many as two dozen in a given year. The nature and extent of the activities of these various groups of psychologists have gone largely undocumented but are known to be substantial.

The interest and support of organized psychology as represented in the policies and activities of such instrumentalities as the American Psychological Association and the state associations have also been important factors in support of the concept of public affairs psychology. Beginning with the reorganization of APA and the appointment of its first full-time Executive Officer in 1946, this national organization of psychologists, now numbering more than 40,000 members, has moved to clarify its role in public policy. The event of major importance was the formal adoption in 1968 of a policy statement (Tyler, 1969) governing the Association's participation at various levels in public affairs. In 1974, the APA took the initiative in establishing an independent Association for the Advancement of Psychology—a group involved in public policy as it affects the interests and expertise of psychologists.

Starting in 1969, APA and the Brookings Institution have cosponsored three small five-day invitational working conferences devoted to the role of psychology in public affairs. The objective has been to develop a cadre of psychologists around the country who occupy a diversity of leadership roles and to provide them with information that would increase their interest and effectiveness in addressing the issues in public affairs psychology.

Another significant event in APA's history was the 1969 Annual Convention which adopted as its central theme "Psychology and the Problems of Society." Selected papers from that meeting were published by APA in 1970 as a 450-page paperback (Korten, Cook, & Lacey, 1970) that serves as something of an illustrative handbook of public affairs psychology. Subsequently, APA began issuing a series of monographs on such public policy issues as population, health services, and aging.

In recent years, state psychological organizations have also increased their activities in the area of public affairs. All of these developments, we believe, are important influences in the legitimization of public affairs psychology.

A continued supply of public affairs psychologists seems assured by the emergence in recent years of formal programs of graduate education aimed at preparation in that specialty area. Well-organized programs are now available at Michigan State University, Pennsylvania State University, Wright Graduate Institute, and Claremont Graduate School. These programs, incidentally, were described in detail at a symposium presented at the 1974 APA Annual Convention in New Orleans under the cosponsorship of the APA Education and Training Board; Division 9, The Society for the Psychological Study of Social Issues; Division 8, Social and Personality Psychology; and Division 2, Teaching of Psychology. We have informal information that additional graduate programs are in the process of development.

Perhaps most important of all, there is evidence that the broad base of active psychologists is itself increasingly receptive to the themes of public affairs psychology. We have survey data showing that the vast majority of graduate students and faculty in academic psychology feel that the discipline should be making more of a contribution to the solution of social problems. Over the last decade, a consensus, not total but substantial, has emerged in support of a psychology that draws its problems for study from the larger society rather than from esoteric theory or disciplinary tradition. Such support is particularly pronounced among younger members of the discipline, but it is by no means confined to them.

Those younger members, however, have important attributes from the point of view of public affairs psychology. They exist in large numbers; they will probably be more likely than earlier cohorts to seek employment outside of academic settings, at least in part because of a shortage of academic positions; and they will mature to hold influential roles in the discipline within the next decade or so. With these developments, public affairs psychology should find even more support among psychologists themselves in the years to come.

Conclusion

We believe that the internal support structures are in place and operative. We share with you a credo offered by Morton Deutsch in his 1969 Presidential Address to the Eastern Psychological Association:

No guarantees can be given to those—from either the right or the left—who are demanding that social science be relevant. We can only guarantee that our efforts will be socially responsible, that our work will seek to be socially responsive to social concerns, and that we will be continuously concerned with fostering the application of psychological knowledge for the welfare of man. (pp. 1091–1092)

Our task as public affairs psychologists is to be imaginative, ingenious, and effective in translating social need into social demand. Perhaps it is a good omen of the new day dawning when we find a classified ad in the January 1975 *APA Monitor* for a "position opening" described as follows:

CONGRESSIONAL FELLOWSHIPS with U.S. Senator Bill Brock. Fellows are advanced graduate students, college professors or other professionals actively working within their areas of expertise to provide substantive materials, leading to policy statements and legislation. Financial assistance is sometimes available for fellows at the rate of $5,000 a year. Fellows generally remain in the office for one year. Application dates are open. Contact Harrison Fox, Ph.D. at 202/225-9579 or c/o Senator Brock, 254 Russell Senate Office Building, Washington, DC 20510. (Classified notice, 1975)

REFERENCES

Classified notice. *APA Monitor*, January 1975, p. 25.

Deutsch, M. Socially relevant science: Reflections on some studies of interpersonal conflict. *American Psychologist*, 1969, 24, 1076–1092.

Korten, F., Cook, S. W., & Lacey, J. I. (Eds.). *Psychology and the problems of society.* Washington, D.C.: American Psychological Association, 1970.

Lasswell, H. The policy orientation. In D. Lerner & H. D. Lasswell (Eds.), *The policy sciences.* Stanford, Calif.: Stanford University Press, 1951.

Moore, W. *The professions: Roles and rules.* New York: Russell Sage Foundation, 1970.

Tyler, L. An approach to public affairs. Report of the ad hoc committee on public affairs. *American Psychologist*, 1969, 24, 1–4.

Znaniecki, F. *The social role of the man of knowledge.* New York: Harper & Row, 1968. (Originally published, 1940.)

24

Sheldon G. Levy

The Employment Environment for Social Psychologists

Social psychologists face the same employment problem as all academics—the lack of traditional academic positions in sufficient numbers to employ the PhDs produced (Cates, 1973; Little, 1972; Vetter, 1973). The problem arises primarily from demographic factors. Declining birthrates over the past 20 years are leading to declines in undergraduate enrollments, while high graduate enrollments are resulting in substantial numbers of PhDs. The imbalance is further exaggerated by several additional factors. Because current faculty are relatively young, few openings result from retirements (Cartter, 1971). Technological improvements in teaching (e.g., programmed learning and videotapes) increase pressure to have fewer faculty available to serve the student population (Carnegie Commission, 1971; Radner & Miller, 1970). Recent economic conditions have increased the tendency to delay retirement and have led administrators to ask fewer faculty to teach larger classes.

A number of ways to cope with this situation are apparent. For example, the profession might seek to encourage an increase in birthrates. Or requirements for a college degree might be increased, thus necessitating more years for completion of an education. The latter idea would be particularly advantageous at the graduate level because it would prevent, at least for a few years, any new PhDs from entering the labor market. Only slightly more feasible is the prospect of increasing the number of majors in psychology. If successful, this alternative would benefit psychologists, but would not solve the overall academic employment problem. Also, graduate enrollments could be restricted. This policy, however, would raise the basic question of whether a free system has the right to prevent qualified candidates from furthering their education. The greater an individual's education the more likely that individual is to be employed (although it may be underemployment); thus, denial of education increases the likelihood of unemployment. Early retirement for current faculty is

Sheldon Levy is a Professor in the Department of Psychology, Wayne State University.

The work of the Division 8 Committee on Employment Opportunities has been a joint effort of its members: Lauren Wispé, John Edwards, Bob Love, and Sheldon G. Levy (Chair).

Statistical significance in this chapter is reported as the probability for the two-tailed value of *t* for the difference between groups. The degrees of freedom were almost always close to 150. They varied somewhat from question to question depending on the number of respondents that answered the particular item.

another solution that must be classified as somewhat impractical at this time. Under present economic conditions this alternative is unacceptable to older faculty. In addition, because faculty are disinclined to ever retire, they would probably teach for minimal pay, which would only serve to reduce positions for new candidates. Finally, increasing the proportion of high school graduates who attend college is of limited potential value because the proportion is already fairly close to a reasonable maximum (Cartter, 1971).

Two avenues for increasing enrollments merit substantial interest. First, college teaching can be expanded primarily through programs of continuing education for the adult population. Second, physical locations for this instruction can be varied; for example, courses can be taught in high-density locations (e.g., factories and office buildings) as well as through mass media, notably television.

While expansion in these directions would be useful, the major potential for employment of social psychologists appears to be in the further development of nonacademic roles. A large number of problem areas exist outside the academic environment for which social psychologists have special competence. (This is also undoubtedly true of several other areas of psychology, such as clinical and developmental.) Rather than restrict graduate enrollments, which would be socially dysfunctional, the solution instead is to demonstrate the social utility of those who are trained.

Following a discussion at its 1971 business meeting, APA's Division 8 (Personality and Social Psychology) developed a committee to investigate matters related to the problem of employment of professional social psychologists. This chapter is an expansion of an earlier report (Levy, 1975) and presents the perspective the committee has developed and the results based on a survey of a sample of the Division membership.

A small and lightly financed committee investigating a major problem is not in a position to directly effect policy changes. Thus, for example, it cannot undertake an information campaign about social psychologists directed toward nonacademic employers without first obtaining a decision at a policymaking level that the Division should engage in this activity. Further, the Division is in a weak position to formulate such policies until it has adequate information about the nature of nonacademic requirements and the extent to which social psychologists can be of value. Similarly, the committee cannot develop a set of recommendations for changes in academic training without much more adequate knowledge about the form that such training should take.

It was apparent that the most appropriate and beneficial committee effort would be to collect information. The first possibility considered was an assessment of the marketplace, including current academic and nonacademic employment needs. Particularly in nonacademic environments insufficient information exists about the capabilities of social psychologists to adequately specify needs. In other words, there might be a great deal of potential use for psychologists that goes unrecognized by various organizations. Therefore, this assessment would require evaluation of the extent to which nonacademic employers were knowledgeable about social psychology and, more importantly, a determination of the organizational activities and needs within the domain of competence of social psychologists.

Given the massive number of organizations from which a sample might be drawn, the committee felt that direct study of this particular problem would require the greatest and most lengthy development and, therefore, first sought other avenues to obtain more rapid information payoffs.

Three projects were undertaken, all of which have been completed. The first project developed panels at regional and national psychological meetings in which psychologists now located in nonacademic environments discussed the nature of their activities and the potential for social psychology. These panels provided some insights that a larger survey of employers would have sought, although obviously on a more restricted level. The discussions led to the judgment that (a) a great potential for social psychologists exists in nonacademic settings and (b) academics seem to be poorly informed about these nonacademic environments.

The insights gained from the panels were incorporated into the next two projects. One project, to be discussed in the next section, was a survey of Division 8 members. The other was a survey of graduate departments of psychology conducted in the fall of 1975. The main purpose of this second survey was to determine the extent to which programmatic changes had been made or were being planned to meet changing employment conditions. Specifically, this survey collected data on the development of applied social psychology courses and programs, departmental contacts with nonacademic employers, and nonacademic placement of graduates. This information should subsequently aid graduate departments in developing innovative training programs to cope directly with changing societal needs for social psychologists. A specific example is the Wayne State University internship program. This program was developed as part of a National Institute of Mental Health (NIMH) training grant to the university's social psychology program. Under the internship, students spend several hours a week during one quarter in an applied location (e.g., industrial or governmental agency) and report to a seminar. Their main function is to be involved in a nonacademic setting and to develop ideas about the way in which social psychological knowledge might be utilized to aid the work of the home agency. In some instances actual projects may be conducted.

Survey of Division 8 Members

The major project of the committee was to survey a sample of Division 8 members in the spring of 1974. Since the Division is large and contains a heterogeneous membership including a substantial number of nonacademics, it was felt that this project could economically investigate a number of areas. The remainder of this chapter describes the information the survey sought as well as some survey results.

The primary goal of the survey was to inform academics and nonacademics about each other's employment environments. Another functionally important goal was to provide information to new PhDs about the conditions of employment that exist in a variety of settings.

Major Information Areas

First, how do environments differ in professional activities and support of professional development. For example, to what extent is one able to keep abreast of new developments in the field, or to communicate knowledge through publications, teaching, conferences, etc.? To what extent is one able to contribute to the well-being of others? Thus, this first general area sought to determine how environments differ in their claims on the talents of the individual and to what extent they support professional fulfillment.

A second major area might be labeled intellectual freedom. This broad area includes such diverse components as the length of the contract (job security), freedom to determine how one's time is allocated, and the extent to which one's ethical obligations as a professional are safeguarded. This last aspect was not investigated because of its complexity. Unfortunately, it is an aspect that psychologists have not yet formally addressed.

A third major area relevant to assessing a work environment is mobility. Mobility involves the ease of intrafield movement as well as the ability to move between academic and nonacademic positions. Mobility is of particular importance for flexibility in employment decision making because it provides the perspective that the decision is not irrevocable.

Finally, the survey examined the tangible rewards of employment including income, travel expense, and overall job satisfaction.

Division 8 Sample

Every fifth name from a complete list of Division 8 members was selected. The survey was sent only to members living in North America. (Some Canadian mail was returned due to a postal strike.) Of the 871 delivered surveys, 494 (56.6%) were returned—an excellent response from the membership, particularly for a mail survey.

The sample was heterogeneous and appeared to reflect different components of the full Division membership. Eighty-nine percent had received the PhD, with the two largest subgroups of psychology being social psychology (31% of the total) and clinical psychology (29%). Thirty-nine percent of the respondents were not employed in an academic environment. Eighty percent were male; 96% were white. The sample may reflect somewhat more established components of the membership because the mean age was 45 ($SD = 10$) and because 59% reported a yearly income of $20,000 or more. The mean number of years since obtaining the PhD was 13 ($SD = 9$) and the mean number of years at the present employment location was 8 ($SD = 7$).

Results of the Survey

In addition to the four major areas of work environment discussed previously, this chapter will examine four subsidiary topics: job satisfaction, additional employment opportunities, relevance of graduate training to current position, and ease of obtaining the present position. The focus will be on those items on which the two groups (academic versus nonacademic) differed from each other at a level at least approaching statistical significance. After this discussion is completed, a brief examination will be made of those items on which the two groups gave comparable responses.

Because Division 8 includes a large number of members who did not receive their PhD in social psychology, the present analyses are based on 116 social psychology PhDs who are employed in academic environments and 37 who are not. It should be noted that the two groups did not differ significantly from each other in age. The nonacademic group was 3 years older on the average, 44 versus 41, but the standard deviations for the samples were 10.2 and 9.1, respectively. In addition, the sex and racial characteristics of the two groups were practically identical. Consequently, differences in job characteristics reported by these two subgroups are likely to reflect true differences in the perceptions of the work environment.

Professional activity and support. It should be noted that the nonacademic psychologists are located in a number of widely varying environments. They have been considered as a group because there are too few members in any one location to allow for adequate statistical analyses. The largest number (12 of the 37) are employed in governmental agencies. Another 7 are in research organizations. The remaining nonacademic social psychology PhDs are distributed as follows: 4 work in a clinic, 4 in a public school or educational association, 2 in an industrial firm, 2 in consulting firms, and 1 in a private agency. (The distribution of clinical PhDs who were in nonacademic environments was similar except that a smaller percentage were in research organizations and a larger percentage were in private practice. Further, 43% of the total responding clinical PhDs were in nonacademic environments compared with 24% of the responding PhD social psychologists.) By far, the greatest distinction between the two groups was the way in which their time was apportioned. As anticipated, academics spent more time reading, researching, teaching, and doing organizational work. On the other hand, nonacademics spent more time consulting both within and outside the organization and doing research for the organization and clinical work. This division between academic and nonacademic subgroups was further indicated in a factor analysis of the professional activity variables across the full sample of 494 cases. Factor I was composed of precisely those variables listed above on which academics spent more time, while Factor II consisted of those variables on which nonacademics spent more time. This division of labor was reflected in two ways. First, academics indicated that they published 1.4 articles per year since obtaining the PhD while nonacademics indicated an average productivity of .8 articles per year. This difference, however, was not statistically significant. In addition, 28% of the academic sample compared with 14% of the nonacademic sample reported they had achieved fellowship status in the Division. This statistically significant difference probably reflects the fact that academics are more likely to be considered for this honor and are somewhat more productive. In addition to time apportionment, academically employed PhDs felt that they had a greater opportunity to learn about new developments in their field and a greater opportunity to interact personally with other significant social psychologists in their field. However, nonacademics indicated a greater opportunity to demonstrate the benefits of psychology to nonpsychologists in a non-teaching capacity. In addition, nonacademics indicated a substantially greater money allotment for professional travel. These results are summarized in Table 24-1.

Intellectual freedom and job security. The only statistically significant differences between the two groups in this category concerned the independent utilization of time. The academics indicated that, on the average, they were able to decide how to utilize their time about 70% of the total, while—surprisingly to the author—the nonacademics' response was 80% ($p < .06$). The academics, however, did indicate they spent more time each week on professional matters (52 hours compared to 44 hours, $p < .0001$). The important point to be made on this topic is that nonacademics re-

TABLE 24-1   *Comparisons of Professional Activities Between Social Psychologists in Academic and Nonacademic Settings*

Activity	Academic	Nonacademic	p
Proportions			
Reading	.11	.05	.14
Teaching	.35	.04	.0001
Research	.23	.15	.05
Consulting	.05	.18	.0001
External consulting	.05	.15	.0001
Organizational work	.12	.07	.05
Internal research[a]	.03	.13	.0001
Clinical work[a]	.01	.13	.0001
Administration[a]	.04	.03	ns
Writing[a]	.02	0	.16
Fellowship status	.28	.14	.05
Means			
Productivity[b]	1.4	.8	ns
Learn new development in field[c]	1.6	2.0	.01
Interact with significant social psychologists[c]	2.6	3.1	.05
Nonteaching benefits to nonpsychologists[d]	3.1	2.2	.0001
Money for professional travel[e]	2.3	3.6	.0001

Note. Statistical significance in this table is reported as the probability for the two-tailed *t* value for the difference between groups. The degrees of freedom were almost always close to 150. They varied somewhat from question to question depending on the number of respondents that answered the particular item.
[a]Categories were developed from open-ended responses and, therefore, some respondents may have included proportions in other categories (e.g., administration = organizational work).
[b]Productivity = number of articles/year since PhD was obtained.
[c]1 = a great deal; 2 = a fair amount; 3 = some; 4 = not much.
[d]1 = a great deal; 2 = a substantial amount; 3 = a moderate amount; 4 = a little; 5 = none.
[e]2 = $100–$249; 3 = $250–$499; 4 = $500–$749.

ported as much freedom on the job as academics. Thus, the two groups did not differ significantly from each other in the length of their present contract or in their assessment of the likelihood it would be necessary to change from their present place of employment. (The two groups gave nearly identical mean responses to these two items.)

Mobility. Academics had been in their present location somewhat longer than nonacademics (8.4 years compared to 6.4 years, $p < .11$). This was reflected in the number of different companies that each group reported having worked for since obtaining the PhD (2.6 for the academic sample and 3.3 for the nonacademic, $p < .04$).

Tangible rewards. In addition to the greater amount of travel money that nonacademics received, they also reported earning more money and receiving larger percentage increases during the previous three years. The academics reported an average adjusted gross income from professional activities in 1973 of $22,500 with a 6.6% annual increase based on the average of the past three years. On the other hand, the nonacademics reported an average income of $26,000 with an annual increase of 9.5%. The p values for the differences in income and the differences in the increases in income were .02 and .0001, respectively.

Job satisfaction. A single job satisfaction item indicated that both groups were reasonably satisfied in their present environment. When asked their preferred location, nonacademics indicated that they preferred a nonacademic environment while academics indicated that they greatly preferred an academic one. Obviously, attitudes in both groups may have been brought into consonance with their behavior, but academics do seem somewhat more committed to their environment than do nonacademics.

Relevance of graduate training. Very surprisingly, nonacademics felt that on-the-job learning was a somewhat less important factor for their current position compared to graduate training than did academics ($p < .05$).

Ease of obtaining present position. Both groups reported submitting about the same number of applications to obtain the present position, but nonacademics indicated slightly more interviews ($p < .16$).

Additional employment opportunities. Of concern are the number of opportunities that exist for additional social psychologists. While academics indicated somewhat more replacement positions to be filled, nonacademics felt that additional social psychologists would be of somewhat greater value to their organizations. This information must be evaluated in light of the fact that the current work unit size reported by the academics was far larger than that reported by the nonacademics (4.8 social psychologists compared to 1.7, $p < .001$). One preliminary conclusion would be that the potential is far greater in nonacademic environments, but the usefulness of social psychologists in meeting organizational goals needs to be made apparent. This conclusion must be considered quite tentative because both groups reported that those who did the hiring were equivalent in their knowledge of social psychologists and that this level was "knowledgeable."

Similarities Between the Two Groups

Apart from the differences in the nature of the professional tasks and the differential income, the two groups were strikingly similar. For example, both groups reported equal attendance and participation in conferences and both reported equal utilization of their professional training and skills ("a large amount"). As indicated before, both groups reported comparable lengths to their contracts and equal likelihood of having to change employment positions. Both groups agreed it would be somewhat difficult to obtain another position as rewarding as their present one, and both groups agreed that it would be slightly difficult to obtain a satisfactory position in the alternate employment domain (i.e., academic to nonacademic and vice versa). These perceptions of mobility do not indicate strong feelings about the difficulty of finding another satisfying position. Both groups indicated equal satisfaction with their present employment but this satisfaction was not overwhelming (self-ratings were between "somewhat satisfied" and "satisfied" rather than "very satisfied"). Both groups felt that they had come from graduate programs that they themselves rated between "very good" and "excellent," on the average.

Finally, as indicated before, both groups were similar in age, sex, and racial characteristics. In addition, the average number of years since obtaining the PhD was comparable (12.1 for the academics and 12.9 for the nonacademics). Nonacademics, however, reported taking a year longer to obtain the PhD than did academics, and this difference was statistically significant ($p < .01$). It is difficult to relate this finding to the two environments and may simply reflect a reporting difference.

Conclusions and Perspectives

The results from this survey indicate that academic and nonacademic groups engage in substantially different activities. Academics devote significantly more of their time to teaching and to research that qualifies for publication in academic journals. Both groups, however, are similar in almost all other respects. Graduate training is equally relevant, job satisfactions are similar, perceptions of mobility are comparable, and job security also seems similar, as well as the freedom to decide how to utilize one's time. These findings may surprise a number of people because they show far more comparability in professional fulfillment between the two groups than was anticipated. On the other hand, the nature of the fulfillment is substantially different.

In evaluating the information obtained from this study, it is very important to note that the employment situation is changing very rapidly. Many of these changes have occurred within the past few years. A survey of the membership is not sensitive enough to determine a number of these factors because the relevant sample component was too small. Additional procedures must be utilized to obtain precise information. The APA's evaluation of the placement of new PhDs is obviously one important effort. Follow-up studies of these individuals and focused sampling of specific employment units are also needed.

Prospects for the Future

With the limitations of this study in mind, two major points seem to be in order as one examines prospects for the future. First, the environments that were described by respondents in this study are those that currently exist, not those that potentially exist. It may be possible to develop nonacademic positions for social psychologists that allow greater opportunity for publishable scientific research.

Second, the panels that were developed by the committee resulted in significant information that was not obtained from the survey. For instance, it was learned that many roles for which social psychologists are specifically well qualified are presently filled, at high levels of remuneration, by individuals with minimal college or postgraduate training. Therefore, it is even more evident that there are major new opportunities to be developed by the profession.

Although those now employed in nonacademic settings were generally satisfied with graduate training, innovative graduate training programs in applied social psychology would be of great value in developing skills to serve the requirements of the potentially large number of positions available in, for example, law firms, judicial systems, consumer agencies, and advertising. The Wayne State University internship program, briefly described earlier, is one such preliminary approach to this problem.

Finally, to reiterate a point made by Lofton (1972): Since recorded history the social problems that affect society have been immense. War, economic injustice, racial prejudice, and religious bigotry are not new phenomena. It would be a depressing irony if that field that is defined as the scientific study of social relations was unable to appropriately train the large number of professionals who are required for the development of meaningful solutions to these problems.

REFERENCES

Carnegie Commission on Higher Education. *New students and new places.* New York: McGraw-Hill, 1971.
Cartter, A. M. Scientific manpower for 1970–1985. *Science,* 1971, *172,* 132–140.
Cates, J. Too many PhDs, not enough jobs. *APA Monitor,* September-October 1973, p. 23.
Levy, S. G. Preliminary analyses of Division 8 employment survey. *Personality and Social Psychology Bulletin,* 1975, *1*(2), 445–449.
Little, K. B. Epilogue: Academic marketplace 1984. *American Psychologist,* 1972, *27,* 504–506.
Lofton, J. A perspective from the public at large. *American Psychologist,* 1972, *27,* 364–366.
Radner, R., & Miller, L. S. Demand and supply in U.S. education: A progress report. *American Economic Review,* 1970, *60,* 326–335.
Vetter, B. Projected psychology PhD's, MA's drop since last year: BA's up. *APA Monitor,* May 1973, p. 3.

25

Kristina Hooper

Psychologists in Architecture

The combination of psychology and architecture is a natural one. Architecture is conceived of by people, it is viewed by people, and it is lived in by people. Psychologists study people. They study how people think and design, they study how people perceive their environments, and they study how people are affected by their environments.

Yet psychologists are generally unfamiliar with the architectural design process, and architects are generally alienated from psychologists as partners in design. This chapter intends to explore the situation, to examine the distance between the architectural and psychological professions, to delineate the architectural process as it might be viewed by a psychologist, and to propose methods by which the present situation might be changed. The ultimate goal is to encourage psychologists to work within the context of architecture so that they might fulfill themselves in an area as yet generally uncharted (by psychologists) and so that they may take an active role in the development of more humane environments.

Architecture and Society

To begin this discussion, we must first explore the field of architecture in general as it fits into contemporary society. Architecture is presently a field in a state of flux. It has changed in the modern era from being viewed as a basically aesthetic and elitist profession to being seen as a very societally relevant domain that is bound up with the responsibilities of social advocacy in the attainment of individual and group goals. As such, it has changed from what may have been considered an applied art to a field concerned with the reflection and expansion of social values. It has moved from the domain of the humanities into the realms of twentieth century social science. Sociology, psychology, and economics, rather than literature, music, and sculpture, have begun to greatly influence architecture. The reasons for this influence are diverse and complex. Central reasons include the recent societal emphasis on the environment and the human role in this environment and the general feeling of affluence that has allowed us to consider, if only in our rhetoric, the comfort of individual citizens. In addition, architects and planners have recently been criticized vehemently by communities, scientists, social scientists, and

Kristina Hooper is an Assistant Professor with the Psychology Board of Studies, University of California, Santa Cruz.

everyday people because of their inability to produce environments that satisfy the needs of modern humanity and because of their apparent insensitivities to these needs.

In response to these many pressures, some architects have looked to social scientists for ways to consider social, cultural, economic, and personal factors in the design of environments. Yet, in practice, social scientists have often been more trouble than they were worth. Outside of carefully delineating the importance of the societal issues and graphically describing the horror of many modern living situations, social scientists have contributed little to the constructive elucidation of the architectural domain. They have instead alienated architects with generalizations and complex theories. More strikingly, they have generally left the architect standing alone with the guilt and burden of issues that have been carefully defined as insolvable.

This situation has driven many conscientious architects into becoming their own social scientists, that is, into achieving competency in the social sciences as well as in design, in engineering, and in other related areas. Yet though this effort is commendable, it is ill spent in a complex modern society in which the issues of any field are changing more rapidly than ever before. Either our society must simplify itself enough so that single individuals can treat the diverse issues of creating environments, or it must admit to the complexities of building at the scale it has chosen and must make decisions in the manner it has constructed. Architects are now planning buildings whose scale, in time and space, is out of proportion to the architects' abilities to comprehend, represent, and communicate these buildings. If this is to continue (though it is not at all clear that it should), the architectural world must equip itself with sets of experts, all of whom are generalists to some extent, who might communicate effectively from different perspectives in ongoing situations.

Psychological Resources and Architecture

The psychologist is one kind of expert who can greatly affect the domain of architecture. The field of psychology can offer much to architects, and, more importantly, it can offer much to society through architects by, for example, its study of the attitudes and behaviors of individuals and of groups. Psychology typically studies how behaviors change in different environments. It studies how groups of people interact in certain physical and social environments. One need only change the perspective a bit to consider what attributes of environments are responsible for certain behaviors and attitudes and how changes in the environment might enhance the quality of individuals' lives and the effectiveness of group interaction.

Another set of resources for the psychologist is studies of human perception. Psychologists investigate how sensory environments affect individuals and how information in the environment is coded by the senses, stored, and retrieved for use at later times. Human perception is important for architects to understand explicitly. The architect and the engineer measure buildings in feet and inches, yet humans measure buildings in terms of big and small. Architects must consider these differences and should create environments intended to be viewed by people rather than to be measured by physical instruments.

Another topic for the psychologist is the basic design process of the architect; the use of visual representations in an architects' thought, the communication of various states of problem solutions, and the battles with creative blocks and goal definitions. This design process is the domain of the cognitive and personality psychologists who study thought and the differences between individual styles of thought.

Clinical techniques can be used to enhance the dialogue between clients and architects and between architects and other professionals. Group and individual encounters can be orchestrated so that ideas can flow most effectively and explicitly between individuals working on common projects.

Another approach to architecture is through environmental psychology, the study of human behavior in a naturalistic environment. This field allows psychologists to move out of laboratories and into large-scale environments and shifts the emphasis of psychology onto the investigation of human behavior in an everyday, normal environment. Environmental psychology also enhances the psychologist's interest in large-scale environments. Studies of environmental perception, crowding, environmental attitudes, and other domains of human–environment interactions explore the general theoretical realms of the relationship between people and their built world.

Yet, though social, perceptual, cognitive, clinical, and environmental psychology can assist the psychologist in working in architecture and with architects, the most important tools for a psychologist are quantitative abilities and the general manner and expertise in approaching complex problems. The process the psychologist has learned is the valuable tool to transfer, rather than the specific content areas of psychology. A well-trained psychologist, independent of a specialty area, is well equipped with methods (qualitative and quantitative) to disarm and tame difficult problems, can find a question to ask that is answerable, can know where to look for evidence for a hypothesis defined in a certain way, and will know how results might be interpreted once they are obtained. These skills can be very effective in the analysis of a design issue and can be very complementary to the skills of an architect. For the ideas and methods of the psychologist to be useful (and salable) to the architects, however, they must be presented within the context of the architect.

The architect's world is based on securing clients and then coordinating effective dialogue with these clients in the design and production of the future environment. This process is not based on the study of general human behavior or on general problems of design, although the investigation of general situations often provides the context with which the architects deal. Architects need to know how to make decisions given the constraints of a particular project. For example, given that a project must house a certain number of people, that it must house a certain set of activities, and that it must cost less than a certain amount, the architect needs to identify the critical aspects of the environment that should be priorities in the design. The architect must determine what would be necessary within those constraints to provide a good environment, aesthetically, functionally, and humanly. Architects must also know how to stretch constraints and change conceptions. For example, they must address the question of whether we need high-rise buildings and whether the economic efficiency justifies the human dissatisfaction that often accompanies these buildings. Yet, in general, a consulting psychologist must deal with an architect who works within a well-defined set of limited time and financial resources, an architect who doesn't have the resources to be philosophic or extremely innovative in approach. Given an understanding of this architectural milieu, a psychologist can be useful to the architect in formulating and testing how humans behave in a particular place. The psychologist must also consider how evaluations and analyses can be distributed to individuals, to communities, and to institutions that are active in the design process.

The Surrender of Myths

To perform effectively and to enter into the architect's world, the psychologist must surrender the myths of the printed page, of the superiority of language, of humility, of infinite time, and of generalizability.

To dispel the myth of the printed page the psychologist must learn that an eloquent, well-controlled experiment, described neatly in standard psychological form, will not necessarily be read by design professionals or by communities. It will not be read unless it is in a form that is approachable and interesting. In communicating ideas verbally, psychologists have to be concise, precise, and free of limited vocabularies and jargon. Otherwise, they should have no delusions of having their work read nor of having it attain any influence in the design process.

The myth of superiority of language over graphic media must also be overcome. Architects are visually oriented (as are many individuals in our society). They are also generally intelligent, creative, and intellectually sophisticated, but they may have difficulty putting their ideas into words or onto paper. In working with architects, the psychologist must accept diagrams written on backs of napkins or complex flowcharts, rather than formats written in complete sentences. Psychologists must adapt because communication with architects is important and also because the graphic media developed and used by architects are extremely sophisticated in the conceptual domain in which they are used (and probably maximally effective in many other realms as well). Psychologists working in architecture must learn to spend as much time drawing diagrams and producing pictures as they normally do editing texts. They must include graphic media within their definition of effective communication channels.

The myth of humility, which falls under the general heading of communication, states that if a person is good, humble, and truthful, his or her wisdom will be recognized. Psychologists have to accept the notion of theater, a notion quite unfamiliar to most psychologists in terms of the presentation of data, so that they can make themselves heard, so that they can make their results understood, and so that the results will be taken into serious consideration. The same acceptance of architecture must be shown. For in the applied world, it is not so much what is said, but how it is said. People do not listen to something or remember it because it is true, but because it has caught their attention and they have found it convincing.

Another myth that psychologists must give up is that time is infinite. Psychologists have studied problems of the human psyche for generations and generations. Often they pause to wonder what they have learned, if anything, and to determine if they really know anything more. Yet they are generally patient in their undertakings and are generally satisfied in adding small pieces to what has been discovered before. Architects are not patient. They deal in a world that has deadlines, a world that has limited resources. If psychologists plan to work with architects, they must learn to work within these very same constraints.

The myth of generalizability must also be considered. Psychologists look for general principles, principles that bind together that which they observe in the world, principles that allow them to make general predictions and to categorize what they view around themselves. Architects need to deal with specifics rather than general principles. They must deal with variance inherent in psychologists' predictive equations. They have to view similarities between situations, between design problems, and between design solutions. Yet they must realize that there will not be complete transfer from one situation to another. They must therefore rely on process strategies of problem solving throughout the design process rather than on attempts to directly transfer old answers. A psychologist who works with an architect must do the same.

Such are some of the myths that psychologists must examine if they are interested in working in the field of architecture. For good reason, the complicated but essential question of how psychologists might actually dispel these myths is still unanswered. This question is complicated because there are no institutional provisions for uniting the two fields. No job descriptions in architectural firms or planning agencies require a PhD in psychology. No degrees are offered in psychological architectural consulting. And, moreover, few observable instances can be noted in which psychologists and architects have worked together effectively. These are not adequate reasons to evade the issue, however. To go beyond these reasons we must move timidly, realizing that the territory is unexplored, yet also knowing that that is what makes the adventure worthwhile. We examine possible roles for psychologists in architecture by first identifying those points in the architectural design process that are well suited to intervention by a psychologist, by exploring those settings in which a psychologist might seem useful, and by then suggesting mechanisms that enhance the interactions of the two professions.

Design Process and Psychologists

The architectural design process is an extremely complex phenomenon, though it has been alluded to in prior sections of this chapter as though it were straightforward. It involves many different actors besides the architect and different problem-solving activities. The process is initiated with a client who has particular conceptions about how a building might be constructed, and it ends with the construction of the building. The client may be a private individual interested in building a house, a university expanding its facilities, an entrepreneur building an attractive new business, or a city producing a new city hall. In any of these cases, the client comes to the architect with sets of criteria, sets of dreams, and a well-defined capacity to pay for a project. The architect is initially responsible for determining the needs and values of the client so that an initial design proposal might be produced. Architects must understand the criteria and their justification, and they must clearly see the dreams of the client before they actualize them. Then with each additional design proposal, architects will attempt to better approximate the clients' expectations within a realistic framework, arriving ultimately at a proposal that fulfills basic functional criteria as well as client desires.

The initial assessment of client needs and values, and then their refinement, is an area where psychologists can be directly useful. First, they can help in the initial interviewing situation, attempting to provide mechanisms for the clients to express their needs. Second, through the development of appropriate media psychologists can help the clients communicate their responses to each design; the architect can then identify appropriate modifications. As the architect attempts to develop these modifications, the psychologist, who deals directly with the creativity of the architect, can develop ways of communicating the architect's desires to the client.

If a project is large-scale, the design proposal will be set before a panel of judges in contexts such as planning reviews or community meetings. This process again offers the psychologist an opportunity to use expertise in ascertaining individual and group preferences and values. It also provides a point where the psychologist can propose reasearch that will test the adequacy of the proposal in terms of behavioral correlates and in terms of levels of human satisfaction. This research can be used to assure that human considerations are intelligently and explicitly considered when design trade-offs are made, a process that can be easily centered only on political and economic considerations. Alternatively, psychologists can cite environmental psychological literature to support certain human aspects of the proposal.

Following the presentation and approval of a project, it will be built by architects in coordination with governmental officials and contractors.

This period of time is not particularly amenable to psychological consideration, except that it is a very stressful time for all involved due to the day-to-day complications of construction. However, following completion of a project, the point where the design process is generally viewed as ending, the potential for psychologists' involvement is magnified. The psychologist can evaluate the success of the project in terms of the people who live in it. Otherwise, the architect will move onto the next project without adequate human feedback to transfer from the old project. This is an important intervention point for the psychologist. The project can be considered an experiment used to provide feedback to the architects and to society in general. Expectations of clients and architects concerning human use of particular spaces can be compared directly to actual usage patterns. The project can at last be directly considered and experienced as a human environment.

Useful Settings for Psychologists

Although it is not completely clear where a psychologist would work in these intervention stages, architectural firms are an obvious possibility. Yet presently few or no positions exist for psychologists in these firms. Jobs in these fields need to be created. Consulting firms offer another possibility to work with architectural and planning firms. Community advocacy groups need psychologists to help in the justification of particular arguments for human needs and values. The architectural or design departments of universities can also provide a setting where psychologists could affect the attitudes of people who are training in the field and could address more theoretical issues of the human–architecture interface with experts in the design fields. Businesses, such as banks, that are involved in construction need psychologists to predict the appeal of their new environments. Similarly, governmental agencies may offer opportunities for psychologists to supervise facility development so that human values will be included.

Interaction of Psychology and Architecture

For psychologists to be useful in any of the contexts mentioned, they must become generally familiar with the architectural world and must secure contact with people involved in the architectural profession. This familiarity can be achieved by attending conferences that include individuals from both design and psychology (e.g., the annual Environmental Design and Research Association conferences or the Aspen Design Conference). To become familiar with the interfaces of these other professions, psychologists can attend architectural schools or become involved directly in urban planning, at universities or in applied situations. Another potential contact source is through the American Psychological Association Task Force on the Environment, which lists individuals (designers and psychologists) who are interested in architecture–human interactions.

These suggestions are but the beginnings of ways to encourage psychological involvement in architecture. The necessity for this intervention is obvious. We need more explicitly human input into the creation of our environment, and psychologists need to enter the design arena in order to effectively provide this input. In addition, the logic of the interaction is clear. Psychologists have skills that would be useful in the design process, because they are trained explicitly in the identification and communication of human needs and values. The difficulties of the interaction, however, should also be clear. Architects and psychologists are trained in very different ways. They generally have different skills and different orientations. The interaction of these two groups is not necessarily natural. In addition, the architectural world does not have positions designed for the presence of psychologists. Yet the situation should not be written off as hopeless, for not only do psychologists need access to architects and to the field of architecture but architects need psychologists. Psychologists have to let architects know this. They have to aggressively approach the field of architecture with their skills in their hands and their minds ready to teach and to learn. They have to make themselves useful so that it becomes obvious that environments should be built for people and that since psychologists study people they can be helpful in sharing the responsibility for the generation and actualization of humane environments.

26

Potpourri: Job Descriptions of
Psychologists in Nontraditional
and Innovative Roles

Editor's Note: In 1974, C. Alan Boneau, the Director of Programs and
Planning of the American Psychological Association, with the assistance
of Marilyn Machlowitz, conducted a survey directed toward the goal of
locating psychologists with innovative careers. Persons believed to be
holding unusual jobs for psychologists were located through APA's wo/
manpower data files and other sources and were surveyed by a questionnaire. Some 600 replies were received. These were analyzed and classified
by Ms. Machlowitz and Connie Ballantine, and from these replies a selection was submitted to the Editor. An additional culling and editing operation was then performed, and the results are presented in this chapter.
While the respondents gave us permission to use their names we decided to
be protective, though I hope not overly so, by not identifying the individuals. It was feared that they just might be inundated with inquiries. If any of
the respondents are unhappy with their anonymity, they should direct
their displeasure to the Editor, not to Dr. Boneau, Ms. Machlowitz, or Ms.
Ballantine, who all worked very hard on this project. In any case, on behalf
of those who may benefit from their replies, I wish to express thanks and
appreciation to all of the respondents.

Following are the items from the questionnaire. Subsequently, the
answers are presented with the headings only.

I. **Employer Description**
   Describe briefly the designation and function of the institution/
   organization/role in which you are working. What services/products/
   activities are involved? Who are the clients/customers? Who foots the
   bill (clients, state governments, etc.)?

II. **Job Description**
   Describe briefly your activities in your position, particularly with
   regard to the extent to which your psychological expertise is utilized
   and your relationship to other professionals and the public. If you are
   performing activities or holding a position you believe to be innovative or nontraditional for psychologists as psychologists, please emphasize.

III. Training

Is a traditional degree in psychology desirable or necessary for these activities? What changes in training would better have prepared you for the position?

IV. Employment Prospects

Does what you are doing represent a potentially expandable job market for psychologists? How might we go about doing that? How many psychologists might be so employed?

V. Other Comments

Social Issues

Consultant to a Public Defender's Office

I. *Employer description.* I serve as a full-time consultant to the investigators and lawyers in the Public Defender's Office on matters relating to their clients in which the services of a behavioral scientist would assist in the defense of clients or would facilitate client management.

II. *Job description.* I am employed by the Community Mental Health Center and am placed in the Public Defender's Office. My services are subsumed under the Center's preventive services activities. My activities, which are diagnostic, evaluative, and consultative, are not innovative, but the setting in which I provide my services is a relatively new one for clinical psychologists.

III. *Training.* I have found my training in psychological diagnostics to be essential in performing my duties. Of course, training and experience in interviewing have also been essential. I guess I do feel that my traditional training in observing, interviewing, and diagnosing psychiatric disorders has been necessary to my activities in the Public Defender's Office.

IV. *Employment prospects.* It seems to me that any large Public Defender's Office could provide more efficient service and enhance the services to defendants if a behavioral scientist with clinical training and experience were added to the staff. Local community mental health centers could provide or offer services to public defenders on experimental, trial, or contractual arrangements. There are 20 judicial circuits in my state. I suspect that all 20 of them could use some consultation from clinical psychologists and that at least 8 or 9 of them would benefit from a half- to a full-time clinical psychologist consultant.

Clinical Psychologist Working in a U.S. Senator's Office

I. *Employer description.* I am employed as a legislative assistant to a member of the United States Senate.

II. *Job description.* My primary function is to act as a catalyst to the Senator's considerable personal interest in health. I also attempt to develop an active communication network between the providers of health care, the major university in our state, and our Washington office. This involves keeping them aware of pending legislation, intervening with federal agencies for them, etc.

III. *Training.* The PhD plus a clinical internship is very helpful, but I could have used some more formal consulting supervision.

IV. *Employment prospects.* This is definitely an expandable job market. There are over 500 offices on Capitol Hill, but I don't know of any psychologist besides myself. There is no doubt in my mind that our profession can have a major impact on the entire national health delivery system, but only by getting involved at the legislative level.

Specialist in Normal Childhood Development Working in Television Programming

I. *Employer description.* I have been working, voluntarily, with a local television channel in the preparation of specialized television programming for young, preschool Jewish children.

II. *Job description.* Being a resource person for specialized programming for preschool children is, I think, a relatively nontraditional role for a psychologist. My psychological and educational expertise is perfectly suited to this kind of activity. Incidentally, I got into this activity because I have been very disappointed all these years by the lack of any major television programming for Jewish children during Chanukah, a December holiday, and Passover, a March–April holiday, and the fact that my children would think that they were second-class citizens as far as their religious preferences were concerned. I decided to do something about this and called a program on our local station. The people in charge of the program were quite receptive and eager to do something, and that is how my association with them began.

III. *Training.* A traditional degree in psychology is desirable for these activities. My educational/psychological background (normal child development, school psychology, etc.) was excellent preparation. I would also have liked "television production" courses.

IV. *Employment prospects.* I believe this field does represent a potentially expandable job market for psychologists. I think there is a field for those interested in developing children's programs, adolescents' programs, and general family viewing entertainment.

Ecological Psychologist Working for an Environmental Research and Development Foundation

I. *Employer description.* The Foundation is a nonprofit corporation organized to do research on the effects of the environment on human behavior. The clients are governmental agencies at the local, state, and federal levels; individual architects; or architectural organizations such as the American Institute of Architects. The mission of the organization is to help build more livable environments.

II. *Job description.* As President of the organization, my chief function is to solicit business for the organization and to act as principal investigator on research and demonstration projects. A significant part of my job is to act as an agent for social change both among psychologists and architects and to make them aware of nontraditional methods such as those of ecological psychology. This has been an uphill battle because most psychologists have a deep investment in explaining behavior by way of individual personality and most architects have an investment in architecture as an art form. Nevertheless, in recent years this area of expertise has been developing and broadening.

III. *Training.* In some ways a traditional education in psychology is a handicap to the solution of any social problem. The training of psychologists tends to focus almost entirely on the laboratory, without cognizance that the laboratory can be a totally artificial creation unrelated to any ecological reality. Most psychologists end up unable to think in terms that would be useful to decision makers. Training in unobtrusive methods of studying daily behavior and social problems would greatly increase the value of psychologists in this area.

IV. *Employment prospects.* It is hard to say how many psychologists might eventually be employed in this area. Right now, many more want to enter this field than there are jobs for, but the future may provide room for more than 100.

V. *Other comments.* As my career has progressed, it has become more and more evident to me that the tools and knowledge of psychology have tremendous relevance to the many social problems of our society. Too much of the time, however, these tools and this knowledge remain "locked" in the university; they must be brought outside.

Psychologist in Accident Research

I. *Employer description.* The organization gathers and disseminates technical safety information on a nationwide basis.

II. *Job description.* The purpose of my job is to review accident literature, to design and execute original research, and to systematically evaluate accident countermeasure programs.

III. *Training.* The "traditional" degree is helpful, but I believe more of a "co-op" approach to graduate education is needed, that is, a program in which work in the real world is mixed with academic coursework.

IV. *Employment prospects.* There is definitely a job market for as many as 1,000 psychologists. They could be employed by indicating the cost–benefit to employers of studying and reducing the tremendous losses caused by accidents, both on and off the job.

Psychologist in Social-Urban Planning

I. *Employer description.* I work for a federal agency whose mission is to assist recipient agencies (local housing authorities, urban renewal agencies, model cities' administrations, local and state planning agencies, etc.) in fulfilling their function to develop the United States' environment by making it safer and more sanitary.

II. *Job description.* I utilize my knowledge of community psychology and social psychology vis-à-vis social-urban planning. I plan to branch out into a new field of planned urban change called social ecology.

III. *Training.* A traditional degree would be a hindrance for my activities in terms of its antiquated requirements. For this reason I chose Fordham University's Urban Education Program, which has an emphasis on the psychology of the urban environment as it affects urban youngsters.

IV. *Employment prospects.* Unfortunately, I don't feel that the government agency I work for, the Department of Housing and Urban Development, could use psychologists *qua* psychologists in its present condition. The government, I feel, is somewhat backward in its image of the field and stereotypes psychologists in the roles of researchers or clinicians. I have had to spend time unobtrusively expanding my own role.

V. *Other comments.* I see the psychologist in any bureaucracy as a catalyst in the implementation of systemic revolution in terms of positive planned change. The psychologist's knowledge of human behavior and sensitivity to the necessity for communication at any level aid in extending the role of the psychologist from the couch to the computer room.

Editor for a Specialized Publisher

I. *Employer description.* I am the Articles Editor for a publishing company which I founded that specializes in publications related to women's liberation. We market the pamphlets and the books that we publish, as well as other books that we buy for resale.

II. *Job description.* As Articles Editor, I review all of the papers and articles submitted for publication. My purpose and the company's purpose is to study and disseminate information about sex-role stereotypes.

III. *Training.* I think that my experience as an activist feminist is more relevant than my training as a psychologist. My PhD training in experimental psychology, however, is useful in evaluating scholarly research.

IV. *Employment prospects.* At the present time, the only employment potential is in women's studies programs. If serious attention were given to Freud's question "What do women want?" the job market would be very large, since no scientific information is available on that question.

Warden at a Federal Center for Young Offenders

I. *Employer description.* I work at a federal youth center for offenders ranging from 16 to 24 years of age. The center offers counseling, vocational training, and basic as well as advanced education. It is funded by the federal government.

II. *Job description.* As Warden I have the overall administrative responsibility for all program areas, including mental health, education, recreation, religion, custody casework, etc.

III. *Training.* My psychology training was a definite asset after I learned how to be an administrator. I would recommend a broad background in budgeting, personnel work, and other administrative activities for someone trying to enter an area such as this.

IV. *Employment prospects.* This field is a potentially expandable job market, but only for those psychologists who can handle the non-psychological parts of the job. The number of such positions is limited, however; thus, the field does not present itself as a "real" job market for psychologists.

V. *Other comments.* Psychologists are definitely needed in correctional work, but only if they are committed to it as a long-term career. Dropping in and out of the criminal justice field does psychology a great deal of harm, and does little to help anyone.

Police Psychologist

I. *Employer description.* I work primarily with the staff and personnel of a large urban police department to provide counseling and therapy services, teaching, research, management consultation, and consultation in regard to crime situations. This is a salaried, full-time position paid by the city government.

II. *Job description.* The police psychologist role is open-ended and includes many of the clinical and industrial psychologist's functions, plus many more. Testifying as an expert witness on pornography, eliciting a psychological profile of a rape-murderer, and using hypnosis with a witness to a homicide to enhance recall are all part of a day's work, in addition to routine assessment, therapy, and organization development.

III. *Training.* A doctoral degree in a behavioral science is basic to this position. In addition, maturity, objectivity, and good on-the-job learning ability are essential. All of my past training and experience have been useful. Perhaps an internship in a police setting would also have been useful.

IV. *Employment prospects.* Police psychology is expanding; an increasing number of departments are hiring psychologists. For example, New York City is in the process of hiring eight psychologists. Among the 40,000 police departments in the country, perhaps as many as 10% could afford and constructively utilize a behavioral science expert. The American Psychological Association could do some public relations work by contacting the local police departments and the International Association of Chiefs of Police to "sell" the relevant skills of psychologists.

Clinical

Clinical Administrator

I. *Employer description.* I serve as Assistant Director of a bureau that provides psychologists, psychiatrists, clinical social workers, and paraprofessionals to serve offenders in all juvenile and adult state correctional institutions and in probation-parole services. These professionals are paid by the state and are not responsible to the wardens, superintendents, and probation-parole administrators of the facilities they serve.

II. *Job description.* My duties are largely administrative and consultative. In the latter role I become involved in some activities that are non-traditional for psychologists. For example, I have been involved with parole board officials and personnel workers in establishing a situational test to serve as part of a promotional examination for evaluating applicants for positions on a state parole board. I have also worked very closely with architects in designing new correctional facilities and in modifying existing ones. The work involves a psychologist in the design of environments and total programs. This association has also resulted in my learning some key architectural concepts and procedures. A third area focuses on legal judicial matters. With the increasing concerns that are emerging for rights of juveniles and adult offenders, for due process regarding juvenile and adult disposition of cases, and for issues such as right to treatment, psychologists in the criminal justice system find themselves working more closely with the courts, prosecutors, and defense attorneys.

III. *Training.* I believe that a traditional doctoral degree in clinical psychology is appropriate and essential. This belief is supported by my experience as an employer of psychologists over the past 10 years. Our bureau recruits traditionally trained clinical psychologists, and we rarely find one with any previous exposure to or experience in working with offenders. With very few exceptions, however, they have acquired the necessary experience and cultural awareness to work effectively with this population. While a traditional clinical degree is essential, it would be worthwhile for psychologists who wish to increase their effectiveness in the criminal justice system to have the opportunity, perhaps on a continuing education basis, to take relevant courses in law, architecture, sociology, neurology, learning disabilities, etc.

IV. *Employment prospects.* My specific position, being largely administrative, probably does not represent a significantly expandable job market for psychologists. The criminal justice system, however, does offer an expandable market. As due process and right to treatment become increasingly established, and as standards for providers of psychological services become implemented, the demand for psychologists in the criminal justice system will likely increase.

V. *Other comments.* It is clear that clinical applicants for our position openings often consider corrections as a last resort or an interim position perhaps to ride out a recession. One reason for this is that psychologists bring to the job a lot of simplistic, incorrect, negative biases about offenders. Once they unlearn these biases and acquire some cultural awareness, they find offenders a fascinating and promising group with whom to work. Another factor has been the negative image of corrections around the country, largely deserved until recently, which has rendered it an undesirable work setting for a clinician. This is changing for the better as correctional facilities accommodate increasingly to the offender's rights. The criminal justice system might be made more attractive to clinicians through an organized effort to counter negative stereotyping of offenders during graduate training. This could be accomplished by paying visits to psychologists who work in the field of corrections, by encouraging the development of more clinical internships in corrections, and by getting clinical staff in psychology departments involved in consultation to correctional programs.

Clinical Administrator

I. *Employer description.* I am the Assistant Commissioner of Public Welfare for Comprehensive Programs and as such have overall program responsibility for the areas of mental health, mental retardation, chemical dependency (alcohol and drugs), aging, low-income families and children, and the physically handicapped. Our bureau is also responsible for the licensing of a large variety of facilities such as foster home and child care institutions and residential facilities for the mentally ill, the retarded, the chemically dependent, and the physically handicapped. The bureau also administers the grant-in-aid program for community mental health centers, the day activities centers for the retarded, and day care facilities for children.

II. *Job description.* First of all, I believe that my position as the "mental health authority" in our state is somewhat unusual; this position is typically occupied by a psychiatrist. Second, I believe the large breadth of my programmatic responsibilities is different, varying as it does from mental health, aging, low-income families and children, etc. I am, of course, fundamentally an administrator and do not engage in direct clinical services as part of my job. At the same time, my professional psychological expertise is most useful in program development in all these areas. The position is unique, as far as I can determine, in terms of the broad responsibilities involved and the mandate to coordinate the various programs into a comprehensive human service system. Finally, I guess my programmatic involvement in programs for low-income families and children is really quite unusual for a psychologist; this involvement is typically reserved for the field of social work.

III. *Training.* My degree in clinical psychology (including as it does a very firm grounding in general psychology, child psychology, etc.) serves me well in this job. I could have used more training in administration, budgetary work, etc.

IV. *Employment prospects.* To the extent that psychologists are interested in broad-based administrative and program planning positions, I believe this type of job has a potential market. Essentially, I think psychologists should be more exposed to these types of functions while they are in training in graduate school. This also would require a broader orientation toward human service delivery systems and types of services than is now provided in training situations.

Hospital Psychologist

I. *Employer description.* I am employed by an acute care, research-oriented university hospital. The hospital provides comprehensive medical care to a large geographic region. General medical fees are covered by insurance; psychological services are provided free of charge.

II. *Job description.* I believe my role is fully innovative for a hospital psychologist. While I provide direct patient intervention for the inpatient and outpatient services, most of my efforts in the hospital are spent facilitating the functions of the medical team and the nursing team. Thus I spend my efforts in team meetings and special meetings developing group processes to cope with general and specific problems that arise in the provision of medical care. In the community, I work in a similar fashion with agencies, schools, medical centers, and individual physicians. For example, rather than take a direct referral, I spend time with the staff to facilitate its handling of the problem. Another variation of this approach was a weekend sexuality workshop I offered to the family physicians from the community.

III. *Training.* My professional training has helped, but I think most clinical and community psychology programs "can't see the forest for the trees." I think the biggest change that is required is for professional schools to loosen their grip on graduate students and allow them to become involved in community issues as a valid part of their training.

IV. *Employment prospects.* I think the field is open. I think many agencies that employ clinical psychologists can be encouraged to permit community-based operations. This would also require some public relations work by the American Psychological Association to entice psychologists out of their offices. Perhaps the only way this may be possible is through the availability of funds for demonstration projects.

Child Psychologist Consulting with
Day Care Centers

I. *Employer description.* I am employed by several day care centers. I train teachers to detect signs of early pathology in 3–6-year-old children. I hold ongoing group sessions with parents to educate them about issues of child development and to provide them with an opportunity to share experiences and articulate their thoughts.

II. *Job description.* I meet with individual parents who are in a crisis and who need support and/or referral. Sometimes the referral is for the child and the mother; often it is the mother alone who needs therapeutic attention. The population I deal with is primarily one-parent families in which the father is totally absent emotionally and/or financially or plays a negligible part in the family. My primary interest is in preventive mental health facilities and in therapeutic intervention in the early years of childhood in populations where the child is likely to be a high-risk candidate for emotional problems.

III. *Training.* I feel the theoretical background and different orientations to which I was exposed have provided me with a flexibility and a reluctance to act in simplistic and/or judgmental ways; I feel these characteristics are crucial to a field as intricate as psychology.

IV. *Employment prospects.* This is certainly a potentially expandable job market for psychologists, but currently funding is extremely difficult. At present, my work in this area is only part-time.

Counseling

Psychologist in Avocational Counseling

I. *Employer description.* I work at a rehabilitation agency that provides physical restoration, vocational evaluation and training, social maintenance programs, speech therapy, etc. There is a wide age range of client-patients, from infants through the elderly. Bills are paid by various insurance programs and other agencies.

II. *Job description.* I initiate and direct research activities for the agency, write grant proposals, and run projects when funding is obtained. I also advise other staff members when they attempt research. My main current interest, however, is avocational counseling, an area in which I have been working for six years.

III. *Training.* Most psychologists as well as other professionals need more training in the dynamics of organizational operations. Some of this knowledge is to be found in the field of industrial psychology and some in the sociology of organizations. Research methods, as outlined in textbooks, are hopelessly naive when applied in the context of an organization such as this. Interns need to be given experiences that will deliberately introduce them to the frustration of trying to get anything accomplished in a bureaucratic organization and teach them how to achieve these accomplishments in spite of bureaucratic rule.

IV. *Employment prospects.* Avocational counseling is a wide open field, and I believe one with great possibilities. Recreation therapists have shown the chief interest in this field, but they have only part of the skills necessary to do the job. A crying need is for psychologists to develop more sophisticated avocational interest inventories. Counseling psychologists could specialize in avocational counseling much as some specialize in vocational counseling. I would anticipate a potential demand for one such specialist for every 50,000 of the general population within the next 10 years.

V. *Other comments.* Many psychologists are blocked from moving into new, fruitful areas because of their own status problems. They are so defensive about their need to be identified as professionals and psychologists that they find it difficult to operate in roles other than the traditional ones into which they have been socialized by graduate school training. In the long run, psychologists will gain the most respect by being people who get the job done, whether it means typing reports to get them out on time, playing with kids on the playground to observe how they behave outside the clinical setting, or whatever.

Rehabilitation Psychologist

I. *Employer description.* I work for the rehabilitation services administration in the U.S. Department of Health, Education, and Welfare.

II. *Job description.* Psychological expertise is utilized in a supervisory relationship—encouraging, motivating, and at times exhorting staff to think through new approaches to the gainful employment of the severely handicapped. My hope is to steer a path of increased opportunities for the severely handicapped to get out of institutions and out of sheltered workshops into regular employment. This means testing new individual and group techniques and developing more practical testing apparatus because the usual aptitude tests are not geared to, for example, a double-hand amputee.

III. *Training.* A traditional degree in psychology is useful, but clinical experience is a must within a rehabilitation setting that involves work goals for the disabled.

IV. *Employment prospects.* There is room for at least 500 psychologically trained administrators of rehabilitation facilities and sheltered workshops in this field. The major need is to obtain psychologists who can use their interpersonal skills to run rehabilitation facilities. These administrative positions start at $15,000 for those with little experience and around $20,000 for psychologists with more experience who would be willing to undertake such a post.

Educational and School

Educational Measurement and Research Psychologist

I. *Employer description.* I work for a nonprofit educational measurement and research organization. Income is from test services, government grants and contracts, and philanthropic foundations.

II. *Job description.* I am a research psychologist working with a number of innovative projects. I have been involved in the evaluation of some nationwide children's television programs. Measuring the impact of children's television and working with producers to develop new delivery systems on television are two major current activities.

III. *Training.* The traditional degree is desirable, and more experience working on large-scale evaluation and research projects would have been useful.

IV. *Employment prospects.* This is potentially an expandable job market for psychologists. They could help both in entertainment and educational programming to specify needs and interests of various subpopulations, pretest materials early in production, and look for impacts, including negative side effects.

Private Consultant

I. *Employer description.* We have a private consulting business providing a variety of services for public schools, colleges, state departments of education, and some governmental agencies. The type of service includes (a) conducting educational surveys and studies, (b) assisting in planning and developing educational programs, (c) assisting in evaluating educational programs, and (d) managing support services in training school personnel and/or in operating educational programs. These services are provided on a contract basis.

II. *Job description.* Some of the following activities and/or skills are used: (a) We apply planning skills in the development of programs. My training in scientific procedures and research procedures has helped in this respect. (b) We evaluate educational programs. My training in statistics, measurement, and research has helped. (c) We conduct studies for schools, state-level departments of education, and other agencies. My research and measurement training has given me some expertise in this area. (d) I testify as a vocational expert in social security determination of disability as well as in workers' compensation cases. My training in guidance and counseling has helped.

III. *Training.* To administer our firm and to obtain contracts it has been highly advantageous to have the PhD degree, although many activities performed by our firm would not require the traditional degree.

IV. *Employment prospects.* With more and more emphasis on accountability, I believe this area is a potentially expandable job market.

Guidance Specialist with Foreign Students

I. *Employer description.* I work for a large city school district. As guidance specialist for foreign students who have English as a second language, I coordinate the guidance program for these students, which includes educational and vocational counseling. The role is primarily one of consultation and is provided to school administrators, counselors, school psychologists, and other school staff. It is a school-tax-supported position.

II. *Job description.* My psychological expertise is used in a consultative role regarding psychological testing, learning, child growth and development, cross-cultural psychology and in conducting an in-service program for school psychologists. I also do some casework.

III. *Training.* At least a master's-level degree is needed. My own training (EdD) was excellent, but I would recommend courses in cultural anthropology.

IV. *Employment prospects.* Public schools desperately need bilingual-bicultural psychologists. Opportunities exist for increased use of psychologists to work with foreign students in the public schools. In cities that function as ports of entry, such populations are growing.

V. *Other comments.* I feel there is a necessity to assess the learning and social adjustment needs of foreign students in our schools and then develop strategies to meet these needs. I feel strongly that we need to know more about the learning styles of foreign students and the evaluation of learning disabilities and communication disorders in them. We need to develop guidance counseling programs that permit these students to have the same opportunities to develop their talents as those students born in the United States. Because many of those students are obtaining poor educational and vocational counseling, they are missing opportunities for which they are qualified.

Industrial and Management

Overseas Industrial Consultant

I. *Employer description.* I am employed as a consultant to industry and government. I advise government and private organizations in many countries on training and development of all levels of management personnel.

II. *Job description.* I aid organizations in establishing assessment center methods to identify and develop management potential. I also aid them in allocating their training and development dollars. One innovative part of my job is working with many organizations, often overseas organizations, at a very high level.

III. *Training.* The traditional degree in psychology is desirable, and I would advise more experience actually observing and working with groups.

IV. *Employment prospects.* I think it is important to point out that the United States is ahead of most countries in applying psychological expertise to the problems of industry and, hence, a large market exists for skills of this kind. The assessment center method is a fast-growing subfield and is something young industrial psychologists should be trained in. Existing psychologists can find a good market for many of their skills in organizations in other industrial nations. The United States is years ahead of other countries in concepts such as test validation.

V. *Other comments.* Even though many foreign psychologists have been trained in the United States, they lack the practical expertise to actually carry out research projects. I find that foreign psychologists when trained in the United States are too theoretical for the organization needing the help. No matter what country I am in, I find myself trying to bring the psychologists down to reality.

Organizational Analyst

I. *Employer description.* I work as a marketing officer for a bank as a consultant to the other officers on organizational problems; I also work as a part-time consultant to health care corporations on financial and organizational planning, as an occasional troubleshooter for small businesses having difficulty, and with educational, business, and health care organizations in training their personnel.

II. *Job description.* My psychological training helps in everything I do. Research training aids in my ability to analyze problems effectively and rapidly and to arrive at potential solutions that need exploring. Educational psychology training aids in approaching all training situations, including training for executives. General psychological training aids in my ability to communicate effectively at a basic level. Overall, my psychological training has helped most in dealing with all situations from a feeling perspective that recognizes real problems rather than apparent and/or superficial problems.

III. *Training.* The traditional degree in psychology is desirable but not at all necessary. In fact, there are times when it has been disadvantageous for clients and/or colleagues to know that psychology was my primary degree because of the typical lay person's suspicion of "being analyzed."

IV. *Employment prospects.* This field represents a potentially expandable job market, but only in conjunction with work in other fields such as business, education, and health care. I have no valid way to estimate the numbers that might be employed but, intuitively, there would seem to be an almost inexhaustible market.

V. *Other comments.* A person could be trained with combined masters' degrees and in some cases doctoral degrees combined with other fields. I feel that the degree title should include reference to the other fields, that is, a degree in "business and psychology." Perhaps the most important factor is the personality of the individual. It should be characterized by a lack of defensiveness, an acceptance of other points of view, and an ability to be aggressive without pressing too much or being abrasive.

Industrial Psychologist in the Insurance Industry

I. *Employer description.* I work for a multiple-line insurance company conducting a wide variety of research activities.

II. *Job description.* I conduct research that is of direct and indirect value to the organization, including traditional industrial-organizational psychology, market and consumer research, safety (traffic) research, and research relating to government regulations of automobiles and insurance reparations.

III. *Training.* I think the traditional degree is necessary with an emphasis on quantitative measurement. The primary benefit that my training provided is an empirical orientation for the study of business organizational problems. Training in statistics and experimental methodology has been especially useful.

IV. *Employment prospects.* I have added three persons with a PhD in psychology to my own staff. Hence, this seems to be an expanding area.

Communication Work Between People and Computers

I. *Employer description.* We are trying to identify design criteria to facilitate communication between a computer and a lay person in order to accomplish useful work. Behavioral experiments are conducted in our work. The Office of Naval Research has partially funded our efforts, but my major employer is the research center of a large computer manufacturer.

II. *Job description.* We are trying to find ways of making it easy for persons in business to tell their problems to a computer and receive some help. We conduct experiments to investigate features of programming languages, to study how people specify procedures in natural English, and eventually to test our ideas about how a certain set of natural language mechanisms could be implemented to provide an exciting, powerful system.

III. *Training.* A person should have more training in "artificial intelligence," linguistics, and computer sciences in addition to the traditional degree.

IV. *Employment prospects.* This field is certainly a potentially expandable job market for psychologists. Since costs in using computers are primarily labor costs, that is, labor for translating a user's problems into computer-compatible form, we can save tremendous sums of money by solving these problems. I suggest contact with industrial companies for funding or cooperative work.

Engineering Psychologist

I. *Employer description.* I am employed in construction, engineering research for the United States Army.

II. *Job description.* As an engineering psychologist I develop habitability and behavioral criteria for design of interior and exterior structures. The innovative character of my work is in systematizing behavioral data to serve as criteria for the design of various building components.

III. *Training.* A curriculum based on physiological and applied psychology with an emphasis on human factors systems, methods, and systems mission-oriented research appears to be most appropriate.

IV. *Employment prospects.* Future employment opportunities may depend upon the aggressiveness of the professionals in the area and how sensitive the public may become to the importance of situational/behavioral criteria for living design.

Miscellaneous

Psychologist in Pharmaceutical Evaluation

I. *Employer description.* I work for a pharmaceutical company and am involved in the clinical development and evaluation of the investigatory compounds that may have potential efficacy as chemotherapeutic agents in the treatment of psychiatric disorders. The object of my role is to aid in the overall design and strategy and to monitor the clinical studies contracted by the company in order to establish the safety and efficacy of compounds in humans.

II. *Job description.* The work entails interaction with basic scientists (chemists, biologists, pharmacologists) and physicians. The multidisciplinary approach is used. Therefore, psychologists do have skills to contribute in this kind of setting with respect to design and evaluation of clinical trials. Since the setting in which I work is primarily a medical and basic science facility, I believe that this role is not quite traditional for "psychologists as psychologists."

III. *Training.* For this particular role, a traditional degree in clinical and experimental psychology is appropriate. In my own particular case a stronger training emphasis in the pharmacological aspects of psychopharmacology would have been welcome.

IV. *Employment prospects.* I believe that this area is a potentially expandable job market for psychologists. One method of expansion would be to train psychologists both academically and practically, through internships or "externships" where the emphasis would be on clinical psychopharmacology, that is, work with humans rather than animals. In the industry in which I work, I know of only two other psychologists in roles similar to mine. I cannot estimate how many psychologists might be so employed but I believe that since the medical-chemotherapeutic-psychotherapeutic treatment concept is already in practice, the monitoring and development of assessments of this treatment model will require psychological personnel in the future.

Psychologist in Nontraditional Education

I. *Employer description.* The organization that I work for is the American College of Life Underwriters, and its primary objective is to provide educational systems, materials, and assessment for those working within the life and health insurance industry. The services provided include the preparation and development of curriculum materials in life and health insurance, production of study guide materials and learning devices, and systems marketing of these materials to those individuals in life and health insurance.

II. *Job description.* I function in a nonacademic, nonindustrial governmental type of organization whose objective is the development of products and services that will increase the learning efficiency and knowledge of individuals engaged in life and health insurance. Although my activities include applying physical techniques, they only go as far as proving the worth from an attitudinal knowledge and cost–benefit standpoint of the programs and services provided by our organization to our students. My activities include the investigation into learning styles of adults and how they differ from children's learning styles; the application of information about learning styles to the development of educational materials; the assessment of individual learning patterns, cognitive styles, cognitive mapping, studies of psychometrics, characteristics of our examination series; and the examination of the value of our products and services in terms of their educational validity, etc.

III. *Training.* A traditional degree in psychology would not prepare one for this type of position. I believe that a person with a set of courses in psychological statistics, design, and psychometrics would have the necessary but not sufficient ingredients for performing this position. What is needed in addition is (a) more awareness as to the operating objectives of organizations, (b) training in areas of cost–benefit analysis, (c) evaluation procedures that work without stringent research design regulations, (d) knowledge of many more traditional statistical techniques, and (e) specifics in observational scale evolution, questionnaire design, and full appraisal of management systems and how they can be applied in terms of interfacing people and products.

IV. *Employment prospects.* I have seen a tremendous growth in the area of these nontraditional educational institutions. We must recognize that there is a "fourth dimension" of organizations; organizations in fields such as accounting, banking and trust, stock exchange, medicine, dentistry, transportation, environmental protection, and utility systems. These organizations all attempt to assist a parent organization whether it be insurance or public utilities in the evolution of its goals and objectives. In many cases, psychologists are needed for the activities concerned with documenting the characteristics of the customers or clients served and for the improvement of existing systems especially in the areas of assessment and instruction. The area of the adult as a professional learner who continues learning throughout a career is an area that has received little attention up to this time but is increasing in recognition. The number of psychologists that can be potentially employed in this field is quite large.

Psychologist in the Field of Fertility-Regulating Behavior

I. *Employer description.* I am employed by a multidisciplinary, nongovernmental, nonprofit research organization that focuses on psychosocial aspects of fertility-regulating behavior.

II. *Job description.* This job is designed (a) to facilitate cooperative, transnational research on psychosocial aspects of fertility-regulating behavior by organizing and coordinating joint studies with colleagues in other lands and with international organizations; (b) to advance the development of fertility behavior adaptable to diverse cultural milieus; (c) to increase understanding of psychosocial, demographic, epidemiological, and public health aspects of abortion-seeking behavior; (d) to strengthen optimal use of fertility-regulating methods; and (e) to publish and disseminate research findings for the consideration of policymakers, clinical service providers, fellow researchers, and interested citizens.

III. *Training.* At the time I was trained I never thought of doing what I am doing now. My "traditional degree" taught me how to look at research, and that helps, but training cannot always anticipate life career patterns and styles.

IV. *Employment prospects.* This is an expandable job market for psychologists—note the history of the APA Task Force on Psychology and Population and the development of Division 34 (Population Psychology). Psychologists will have to get university psychology departments more involved and then get them to recognize fertility behavior as a serious topic for psychological research and services.

Psychologist in a Medical Publishing Company

I. *Employer description.* I am employed by a medical publishing company. The prime products are medical publications designed for the first-line medical practitioner. A second major area of corporate activity is training programs for paraprofessionals in the health care field. The prime clients are pharmaceutical companies and physicians.

II. *Job description.* My primary duty is as publisher of a medical publication that goes to first-line family physicians. In the design of the magazine, a number of psychological principles have been employed, such as "express stops." These are small summary paragraphs of about 700–1,000 words that appear within the text. One can read the summary and decide whether to pursue that area of the article in detail. The company has also published flowcharts that represent key diagnostic and therapeutic points for various medical problems and diseases and has produced a training program based on learning theory and the utilization of a number of reinforcement concepts.

III. *Training.* If by the "traditional degree in psychology" one means a degree from programs containing a high number of social psychology courses, abnormal psychology courses, and other "soft science" courses, I'd say that the "traditional" degree is not desirable or necessary for the activities I perform. If by "traditional degree in psychology" however, one means a good basis in learning theory and statistics and one or more "hard sciences" I'd say that such a degree is desirable. I went through a university at a time when the program was very strong; included in the graduate sequence with statistics, experimental design, and theory were requirements in the areas of mathematics and hard science. The graduate program was extremely strong in areas of learning theory, tests and measurement, statistics, and lab courses. As far as my own training is concerned, I wouldn't change any of it.

IV. *Employment prospects.* I think that what I am doing and what I could be doing if I had more time truly represent an expandable job market for psychologists, but not for clinical psychologists. I see the greatest potential use of psychologists in the area of learning and training as well as communications.

V. *Other comments.* I've been looking for good people for our organization for seven years and have found that the kinds of psychologists I would like to employ are very scarce. Many of those that do have the kind of training I desire have very little interest in the applied life.

Behavioral Researcher in Highway Safety

I. *Employer description.* I am employed by a bureau of the federal government.

II. *Job description.* This job entails the preparation of staff studies and the development of recommendations for action dealing with problems such as alcohol, pedestrians, driver education, bicycles, and motorcycles.

III. *Training.* I received my PhD in industrial psychology and took a minor in statistics. But the question of how much of my training was relevant is difficult for me to answer because in various jobs in this field I have essentially made the job and, in the process, have used all of the training and experience that I had.

IV. *Employment prospects.* I think more psychologists might be employed in the area of highway safety research in the future; I think there are more so engaged now than ever before. It is very difficult to estimate how many more might be so employed because this depends on the funds available, and this in turn depends on the way the decision makers view the problem. There is a great need to enlighten the administrators and to enlighten the Congress. I am happy to see that the American Association for the Advancement of Science has initiated a program to promote the interaction of scientists and members of Congress. Scientists on the staff of congressional committees are extremely rare, and I think this is a priority need for scientifc societies. There is a crying need for psychologists in this field that goes largely unrecognized, and the national interest suffers. I'm not confident about how to go about moving more psychologists into such fields, but my feeling is that training in the methods of science, particularly quantitative experimental and social science, and training to address social issues with investigative methods of science would be basic. The problems of society are generally not amenable to the skills of one discipline; they are multidisciplinary in nature. It is the tragedy of our era that each discipline sees the world in terms of variables and bodies of logic that are unique to that discipline.

Museum-Visitor Researcher

I. *Employer description.* I am employed by a number of museums including the Smithsonian Institution. I have been working with museums on topics in visitor behavior research, and my services are paid for out of the museum fund.

II. *Job description.* My work with museums emphasizes the role of museums as social institutions in the community. In my work I also encourage visitors to make use of unique environments. Part of this work now focuses on the family and informal social learning in specific environments. In addition, I am continuing to serve as a workshop resource person on applications of psychology to designed exhibits, museum programs, etc.

III. *Training.* Basic work in research methods and social psychology has been useful. More preparation in field research strategies and the practical problems of working with nonpsychologists in nonacademic settings would have been of value.

IV. *Employment prospects.* I have received several offers from museums to join their staff on a one- or two-year basis to set up a program in visitor research and services. There could be employment of psychologists by museums on such a short-term basis if psychologists with ample leave time could coordinate with museums.

V. *Other comments.* I hope the American Psychological Association will give some thought to psychologists working in the leisure-time area and to those working on the kinds of problems and wo/manpower needs that are going to be a part of a "postindustrial" society.

Museum Consultant

I. *Employer description.* I am employed by groups of museums offering exhibits and related educational programs to the general public. These groups are supported by federal government funds, plus funds from private donors and foundations.

II. *Job description.* Initially I was hired to advise on the creation of the plans for the Smithsonian Institution's first inner-city branch museum. In collaboration with neighborhood leaders and Smithsonian staff, I wrote the plans, selected the location, and played a major role in the launching and development of the branch museum. I later did research on problems related to exhibit impact. More recently, under a grant from the National Science Foundation, I created a totally new kind of exhibit for the Smithsonian National Museum of Natural History. The exhibit is called the Discovery Room and offers visitors an opportunity to touch and handle a wide range of beautiful and unusual natural history specimens.

III. *Training.* I believe that my training and prior experiences as a psychologist working in the community provided me with both the knowledge and the approach to solve the problems that I tackled at the Smithsonian. Since many museum administrators and curators are trained to the PhD level in their respective fields, a psychologist-collaborator does need a PhD degree as well as a secure, scholarly knowledge of his or her own field.

IV. *Employment prospects.* The knowledge and methods of psychology can be used in many ways in museums, in the creation of exhibits, in related educational programs, and in evaluation of such programs. As Arthur Melton pointed out in the early 1930s, museums are also superb field settings for the study of basic psychological questions related to motivation, perception, cognition, and learning. There are thousands of museums both in the United States and abroad, but I don't believe most museum directors and psychologists are ready for each other at present.

V. *Other comments.* I would like very much to write an article on the field with a review of some of the literature on exhibit evaluation. The field has an interesting history; for example, Fechner in the 1870s used a rudimentary public opinion poll to elicit reactions of museum visitors in an aesthetics experiment that he conducted in a public museum in Germany.

Consultant in Animal Psychology

I. *Employer description.* I am engaged in private practice and accept clients, pet owners, by veterinary referral only. The fees are paid by the clients.

II. *Job description.* I deal with three categories of behavior problems in patients, the animals: (a) behaviors arising from faulty training methods, (b) frankly abnormal behaviors, and (c) behaviors that may be due to physical pathology in which I am asked to provide data that may serve to support or refute a particular diagnosis, such as a central nervous system dysfunction. I do not directly train or treat patients; I attempt to diagnose and prescribe; the change agent must be the client. I believe that my practice represents a novel departure from the academic field of animal behavior in two major ways; first, the promotion or restoration of normal behaviors in intact animals through the application of principles and techniques acquired in research settings in which animals served as subjects. In my work, animals as patients are the recipients of services. Second, as opposed to a rigidly controlled environment, I am obliged to work within the physical and psychological constraints of the human household, and frequently with animals where the genetic and developmental history is unknown. Whereas in the experimental situation the human variable is minimized, I must give full recognition to the owner–pet interaction and exercise all the clinical skills at my command to deal properly and effectively with that human factor.

At present, I have been well accepted by veterinarians, animal trainers, and breeders. I have given invited addresses to several professional societies and to various animal associations.

III. *Training.* A PhD degree from an accredited university is mandatory. The major field should be physiological-comparative psychology, but a broad background in other areas such as perception, motivation, learning theory, developmental psychology, personality, and psychopathology is necessary. In addition, courses such as behavior genetics, neuroanatomy, neuropathology, and pharmacology should be strongly considered. I believe that a new curriculum within psychology, one that encompasses the courses cited and perhaps some courses in conjunction with schools of veterinary medicine, should be established in universities to prepare students for my specialty. An internship should be included.

IV. *Employment prospects.* I do believe that this specialty holds promise for the employment of future psychologists, providing, of course, that the sort of training noted above can be provided. Currently, I am supporting the practice, which is on an evening and weekend basis, by earning salaries through a research position within an institution where my role is far more traditional. Eventually, I expect to expand to a full-time operation. Considering the pet population explosion in this country—which has led to increasing specialization within veterinary medicine and has resulted, concomitant with growing urbanization, in an acceleration of behavior disorders among such animals—the need for psychological services must be recognized and met. I think the demand already exists, but psycholo-

gists are not perceived as the best-equipped suppliers. Psychologists themselves, becoming available as practitioners, must alert and educate the
public. In the human realm, the physician, the educator, and more recently
the psychiatrist and clinical psychologist can answer the behavioral needs
of people. Analogous specialists, concerned with infrahuman behaviors,
are the veterinarian and the animal trainer, respectively, with the third
role represented by the animal psychologist. In each of the realms, I see the
psychologist as suited to coordinate the other two specialties with his or
her own, in order to develop and maintain a team approach.

V. *Other comments.* I am concerned deeply over the legal and ethical
standards that must evolve to protect this specialty and the general public
from charlatans. I am a certified psychologist in the State of Maryland and
am licensed to practice psychology in the District of Columbia. I do not
advertise. My professional credentials are known to the veterinarians to
whom I announced my services and to members of the groups to whom I
have spoken. I will continue, in every way possible, to warn those with
whom I come in contact to check the qualifications of any "animal
therapist," "animal behaviorist," or any other who professes skills in the
specialty of animal psychology prior to becoming actively committed to
their programs.

Social Psychologist in Volunteer Work

I. *Employer description.* I am national chairperson of Volunteers for the
Red Cross. As such I relate to about 7,000,000 volunteers and about 700
staff people who work with them. Among my concerns are motivation,
recruitment, training, management, and recognition.

II. *Job description.* I feel that my psychological expertise is crucial in all
of my work. Voluntary organizations and volunteering are important factors in American society but are seldom recognized as such. In a real sense
they depend almost totally on psychology: motivation, satisfaction, and
the ability to help people express their real concerns and to develop skills
and interests beyond their work roles. At the moment, one of my special
interests is the translation of management know-how from the world of
business to the work of voluntarism. This activity, it seems, is filling a real
need.

III. *Training.* I found that the work I did in psychology for my degree has
been very useful. I would like to see some actual courses in voluntarism as
a part of both educational and social psychology, but a solid grounding in
traditional psychology has been very useful to me.

IV. *Employment prospects.* I think it could become a very good field.
Many of my friends in the group dynamics area are active with voluntary
associations—consulting and training. I'd like to see more psychologists
who go into management training learn about voluntary organizations as
well as business organizations.

V. *Other comments.* This field of voluntarism is a natural for psychology because it is primarily concerned with people. But schools of manage-

ment and sociologists will take it over if psychologists don't move in quickly and aggressively.

Nursing Home Consultant

(Editor's Note: This person has a more traditional job, but is also a consultant to several nursing homes, and the following comments are included because of this innovative area of involvement.)

There is an expanding area for psychologists in the field of nursing homes. Government regulations requiring psychological consultation for these homes are getting more stringent. I believe that group work and organized activity for ill old people when they enter such a home can retard or prevent senility. The American Medical Association has finished a three-day Quality of Life for the Aged seminar in Chicago emphasizing this issue.

Many nursing homes belong to corporations, and it seems that a psychologist could be employed as a full-time consultant for five or six homes a week or less. The administrators need to be convinced that this is financially feasible.